C.D. Broad: Key Unpublished Writings

C. D. Broad (1887–1971) was a British philosopher who taught for many years at Trinity College, Cambridge. Possessing extremely wide-ranging interests, Broad made significant contributions to the mind-body problem, perception, memory, introspection, the unconscious, the nature of space, time, and causation. He also wrote extensively on the philosophy of science, ethics, the history of philosophy, and the philosophy of religion and had an abiding interest in 'psychical research'—a subject he approached with the disinterested curiosity and scrupulous care that is characteristic of his philosophical work. Whilst overshadowed in his own time by figures such as Russell, Moore, and Wittgenstein, he is acknowledged to have anticipated important developments in several fields, such as emergence in philosophy of science, sense perception, and the 'growing block' theory of time in metaphysics.

Although Broad published many books in his lifetime, this volume is unique in presenting some of his most interesting unpublished writings. Divided into five clear sections, the following figures and topics are covered:

- Autobiography
- Hegel and the nature of philosophy
- Francis Bacon
- Hume's philosophy of the self and belief
- F. H. Bradley
- The historical development of scientific thought from Pythagoras to Newton
- Causation
- Change and continuity
- Quantitative methods
- Poltergeists
- Paranormal phenomena.

Each section is introduced and placed in context by the editor, Joel Walmsley. The volume also includes an engaging and informative foreword by Simon Blackburn. It will be of great value to those studying and researching the history of twentieth-century philosophy, metaphysics, and the recent history and philosophy of science, as well as anyone interested in Broad's philosophical thought and his place in the history of philosophy.

C. D. Broad (1887–1971) taught for many years at Trinity College, Cambridge. A philosopher of extremely wide-ranging interests, Broad made significant contributions to philosophy of mind, metaphysics, ethics, and the history and philosophy of science. He also had a longstanding interest in 'psychical research'—a subject he approached with the disinterested curiosity and scrupulous care that is characteristic of his philosophical work. The author of several books, his most important works are *Scientific Thought* (1923), *The Mind and Its Place in Nature* (1925), and *Examination of McTaggart's Philosophy* (1933–1938).

Joel Walmsley is a Lecturer in the Department of Philosophy at University College Cork, Ireland. He is the author of *Mind and Machine* (2012), and co-author of *Mind: A Historical and Philosophical Introduction to the Major Theories* (2006).

C.D. Broad

Key Unpublished Writings

Edited by
Joel Walmsley, with a Foreword by Simon Blackburn

LONDON AND NEW YORK

Cover image: C. D. Broad, 1968. © Anthony Howarth. Reproduced with kind permission. With thanks to the Wren Library, University of Cambridge.

First published 2023
by Routledge
4 Park Square, Milton Park, Abingdon, Oxon OX14 4RN

and by Routledge
605 Third Avenue, New York, NY 10158

Routledge is an imprint of the Taylor & Francis Group, an informa business

Selection and editorial matter © 2023, Joel Walmsley

Foreword © 2023, Simon Blackburn

C. D. Broad chapters © 2023, Trinity College Cambridge

The right of Joel Walmsley to be identified as the author of the editorial material, and of the authors for their individual chapters, has been asserted in accordance with sections 77 and 78 of the Copyright, Designs and Patents Act 1988.

All rights reserved. No part of this book may be reprinted or reproduced or utilised in any form or by any electronic, mechanical, or other means, now known or hereafter invented, including photocopying and recording, or in any information storage or retrieval system, without permission in writing from the publishers.

Trademark notice: Product or corporate names may be trademarks or registered trademarks, and are used only for identification and explanation without intent to infringe.

British Library Cataloguing-in-Publication Data
A catalogue record for this book is available from the British Library

Library of Congress Cataloging-in-Publication Data
Names: Broad, C. D. (Charlie Dunbar), 1887–1971, author. | Walmsley, Joel, editor. | Blackburn, Simon, 1944– writer of foreword.
Title: C.D. Broad: key unpublished writings / edited by Joel Walmsley; with a foreword by Simon Blackburn.
Description: Abingdon, Oxon; New York, NY: Routledge, 2022. | Includes bibliographical references and index.
Identifiers: LCCN 2022005214 (print) | LCCN 2022005215 (ebook) | ISBN 9780367532529 (hardback) | ISBN 9780367532543 (paperback) | ISBN 9781003081135 (ebook)
Subjects: LCSH: Broad, C. D. (Charlie Dunbar), 1887–1971. | Philosophy, English—20th century.
Classification: LCC B1618 .B751 W35 2022 (print) | LCC B1618 .B751 (ebook) | DDC 192—dc23/eng/20220504
LC record available at https://lccn.loc.gov/2022005214
LC ebook record available at https://lccn.loc.gov/2022005215

ISBN: 978-0-367-53252-9 (hbk)
ISBN: 978-0-367-53254-3 (pbk)
ISBN: 978-1-003-08113-5 (ebk)

DOI: 10.4324/9781003081135

Typeset in Joanna
by codeMantra

Contents

ACKNOWLEDGEMENTS   vii
FOREWORD   ix
Simon Blackburn

Editor's General Introduction   1
Joel Walmsley

Part 1
Autobiographical Notes (24 August 1954 to 31 December 1968)   7
Introduction to Part 1   9
Joel Walmsley

  1.1. Autobiographical Notes (August 24 1954 to December 31 1968)   13

Part 2
Philosophers and the History of Philosophy   103
Introduction to Part 2   105
Joel Walmsley

  2.1. Hegel's Views on the Nature of Philosophy   111
  2.2. Hume's Theory of Belief   130
  2.3. Hume's Doctrine of the Self   145
  2.4. The Philosophy of F.H. Bradley   163

2.5. Philosophy 1900–1950	182
2.6. Bertrand Russell's 90th Birthday	188
2.7. Francis Bacon (1561–1626)	196
2.8. The Historical Development of Scientific Thought (From Pythagoras to Newton)	218

Part 3
Science and Metaphysics   235

Introduction to Part 3   237
Joel Walmsley

3.1. Introduction of Quantitative Methods	240
3.2. Notes on Causation	260
3.3. Some Remarks on Change, Continuity, and Discontinuity	275
3.4. The Logical Analysis of Change	295

Part 4
Psychical Research   305

Introduction to Part 4   307
Joel Walmsley

4.1. Ostensibly Paranormal Physical Phenomena	312
4.2. Poltergeists	330

Part 5
Miscellany   355

Introduction to Part 5   357
Joel Walmsley

5.1. The Necromantic Tripos	360
5.2. Problem in Family Relationships	365

REFERENCES   369
INDEX   371

Acknowledgements

A great many people have helped me to bring this project to fruition, and so I would like to record my sincere gratitude to them here; the growing block of the universe would not have included this volume as a continuant without the following necessary conditions.

I would like to thank the Master and Fellows of Trinity College, Cambridge, especially Jonathan Smith at the Wren Library, along with Adam Green and Jonathan Kirwan. I am also grateful to Tim Crane and the *New Directions in the Study of the Mind* project for the travel funding to facilitate this book: this was made possible through the support of a grant from the John Templeton Foundation, and the opinions expressed in this publication are those of the author and do not necessarily reflect the views of the John Templeton Foundation. Particular thanks must also go to: Simon Blackburn for the foreword and for alerting me to Lewis Carroll's version of the 'Problem in Family Relations' in Chapter 5.2; Landon Elkind for help with the *Principia Mathematica* typesetting complications in Chapter 3.4; Anthony Howarth for the cover photograph; Ted Jackson (Manuscripts Archivist at Georgetown University) for the 'Necromantic Tripos' paper. More generally, I am grateful to colleagues and students at University College Cork, and beyond, for their encouragement – and sometimes, I'll admit, *tolerance* – including Vittorio Bufacchi, Cara Nine, Don Ross, Alessandro Salice, Alfred Moore, Dan Deasy, Aideen Casey, and Corey Cashman.

Finally, I am extremely fortunate to have had the invaluable support and guidance of Tony Bruce and Adam Johnson at Routledge, and I'm grateful that they seem to have shared my view – whether, as Broad might have said, veridical or delusive – of the ostensible merits of this project.

Foreword

I think it was an accident that when I went up to Trinity College, Cambridge in 1962 I found myself on the same staircase as C.D. Broad. He was then in his mid-70s, and appeared as a shy, rotund, and bald figure, rather like a benevolent gnome. I do not remember how we became acquainted, but with time I learned who he was and began to plough, in a faltering way, some of the fields that he had tilled for more than the previous half-century (he came up in 1906). I was naturally greatly in awe of him, and as a diligent student I pored over The Mind and its Place in Nature, Five Types of Ethical Theory, and other writings. Over time he opened himself up to the undergraduates on his staircase, inviting us and our friends to excellent dinners provided by the College kitchens and brought to his magnificent rooms, once those of Isaac Newton. On these occasions, he came alive in ways that were only occasionally visible in his written works. He was mischievous, especially about his distinguished colleagues, but also about university life in general, as his spoof regulations for a Necromantic Tripos in this collection show. He was also astonishingly well-read and had a wonderful memory, which embraced a large supply of scurrilous light verse. He had no vanity, but once told me that if all the works of W.S. Gilbert were destroyed he thought he could write them out from memory. I think I felt some rapport with him because I, like him, had been bound for the natural sciences. He did not escape until he had taken Part I of the Tripos, whereas being more impatient I had changed to Moral Sciences, as philosophy was then called, immediately on entry.

His wit was fed by a fair share of prejudices – after all, he had been born in 1887. One of these was his dislike of Wittgenstein, of whom he acidly wrote: 'I have to say that nothing impressed me as much about Wittgenstein, as the impression he made upon such fine characters and such eminent philosophers as Moore and von Wright'. He also disliked Oxford, the Roman Catholic Church, no doubt much else besides, and was patronising about women. So when he was informed that Elizabeth Anscombe, a pupil of Wittgenstein who also ticked all the other boxes, had been appointed to succeed John Wisdom as the Professor of Philosophy, one might have expected some kind of explosion. Instead of which he merely commented: 'Ah, yes, she may call herself Miss Anscombe, but in the eyes of her God, she is plain Mrs Geach'. Few philosophers of his age (nearly 83 at the time) or indeed any age could have brought down so many birds with one barrel.

Nevertheless, he regarded himself as slow in conversation and his lectures were invariably texts that he had previously written out. For this reason, he took little part in the Moral Sciences Club, which was frequently something of a bear-pit, especially when dominated by his special bête noir, Wittgenstein. But he did turn up once for a Moral Science club photograph, which had been arranged on King's College lawn. Seeing the somewhat cadaverous Professor John Wisdom hurrying in from a distance Broad waited until the right moment, and then announced in a loud voice: 'Ah, I see Wisdom coming. Now I know what it will be like at the resurrection of the dead' – this in spite of his being some 17 years older than Wisdom.

It has to be admitted that this sparkle does not always animate his written works. For instance, his autobiography in the Schilpp volume *The Philosophy of C. D. Broad* is for the most part a remorselessly dull description of previous generations of his family, and it cannot be said that the pace improves in the supplement presented here, taking him from 1954 to within three years of his death. At least, I rather doubt if I would be the only reader whose head nods over the details of his various contemporaries and various jobs in the College, and that is in spite of my having the advantage of belonging to the same institution. It is as if within the wide angle of his vision there is no mechanism of selection, no concession to the thought that readers might be more interested in one thing rather than another. There is no light and shade: everything deserves, and gets, equal treatment. The same trait is visible in some of his books. The upside, of course, is that when fields are ploughed so relentlessly, any nuggets that are there to be had have a good chance of showing up.

The philosophical world Broad had entered at the beginning of the twentieth century was not so very different from that which I entered so much later. Cambridge, and perhaps especially Trinity, regarded itself as the home of analytic philosophy, whose guiding stars were Bertrand Russell and G.E. Moore. Analytic philosophy was painstaking, scientific, empirical, and critical. Not only its primary but arguably its only focus was the individual proposition and its make-up. Its methods were largely *a priori*, descending from the Socratic idea that if you meant something by some assertion then with sufficient thought and attention you should be able to identify exactly what you meant. Much of its energy was spent in distinguishing various options for what might be meant, and patiently pruning away that ones that really would not do. Its main tool was logic, and the goal would be an account of what a proposition meant, presented through necessary and sufficient conditions for its truth.

The value of the approach lay in the concentrated attention to what we say and think. Its drawback was ignoring the contexts within which these sayings and thoughts exist. Against this background, it is unsurprising that Broad had little sympathy with pragmatism, genealogy, or other movements that do not take the ways we think for granted, but endeavour to explain them. As well as the later Wittgenstein there were others in Cambridge from whom he could have learned better – notably Frank Ramsey and later Charles Stephenson (he eventually took notice of Stephenson's work, although remaining lukewarm about it).

The analytic flame still burned fiercely in the person of my own supervisor in Trinity, Casimir Lewy, who was also sceptical about the influence of Wittgenstein and whose own academic contributions revolved around certain problems of logical theory, and those of editing the legacy of Moore himself. I think it is fair to say that Broad never really escaped from the analytic paradigm in spite of the willingness to explore every aspect of a problem that was perhaps the principal signature of much of his work. A salient example is the end of *The Mind and Its Place in Nature* where he is left with no fewer than 17 different theories about its topic, created by permuting answers to questions of whether mentality and materiality are differentiating attributes, emergent according to various standards of emergence, reducible one to another by various standards of reduction, or indeed delusive. There is no victory parade for any one theory. But the hard concentration he brings to topics often brings its own reward. His work on emergence lives on in the philosophy of mind.[1] And his note on causation collected in this volume stresses the ways in which our own agency in the world, our experience of 'lifting, chopping, pushing, etc.', lies behind our causal interpretations of events anticipated work which only flowered in the academic community very much later.[2]

Broad was openly contemptuous of anything that he saw as a dogmatic and hasty dismissal of open possibilities, a trait that some would say led him to waste an inordinate amount of time in pursuit of telepathic communications, precognition, and other ghostly phenomena of psychical research. Even poltergeists, which he himself called the oiks of the spirit world, are given a fair hearing in the paper collected here. The world of psychical research, like that of conspiracy theories, is beset by wishful thinking, false memories, and illusions, and is a happy hunting ground for fantasists and outright charlatans. As with reports of miracles, fair-mindedness is apt to result in more tolerance towards the fantasists than perhaps they deserve. Yet unlike most other pursuers of the topic Broad largely kept his balance. For instance, on the topic of life after death, while he admits that he should be 'slightly more annoyed than surprised' to find himself experiencing it, the final sentence of his book of Perrott lectures on psychical research tells us that 'One can only wait and see, or alternately (which is no less likely) wait and not see'.

I am sorry to say that in its Cambridge clothing analytic philosophy also encouraged a somewhat patronising attitude to previous thinkers who did not share its love of definitions and necessary and sufficient conditions, or the question of what constituted the truth of one proposition or another. This could all lead to blind spots in the history of philosophy. For example, in his essay on Hume in *Five Types of Ethical Theory* (1930) Broad launches straight into asserting that Hume defined the good as that which is admired by most people, and of course has no difficulty in rejecting it. Yet Hume's approach to ethics bypasses anything so silly. Hume did indeed think that ethics needs to pay attention to what it is that we actually admire, but he was also hospitable to the possibility that we might not always admire what we should (he explores the same issues in aesthetics in the great essay *On the Standard of Taste*). Broad later became more interested in the history of philosophy, writing many essays on Descartes, Newton, Bacon, as well as providing in his lecture notes material later turned into books on Kant and Leibniz. His introduction to Leibniz's system is widely respected, and generally preferred for example to that by Russell.

Whether it is a professional deformation, or somehow intrinsic to the subject, philosophy is apt to fragment into a list of positions and '…isms'. And it is surely true that ever since the worldly Aristotle opposed the transcendental Plato, the most admired philosophers have stood for something, and fought against something else. Broad's open-mindedness and reluctance to come to definite conclusions can be seen as a strength, but I fear they have denied him the place in that pantheon that his other virtues might have been expected to earn him.

Simon Blackburn, December 2021

NOTES

1 See McLaughlin, B. (1992), 'The rise and fall of British emergentism' in A. Beckerman, H. Flohr and J. Kim (eds.) *Emergence or Reduction?* (Berlin: de Gruyter).
2 A seminal paper is Peter Menzies and Huw Price, (1993) 'Causation as a Secondary Quality' *The British Journal for the Philosophy of Science* 44(2):187–203.

EDITOR'S GENERAL INTRODUCTION

Joel Walmsley

Shortly after his retirement – at the end of a 1959 volume dedicated to an exploration of his work – C.D. Broad wrote:

> ... though philosophies are never refuted, they rapidly go out of fashion, and the kind of philosophy which I have practised has become antiquated without having yet acquired the interest of a collector's piece[1]

Broad *was* self-deprecating (and sometimes humorously so); in a letter to Mind, responding to a review of the volume from which this quotation is taken, he referred to the series as 'Schilpp's Library of Moribund Philosophers' (rather than the actual series title, The Library of Living Philosophers).[2] This was not intended as a slight on any of the other philosophers to whom volumes in the series had been dedicated; indeed, several other reviews of the Broad volume noted that he was perhaps *too* harsh in his autobiographical self-appraisal. In any case, despite the modesty of this quip, it is now clear that it is incorrect; over 60 years later, the present volume stands as a counter-example to Broad's self-referential claim. The pieces herein will be of considerable interest, and not only to mere 'collectors'.

It is fair to say that Broad's work has been neglected, for reasons that are perhaps unsurprising. Almost the entirety of his career was spent in Cambridge at a time when the scene was dominated by figures – particularly Russell, Wittgenstein, and Moore – who inevitably overshadowed him. Yet

DOI: 10.4324/9781003081135-1

Moore himself (in his own Schilpp volume) writes 'Of all living philosophers, it is Broad's work, next to Russell's and Wittgenstein's, that I have thought it worthwhile to study most carefully'.[3] And Broad's work – both that which is already available and the previously unpublished work which appears in this volume for the first time – contains much which can be profitably studied by contemporary philosophers.

In Broad's own style, let us enumerate some examples. In philosophy of science, the resurgent interest in the concept of 'emergence' is usually prefaced with the acknowledgement that Broad did much to clarify and develop the idea in his 1925 book *The Mind and Its Place in Nature*. His account is both the deepest of those provided by the so-called 'British emergentists',[4] and the one that is most recognisably continuous with present debates. In philosophy of mind, Broad developed an early version of the 'knowledge argument' about phenomenal consciousness[5] (something acknowledged by Frank Jackson, who subsequently named and refined it). Van Inwagen (2008) cites Broad as the first to formulate the influential 'consequence argument' for the incompatibility of free will and determinism, and Broad's careful distinctions and clarifications in his (1934) *Determinism, Indeterminism, and Libertarianism* are still in use. In the history of the sense-data theory of perception, and its ongoing discussion, Broad's (1952a) paper 'Some elementary reflections on sense-perception' is an essential source. Broad's *Five Types of Ethical Theory* continues to inform both the views he discusses and our understanding of the philosophers to whom he attributes them. And Broad's 'growing block' theory of time has been reconsidered in several more recent treatments (Earman 2008, Thomas 2019, Oaklander 2020).

Additionally, aspects of Broad's philosophical style – especially his characteristic exhaustiveness and his witty expression – make him both distinctive and (to this reader, at least) a pleasure to read. On the former, Broad is recognised for his systematic rigour and quest for analytic clarity. For example, in keeping with Broad's own self-assessment (but with a slightly more complimentary tone), A.J. Ayer writes:

> Philosophical fashion has not been kind to Broad... Even so, I think that his work is under-rated... Where he excelled was in drawing up a brief. The subject is discussed from every angle, the various possibilities set out, the precedents cited, the fallacious arguments exposed: nothing is skimped: looking for reason, we are not fobbed off with rhetoric: there is never a hint

of 'something far more deeply interfused'. This is, perhaps, his weakness, that he does not burrow under the surface, but only few can do this with profit, and it is much to have the surface properly scrubbed.[6]

This methodological feature is highly characteristic both of Broad's published work and of the papers in the present volume. Those papers in Part 3 **"Science and Metaphysics"** – on the analysis of causation, change, continuity, and discontinuity – are especially good examples of this side of Broad's style.

Finally, although Broad's painstaking methodology can sometimes come across as dry, his writing frequently juxtaposes a marked verve and good-humour, punctuating the prose with amusing examples, classical allusions, and witty asides. Philosophical humour is a matter of taste, of course, but Broad's aphorisms are often quoted with approval (e.g., the final paragraph of his (1926) The Philosophy of Francis Bacon, or his sometimes snarky comments about Wittgenstein). Broad's quips can be acerbic (particularly when they're directed at other philosophers; for example, in the essay 'Philosophy 1900–1950', Chapter 2.5 below, he describes Bosanquet's prose style as 'resembling glue thickened with sawdust') but he does have a knack for condensing a point into a memorable phrase. Even the index to his (1930) Five Types of Ethical Theory contains subtle jokes, such as the matching cross references 'Bentham, Jeremy; tentatively compared to God, 160' and 'God; tentatively compared to Jeremy Bentham, 160' or the entry 'Socrates; less widely appreciated than Mr. Charles Chaplin, 173'. Suffice it to say that there are many more such gems to be found amongst the 'collector's pieces' in the present volume.

Broad was notorious for writing out his lectures in full and reading them out loud verbatim to his audience. Broad himself is quite frank about this fact: in his 'Autobiographical Notes' below (p. 79 of this volume) he writes, 'In speaking, I am quite hopeless, unless I have written out the speech beforehand'. It would seem that this custom was well-known amongst – and somewhat derided by – Broad's colleagues and students. Graham Farmelo, in his biography of Paul Dirac (the latter of whom was a student of Broad's in Bristol between 1920 and 1923) writes that Broad '… always appeared with a carefully prepared script, and he used to read every sentence twice, except for the jokes, which he read three times'.[7] This claim repeats something that is also found in Edmonds and Eisenow's (2001) book Wittgenstein's Poker, with a somewhat withering addition: 'The jokes were read out three times. That, says Maurice Wiles, who attended Broad's lectures, was the only way one could tell what was a joke'.[8]

Similar stories are repeated by Max Black,[9] and Karl Britton,[10] the latter of whom (despite seeming to have appreciated the practice) comments:

> Broad remarks that his lectures were always written out in full before delivery, and that this made it easy for him to turn his lectures into books. Those who attended them may be inclined to say that it was a matter of turning books into lectures, rather than lectures into books.

Whatever one's stance on the pedagogical merits of this practice, the practical consequence is significant and fortunate for the present volume. When Broad died in 1971, he left a large collection of manuscripts, papers, notes, and diaries to the Wren Library at Trinity College, Cambridge. Amongst those boxes of papers, there are a great many complete but unpublished manuscripts that had served as the basis of Broad's lecturing practice. The present volume compiles a selection of the best of these papers, in order to make them accessible for the first time.

I have divided this volume into sections which are organised thematically, rather than chronologically. On the one hand, since the papers are all self-standing, this division will make them easier to dip into for consultation on a particular topic or cluster of topics. On the other hand, this is because several of the manuscripts are effectively impossible to date; Broad seems to have switched from handwriting to typing most of his scripts sometime in the 1930s or 1940s, but this is not always the case, particularly when it comes to the successive stages of his apparent drafting process. Although one can date some of the papers on the basis of other information (e.g., the details of his travel in the 'Autobiographical Notes' of this volume), that has not always been possible. I have therefore supplemented each section with an editorial introduction summarising both the contents and origin of each paper, as well as offering some brief comments on their context in relation to Broad's other published work.

In general, I have tried to employ a very light editorial touch, erring on the side of fidelity to the originals and to completeness, but where editorial changes and omissions were prudent or necessary, I have commented on them in the introduction to each section. Broad's manuscripts are – unsurprisingly, given his methodical approach – remarkably free of error, but his handwriting (as may be seen in Figures 2.1 and 4.1) is dense and sometimes difficult to read; if there are mistakes in transcription, a reasonable inductive inference would permit blame to be placed with the editor rather than with the author. In addition, a consequence of Broad reading his talks before subsequently turning them into papers and books is that they are almost entirely devoid of the now-familiar scholarly machinery of footnotes, citations, and bibliographies. But where such items appear, I preface them with 'CDB' or 'JW' in order to avoid any ambiguity about their author.

NOTES

1. Broad (1959b, p. 830).
2. Broad (1962a, p. 251).
3. Moore (1942, p. 34).
4. McLaughlin (1992).
5. Jackson (1982).
6. Ayer (1977, pp. 117–118).
7. Farmelo (2009, p. 39).
8. Edmonds and Eisenow (2001, p. 55).
9. In Misak (2020, p. 358).
10. Britton (1978, pp. 297–298).

Part 1

AUTOBIOGRAPHICAL NOTES (24 AUGUST 1954 TO 31 DECEMBER 1968)

INTRODUCTION TO PART 1
Joel Walmsley

The first part of Broad's autobiography, covering most of his life, was written in 1954 and published in 1959 in *The Philosophy of C.D. Broad* (in Schilpp's Library of Living Philosophers series). The present addition to that historical record is taken from a manuscript dated 24 September 1969 (completed when Broad was aged 80), of which there are several typed copies amongst the Broad papers in the Wren Library at Trinity College, Cambridge.

The first instalment of Broad's autobiography was a good deal longer – and more ambitious – than those provided by philosophers in the other volumes of the Schilpp series. Philosophical autobiography, like Broad's particular brand of philosophical humour, is a matter of taste, and it is therefore perhaps not surprising that Broad's earlier autobiography generated, let us say, *mixed* reactions.

On the one hand, some critics seem to have regarded Broad's autobiography as vain, or self-indulgent, or simply irrelevant. Gilbert Ryle, in his review of the Schilpp volume, writes scathingly that:

> Broad's autobiography, whether intended or not, is a mistake. Most of its 65 pages commemorate his forgettable female relatives, and contain little to satisfy those who want to know what intellectual ferments were working in and around Broad in his days as a student or teacher in Cambridge... Self-portraits are, I think, bound to be caricatures ... I wish that Broad had not attempted the task.[1]

DOI: 10.4324/9781003081135-3

Similarly, Britton suggests a kind of vanity, or excessive self-regard, as amongst Broad's motivation:

> Like many unmarried people, he was tremendously occupied with his forebears and relatives, although only in a few cases did those mentioned by Broad have any apparent influence on his career... It is clear that Broad was very much taken up with himself: his writing of this autobiography shows how fascinating a subject he thought himself to be.[2]

On the other hand, some readers took a more positive view, in line with the unapologetic self-assessment that Broad expresses in the opening paragraphs of the second instalment below. Ewing describes it as 'written in a lively, interesting, even brilliant style'[3] and White, for example, notes that:

> Broad's autobiography is a good deal longer, more entertaining and witty, more personally revealing, but less philosophically interesting—unless you take a psycho-analytic view of philosophy—than is common in these volumes.[4]

Those who are familiar with the first instalment of Broad's autobiography will find that the contents of the present edition are continuous both temporally and stylistically. However, this time, the portraits of *others* that Broad includes may be of wider interest since they concern other well-known scholars and fellows of Trinity College ('Other Trinity Octogenarians Still Living' and 'Old Friends Who Have Died') rather than the long list of unknown and perhaps forgettable family members who appear in the 1959 edition. We also find details of Broad's post-retirement travels, and his ongoing interest in 'psychical research' (both of which help to put some of the papers in this volume in context), as well as an account of his illnesses, other aspects of his life at Trinity College, and some concluding candid general reflections.

I *have* taken the liberty of omitting some material from the manuscript of the present 'Autobiographical Notes', for the sake of length, interest, and good taste. On the one hand, the language in which Broad expresses his views about the connection between immigration and population growth, though officially appropriate for the 1960s, does not deserve to be reprinted in the 2020s. His sentiments – disappointing, but predictable – remain clear, and so no insight into his character and motivations is lost with these omissions.

On the other hand, the original manuscript contained three very long, detailed (and sometimes dreary) accounts of Broad's membership of various committees. These included the Governing Body of the Perse School (on which Broad was Trinity College's representative), the permanent committee of Newnham College (on which Broad was an external member), the Trinity College Finance Committee, and the Trinity College Kitchen Reconstruction Committee (1955–1968) and the Central Heating Committee (1963–1968), the latter two having over 20 typed manuscript pages devoted to them. Rather than reproduce those lengthy (and, frankly, tedious) chapters, I simply excerpt three items of conceivable interest here.

First, it should be noted that Broad generously contributed a considerable sum of his own money (£4,000 in total, in instalments between 1963 and 1968) towards the construction and furnishing of a new 'Sick Bay' at Trinity College. When some space in Nevile's Court became vacant because of the Kitchen Reconstruction that he oversaw, Broad suggested this development, and both the committee and the College Council accepted it. He writes, with a characteristic wry tone:

> We have now got a magnificent Sick Bay, on ground level, replete with every modern convenience. I think it may fairly be claimed that even the most pampered products of the Welfare State would not mind 'being seen dead in it.' I was not surprised when the College Nurse told me that she often finds it difficult to get undergraduates, who have been temporarily moved into the Sick Bay, to quit it and return to the comparative squalor of their own rooms.

Second, concerning the inevitable conflicts that arose between the Fellows, the College Council, the Kitchen Reconstruction Committee, and the firm of engineers and builders who were contracted to complete the work, Broad finds some literary solace in the words of Virgil:

> Of such controversies as the above it may fairly be said:
>
> > *Hi motus animorum atque haec certamina tanta*
> > *pulveris exigui iactu compressa quiescunt.*[5]

Finally, on a related note, concerning a meeting on 16 February 1967, at which the Central Heating Committee presented its proposals to the rest of the college, Broad writes:

It would ill become me to expose the *pudenda* of a College Meeting; I would not like to risk being compared with the patriarch Ham in his deplorable behaviour on a certain notorious occasion *vis-à-vis* his father Noah. (*Genesis* 9:21–25). It will suffice to say that there was the usual mixture of plain silliness; of clever-silliness (which is rather characteristic of debates in academic circles); of a certain amount of personal malice thinly disguised as solicitude for the welfare of undergraduates and for other high impersonal ends; and of sensible enquiries, suggestions, and criticisms.

Contemporary members of university committees across the world may well opine, *plus ça change, plus c'est la même chose!*

NOTES

1. Ryle (1962, p. 186). It seems pretty clear, therefore, that Ryle is the 'very distinguished philosopher in Oxford' that Broad mentions on the first page of the 'Autobiographical Notes' below.
2. Britton (1978, p. 308).
3. Ewing (1963, p. 79).
4. White (1960, p. 11).
5. Virgil, *Georgics*, Book IV 'These passions of their souls, these conflicts so fierce, will cease, and be repressed by the casting of a little dust'.

1.1

AUTOBIOGRAPHICAL NOTES (AUGUST 24 1954 TO DECEMBER 31 1968)

All censure of man's self is oblique praise. It is in order to show how much he can spare.

(Dr. Johnson)

INTRODUCTION

On 24 August 1954, I completed, at Karlstad in Sweden where I was then staying, the manuscript of the *Autobiography*, which was to be published in the then-forthcoming volume *The Philosophy of C.D. Broad* in Schilpp's series *The Library of Living Philosophers*. I was then in my 67th year. The volume was published eventually in 1959, and the *Autobiography*, as is the rule in this series, was the first item in it. It occupies there pp. 3–68, both included.

Reactions to this *Autobiography* were very varied. One at least of my friends, a very distinguished philosopher in Oxford (not Professor H.H. Price), thought it deplorable and expressed to me his regret that I should ever have published such a thing. On the other hand, quite a number of readers, including some of my friends and colleagues at Trinity College, Cambridge, have obviously enjoyed it.

Speaking for myself, I have no regrets whatever about it. The composition of it occasioned in me a good deal of introspection and retrospection, which

I should in all probability not have otherwise undertaken. This, and the recording of some of the results in writing, was, I am sure, wholesome for me. For it brought to the surface a good deal of unpleasant material, which had been floating about just beneath it, and which it was good for me to face deliberately and as an inter-connected whole.

As to the publication of my resulting reflexions, I cannot see that anything that was printed was in the least offensive or improper. In this connexion, I may remark that one young don at another Cambridge College, a complete stranger to me, told that it had been a great relief to him to discover that certain uncomfortable symptoms, which he had thought to be peculiar to himself, had in fact played a considerable part in the life of the author of the *Autobiography*.

The account of immediate and remoter ancestors and collaterals, and of their circumstances, is naturally of much more interest to myself and my younger relatives than it is to strangers. Nevertheless, I do not consider that the publication of what I had to say on this topic was impertinent. For an account of the ups-and-downs of a fairly typical middle-middle-class English family during the immediately previous 150 years or so was surely even at the time of some interest to the social historian. It is of interest from its very ordinariness, and that is a point which it is likely to have to a greater and greater degree as the period in question recedes into the more and more distant past.

Lastly, it seems to me that the *Autobiography* contains some of the best writing, stylistically, of which I have ever been capable. it would, therefore, be a *meiosis* to say that I feel no regret about having written and published it. I am positively glad that I did so, and I think that I have good reasons for that feeling.

I pass now from the old *Autobiography*, completed in 1954, to its present sequel, continued up to the end of 1968. The history of my undertaking it is this. One of my colleagues and a friend of very old standing, A. M. Binnie, after reading the published chapter, has often pressed me to continue the story up to date. I have returned more or less evasive answers on many occasions. But I generally find myself succumbing in the end to Binnie's importunities, when I do not think them too unreasonable. And in the present case, having survived another 15 years, I find myself with the leisure to carry out his instructions, without the intellectual energy to employ myself in anything more exciting and with some slight positive inclination to indulge in a little further autobiography. So, after reading through and making abstracts from my diaries for the period in question, I now record what seems interesting to me, in the hope that parts at least of it may be of some interest to certain of my colleagues and to some other friends of mine, if to no one else.

OTHER TRINITY OCTOGENARIANS STILL LIVING

I will begin by saying something of the Fellows of Trinity, still alive and vigorous at the time of writing, who have passed their 80th birthdays during the period in question.

First, I must mention one who is no mere octogenarian, but reached the age of 90 in 1962, and has lately had his 97th birthday. This is the third Earl Russell, better known to the public as 'Bertrand Russell'.

On 18 May 1962, the Fellows of the college assembled in the Combination Room after dinner to drink Lord Russell's health. We should have been delighted if he had been able to be present, but he had had to decline our very cordial invitation because he was, very naturally, involved as the central figure in the more formal and more widely representative celebrations of the event which were taking place in London. There was a record attendance of Fellows and their guests in the Combination Room, and it was only just possible to seat the whole company. Both the Master (Lord Adrian) and the Vice-Master (Patrick Duff) were unavoidably absent from Cambridge, and it fell to Kitson Clark to preside. The Council had invited me to make the speech proposing Russell's health. I felt it to be a great honour to be entrusted with this duty, and it was extremely pleasant for me to have this opportunity of expressing, *inter alia*, in presence of my friends and colleagues, my gratitude to Russell for all his kindness to me as a young man, for the stimulation of his wit and humour, and for the immense debt which I owe, in respect of my philosophical work, to his lectures, his writings, and his conversation.

A copy of this speech is kept in the Library, and it is available to be read there by any Fellow of the College who may care to consult it.[1] In the course of it, I tried to give an accurate and objective account, based mainly on G.H. Hardy's privately printed pamphlet of 1942 entitled *Bertrand Russell and Trinity*, of the tangled tale of the relations between Russell and the College during and after the First World War.

Anyone who may be interested in a fuller account of what I think I owe as a philosopher to Russell and his writings is advised to glance at the paper 'Some Personal Impressions of Russell as a Philosopher', which I contributed at the Editor's request to the collective volume *Bertrand Russell, Philosopher of the Century* published by Allen & Unwin in 1967.

Finally, I would refer any reader who may be interested to a recent article of mine in the *Philosophical Review* for October 1968. It is entitled 'Bertrand Russell's First 42 Years in Self-Portraiture', and was occasioned by Vol. I of Russell's *Autobiography*. It deals with the following topics: his ancestry and blood relations, his boyhood, his early years at Cambridge, his first marriage, his subsequent extra-marital relations, mysticism, and his philosophical work.

Leaving now our one nonagenarian, I turn to those Fellows of the College who have reached the age of 80 during the period under review and are still living in College and associating daily with the rest of the Society. There are no less than seven of these. I will begin by mentioning them in the order in which they reached their 80th birthdays. The list is as follows: Rev. F.A. Simpson (22 November 1963), Professor H.A. Hollond (4 October 1964), Professor J.E. Littlewood (9 June 1965), Professor Sir G.I. Taylor (7 March 1966), Mr A.S.F. Gow (27 August 1966), Professor C.D. Broad (30 December 1967), and Mr T.C. Nicholas (17 August 1968). Of these, all except Simpson were at Trinity as undergraduates, gained their Fellowships in one or another of the annual competitions between 1908 and 1912, and have spent most of their subsequent active lives in the service of the College or the University or both. I will now take those other than myself in turn.

Simpson was an undergraduate at Queen's College, Oxford, and graduated at that university. He came to Trinity in 1911 by invitation to join the History Staff of the College. He has been a Fellow from then onwards. On the historical and literary side, he is famous as the author of *The Life of Louis Napoleon*, which is unfinished, but has become a classic. He is also well known as the author of two devastating articles, 'Max Beerbohm on Lytton Strachey' (*Cambridge Review*: 4 December 1943) and 'Methods of History' (*Spectator*: 7 January 1944), in which he exposes the dishonesty of Lytton Strachey in the latter's account of Manning in 'Eminent Victorians'.

He soon became, and has ever remained, one of our most outstanding figures, in the eyes of his colleagues, of the undergraduates, and of the College servants. He is greatly interested in gardens in general, and in trees and shrubs in particular, and, for all that I know, he may well have expert knowledge on these matters. At any rate, he is wont to walk about armed with an apparatus which enables him to snip off leaves, twigs, etc., leaving them lying on the ground for lesser men to collect. He has been for many years a kind of perpetual member of the Gardens Committee. I have often been able to watch from my window parts of the prolonged meetings of that body out-of-doors. From what I have observed myself, and from what I have been told by members of the Committee, I conclude that Simpson's membership has been an infernal nuisance to the others.

One of Simpson's eccentricities, at any rate to an external observer like myself, has been his friendship with the present Bishop of Southwark. The latter was in Cambridge for a number of years as Canon Stockwood, Vicar of Great St. Mary's. I must say that, on the rare occasions when I met him, he always seemed to me to be pretty bogus. One would have expected that his particular combination of left-wing politics with rather theatrical Christianity would have made him particularly repellent to Simpson. But, in fact, he soon became and has remained one of Simpson's nearest friends, and has regularly been brought by the latter as his guest to our Christmas Feasts. Perhaps all this is a mystery to me because of inadequate knowledge. For I note that Harry Williams, who is himself a thoroughly genuine Christian, and is not one to be easily taken in by bogosity, appears to share with Simpson this deep and to me, most surprising fondness for 'Mervyn' – as those who have the privilege of counting that churchman among their 'boy-friends' are wont to call the Bishop of Southwark.

Simpson has been, and on occasion still is, an extremely good talker. Nowadays, however, as is common enough in advanced years, he has largely lost the gift of condensation, and his conversations tend to be tediously prolonged and repetitive. Perhaps the characteristic in him which most strikes a colleague, and which the college servants must have had many occasions to mark, is the naive self-indulgence and the lack of consideration for others which he has for so many years exhibited. What I have in mind was well expressed long ago by the late D.A. Winstanley in two comments on Simpson, viz., 'A fallen angel, who has fallen on his feet', and 'When he gets to Heaven, he'll find he has to rough it'. While such tendencies exist no doubt in many of us, the majority of us manage to indulge them less openly and naively. Moreover, most of us are not, like Simpson, professional Christians, and are therefore under less of a *prima facie* obligation to keep up at least the appearance of being guided by the Sermon on the Mount.

I conclude the above not very flattering reflexions with the following *caveat*. They are those of a more or less superficial observer. I have never known Simpson at all intimately. If I did, I might understand and forgive much that now appears objectionable. I have certainly from time to time learned of facts which suggest that he has shown very great generosity towards certain others. I can only end with the platitude: 'It is a queer world, and we are an odd lot'.

The next name on my list is Professor H.A. Hollond. Of his eminence as an academic lawyer, I cannot speak with any authority, but I know that it is very great indeed. I have enjoyed his friendship and his constant personal kindness ever since I was a timid and rather *gauche* undergraduate and he was already an outstanding Scholar of the College, first in Classics and then in Law. We attended, if I remember right, McTaggart's lectures on the History of Philosophy together; Hollond as an interested amateur, and I in preparation for my Tripos. Soon after the First World War, Hollond became Secretary of the Cambridge University Commissioners (1923–1927). As such he was very largely responsible for drafting the present University Statutes. At the same time, each individual College had to revise fundamentally its own Statutes, and Hollond did invaluable work for us in this. He was Dean of College for 18 years from 1922 onwards, and he was Vice-Master from 1951 to 1955.

So much for his official services to the College. These are but a small part of what he has done for us throughout the years as a member of the Council and of other important College committees. I have always admired, in this connexion, his skill in getting us around apparently insuperable legal difficulties by a process of 'deeming'. I often call to mind the following remark, which he once made to me concerning his experiences as the one professional lawyer on a number of committees composed of laymen. In nine cases out of ten, he said, laymen show quite unnecessary timidity in presence of written Statutes or Ordinances, which are supposed to be binding on them. In the tenth case, however, they are liable to do something which makes a lawyer's hair stand on end.

It remains for me to say something of his personality as known to me. I think that his outstanding merit as a member of our community has been his skill in formulating, and his tact in carrying through, compromises which have healed existing rifts in the Society or have averted threatening ones. Immediately after the First World War, when there were bitter dissensions over the actions of Bertrand Russell and the reactions which the College

Council had made to them, Hollond succeeded in what might have seemed the hopeless task of re-introducing unity and good feeling. And it was he who in 1944 was largely responsible for getting the Council to issue that invitation to Russell which led to the latter's returning to Trinity as a Fellow for a number of years and eventually becoming a life-Fellow under Title E.

I think that Hollond really enjoys the company of his fellow men. He can talk easily with anyone whom he is likely to meet. In conversation, he makes no attempt to scintillate or to 'throw his weight about', and he puts even the most diffident at their ease. He gets them to talk and is obviously interested in what they have to say. This is a gift which I admire the more as I lack it almost completely myself.

Hollond and I have always shared an interest in psychical research. This goes back a long way in his family. One of his uncles, John R. Hollond, at one time M.P., was one of the original Vice-Presidents of the Society for Psychical Research[2] at its foundation in 1882. He rendered very valuable services to the Society for many years, while he still enjoyed good health. He remained a member up to his death in 1912, but had been prevented by long illness during his later years from taking any active part in either research or in administration.

The Hollond family have been for at least a couple of centuries outstanding representatives of that English upper-middle class, to which we have been so greatly indebted in so many ways, and which for the last 50 years we have been high-mindedly taxing out of existence. Hollond's ancestors have combined wide general interests and high general intelligence with those special abilities which enabled them (as the Church Catechism so well puts it) to get their own living and to do their duty in that state of life to which it has pleased God to call them. In illustration of this, I would call attention to a poem entitled The 'Monstre' Balloon in the Ingoldsby Legends, written by Richard Harris Barham and published in the early 1840s. This refers to a famous ascent from Vauxhall Gardens in 1835–1836, in which the balloonists were a Mr Green and a Mr Monck-Mason. In it occur the lines:

> Mr. Holla̱nd, on one side, who hired the machine.

Though the name is wrongly spelled, the person referred to is an ancestor of Hollond's of that period, who put up the money which made the flight possible.

I cannot leave Hollond without mentioning the following fact about him. In spite of the fundamental vitality which underlies his constitution, there can be few men of his intelligence who have devoted more attention than he to the odd and 'cranky' methods of retaining and restoring health. And there can be few who have submitted themselves more often to the ministrations of always expensive and often unplausible practitioners of one kind or another. One can say of him that, unlike so many of us, he would prefer to recover under the dubious treatment of a quack rather than to die forfeited by all the consolations of orthodox medicine.

I turn now from Hollond to his contemporary, and friend since undergraduate days, J.E. Littlewood. Littlewood's name will always be associated with that of his older colleague and collaborator, G.H. Hardy. Hardy died in 1947 at the age of 70. But Littlewood is still going strong, and is, as I understand, still making first-rate contributions to certain topics in pure mathematics. His knowledge and his interests are quite extraordinarily wide, and he makes a most agreeable table companion, ready and willing to contribute valuably and entertainingly to conversations on any subject with any colleague from the oldest to the youngest. I should say that his interests in mathematics are much wider than Hardy's. The latter felt, or professed to feel, a contempt for all but the purest of pure mathematics. Littlewood, on the other hand, is interested in and has a first-hand mastery of, modern mathematical physics, whether macroscopic or ultra-microscopic. He shares with Hardy the power of expressing his thoughts, on any topic which he cares to write about, in beautiful clear and felicitous English.

Littlewood has always avoided taking any public office in College, and has never himself become a member of Council or of any important College committee. One knows that he could have done first-rate work in such positions, had he chosen to be burdened with office, and that he has deliberately decided to spend his time and energy in other ways. He is always the last, or the last but one, to come in to dinner in Hall. He therefore sits at the lower end of one or other of the High Tables, generally among his juniors, taking up the dinner at the stage which it has then reached. He is, on the other hand, an absolutely regular attendant at the optional dessert in Combination Room afterwards, and he often presides there, with the utmost felicity, if both the Master and the Vice-Master should be absent. He is also a regular attendant at all College Feasts which occur while he is in residence.

He has been all his life an expert in many sports and bodily exercises, rather than in games: and these have generally been such as to demand a high degree of skill and courage. In particular, he has excelled at rock climbing. He still spends a long holiday every year in the mountains of Switzerland, and, until quite lately, he was active while there in climbing and in skiing. Nevertheless, he is not, and for many years has not been, in the enjoyment of buoyant bodily health, he has suffered from prolonged periods of depression, due to obscure bodily causes, and he has for long had to combat these with medicine and with special diet. He has been lucky in his later years to have found a doctor who seems to understand and to be able to alleviate his symptoms.

I would add that Littlewood, like Hollond and myself, has for long taken a critical interest in psychical research. Hollond and I have been able to do this only as outside observers, having had no ostensibly paranormal experiences, and showing no trace of possessing ostensibly paranormal powers. But Littlewood, particularly in his later years, has taken part in repeated long series of 'card-guessing' experiments, with a niece of his as 'agent' and himself as 'guesser'. These have consistently produced, under conditions which seem *prima facie* to rule out explanation by normal sensory clues, a proportion, and a distribution, of correct 'guesses' by Littlewood, which it would be fantastic to ascribe to mere chance-coincidence.

Whatever view we may hold as to the correct interpretation of these results, we should note that the experiments have led Littlewood to undertake some very high-grade work on mathematical questions of probability. The results of these are, of course, applicable and highly relevant to experiments where there is no question of possible paranormality. The complete mathematical paper, entitled 'On the Probability in the Tail of a Binomial Distribution' appeared in *Advances in Applied Probability*, November 1969. An abridgement, containing results and Tables, without mathematical proofs, is to be found in S.P.R. *Journal* Vol. 44, No. 737, Sept. 1968. (I found, on going through this, that it *must* contain some errors, probably in the original M.S. I pointed this out to Littlewood, and the necessary corrections were supplied by him in a Note which was published in S.P.R. *Journal*.)

Sir G.I. Taylor is the next on our list of living octogenarians. To my very great regret, I was prevented by a previous engagement of long standing from dining in Hall on 7 March 1966, the night of his 80th birthday. Not only is he Trinity's most distinguished living applied mathematician, with infinite resource and ingenuity and quite outstanding technical achievements both in war and in peace. He is also the most delightfully unassuming and completely 'natural' person whom one could hope to know. He has, moreover, repeatedly shown great physical courage, not only (as one would expect) in the course of duty, but also in the dangerous pastimes in which he has spent and still spends his leisure.

I pass next to Andrew Gow. Of all the seven Fellows enumerated each except him was present when we drank his health on his 80th birthday. Anyone who knows him would realise how such he would hate to be the object of any kind of public ovation. Moreover, he has borne for years, with heroic stoicism and amazing self-discipline, the ever-growing disabilities of arthritis. This has gradually crippled his body, without producing the slightest observable deterioration in his mind. He characteristically took the opportunity to be away from Cambridge, on a visit to friends, during the period covering 27 August 1966. On that occasion, the speech in his honour was held by Hollond, a fellow Rugbeian of slightly older vintage.

In my already published *Autobiography*, I have expressed my admiration for Gow's work for the College curing the Second World War, especially in the organisation and the running of its A.R.P. department. His circular letters to his old Tutorial pupils throughout that war were a joy to them and will be a most valuable memorial to posterity. I would only add that my admiration for his character and his abilities has been increased by seeing how he has reacted to an affliction which a lesser man might well have taken as an excuse for idleness and self-indulgence.

Ignoring myself for the present, I come finally to our youngest living octogenarian, T.C. Nicholas. Nicholas became a fellow in 1912. His geological studies had made him expert in everything to do with surveying country and making and using maps. Throughout the First World War, he was on active service, first in the Middle East and later in France, as an officer in the Field Survey. In that capacity, he was intimately concerned in keeping such order us could be kept, and in saving what could be saved, during the retreat following on the near break-through by the Germans in the neighbourhood of St. Quentin in March 1918. He managed to survive and to escape, and very soon after the end of that war, he returned to Trinity as College Lecturer in Geology, a post which he held for ten years. On the retirement of Innes from the Senior Bursarship in 1923, Nicholas was appointed his successor, and he held office from then until 1956, when he was succeeded by Bradfield.

During the Second World War, in which his son Bryan was on active service, Nicholas, besides performing the duties of the Bursarship under peculiarly difficult conditions, made a characteristic contribution to the national defence by his expert work as a member of the Observer Corps.

I hardly knew Nicholas until my return to Trinity in October 1923, and it was not until he became Senior Bursar in 1929 that I began to know him well. Since then I have got to know him better and better, and to admire him and his work for the College more and more.

In order to describe the functions of the Senior Bursarship, and their development during Nicholas' period of office and since then, I will begin by classifying briefly the main categories under which the bulk of the corporate property of the College at present falls. They are as follows:

Corporate Property	
(I) Real Estate	(II) Stocks and Shares
(1) Agricultural Land	(1) Fixed-interest Securities
(2) Gravel and other Minerals	(2) Equities
(3) Shops, Houses, Offices, etc.	

When Nicholas took over from Innes there was one important item in the Corporate Income which no longer exists. This was Tithes. The College was one of the largest lay tithe-owners in the country. This item ceased to exist while Nicholas was Bursar, owing to legislation, and the capital value was assigned to the College in the form of payment in government stock. Apart from this peculiarity, the corporate property when Nicholas became bursar fell under only three of the above headings, viz., Agricultural Land, Minerals, and Fixed-interest Securities.

One very important development, which went on steadily under Nicholas' Bursarship, was gradually to get rid of poor or mediocre agricultural land and to replace it with land of very high quality. Another was to arrange for the development of deposits of gravel which already existed on certain of the old estates and to acquire new properties having good prospects in that respect. In both these developments, Nicholas' special knowledge and skill as a geologist were of immense value to the College.

It became more and more evident as time went on that it was desirable to reduce the item of Fixed-interest Securities in the above list. For with the continual process of inflation these had more and more come to merit the name of 'insecurities'. There was a long-ish period, however, when the College was not legally entitled to invest any of its money in equities. During this period it was discovered (I think first by Maynard Keynes) that there was no legal objection to investing in shops, factories, offices, etc. So the next development, under Nicholas' bursarship, was the purchase of such property, as opportunity arose, in London and in the provinces. Finally, during the latter part of Nicholas' period of office, it became legally possible for the College to invest in equities.

Nicholas never claimed to have expert knowledge, beyond that of a shrewd and experienced man of business, about shops and other forms of town property. Still less did he pretend to have that very special knowledge and that peculiar skill needed for successful speculative investment in equities. The invaluable service which he rendered to the college in these matters was this. He caused to be established the Estates Committee and the Finance Committee. The latter was composed from the first partly of Fellows of the College and partly of external experts closely connected in one way or another with the College and having its interests very much at heart. The London members of the finance committee have supplied, and continue to supply, the senior bursar with most valuable expert advice on investment and changes of investment in equities.

As I was for many years a member of both these committees, I learned to know Nicholas well, and to admire his services to the college in his bursarial capacity. But I would like, before leaving the subject of Nicholas, to say something of his personality.

Probably the strongest of his personal interests is music. He married early, and his wife was a skilled performer and teacher of music. He too has always been an appreciative and critical listener and a highly competent performer.

The house which they for many years occupied in Park Terrace always seemed to me to be one of the most attractive in Cambridge, and it was a great pleasure to enjoy their hospitality there. Park Terrace was built at a time when the art of combining beauty, convenience, and simplicity had not yet been lost. It overlooks the extensive and unspoiled open space of Parker's Piece, and it fits perfectly into its situation. Here the Nicholas's and their children (a boy and two girls) lived for many years. In course of time, the children married and left Cambridge. Gradually, the house became too big for the parents, and slowly Mrs Nicholas, who was somewhat older than her husband, began to lose her mental powers, to have bodily accidents, and to need constant attention. In all this Nicholas behaved with characteristic kindness, patience, and efficiency, taking upon himself more and more of the duties of running the household. An intermediate stage came, when it was necessary to leave the old house in Park Terrace, and to move into a much smaller house. Finally, even this expedient became no longer workable. Mrs Nicholas is now living in a home in Northampton, and Nicholas is now residing in College, though he is able to pay frequent visits to her.

I would conclude by remarking that Nicolas, like Hollond, is a genuinely sociable person. He obviously enjoys the company of most of those whom he meets. He takes a real pleasure in College feasts. And at ordinary dinners in Hall he readily gets on friendly terms with anyone, old or young, Fellow or guest, whom he happens to sit beside. He makes no attempt to shine or to sparkle or to shock in conversation, but is always ready to talk in a pleasant way and to put his neighbour at his ease.

OLD FRIENDS WHO HAVE DIED

I have now said as much as I wish to say about those octogenarian Fellows of the College, other than myself, who are still active among us at the time of writing. Naturally, in the period of nearly 15 years under review, many old friends have died. I will first mention those who have meant much to me, and will then say a little about each of them. In order of their deaths I would name the following, viz., Donald Robertson (18 October 1961), G.M. Trevelyan (17 November 1962), C.G. Darwin (22 February 1963), Dennis Robertson (13 June 1963), H.O. Evennett (14 November 1964), Hester Adrian (13 June 1966), Karl Pantin (14 January 1967), and Alan Ker (4 January 1967). Of these Trevelyan was very much older than I; Evennett, Pantin, and Ker were considerably younger, whilst the two Robertsons and Charles Darwin were more or less my contemporaries.

Of Trevelyan, I will say only the following. He was Professor of Modern History in Cambridge from 1927 to 1940. In 1940, he became Master of the College in succession to J.J. Thomson, and he and Mrs Trevelyan did wonders in the Lodge during the extremely difficult war-years and in those of even greater penury and restriction which immediately followed. Under the rationing system, as applied to the College, undergraduates got far less to eat than young men of similar age in the army or in factories. They were, in fact, to put it quite plainly, grossly underfed. Trevelyan made one attempt after another, addressing himself to the highest quarters, to get this anomaly rectified. It was all in vain because Colleges fell outside or between the categories in terms of which alone the rationing authorities would or could think. Meanwhile, Mrs Trevelyan used to scour the country in order to pick up cakes, buns, etc., and thus managed at least to entertain undergraduates to occasional tea parties at the Lodge, at which they could temporarily stuff the habitual vacancies in their stomachs.

Trevelyan retired from the Mastership in 1951, when he was succeeded by Adrian. He then returned to the house in Cambridge in which he had lived before he became Master. Mrs Trevelyan died in 1956, after a long and gradual failure of health and strength. Trevelyan himself lived on until November 1962. He gradually lost his eyesight, but was remarkably vigorous intellectually until very near the end.

I have extremely pleasant memories of luncheons with the Trevelyans, followed by long walks, during the period from 1927 up to the outbreak of the Second World War. I think that they may fairly be described as ideal of their kind. After an excellent lunch, we would be driven by the chauffeur to point A; and he would be directed to drive thence to point B, some miles distant, and to await us there. Trevelyan and I would then walk from A to B during which period his conversation would be most stimulating and very varied in its topics. On arriving at point B we would find the car and the chauffeur, and we would then be driven back to an excellent tea at the Trevelyan home.

During the war, I saw a great deal of Trevelyan, not only as a much older personal friend, but also in various official capacities, since I was then acting as Junior Bursar in the absence of David Hinks on war service. I have a strong feeling of gratitude and appreciation for constant helpfulness and consideration for me. After he had ceased to be Master I used once more to visit him often in his home. The days of luncheons, followed by long walks in the country, initiated and terminated by drives in the chauffeur-operated car, were of course over. But Trevelyan had a great love and a great knowledge of English poetry, in particular, that of Meredith and of Swinburne. He delighted to quote it by heart, to read it aloud, and to have it read to him. I used to enjoy these occasions, generally after tea, very much.

I well remember reading aloud to him at his request on one occasion Swinburne's 'Garden of Proserpine', which contains the lines:

> From too much love of living,
> From hope and fear set free,
> We thank with brief thanksgiving
> Whatever gods there be
> That no man lives for ever
> That dead men rise up never
> That even the weariest river
> winds somewhere safe to sea.

Trevelyan knew of my interest in psychical research and of my long connexion with the S.P.R. He had too much good sense, and too much knowledge of the intellectual and moral calibre of men like Sidgwick, Gurney, and Myers who had founded the S.P.R., to think the worse of me for this. But, on this occasion as on others, he told me that he for his part felt certain that neither he nor anyone else would survive bodily death. I could only answer that I most sincerely hoped that he was right on this matter, but that I unfortunately, with my greater knowledge of certain apparently relevant facts, could not feel so sure as he did.

Trevelyan was a hot-tempered and an impatient man. He did not suffer, or pretend to suffer, gladly those whom he considered to be talking or acting like fools or like knaves. He had no hesitation in barking out pretty strongly expressed disapproval on such occasions, whether the culprit were a Fellow of the College or a guest brought to dinner at the High Table. I think that this was often a highly valuable property when he was chairman of the Council, or of other College committees, during his Mastership. The knowledge that one might well be blasted from the Chair tended to make even the most tiresome of the Fellows a good deal less inclined than they would otherwise have been to delay business by clever-silly talk.

Mrs Trevelyan, in her long last illness, became very difficult, and she must often then have sorely tried the patience of a hasty and hot-tempered man like her husband. I have often, when taking tea at their house at that time, admired and been touched at the perfect courtesy and patience which Trevelyan displayed towards her. After her death in 1956, Sister Thomas, who had looked after her devotedly, stayed on and kept house for Trevelyan up to the last. It was quite admirable arrangement.

Before leaving the subject of Trevelyan I must mention the extremely characteristic events which marked the celebration by the College of his 80th birthday on 11 February 1956. The weather was frightfully cold. At 12 noon such of the Fellows as could face the chill assembled in the north-west corner of the North Paddock. (I remember that I took the precaution of wearing a pair of ear-protectors which I had bought when staying in the United States.) There Trevelyan, far older than nearly anyone else present, sturdily dug a hole with a spade and planted a young oak-tree. The ground must have been as hard as iron. In the evening he dined in Hall with the Fellows, and we drank his health. Directly afterwards he left us, in order to go home and hear the tributes to himself which the BBC was to broadcast at 10.10 pm. I am glad to say that he was none the worse for what might have seemed to be a pretty trying day for a man of 80.

I pass now from Trevelyan to Donald Robertson. He was born on 23 June 1885 and was already a classical scholar of the College when I came up in October 1906. He was a friend of my cousin, A.W. Gomme, also a distinguished classicist at Trinity, and it was through the latter that I first got to know him. He was from the first extremely kind and friendly to me.

Robertson was primarily an outstanding Greek scholar. But his interests and his knowledge were extraordinarily wide, and they continued to expand throughout his life. When I first met him his main extraneous interest was in gypsy lore. He had associated much with English gypsies and had learned their form of Romany. He had acquired from them, *inter alia*, the art of roasting dead hedgehogs in a covering of clay, which (he alleged) removed their spikes and left a delicious edible residue within. Much later in his life Robertson made a thorough study of Icelandic, and read all the sagas in the original. Later still he took up Persian, and acquired a mastery of that language and its literature.

Robertson married quite soon after getting his Fellowship. For many years, after the First World War, he and his wife and their children lived in a house in Bateman Street. At the beginning of the Second World War Mrs Robertson became an air-raid warden. Early in that war, in one of the few raids on Cambridge, she was killed while on duty in the streets. Thereafter Robertson moved into College and lived for many years in the vast set of rooms on C Great Court, which had been occupied by Ernest Harrison up to the date of the latter's death. Quite late in life, Robertson married again, this time the young widow of a Fellow of the College who had died at an early age. So, in the last years of his life he again lived in a house in Cambridge, though he continued to dine in Hall fairly regularly. While living in College he took an active part in its business, and he was an efficient and popular Vice-Master between the years 1947 and 1951.

As a young man, Robertson had a very happy gift for producing excellent light verse on somewhat delicate topics. As such poems are unlikely to have been preserved among his published works, I will quote from memory three of them. The first needs no explanatory comments:

> If a bee stung the Master's *pudenda*.
> And those parts were in consequence tender,
> Would 'A hot mustard-plaster
> For the use of the Master'
> Appear on the Council's agenda?

The second refers to the distinguished joint-authors of a standard dictionary of classical antiquities, and to the late King Edward VII:

> If Daremberg bedded with Saglio,
> And the scene were engraved in intaglio,
> And worn in a ring
> By our popular King,
> What delight it would give his seraglio!

The third is concerned with the development of religious beliefs, and its influence on morality:

> Although the sin Jehovah hates the most
> Is disrespect toward the Holy Ghost,
> He is not (like his predecessor Zeus)
> Blind to the ill-effects of self-abuse.

So much for Donald Robertson. I come next to C.G. Darwin. He was born on 19 December 1887, and was therefore almost exactly contemporary with myself. He was the son of the eminent mathematical astronomer Sir George Darwin, long a Fellow of Trinity, and his paternal grandfather was the great Charles Darwin. The family home in Cambridge was the house, beside the backwater south of Silver Street, which is now incorporated in Darwin

College. It, and the life in it and in donnish circles in Cambridge during the brief period when dons were gentlemen, is most amusingly described in Gwen Raverat's classical book 'Period Piece'. She was an elder sister of C.G. Darwin. The latter was at school at Marlborough, and came up to Trinity as a mathematical scholar in October 1906, when I entered the College as a scholar in natural science.

We soon became good friends and remained so for the rest of Darwin's life, though neither of us would have counted the other among his intimates. I saw most of Darwin when we were both undergraduates. He just missed getting a Fellowship at Trinity, and returned to us only in his old age, after holding a number of very distinguished offices. On his return, he lived in his childhood's home by the river, and there he died.

I remember him best for his humour and his ready wit in our undergraduate days. He told me (with what truth 1 do not know) that be was once standing reverently by the side of the path in the Great Court along which the Judge on Assize was proceeding from the Master's Lodge to the Great Gate on his way to his performance of his judicial duties. Darwin, as the Judge's procession passed him, saw an agonised expression appear on the latter's face, saw him raise his band to his mouth, and heard him exclaim: "Christ! I've forgotten my teeth!"

Darwin once asked me if I knew the motto of Jesus College. I confessed that I had no idea of it. He said: "It is contained in the line of the hymn:

'I came to Jesus, and I drank....'"

(This was certainly most appropriate to the College at that time, when it was famous for tough undergraduates, often the sons of wealthy manufacturers in the North of England, whose most respectable occupations were rowing and drinking. It may very well be quite inapplicable nowadays.)

I cannot resist adding the following very odd story which Darwin once told me. When he was still a schoolboy Dr Donaldson was Master of Magdalene College, and his wife was Lady Albinia (née Hobart-Hampden). The Donaldsons gave a party at the Master's Lodge, and Charles Darwin and at least one of his sisters were present as guests. The host and hostess did or said something which offended the Darwin children. Next day the latter, in a mixture of annoyance, fun, and half-serious experiment, made a wax mommet of Dr Donaldson, stuck a pin through it, and buried it in a bed in the garden of their home. Within a couple of days, Dr Donaldson had a quite serious fall from his horse. The Darwin children were slightly disturbed, but laughed it off as a mere coincidence. Almost immediately afterwards, however, they heard that Lacy Albinia had been stricken by a serious attack of influenza. Charles and his sisters decided that no further risks should be taken. They dug up the mommet, removed the pin from it, and dealt with the situation in accordance with certain traditional methods for taking off a spell, about which they had read. The Master then rapidly recovered from his fall, and Lady Albinia from her influenza.

Many years later, in 1926, J.G.S. Donaldson, the son of these two targets of the Darwin experiment in sympathetic magic, came up to Trinity as a freshman, He studied Moral Sciences, and we soon became and have ever since remained very good friends. At that time his father was dead, but his mother was alive and in good health. I visited on several occasions in those days their country home near Cromer. When I got to know Lady Albinia well enough to be sure that she would not be hurt or offended, I narrated the story to her. She confirmed it at least to the extent of admitting that her husband had had a bad fall from his horse and that she had immediately afterwards had a severe attack of influenza, at about the right date to fit in with Darwin's story.

Darwin died suddenly, sitting in his chair at home, in February 1963. If this life be all, it is certainly the kind of ending which one would most wish for oneself and for others. Nor does it seem that there would be much reason to wish otherwise, even if some at least of us survive in some sense, for a while at any rate, the death of our present bodies. (This suggestion Darwin would have regarded as too absurd to be worth serious consideration.) For we have no reliable information whatever as to whether it would be an advantage or a disadvantage in one's next life, if any, to have ended one's present life suddenly or to have faded away gradually or to have died after a long illness.

Leaving Darwin with this tentative valediction, I turn now to Dennis Robertson. He was born on 23 May 1891. His father had been for a time Headmaster of Haileybury, and later became a country clergyman in Cambridgeshire. One of his two elder brothers was for many years a much-beloved master at Winchester, to whom there now exists a memorial in College. Dennis Robertson himself was one of the most brilliant of that galaxy of Scholars of Eton College, most of whom were doomed to an early death in the First World War. He entered Trinity in October 1908 as a Scholar in Classics. After brilliant achievements in that subject, he turned to

Economics; gained his Fellowship for a thesis on an economic topic; and, after the First World War, in which he served in the Middle East, became one of the most eminent English economists of his day.

I knew Dennis Robertson fairly well when we were undergraduates and came to know him far better in his later years. He was one of the gentlest and kindliest men whom I have ever met, with an extremely high sense of duty towards his pupils and his colleagues. He was a master of English prose, as his published writings abundantly testify.

Leaving aside his achievements in his professional work, I will confine myself here to recording a few personal details about him. He had plenty of wit and humour, and an exceptional gift for writing polished light verse. I have heard or read, and greatly enjoyed, many examples of this. Unlike the light verse of many of his contemporaries – in particular, that of his fellow Etonian and fellow Scholar of Trinity, Philip Bainbrigge, who was killed in the First World War – Robertson's verses were always, so far as I am aware, completely chaste both in matter and in expression. His tastes were homosexual; his life was, I should suppose, completely continent. Personally, he was highly ascetic and lived up to the last in what seemed to others to be decidedly uncomfortable conditions.

Robertson was an extremely good amateur actor. From the time when he was still quite young, he excelled in the role of rather doddering old men. I have a vivid recollection of his representation at an A.D.C. concert in 1909 of the character of 'The Master of King's Hall' in a performance of Winstanley's and Pym's mock melodrama *Fellow or Felon*. I have also a clear memory of him on a similar occasion in 1911 acting the part of the Prime Minister 'Lord Trumpington' in Winstanley's *The Shame of the Shelfords*.

As an undergraduate and a young B.A., Robertson took a fairly active part as a Liberal in local politics. I remember his telling me the following story concerning a by-election either in Cambridgeshire or in Huntingdonshire. He was standing one evening among a crowd assembled in the marketplace of a certain town to hear the result announced of a recent polling. At one side of the square was an ancient church, and in front of it stood a statue of Oliver Cromwell facing the marketplace. Next to Robertson was a young farmer, of Liberal principles but plainly not a total abstainer. He poked Robertson in the ribs, and confided to him the following political and historical sentiment: 'There's Oliver, the best Liberal of them all. There he stands, his face to the People, and his arse to the Church!'

Towards the end of his life, Robertson began to have trouble with his heart. One noticed that he became breathless and distressed when he had to mount any stairs. As I have said, he was a highly ascetic person, who certainly took little care for his own comfort, and he probably neglected elementary precautions about his health. One day in the first half of 1963, he had a heart attack in his room. He was taken to the nursing home and died there within the next 24 hours. It was for me the loss of an old and valued friend, towards whom I felt, not only affection for himself, but also the deepest respect and admiration for his character and his gifts.

The next friend whose death I will record is H.O. Evennett (born 15 May 1901). He was a Roman Catholic, and came up to Trinity from Downside in 1920. His academic studies were in Modern History, and he gained his Fellowship in that subject. The field in which he became the acknowledged English expert was the history of the Council of Trent and its background. During the Second World War, he was living near Bletchley, engaged in government work there. Soon after his return to Trinity he became a Tutor, and held that office from 1945 to 1955.

Evennett was an extremely accomplished pianist. He might easily have been a professional musician instead of a don at Trinity in history. He hovered for some years between the two alternatives, and after he had (to our great good luck) come down on the historical side, he continued regularly to play the piano in his own rooms and, on occasion, at concerts.

I did not know him when he was an undergraduate. But I got to do so better and better from when he became a Fellow to his death in 1964. The following very contingent circumstance formed one minor link between us.

From the 1800s my father had a great friend, Mr Henry Harris, a rich man who lived at a house called 'The Holt' at Aspley Guise, near Woburn Sands, in Bedfordshire. For many years, so long as Mr Harris lived, my parents used to pay a longish visit to this house each Easter. From the time when I became old enough to be no great nuisance (say ten years of age), I used to be taken with them on these visits, which I greatly enjoyed. 'The Holt' was a big house with plenty of stables, horses, and carriages. It had extensive and beautiful grounds, and Mr Harris specialised in conservatories and ferneries. My father was an amateur expert in this, and he had played a prominent part in the design and the construction of these. Dukes were still dukes, and I well remember long carriage-drives in the grounds of Woburn Abbey, as it then was and as it will never be again. I remember also walks in the woods near Aspley Guise, belonging to the then Duke of Bedford. Now it so happened that the house which Evennett and his sister took, while Evennett was working at Bletchley during the Second World War, and in which his sister remained afterwards, was closely adjacent to, or actually built upon part of, what had been the grounds of 'The Holt'.

When Evennett and I had come to know each other well, I would sometimes 'rag' him by solemnly offering him helpful literary suggestions which I knew quite well that he would not accept. When, for example, he was about to publish his book *The Cardinal of Lorraine and the Council of Trent* (C.U.P. 1930), I suggested that he should put on the title page the following quotation from Chap. XV of Gibbon's *Decline and Fall of the Roman Empire*:

> The theologian may indulge the pleasing task of describing religion as she descended from heaven, arrayed in her native purity. A more melancholy duty is imposed on the historian. He must discover the inevitable mixture of error and corruption, which she contracted in a long residence upon earth, among a weak and degenerate race of beings.

(I observe that the simpler and less controversial words which Evennett in fact put next to the title-page were: "To Dom Lucius Graham.")

Any Tutor, in the course of his duties, has occasionally to cope with some unexpected complication involving, one or other of his pupils. Evennett once confided to me that one of these had recently 'fallen for' one of the kitchen apprentice boys and that he was concerned tutorially to try to unravel the situation. (It struck me at the time that such a complication must be very unusual, since these boys are kept strictly in *purdah*, and most undergraduates are quite unaware of their very existence.) However, I offered to Evennett to write, on his behalf, a soothing letter to the distracted parents of his pupil, pointing out to them the brighter side of such an imbroglio. Whilst 'succulence' (I proposed to say) is indeed the most ephemeral of human goods, a light hand at pastry is something that may be expected to last for almost a lifetime. To my no great surprise, Evennett declined my offer, and dealt with the situation in his own tactful and effective way.

During the latter years of his life, Evennett suffered increasingly from ill-health of various kinds. This began with a series of different illnesses, and at least one operation, which seemed to be disconnected with each other.

Towards the end, however, what was more and more seriously amiss was his heart. He moved into the rooms D3 King's Hostel, and there had a lift built, since he could no longer mount stairs. During this period, he would still dine in Hall, but getting to it was a complicated process. He would walk on the level to the front door of the Master's Lodge, would then ascend by a lift therein to the level of the Combination Room, and would then walk through the latter and down the stairs to the door entering the Hall from the half-landing at its northern end. At length, his heart became too bad for him to live in College. He moved into the Hope Nursing Home, which is a Roman Catholic institution, and died there after a long period of decline. He was one of the nicest and the best of men whom I have ever known. After his death Gow moved into his old rooms; and the lift, which Evennett had built for himself, has been a godsend to Gow with his arthritis.

I will say only a few words of Pantin, who died, after a long and distressing illness, in 1967. He came to Trinity from Christ's many years ago. He was a very distinguished zoologist, of high general intelligence, and with strong philosophic interests. I came across him a good deal in connexion with 'The Eranus', an ancient society which has met for many years twice a term in my rooms. We greatly enjoyed Pantin's papers, the demonstrations which accompanied them, and the discussions which followed. They were generally illustrated with actual specimens of living non-mammalian fauna. I was often a little afraid that I might find a stray one of these in my rooms afterwards, but I never did. Pantin lived long enough to give, and afterwards to prepare partially for publication, an admirable series of Tarner Lectures. Happily, he left the M.S. in so nearly a perfect form that his widow has been able to edit it as a book.

Alan Ker, like Pantin, cane to Trinity from elsewhere. He had been a don at Oxford, and a schoolmaster at (I think) Rugby. He was a distinguished classical scholar, and he became, like Evennett, a highly successful and much-beloved Tutor. He was an entertaining talker and an admirable mimic. His experience in the Higher Civil Service during the Second World War provided him with a number of distinguished models on whom to exercise these gifts.

I had one very early connexion with Ker, of which I was first reminded when he joined us at Trinity. My first job after getting my Trinity Fellowship in 1911 was as Assistant to G.F. Stout, then Professor of Philosophy at St. Andrews. Stout and his wife were extremely kind and hospitable to me, and

I was very often at their house 'Craigard' to tea and on other occasions. Now Mrs Stout had been a Miss Ker, and Alan Ker was a nephew of hers. He was at that time a small boy, attending a preparatory school at St. Andrews, along with his cousin and contemporary Alan Stout (now Professor of Philosophy in the University of Sydney.) The two boys were constantly in and out of the Stouts' house. It was then that I first met Alan Ker, and I had altogether lost sight of him since those days until he came to Trinity as Lecturer in Classics.

By 1967, Ker had lately come to the end of his Tutorship. He was looking forward to many years to be devoted to renewed research in classical subjects. Instead, he died one night in his sleep at the age of 63 from a sudden heart attack. His death was a shock and a loss to all who had known him. At the memorial service to him in the College Chapel on 18 February 1967, there were present, not only many of his colleagues, but also a large number of his former pupils who had come to pay their last tribute to their late Tutor.

Among those who have died during the period under review, I come finally to Hester Adrian. She was born in 1899. Her father was H.C. Pinsent, a well-known solicitor in Birmingham. Her mother, née Parker, became Dame Ellen Pinsent. Her brother, David, was an undergraduate at Trinity immediately before the First World War; became a great friend of Wittgenstein's and lost his life in an aeroplane towards the end of that War. In 1923, she married B.D. Adrian (now Lord Adrian of Cambridge), who has been a great friend of mine ever since we were both undergraduates. In consequence of his marriage, he vacated the rooms E 4 Great Court (Sir Isaac Newton's rooms) in which he had been living, and took a house in Grange Road. It was just at the time when I returned to Trinity in order to succeed McTaggart as College Lecturer in Moral Science. I was lucky enough to be able to take over these rooms from Adrian, and I have lived there ever since.

Before the Second World War, the Adrians lived first in this house and then in a much larger one, both being on the eastern side of Grange Road. During the war, they lived for a time in a flat in Grange Court on the opposite side of that road. When Adrian succeeded Trevelyan as Master of Trinity in October 1951, they of course moved into the Master's Lodge, and that was their home in Cambridge until Adrian ceased to be Master in June 1965. In preparation for his retirement Adrian had been building a house for Hester and himself, called 'Burrell's End' close to Binn Brook, and on part of the grounds of 'Burrell's Field' which already belonged to the College. Here they lived for the rest of Hester's life.

Fairly early in their married life, the Adrians were involved in a very serious mountaineering accident, which might easily have proved fatal to both of them, and which involved grave permanent injury to Hester. They were climbing together somewhere in the Lake District, accompanied by Claude Elliott, when the accident happened; and they had to lie out in the open for five or six hours before they were discovered and rescued by a party alerted by Elliott. Adrian escaped lasting injury, but Hester had to have one of her legs amputated above the knee. Her reactions to this terrible deprivation were typical of her and were a constant source of admiration to me. She learned to cycle and to drive a car, in spite of her injury, and she regularly practised both those arts in the highly crowded and dangerous conditions of the Cambridge streets.

Hester's mother, Dame Ellen Pinsent had been a pioneer in the development of public services for mental disease. She was first an honorary Commissioner of the Board of Control, and later (1921–1932) a Commissioner. She died in 1949 at the age of 83.

Hester followed her mother's footsteps in her public work. She had been a member of two Royal Commissions, viz., that on Mental Health (1954–1957) and that on The Penal System in England and Wales (1964–), and from 1959 onwards she was President of the Howard League for Penal Reform.

She took a prominent part in the affairs of the City of Cambridge, being of special value because of her expert knowledge in certain directions. She was a Justice of the Peace for the city from 1936 onwards; was Chairman of the Board of Magistrates from 1956 to 1958, and Chairman of the Junior Court Panel from 1954 to 1958; and was a Manager of the Cambridge Special Schools from 1935 to 1964, and Chairman from 1960 to 1964.

She played a most important part in the institutions concerned with the care and treatment of the mentally defective in the City and in the County. She was, for example, a member of the East Anglian Regional Hospital Board for many years, and was for long Chairman of its Mental Health Committee. From quite early in its history, she was deeply involved in the work of the Cambridgeshire Mental Welfare Association, being its Hon. Secretary from 1924 to 1934, and its Chairman and President from 1948 onwards.

The above will give some idea of her services in the special fields in which she was an acknowledged expert. Those services were publicly recognised in 1965 by the award of the D.B.E. But she was not just an outstanding public figure. She ran her home admirably, and it was always a pleasure to visit the Adrians, whether alone, in a small intimate party of old friends, or at a formal dinner party. One could count on thoroughly enjoyable conversation, which was always interesting and stimulating, but never in the faintest degree 'high-brow' or self-consciously uplifting.

Some of my pleasantest memories are of the annual 'birthday' dinner parties, dating back to many years before Adrian was married, which I have given and still give shortly after my actual birthday on 30th December. At these, Adrian has been from the first, and he and Hester were throughout their married life, the guests of honour. The rest of the company, besides myself as host, has been composed of a couple of old friends and colleagues and their wives. We start with as good a dinner as the Kitchens can provide, and continue the evening after dessert sitting around the fire and chatting in my rooms until it is time to say goodbye. Hester used to be at her very best on these occasions. After my guests have left I clear up everything in my rooms, and get to bed in the not so small hours of the morning. I take, and I think I have earned, my breakfast in bed the next day.

Hester, like Alan Ker, died suddenly and unexpectedly of a heart attack while in her home. At the time of her death, she was in her 67th year, and it seemed reasonable to expect that she would have many more years of active life. One can at least console oneself with the thought that she was spared the horrors of a long and painful illness, or of a slow decline. The memorial service in Chapel was held on 13 June 1966, and it was a most moving ceremony. After her death, Adrian moved into College, and took up residence in the beautiful oak-panelled rooms G 2 Nevile's Court. These had recently been vacated by Hollond, when the latter moved out of college to the house at 3 Madingley Road which is now his very beautiful home.

TRAVEL

My travels during the period under review may be divided first into (A) English, and (B) Scandinavian. And my Scandinavian travels, in turn, may be sub-divided into (1) visits to Scandinavian countries other than Sweden, and (2) visits Sweden. I will treat them in that order, and thus begin with (A) English Travel.

(A) *English Travel.* During the earlier years of the period, I went regularly to Bristol for about a fortnight each year. Thus, I was there from 22 June to 5 July in 1955, from 3 to 18 April in 1956, from 10 to 18 April in 1957, and from 26 March to 10 April in 1958. Then there was a gap until 1963, when I was there from 2 to 9 July. Since then I have not returned to Bristol or its neighbourhood.

I am extremely fond of Bristol and regard it almost as my native place. Though I was not myself born there, my father and my paternal aunts and uncle were, and it was for at least a couple of centuries the home of my father's ancestors. I used to visit the place regularly, as a guest of an old aunt of mine, as a schoolboy and as an undergraduate. I was Professor at the University there for a shortish time in the early 1920s; and my mother spent her later years living at Langford, about ten miles from the city, until her death in 1939 just at the beginning of the Second World War. Whilst I was Professor there, I made some very good friends, in particular, Mr and Mrs Donald Hughes, whom it was always a great pleasure to meet again. During my recurrent annual visits I would generally occupy a room as guest in Mr Hughes' house in Berkeley Square; coming and going as I liked, and getting my own meals there or outside, but seeing and talking with him most evenings.

I deliberately stopped my recurrent visits to Bristol for a mixture of reasons, which I will now try to enumerate. The first two are rational enough. (1) Bristol is an extremely hilly place; and, moreover, the rooms which I used to occupy at 23 Berkeley Square were either in the basement or at the very top of a tall house. As I got old, and began to have to take care not to strain my heart, I found these two circumstances more and more trying. (2) I came to reflect that my acquaintance with my own country was extremely patchy. It compared, for example, very ill with the wide distribution of my annual visits to Sweden. I reflected that it was rather silly to confine myself to repeated visits to places, such as Bristol, which I had known like the back of my hand since boyhood; and that, if ever I were to do so, I had better begin to make myself familiar with a wide selection of places in England.

These two reasons would have been enough by themselves to justify me in henceforth visiting Bristol only occasionally, and in staying at some conveniently situated hotel when I did so. But there was a third reason, or at any rate motive, which caused me to make a more radical breach with my previous custom. It was the following.

In my *Autobiography*, I mentioned, with some of the gratitude which they had deserved from me, my mother's devoted servants, Mr and Mrs Doughty. I mentioned, too, that Mrs Doughty after her husband's death, was living in a flat in a house in Clifton which belongs to me. She is still living there, at the time of writing, and must be at least 85 years old. She is an extraordinary mixture of, on the one hand, extravagant and rather embarrassing generosity (both in money and in kind) towards myself, and, on the other, of continual bickerings with, and complaints about her neighbours, the tradespeople, the workmen about the house, and indeed all with whom she has daily dealings.

I found more and more that, when I was in Bristol, she tried to monopolise me. She would invite me to one meal after another, which she had obviously taken the greatest pains to choose and to cook to my liking: and would afterwards pour out a continuous stream of complaints about all and sundry with whom she had been in touch, many of whom were of course quite unknown to me. It was this, more than anything else, which eventually made me decide to keep well away from Bristol for the future.

Mrs Doughty and I remain in fairly regular contact by letter. At Christmas, she insists on sending me an extravagantly generous present of money paid in cash. This I find acutely embarrassing, since she must need the money much more than I do. But I spend it on one thing and another, which I should probably otherwise not have bought, and eventually give her a rough account of what I have done with her gift.

Then there is the black-currant jelly complication. She knows that I very much like black-currant jelly and that I used to eat a lot of it when at home at Langford in the vacations. Accordingly, she makes each year a large amount of this, of the most exquisite flavour and composition, and sends me at frequent intervals a parcel containing from four to six pots. (One or more is generally broken; and I have a long and messy job each time separating the fragments of glass, dissolving the attached jelly, and eventually pouring the solution down my gyp-room sink. I, of course, never mention this in my subsequent letter of thanks.)

While I was able to eat the jelly I much enjoyed it, and between myself and the numerous undergraduates who helped me when they came to tea, we managed roughly to equalise consumption and supply. But latterly I have been forbidden to eat things containing much sugar. Mrs

Doughty would be heartbroken if I asked her not to send me any more jelly, and so the difficulty of disposing of that which has arrived and has survived breakage in the post has become fairly formidable. Fortunately, two of my colleagues, each with a wife and family, give me a good deal of help in this problem. I also get some occasional assistance from a research student, whom I knew very well when he was an undergraduate, and who is now married. Help from this source is unfortunately limited by the fact that the lady whom he married is forbidden to eat anything containing sugar, She is also (as I understand) provided by nature with what I may call a 'built-in contraceptive', so is unlikely to produce offspring to consume jelly in future.

Apart from these former visits to Bristol, my English travels fall under two headings, viz., short and occasional, and longer and recurrent. I will now take these two in turn.

My short occasional absences from Cambridge have been of the following two kinds:

(i) In the first place, I always try to get away for a couple of nights at the time of the Trinity May-week Ball and that of St. John's which immediately follows it. I generally go to some fairly nearby town, such as Saffron Walden, or Thetford, or Bury St. Edmunds, which is pleasant in itself and has agreeable surroundings. I like to get away from Cambridge in the May week, not merely to avoid the noise at night. This is not really very serious in my bedroom, with double windows, facing over a lawn towards Trinity Street. What most strongly draws me away at that time is that I find the atmosphere of Cambridge in May Week terribly depressing. The thought of so many nice young men, most of whom will, from the nature of the case, never be so nice again, hectically celebrating their last hours in *statu pupillari* before being absorbed into the great world outside, is almost too sad for me to face on the spot. I am well aware that, rationally considered, this feeling of mine is rather silly. But *ich kann nicht anders*.

(ii) My other short occasional visits to other places have generally been made on invitation, in order to give a lecture or address there. The following are some examples.

From 14 to 16 February 1955, I was first in Glasgow and then in St. Andrews. At the former I gave a lecture on 'Human Personality and the Possibility of its Survival' at the College Club³; and at the latter I addressed the philosophy students on 'Hume's Theory of the Self'.⁴

On 15 July 1957, I made a rather interesting visit to Dillington House, near Ilminster in Somerset, at one time the residence of George III's Lord North. At it were assembled boys and girls from the primary schools of Somersetshire, on a week's course. That evening I gave to them a lecture on 'The Development of Scientific Thought (Pythagoras to Newton)'.⁵ Next morning we had a discussion class, and after lunch, I returned to London. It was a very pleasant occasion. The young people were friendly, well mannered, and intelligent. The house and grounds were beautiful. And there were a number of interesting older people there, including one whose hobby was to construct telescopes, and who gave some fascinating demonstrations with one which he had made.

Later in 1957, viz., 10–11th November, I was in Edinburgh, in order to give to the Royal Society of Edinburgh the John Scott Lecture. My subject was 'Change, Continuity, and Discontinuity'.⁶ I had a most enjoyable visit, and met *inter alios* my former Trinity colleagues, Kemmer and Feather, and my future Trinity colleague, Polkinghorne.

Next year, I was again in Scotland. This time, 28 and 29 October 1958, I was in Dundee. On the 29th, I gave a lecture to the Philosophy of Science Group at University College on 'Soal's Work with Mr Shackleton and with Mrs Stewart'.⁷ I had been Lecturer on Logic there many years earlier, during the First World War. I found it most interesting to renew my acquaintance with the city and the College, and to note the many changes and the great improvements which had taken place.

The year 1961 was the fourth centenary of the birth of Francis Bacon. I was invited by the University of Leeds to give them an address about him, and I did so on 30th January.⁸ Already, in September 1926, I had given a lecture in the Senate House at Cambridge, on Bacon's *Philosophy*, in celebration of the tercentenary of his death, and this had been re-published in my book *Ethics and the History of Philosophy* (1952). So this time I chose to talk about the political and the private life of that most remarkable, but not wholly exemplary, man of genius. This address has not as yet been published.

There remain just three more occasional lectures away from Cambridge to be mentioned. All of them were on topics connected with psychical research. In 1963, I went to Nottingham on 15 October spent the night in a cottage on the University Park (situated in the grounds of the late Sir Jesse Boot's mansion), and read a paper to the Philosophy Club on 'Problems of Ostensible Precognition'. Very soon afterwards (24 October). I was again away. This time, it was at Wells. I stayed there with the Principal of the Theological College, had supper with some of the students at their lodgings in Vicars' Close, and then lectured in the College Library on 'Precognition'. (This outing was made memorable by two facts. In the first place, I lost my return ticket and had only just enough money to enable me to get back third-class to Cambridge. And, to crown this, the *Diesel* engine, drawing the train from Bath to Paddington, broke down at Hayes, and after a very long delay, we had to be ignominiously dragged for the rest of the way by a steam-locomotive.) Finally, on 11 May 1966, I went to Hull, a city which has always interested me through its connexions with Andrew Marvell and with William Wilberforce. I read a paper to the Hull University Society for Psychical Research on 'Human Survival'.

I now leave my occasional visits to places in England outside Cambridge and pass to my longer and more systematic expeditions to various parts of England. These may be enumerated in chronological order as follows. From 31 March to 6 April 1959 I was successively in Bury St. Edmunds, Ely, Kings Lynn, Spalding, and Lincoln; from 5 to 19 April 1962 in Winchester and Salisbury: from 28 March to 1 April 1963 in Wells; from 2 to 15 April 1964 in Rye and Tunbridge Wells; from 31 March to 14 April 1965 in Canterbury and Folkestone; from 23 March to 6 April 1966 in Chester and Shrewsbury, and from 1 to 22 September of the same year in Chepstow, Hereford, and Worcester; from 29 March to 5 April 1967 in Norwich, and from 28 September to 19 October of the same year in Ipswich, Colchester, and Lewes; and, finally, from 27 March to 10 April 1968 in Huntingdon and Bedford, and from 4 to 25 September of the same year in Leamington, Matlock Bath, and Buxton.

The general plan of these expeditions was as follows. I would go away either well before or soon after Easter, and in the early autumn, when most people will be at home and at work. I always avoid holiday resorts or 'show-places'. And I would book, long in advance, quiet rooms in hotels at the various places at which I was going to stay. Once I was settled in a place I would first explore it thoroughly, and then make expeditions by bus or by rail to other places of interest in its neighbourhood.

In this way, I have gradually got to know quite a considerable selection of inland districts dotted about over England. The high lights have been ancient cathedral cities, such as Canterbury, Chester, Hereford, Lincoln, Norwich, Salisbury, Wells, Winchester, and Worcester. These have always contained a great deal of historic interest besides their cathedrals and the adjuncts of the latter. For bishoprics were generally founded originally in ancient cities, going back often to Roman times, and those cities have often since been the scenes of important events in English history.

(B) *Scandinavian Travel*

(1) *Countries Other Than Sweden.* I turn now to my Scandinavian travels. I will first say something about my visits to Scandinavian countries other than Sweden, viz., Denmark, Finland, and Norway:

(i) I will begin with Norway, as this was the first Scandinavian country other than Sweden which I visited during the period under consideration. I was there on two occasions during this period.

On my first visit to Norway, I was in Oslo from 21 March to 4 April 1955. I went there by invitation of the University to give various lectures. My stay there was made particularly pleasant by the kindness of a former pupil in Cambridge, Knut-Erik Tranøy, and his parents. Tranøy was at the time a Lecturer at the University, and he has since become a Professor at the University of Bergen.

At first, I stayed on my own in rooms provided for me at the Studenthjemmet Hotel, but on 28 March I moved to the house of Tranøy's parents and was made one of the family until I left Oslo. I also met again a young man called Ingemund Gullvåg, whom I had known well at Cambridge when he used to attend my lectures there. Karl-Erik Tranøy, his brother, and Ingemund had all been, in several ways, in the resistance movement when the Germans were in occupation of Norway. Karl-Erik, in particular, had suffered pretty severely at their hands, and I always admired the sanity and balance which he showed on viewing this part of his life in retrospect.

I gave in all three lectures to the University, viz., one on 'Self and Others'[9] (22 March), and two on 'The Nature of Philosophy'[10] (23 and 30 March). I also gave one to the Philosophy Society on 24 March, entitled 'Some Notes on Causation';[11] and one on the following morning (of the title of which I have no record) to the Norwegian Academy of Sciences. And, to conclude my tale of lectures, I gave one on a topic in psychical research, viz. 'Mrs Leonard's Mediumship',[12] to an audience of students at the Institute of Social Research.

While in Oslo I was almost overwhelmed with hospitality, both by Norwegians and by certain English residents. But to me, the most interesting experiences were being shown round the city and some of the surrounding country by Karl-Erik, who of course had known it from infancy. Among other notable things, we saw the Viking ships, which had been recovered in remarkably good preservation from Oslo Fjord; and the 'Fram', in which Nansen had made his famous polar expedition when I was a small boy.

On 4 April 1955, I left Oslo and flew to Copenhagen. My American friend, H.A. McNitt, whom I had first met when I was at Ann Arbor, Michigan, in 1955, and his wife, were at that time quartered in lodgings in Copenhagen. I stayed in a room which they had booked for me at an hotel, but I spent most of my time in their company. McNitt by that time knew Copenhagen very well, and we visited many places of interest together. On 8 March, for example, I met the McNitts early at the railway station, and we went to Helsingør, the Elsinore of Shakespeare's 'Hamlet'. We went over Kronoborg Slott; and from there by train to Hillerød, where Frederiksborg Slott lies in a great park, but we arrived too late to enter the castle. Generally, the McNitts and I dined together at one or other of the excellent restaurants with which Copenhagen abounds. Sometimes I was their guest, sometimes their host, and at other times we just dined together each at his own expense.

I was immensely struck by the number and magnificence of the royal castles which I visited. They included, besides those which I have already mentioned, Rosenborg Slott and

Amalienborg Slott. I got the impression that Denmark must have been immensely wealthy and powerful at a time when Sweden was very much of a poor relation. (It should be remembered that Denmark owned all of what is now the southern part of Sweden, and controlled the sea traffic through what we call 'The Sound' from the North Sea to the Baltic, up to the time of the Peace of Brömsebro in 1645, and that she continued to own Norway until 1814, when she had to cede it to Sweden under the Treaty of Kiel.)

I returned to London on 12 April 1955, with a bad cold, but after a very memorable three weeks spent first in Norway and then in Denmark.

I was again in Norway for a short while in August 1958. This time it was for a brief visit on my way to Sweden. I flew to Oslo on 13 August 1958 *en route* for Trondheim. Karl-Erik Tranøy was not then in Oslo, but I was met by his father and his brother Jörgen, who very kindly took me to the paternal home and gave me supper there. I spent the night at a hotel and flew early the next day to Trondheim. I stayed at the Hotel Britannia there for a couple of nights. Trondheim has a magnificent cathedral and is the city where the Kings of Norway are crowned.

On 16 August, I left Trondheim by rail and made the impressive journey through the mountains to Storlien, which is a border-station where the Norwegian and the Swedish state railways meet. What follows belongs strictly rather to travels in Sweden than in Norway, but it will be convenient to describe it here.

From Storlien I travelled by a Swedish train to Östersund, in the province of Jämtland, where I had arranged to make a longish stay that year. During this part of the journey, the train was boarded by a number of young Swedish soldiers who had been on an exercise in the mountainous country around Åre. They were nice, friendly boys. But they were heavily dressed; the train was extremely hot, and they probably had not had much chance for a thorough wash for some time past. As a result, I could not help being forcibly reminded of the advertisement in London tube stations with the legend: 'Someone's not been using *Amplex*'.

On the train, I met, and got into conversation with, a young man called Bo Lindhammar. He was a student at Uppsala. His home was in Östersund, and he was proposing to break his journey there and visit his people before travelling onwards to Uppsala. He was extremely kind and helpful, carrying my two suitcases for me from Östersund station to my lodgings, and showing me the way. Later on, when I was in Uppsala on 18 September of that year, I gave him lunch, and afterwards went to the rooms in which he was living. These were of considerable interest, being situated in the extremely rickety old wooden building which has been known to generations of Uppsala students as '*Imperfektum*'.

So much for Norway and Denmark (with a bit of Sweden tacked on at the end): I turn now to Finland:

My first visit there was during the eight months which I spent in Sweden in 1946. I was the guest of the von Wrights, partly in Helsingfors[13] and partly in their country home. During the period at present under review, I was twice in Finland, viz., in 1962 and in 1965. On each occasion, I travelled thither from Stockholm, where I was living at the time.

On the first of these occasions, I was in Helsingfors from 25 to 29 September 1962. I was officially a guest of the University, and I had a room in the house which is reserved for such guests. On the evening of 26 September, I gave the lecture which I had been invited to deliver. It was entitled 'Obligations, ultimate and Derived',[14] and was given in the hall of the former *Borgarståndet* (Order of Burghers). Though I was in principle the University's guest, I received continual hospitality from the von Wrights in their own house and elsewhere. The high light of this was a large dinner party on 27 September, at which the von Wright children acted as waiters and waitresses, and acquitted themselves admirably.

The second time when I visited Finland in this period was late in September 1965. On that occasion, I was in Åbo and not in Helsingfors. I was there at the invitation of the University, and, as their guest was quartered at a hotel, but I enjoyed also much personal kindness and hospitality from two individuals, viz., Professor Krohn and John Magnus von Wright.

I was guest at a pleasant dinner-party at the Krohns' flat on the night of my arrival (26 September 1965). The next morning I was at a luncheon party at John Magnus von Wright's flat. He is a distinguished experimental psychologist and a cousin of my old friend Georg Henrik von Wright. He had worked for some years at Oxford, and I had got to know him then on his occasional visits to Cambridge.

On the evening of 27 September, I lectured at the University on 'Hume's Theory of Belief',[15] after which Krohn took me to a pleasant supper at the *Swedish* Club. On the following evening, I gave a second lecture at the University, this time on 'Hume's Theory of the Self'.[16] On this occasion, to ensure racial equilibrium, Krohn took me afterwards to an equally pleasant supper at the *Finnish* Club.

I had a busy day on 28 September. John Magnus met me in the morning at my hotel and took me to see the magnificent Åbo Slott, where the Swedish governors of Finland used to live during the many centuries in which the country was a Swedish possession. I was shown this in great detail, and it was a most rewarding experience. After that, at 12.15 pm, I gave a lecture to John Magnus's psychologists on 'Soal's Experimental Work on Extra-sensory Perception'. I then rested, and in the evening gave the lecture on 'Hume's Theory of the Self' which I have mentioned above.

I returned on 29 September by air to Stockholm *via* Mariehamn. The weather was atrocious, and I was relieved to get back safely.

(2) *Travels in Sweden*. I will now say something about my visits to Sweden during the period under discussion. As I mentioned in my *Autobiography*, I first visited that country in 1946, and then made a long stay there. From then onwards I returned every year up to and including 1965. After that I have ceased to a travel outside Great Britain.

The general outline of these Swedish holidays has been as follows. I have usually been away from England on such occasions from the middle or the end of August until the beginning of Full Term early in October. In a typical visit to Sweden, I would begin by staying from the date of my arrival until about the end of the first week in September at one or more places other than Stockholm and its near neighbourhood. In choosing these I always avoided pleasure resorts and holiday places, and would try to stay in quiet ordinary towns. Usually, I would stay in lodgings, but occasionally in hotels. Arrangements would have been made for me in advance through friends in Sweden, very often through Ulf Hellsten. I would visit different provinces of this very extensive country in different years.

Thus, I was in Härnösand (1955), in Helsingborg (1956), in Vänersborg (1957), in Östersund (1958), in Göteborg and then in Mariestad (1959), in Östersund again and then in Sala (1960), in Kalmar (1961), at Julita Herrgård and then in Strängnäs (1962), in Falköping and then in Eskilstuna (1963), in Örebro and then in Enköping (1964), and finally in Åmål and then in Kristinehamn (1965). In the years 1946–1954, both included, I had already stayed in a great many parts of the country, including a province so far north as Lappland. So I can claim to have sojourned, in the aggregate, in a pretty fair selection of Sweden. Naturally, while I was centred on any place, I would pay visits to interesting spots in its not too distant neighbourhood.

After the end of the first week in September, I would move into Stockholm, to which most of my friends living there would by then have returned from their holidays, and I would make it my headquarters for the rest of my visit. In my earlier visits to Stockholm, I had lodged time after time with Disponent and fru Nyström. I had fared excellently there, and they soon became, and afterwards remained, very good friends of mine. But in 1953 began the generous and magnificent hospitality which Dr (afterwards Professor) Gösta Berg and his wife fru Hazelius-Berg extended to me in every successive year until I ceased to visit Sweden after 1965. I feel that I must say something about this extraordinary kindness on their part and good luck on mine.

In order to do this, I must first digress a little. Almost everyone who has ever visited Stockholm must have been taken, or advised to go, to *Skansen*. It is situated on the vast area of crown-land in southern *Djurgården*, and is reached from the city by crossing the bridge called 'Djurgårdsbron' which leads in a southerly direction from the junction of the eastern end of *Strandvägen* and the southern end of *Narvavägen*. *Skansen* is an extensive high, precipitous area, with a kind of tableland on top, from which extensive views can be had of the city and the surrounding land and water. As its name implies, it was formerly a fortified place, and it must have been an extremely strong one.

Late in the XVIIIth or early in the XIXth Century, the part of it nearest the city became a place where wealthy Stockholmers built for themselves luxurious semi-rural retreats with magnificent views. The two finest of these houses, *Jakobsberg* and *Sagaliden*, play an essential part in what follows. In the latter part of the XIXth Century, owing to the efforts of Artur Hazelius, a direct ancestor of fru Hazelius-Berg, *Skansen* was made into an enclosed park, into which the public can enter by payment. It contains pleasant gardens, an excellent restaurant (*Solliden*), and a zoo. But what is most characteristic of it, and what primarily interested Artur Hazelius, is its wonderful collection of old houses and other buildings, removed bodily from all over Sweden, and set up appropriately throughout the grounds for a very extensive open-air museum of the country as it formerly was. Hazelius was also largely responsible for the foundation of *Nordiska Museet*, a magnificent building which lies outside *Skansen* and adjacent to it on the right-hand side of the main road from *Djurgårdsbron* into *Djurgården*.

The above account of *Skansen* will be seen to be highly relevant when I say that Gösta Berg was intendent of *Skansen* and afterwards became also head of *Nordiska Museet*. In those capacities, he had as his official residence two in turn of the fine old houses within *Skansen* which I have already mentioned. When I first came to know the Bergs their home was *Jakobsberg*, a very fine and beautiful house. Later (I take it when Gösta Berg became head of *Nordiska Museet*) they moved to the still finer and more beautifully situated *Segaliden*, with its magnificent view from high up over Stockholm.

Now in each year from 1953 to 1965, both included, when I visited Stockholm, my home throughout the period would be one or other of the bedrooms in Gösta Berg's official residence within

Skansen at the time. The family would supply me with an ample breakfast in the morning. I would take my other meals out, and I was free to come and go all day and every day just as if I were in my own home. I would be provided with a ticket and a key to Skansen and a key to the house, so that I could come in at any time without trouble to myself or disturbance to others.

It would be difficult to imagine a greater privilege than that which was thus given to me. For all this, the Bergs absolutely refused to allow me to make any payment. The utmost that I was allowed to do in the way of recompense was to send to Gösta Berg, on my return to England after each such visit, a few books which I thought might be of interest to him. I should think that such generosity as I experienced must be pretty well unprecedented. I certainly am most deeply grateful for it.

My first introduction to the Bergs began, like so many of the most important phases in one's life, in the most contingent way possible. On 6 July 1949, as I was returning to College, I happened to pass a lady, accompanied by two schoolboys, looking into the window of Matthew's shop. I noticed that they were talking Swedish and I ventured to accost them in that tongue. Finding that I was at least outwardly respectable, they consented to come to my rooms, to be regaled there with cake and lime juice, and then to be shown around the College. The lady proved to be fru Kallner, and the boys were her eldest son Gunnar and his rather older friend, Pelle Jörpes, son of Professor Jörpes in Stockholm. Her husband was Dr Sixten Kallner of Stockholm, a very distinguished medical man. The boys stayed on in Cambridge for some time longer in that vacation, and I used to have them to tea and to play at bowls with them from time to time.

Now it happened that Dr Kallner was the private physician of the Berg family, and also the official physician to the personnel employed on Skansen. In the following summer Gösta Berg had the idea of sending his son Jonas, then a schoolboy in Stockholm, to England for a few months in order to improve his English. He spoke to Dr Kallner about this, and the latter wrote and consulted me. As a result of all this Gösta Berg, whom I had never yet met, got in touch with me by letter. It was arranged that Jonas should come to Cambridge in the middle of March 1950, and should stay there for a couple of months. Jonas in fact arrived on 16 March 1950, and was met at St. Pancras Station in London by me and Terry Moore, an undergraduate friend of mine at Trinity. After giving him lunch at my Club, and showing him around London a little, we brought him back with us to Cambridge. He began by spending a few days in College as my guest and thereafter lodged with a family in the town until he returned to Sweden early in May 1950. During that period I entertained him from time to time, and Terry Moore saw much of him and introduced him to his own young friends.

During the summer of 1952, a young Swede from Stockholm, named Björn Qvarnström, was living and working in Cambridge. He was a great friend of Jonas Berg, and on that basis, he rang me up. We first met on 30 July 1952, and we soon became, and have ever since remained, very good friends. This naturally formed another link between me and the Bergs. Later in 1952, When I was staying in Stockholm and lodging with the Nyströms, I saw a good deal of Jonas and Björn. They assured me that, if ever I should want to stay in Stockholm at a time when the Nyströms could not take me in, they would arrange alternative accommodation for me.

In 1953, I was to go to the United States in the autumn for a sabbatical year, and so I should not be able to pay my usual autumn visit to Sweden. So I decided to pay an earlier and shorter visit that year, and to confine it to Stockholm. I arrived there on 16 March 1953, was met by Jonas and Björn, and was taken to *Jakobsberg*, the official residence on *Skansen* in which the Bergs were then living. This was my first stay in Stockholm as a guest of Gösta Berg and his wife. Every year afterwards, up to and including 1965, which was the last time when I visited Sweden, a similar hospitality was extended to me. For several years my temporary home was at *Jakobsberg*. When that ceased to be Gösta Berg's official residence, and he moved into the yet statelier *Sagaliden*, I enjoyed the same privileges there.

I will now describe first in outline a typical stay in Stockholm, and will then say something of my visits to other parts of Sweden.

I have a number of good friends of long standing in Stockholm, and they have always been most hospitable to me. One part of my regular routine was a dinner with each of these at his home, and occasionally a return dinner by me at some restaurant.

I must mention in particular one of my earliest, and still my best, friends in Stockholm, viz., Ulf Hellsten. I have known him since he was at Trinity during the latter part of the Second World War. We have always seen a great deal of each other on each of my annual visits.

Apart from the fact that I have often dined with him and his wife and children, and occasionally spent a night or two, at the houses at which they have successively lived, first in Stockholm itself, and then on Lidingö, there have been the following regular meetings. Ulf's birthday is on 19 September. Always at that date or very soon afterwards, I would entertain him and his wife Yvonne to an extremely good dinner at one or other of the better restaurants. Then, again, Ulf and Yvonne have a very pleasant place in the country beside an internal sea called *Spaksjön*. This lies in the wilds in the extreme N.E. of the province of Dalarna on its boundaries with that of Hälsingland on the north and that of Gästrikland on the east. Here the family are wont to spend much of their holidays. During each of my visits to Stockholm Ulf would drive me in his car, through Uppsala and Gävle, to Spaksjön for a weekend. I must confess that I find a very long drive in a car (and this one took several hours) very tiresome, and I was always glad when these journeys were over. But living in the house, and walking about in this utterly wild and remote region, to which nothing at all comparable has existed for centuries in over-crowded England, was always an unforgettable experience.

While living in Stockholm I would nearly always go at least once for a night to Uppsala, stay with some friends there, and pay visits to others. On these occasions, I would generally read a paper to the University's Philosophical Society. These meetings usually took place in a stiflingly hot room. They were followed by a discussion, and then we generally had an enjoyable tea supper together before breaking up for the night. At Uppsala, I would generally stay in the house on *Villavägen* of my very good and long-standing friend fru Laurell, widow of Professor Laurell and mother of my friend Helge.

Another recurrent feature of my visits to Stockholm would be a lecture, on some topic connected with psychical research, to the *Sällskapet för Parapsykologisk Forskning* (Society for Research in

Parapsychology) there. The Society was founded and very efficiently run by fru Eva Hellström. It contained many highly intelligent members, and Ulf Hellsten was for long its Hon. Secretary. I would generally give my lecture in Swedish, which Ulf had gone over and corrected beforehand. He and I would generally eat a modest dinner together at some restaurant before the lecture. After it there would be discussions, ending with an enjoyable tea supper.

Lastly, I would sometimes give a lecture on some philosophical topic to Stockholms Högskolas Philosophical Society. I am bound to say that I thought the discussions after these pretty poor, on the whole. But this was compensated for by the fact that I would afterwards be taken out and entertained to an excellent supper, with good talk, at some pleasant restaurant.

So much for Stockholm; I pass now to my visits to other parts of Sweden. I shall make no attempt to describe all these in detail. I will confine myself to the following three, which seem to be of some special interest:

(1) In 1955 I stayed for some time in Härnösand. This lies in the province of Ångermanland, on the west coast of the Gulf of Bothnia, and on the southern edge of the estuary of the great Ångerman River. It is an oldish city and is the centre of a bishopric. Now it happened that the Bishop of Härnösand at the time was Dr Hultgren. He and Gösta Berg had been at school together at Örebro, and had remained lifelong friends. Gösta Berg gave me an introduction to the Bishop, and the latter was most kind and hospitable to me. He entertained me to dinner, and he drove me around to various parts of his vast diocese. Later on, Hultgren became Archbishop of Uppsala. He then kindly invited me to stay for a few days with him there. During this latter visit, I had the opportunity of driving in his company about the province of Uppland, and of seeing, under specially favourable conditions, something of the magnificent mediaeval churches with which that province abounds.

Hultgren is a very distinguished scholar, and, in particular, is an expert on St. Augustine. As such, he knew and admired Burnaby's works, but he was wholly unacquainted with the author. When he found that Burnaby was a friend and colleague of mine, of many years' standing, his respect for me was (if possible) increased. Later on, when Hultgren was spending some time in England, I had the pleasure of introducing these two Augustinian scholars to each other in Cambridge.

The acquaintances whom I made in Härnösand were not confined to the higher Lutheran clergy. Lodging in the same house as I was a young man called Karl-Gustav Nylander. While we were there our landlord and landlady went away on holiday with their children and left us two by ourselves in the house. I got to know my fellow lodger, Karl-Gustav, very well. He was on a course at a technical college in Härnösand. In the evenings we would sit together, and I would often help him with his mathematical exercises, which were not always above my head. I gradually got on easy terms with him, and soon discovered the following odd facts about him. He belonged to a family of small peasant farmers in the neighbourhood, and they were all enthusiastic members of an extremely queer Swedish evangelical sect called Pingstvänner (Whitsun-friends).

This sect was quite widely spread throughout Sweden and plainly was in control of considerable capital sums. It had its own wireless station, somewhere in North Africa, and at the times when this was broadcasting Karl-Gustav would sit glued to his receiver. At meetings of the Pingstvänner, it was very common for members of the congregation to get into an ecstatic state and to 'speak with tongues'. Karl-Gustav told me that he had very often been present on such occasions, and I gathered that he had now and then 'spoken with tongues' himself. In spite of all this, he was in all other respects a nice, sensible, efficient, and rather 'tough' young man, and we got on very well together. I do not know what has become of him since then.

I made one other friend in Härnösand besides the Bishop and the Pingstvän. This happened in the casual, contingent way in which quite important phases in my life have often started. One afternoon, in the course of a long walk, I was panting up a long, steep, hilly road. A young man happened to be engaged in pushing his bicycle up the same road, more or less side-by-side with me. We accosted each other, and I soon learned that he was called Karl-Erik Olsson, and was working in Härnösand on the same technical engineering course as Karl-Gustav Nylander. After that, we met fairly often while I was in Härnösand. We used to go for long walks together, and he used from time to time to dine with me at a pleasant restaurant in a public park outside the town.

Karl-Erik's origin was very like that of Karl-Gustav. He came from a family of small peasant farmers in a place not far from Östersund in the province of Jämtland. He had a minor job on the Swedish State Railways, and he was temporarily in Härnösand on a technical course in engineering. He was not, like Karl-Gustav, a member of any extremely odd sect such as the *Pingstvänner*. But he was, as I soon found, what we should call a highly puritanical Nonconformist. He was, for example, and has always remained, a rigid teetotaller. He did not feel it his duty to obtrude or to propagate his views, and I of course always respected them.

Since then we have always kept in touch with each other. I saw a good deal of him on the two occasions when I stayed in Östersund, viz., in 1958 and 1960. He was then working as an engineer in the service of the Swedish State Railways in that part of the country and was living in Östersund. In June and July 1959, he paid a visit (his first) to England, and he stayed with me in College from 1 to 3 July. He has steadily improved his technical qualifications, and now holds a responsible post as a railway engineer. He has been moved about from one part of the State Railways to another. He has now been married for some time and is living at Örebro in the province of Närke.

We still keep in quite regular contact by letter. I think it is fair to say that most Swedes (in common with most inhabitants of countries where communication is mainly by telephone) are poor letter-writers. Karl-Erik is a most notable exception to this general rule. He cannot have had much general education, but he seems to be a born letter-writer. His letters are always full of interest in their content, and (so far as I can judge Swedish) admirably expressed. It is a pleasure to get them, and in due course to answer them.

It may seem odd that these two young men and I, with such extremely different backgrounds, managed to get on so well with each other. I think that an essential negative favouring condition was this. They, though highly religious in their several ways, never attempted to push their religious views on me. And I, though completely non-religious, both in sentiment and belief, never obtruded my non-religion on them.

(2) A second place visited by me, which I will describe in some detail is Julita in the province of Södermanland. I was there from 17 August to

3 September 1962. Södermanland is a part of Sweden famous for the presence of many fine, ancient *herrgårdar*, i.e., country estates at which there live, or have lived until the fairly recent past, the equivalent of an English county-family. As in England, more and more of them under modern conditions have had to be handed over to the ownership of the partial control, of public or semi-public bodies.

Julita Gård is an instance in point and a particularly happy one. It is situated on the north-eastern shore of Lake Öljaren, which itself lies south-east of Lake Hjälmaren, one of Sweden's very big internal seas. The nearest town of any size is Katrineholm, on the main railway line to Stockholm from the south-west. The house, a very beautiful example of its kind, goes back to the XVIIth Century; but the estate dates much further back. In the middle ages, and up to the time of the Reformation, it was the site of a large and important monastery, considerable traces of which still exist in the grounds.

The old line of owners came to an end in the 1870s, after the estate had been handed down for many generations. The house and grounds and the agricultural property were then bought by a wealthy family of Stockholm merchants called Bäckström. For a great many years it was owned and occupied by a Lieut. Arthur Bäckström. He was a wealthy man, who delighted in spending money on the house and grounds, and on collecting appropriate furniture, etc., for it. When he died, at the age of 80, in 1941, he left the whole estate to Nordiska Museet. The house and its gardens have become a show-place, and the main rooms, which the public are allowed to visit in conducted parties, are left furnished as they were when Lieut. Bäckström was living there.

The very considerable agricultural estate, which is an essential part of the property, is worked for profit on the most up-to-date lines; and the whole property is managed for Nordiska Museet by an expert employed by them. He lives in a house closely adjacent to the Great House. At the time in question, he was Kaptén Danielsson. The nearest English analogy to Julita Gård, as it now is, which comes to my mind, is Ickworth in Suffolk, formerly the seat of the Herveys, and now run by the National Trust.

Now Gösta Berg, as head of Nordiska Museet, made to me the generous offer that I should live in the Great House at Julita as a guest from 17 August to 3 September 1962. I of course accepted this with alacrity. I had a magnificent sitting room and a no less magnificent adjoining bedroom, and I used to take my meals in the restaurant at the other end of the grounds, which was open to the public. I received the greatest kindness from Kaptén and fru Danielsson, and from all the estate-servants with whom I had to do. I was shown all over the Great House. I saw many parts of it which are not open to ordinary visitors, including the room in which Lieut. Bäckström died, and another which is supposed to be haunted by the ghost of a daughter of one of the earlier proprietors, who had made a *mésalliance*.

Nordiska Museet owns, presumably in connexion with Skansen, a number of specimens of that rare and fordable beast, the European bison. Some of these are kept at Julita within extremely heavily fenced compounds; and they formed an interesting sight, provided that one was on the right side of the fence. They were about the ugliest brutes that I have ever seen, with the possible exception of some of the undergraduates of the University of Essex whom I observed in 1967 when I paid an unofficial visit to that seat of learning from Colchester.

The only drawback to my stay at Julita was the awful weather which prevailed all over that part of Sweden in the late summer and early autumn of 1962. It rained almost every day, and often almost all day. It was not until my visit to Derbyshire in 1968 that I encountered anything comparable in horror to this. Then the weather conditions at Julita were certainly equalled, and if possible surpassed, in badness.

(3) The only other place in Sweden which I will mention in detail is Vänersborg, where I stayed from 27 July to 7 September 1957. It lies in the province of Västergötland, just on the border between the latter and the province of Bohuslän, at the south-western tip of Lake Vaner. The town is known all over Sweden as '*lila Paris*' (little Paris), from a delightful song about it with that title, of which the words and music were written by Birger Sjöberg early in the present century. This song is one of a collection by Sjöberg, entitled '*Fridas bok*' (Frida's Book), which gives an enchanting picture of Vänersborg as it was at that time for one of its own very sensitive and poetical citizens, whose feet were nevertheless always kept well on the ground of actual daily life there.

Ulf Hellsten's youngest brother, Helge, had been settled in Vänersborg for some years as surgeon at the local hospital and lived with his wife and family in one of the houses attached to it. I had known him some years earlier when he was still a medical student in Stockholm and was as yet unmarried. As soon as I arrived in Vänersborg the Helge Hellstens treated me with great kindness and hospitality. But later developments, as we shall see, were to make Helge, in his professional capacity, a pillar of help, and to cause me to thank my stars that he should be living and practising in Vänersborg.

I had been living in lodgings in a house in Vänersborg, and all had gone well until the early morning of 22 August 1957. I then awoke with a very severe pain in the left side of my stomach. The sequel to this, and the rest of my stay in Vänersborg, belong to the Chapter on Illnesses, and to this, I now turn.

ILLNESSES

Though I have never been in strong and vigorous health, and have always made this an excuse for evading duties and responsibilities which I wished to shirk, I had never had any severe illness since the one that nearly killed me in early childhood, until that happened in Vänersborg. I was then approaching the end of my 70th year.

After awaking with severe stomach pain early in the morning of 22 August 1957, I called in a local Swedish general practitioner, as I did not want to bother Helge if the trouble should prove to be merely transitory. The doctor hummed and ha'd; came to the conclusion after examining me, that I had not got appendicitis, as I had feared; and left it at that. But on 24th August, I again had a very bad attack of stomach-pain, after breakfast. I thought then that it was time to get in touch with Helge. He acted promptly and efficiently. By 6.30 pm, he had fetched me to the hospital and had installed me in a very nice private room there. (This was the first time in my life that I had ever been a patient in a hospital or a nursing home.) I shared this room with a friendly young Swede, who was recovering very slowly from the effects of a terrible motor accident, in which he had been involved as a passenger some months before.

The pain stopped at about 10 pm that night. In the morning of 25th August, my stomach was X-rayed, and nothing was found to be amiss with it. Next morning, after a great deal of very tedious waiting-about, my bowels were X-rayed, and found to be quite healthy. But, unfortunately, something else had taken place in the meanwhile, which had the most unhappy and long-lasting effects. In the evening of 25th August, a young doctor, who was at that time in control, insisted that urine should be drawn from me with a catheter. I had, and I still have no idea why he thought this to be necessary. Whether or not as a result of this, I developed a high temperature on 26 August and had a bad night. On the 27th, there had developed great irritation in the bladder. In spite of this, the same young doctor insisted on my being again treated with the catheter before I went to sleep. My stomach pain developed again in the evening.

By 29th August, things were again progressing more or less normally. On the 30th, there was an extremely elaborate X-ray examination of my kidneys. Nothing was found to be wrong with them.

On 31st August, I left the hospital, by Helge's permission, and returned temporarily to my lodgings for the weekend. During this period, I packed my belongings. On 2nd September, Helge very kindly took me to his home as guest, and I stayed there until 7th September. By then, everything seemed fairly normal, and I left Vänersborg for Stockholm. I never learned what was the cause of the severe and recurrent stomach pains; and, up to the time of writing, I have had no repetition of them.

After settling down in Stockholm, I wrote to Dr Kallner, describing my past symptoms, and asking for an interview with him. On 18th September, I spent a long time at his consulting room. My urine and my blood were carefully tested. As a result, he diagnosed that I was suffering (a) from diabetes and (b) from a nasty infection in the bladder with *bacillus coli*. He considered that a suitably restricted diet would do all that was needed for the former, and he prescribed an anti-biotic called 'Elkosin' for the latter. I noticed that he asked me almost at once whether I had been subjected to treatment with a catheter, and that he appeared to be highly indignant to learn that I had. On 7 October, shortly before leaving Stockholm and returning to Cambridge, I had another interview with Dr Kallner. At that time there was no excess of sugar and no sign of infection in the urine. I was advised to stop taking Elkosin, unless and until symptoms of infection should recur. It was characteristic of Dr Kallner, in his relations to me, that he would not take any fee, either on these occasions or on any future ones.

I had, of course, informed my Cambridge medical attendant, Dr Woods, of these events. I saw him soon after my return to Cambridge, and from time to time provided him with samples of urine to be tested. The net result over the next couple of years was this. The diabetic symptoms soon subsided, and I am afraid that I became less and less careful in my diet. But the infection with *bacillus coli* was recurrent at intervals.

I could easily recognise this for myself when it happened, and Woods's subsequent tests never failed to confirm my own previous impressions. When the infection was becoming serious I would feel a characteristic irritation in my penis, and my urine would have a characteristic unpleasant smell. Various kinds of anti-biotic were tried. Each was effective for a time, but the infection always returned after an interval. It thus looked as if there were a persistent source of infection, and as if the bacilli from it gradually became more or less immune to one anti-biotic after another.

Next year (1958) in Stockholm I again had interviews with Dr Kallner. At the first of these (22 September), it appeared that there was no appreciable excess of sugar, but quantities of *bacillus coli* and some pus. Dr Kallner prescribed an anti-biotic called 'Terramycin'. At my second interview (29 September), there was no sugar and very little infection. I was advised to continue for a while with Terramycin and then to revert, when necessary, to Elkosin.

Things went on in much the same recurrent way through the rest of 1958, the whole of 1959, and the earlier part of 1960. It began to be suspected that there might be something amiss with the prostate. Woods examined this on 19 October 1959, but saw no reason to advise an operation in the near future.

When I was in Stockholm in September 1960, I had a conversation on the whole matter with my friend Dr Helge Laurell, who was then working at the famous Stockholm hospital *Serafima Lasarettet*. He insisted on the dangers of neglecting possible prostate trouble and advised that I should be thoroughly investigated by an expert. He arranged for me to interview Dr Giertz at *Karolinska Sjukhuset*, who is reckoned to be the greatest authority in Sweden on such matters. On 29th September, Dr Giertz (brother to an eminent Bishop of the Swedish State Church) examined me with a skill and thoroughness worthy of his own reputation and his brother's ecclesiastical position. He pronounced that my prostate was *not* notably enlarged, and was *not* in a cancerous state, but *was* infected and discharging pus. He advised me to get in touch with a urologist as soon as I should be back in England. In the meanwhile, he prescribed a fascinating new kind of tablet. This was great fun, as these tablets made my urine bright red, but, unfortunately, when they were exhausted I could not get anything of precisely the same kind in England.

I had informed Dr Woods by letter of all this. I returned to Cambridge on 13 October 1960, and Woods then put me in touch with the most eminent of the local Cambridge urologists, Mr Withycombe. I wrote for the latter a preliminary account of the history of the case, as known to me, and I had my first interview with him on 3 February 1961. He arranged for me to be X-rayed by Dr Berridge, who is an expert in that kind of work.

The sitting, or rather lying, at Dr Berridge's consulting-room, took place, after the usual preliminaries, on 9 February. He informed me that there was nothing amiss with the kidneys, but the bladder was not emptying properly. He forwarded the photographs, no doubt with his own detailed comments, to Withycombe.

I had my second interview with the latter on 14 February. I would like to say here how very greatly I appreciated his behaviour towards me both then and thereafter. The essential point is that he treated me as a reasonably intelligent individual, and not as a mere bit of 'operation-fodder'. He went over the photographs with me, and explained them, and he stated the various alternative courses of action, and the pros and cons of each.

The verdict was that my prostate was not very much enlarged, but it contained calculi and was the seat of a long-standing infection. He said that it was not essential that I should have an operation in the near future, but I gathered that I should probably need one sooner or later. He left the decision to me, and I had no hesitation in deciding for an operation at the earliest convenient date. I am pretty sure that he thought that I had made the right decision.

On 26 February 1961, I went into the old Addenbrookes Hospital and took up residence in a private room there. On 28 February. Withycombe performed the operation. Things went quite normally until 12 March, when I developed an infection in the urine. Such a setback is probably usual and before the days of anti-biotics, it was very dangerous and often fatal. Nowadays, apparently, it does not present much difficulty to the experts. After an uncomfortable day on 13 March, when I was light-headed, my temperature returned to normal. What remained was tenderness in the left testicle, which was somewhat enlarged.

On 19th March, I left hospital and returned to my rooms in College, provided with suitable temporary auxiliaries. These included a suspensory bandage, known apparently in the medical profession as a 'Jock-strap', and a polythene bottle to receive my frequent urinal tributes. The left testicle gradually returned to normality under the healing influence of a particularly swell anti-biotic called 'Ledermycin'. On 2nd April, I dined in Hall for the first time after leaving the hospital. On 18th April, I had an interview with Withycombe, who examined me carefully and decided that he did not need to see me again professionally unless further symptoms should develop. By 3rd May, I was able to deliver to the British Academy their annual Dawes Hicks Lecture. The subject was 'Hume's Theory of Space',[17] and I hope that I was well enough to show that that is pretty fair rubbish.

Thus ended very happily the only major operation which I have undergone up to the time of writing. I understood from Withycombe that the prostate proved to be greatly affected with calculi and was in a pretty bad state, and that it was a very good thing to be rid of it. I only regretted not being allowed to keep it in a glass bottle on my bedroom mantelpiece.

The operation has certainly been completely successful in curing the recurrent infection which had gone on for so long. I would not say that it has had any spectacularly good effects in other respects. On 27 July 1961, I had an interview with Withycombe, at my own request, about the continuance of rather frequent urination. He prescribed certain pink tablets, of which I can only say that, whenever I have tried them, I have found their side effects far worse than the condition which they are supposed to alleviate. I had a second interview with Withycombe on 10 August 1961. He found that there was no trace of infection in my urine. He also told me that the healing after an operation for removing the prostate may lead to a constriction of the urethral passage. I have very little doubt that this has happened in my case. Withycombe said that this can, if necessary, be dealt with by means of instruments. But he did not advise such treatment at the time, and I have so far managed without asking him to consider having recourse to it. No doubt, a time may come!

So much for urino-genital matters; I pass now to the only other bit of ill-health which has been serious enough to deserve special mention. This is occasional attacks of dizziness, which have occurred in bouts from time to time, and which remain rather a mystery to my professional advisers.

The first which I noticed happened on 19 August 1960, when I was staying in lodgings in Östersund. I woke up that morning sweating profusely and feeling dizzy. There was no recurrence of such symptoms at the time, and it may well have been nothing but a temporary liver-attack.

It was not until 13 April 1964 that I had another onset of giddiness. This happened when I was out walking in the country, and it frightened me considerably. I was at the time staying at an hotel in Tunbridge Wells, and that afternoon I had taken a longish walk to visit what are called 'The High Rocks'. While there I had a sudden and violent attack of dizziness and should almost certainly have fallen if I had not managed to sit down on the ground. I had a stick with me, and I managed to walk the 1½ miles or so back to the hotel with its help. I returned to London on 15 April and to Cambridge the day after. For some time, I was liable to occasional mild attacks of giddiness when walking in the street. But my condition, in that respect, soon became normal, and then remained so for a longish period.

The next attack was not until 13 October 1967, and this was the beginning of a longer period of more uncomfortable symptoms. I had been away from Cambridge on holiday since 22nd September, first in Ipswich and then in Colchester. On 12th October, I moved on to Lewes, where I stayed at a hotel. Early in the morning of 13 October, I awoke, at about 6 am, with a turn of dizziness, accompanied by profuse sweating. So far this closely resembled my experience in Östersund on 19 August 1960, which had no particular sequel. But this time, it was the prelude to something much more persistent. For the rest of my stay in Lewes, I had recurrent severe attacks of dizziness and did not venture to go out into the street without a stick.

I got back to London on 19th October and to Cambridge on the 20th. I was most thankful to be once more in my own room. The symptoms continued. In particular, I noted repeatedly an attack of dizziness each morning on coming upstairs from my bathroom to my bedroom, and again on getting up from my chair in my bedroom immediately afterwards.

I wrote an account of all the above-mentioned events for Dr Woods. The symptoms looked as if they might arise from a defect in the blood supply from my heart. So he arranged for me to be thoroughly overhauled by the eminent local cardiologist, Dr Fleming. I had a long session at his house with Dr Fleming on 31 October 1967, and he certainly made a most thorough investigation. He told me at the time that he found nothing to account for my symptoms, and he wrote a detailed report to Dr Woods to the same effect.

In my diary for 11 November 1967, I wrote an account of the pattern into which my symptoms had by then settled. The essential points are these. Just at the end of the dressing process, in the bathroom on the ground floor of my staircase, I would begin to feel slightly dizzy. I would come upstairs to my bedroom and have a definite short spell of dizziness, accompanied as a rule by sweating and a feeling of nausea. I would sit down for a minute or two, and this would pass off. Then I would have my usual light breakfast, sitting in my armchair in my dining room, during which I would generally feel quite all right. Just at the end of breakfast, I would begin again to have symptoms of dizziness, accompanied as a rule by sweating and a feeling of sickness. I would then sit down, and would soon be feeling all right again, except that I would sometimes feel very sleepy for a while.

It was not until 2 November 1967 that I was able to write in my diary; 'Symptoms of giddiness seem to be pretty well over…' Since about then I have had only occasional and very slight recurrences. But one never knows what may happen, and nowadays I like always to have a walking stick or an umbrella with me, when I am out of doors, in case of an attack coming on suddenly in the street. Obviously, the medical men whom I consulted had no idea, after most careful investigation, of the cause of the symptoms. And I feel that what has begun so suddenly and inexplicably on several occasions in the past may recur at any moment in the future.

I will conclude my tale of illnesses up to date by a brief account of the latest trouble falling within the period under review. As I have mentioned above, Dr Kallnor, as early as 18 September 1957, discovered that I was suffering slightly from diabetes, and put me on a diet, though he did not think it necessary to prescribe medicine. I followed his directions as to diet pretty carefully for some time. Gradually, I came to ignore them altogether; and it must be said in my defence that samples of urine, taken and tested from time to time, were alleged to show no sign of excessive sugar content.

Early in January 1968, however, it became pretty obvious to me that I was experiencing definitely diabetic symptoms to a hitherto unexampled degree. In particular, I suffered from a dry mouth and constant thirst. On 27th January, I saw Dr Woods about this. He at once diagnosed diabetes: put me on a strict diet, and arranged for me to see Dr L.C. Martin, a local specialist on such diseases. I had a long session with the latter, who made an extremely thorough and detailed investigation. After that, I was put on a diet, and have kept pretty close to it ever since. No special medicine has been needed.

This has introduced me to a new minor amusement in life, in the form of an apparatus called 'Clinitest', which I bought on Dr Martin's advice. With this one tests on various days, and at various times of the same day, the sugar content of one's urine, by dropping a tablet into a test tube containing five drops of urine diluted with ten drops of water. As the tablet dissolves, the solution fizzes and boils, and goes through various changes of colour. When this process is completed, one compares the final colour of the solution with a set of variously coloured spots on a chart, and thus determines the percentage of sugar present. I have for long past done this regularly every sixth day, on three occasions (before and after lunch, and after dinner) on that day. I then note the results and keep a record of them to submit at longish intervals to Dr Woods. If most human beings were at most times as innocently occupied, things (it might not unfairly be said) would be very different.

I am well aware that the details of one's own diseases, though of fascinating interest to oneself, tend to be extremely boring to others. I must therefore apologise to any possible reader for the length and prolixity of this Chapter. I found it delightful to write, and *he* can skip it. So no great harm will have been done by it.

PSYCHICAL RESEARCH

In my earlier *Autobiography* I mentioned, and discussed rather fully, my early and continuing interest in psychical research. This has in no way diminished. On the contrary, I think I may say that, as my interest in and attention to contemporary philosophy have declined, my interest in psychical research has increased, and such philosophical abilities as I still have have been more and more directed to theoretical problems arising out of its ostensible findings.

In 1935 and 1936, long before the period at present under review began, I was President of the S.P.R. I then gave, as my Presidential Address, an elaborate lecture entitled 'Normal Cognition, Clairvoyance, and Telepathy'. This, in a somewhat extended form, has been published in my book *Religion, Philosophy, and Psychical Research* (1953). It is wholly concerned with *philosophical* questions arising out of the very notions of 'clairvoyance' and of 'telepathy'. I think that it contains as good analytic-philosophical writing as I have at any time been able to produce.

On 15 May 1958, I give the *Myers Memorial Lecture* at Caxton Hall, London, for the S.P.R. I chose as my subject 'Personal Identity and Survival'. The lecture was, as usual with such addresses, printed and issued as a pamphlet by the S.P.R.

Shortly before this, I had become President of the S.P.R. for a second time, and I held that office during the latter part of 1958, the whole of 1959, and the earlier part of 1960. The practice of the S.P.R. is to have canvassed alternative possible Presidents and to have practically decided on a certain one, some time before the Annual General Meeting, which takes place in March or April of each year. Immediately after the A.G.M., there is a short Council Meeting, at which the President for the following 12 months is formally elected. I became President immediately after the A.G.M. of 26 April 1958 and was re-elected for further 12 months after that of 21 March 1959. I continued until the A.G.M. of 26 March 1960, when I was succeeded by my old friend Professor H. H. Price of New College, Oxford.

On 13 November 1958, I save my Presidential Address at 26 Portland Place in London. I chose my subject: 'Dreaming; and some of its Implications'. I have at least one qualification for writing on this subject. I hardly ever sleep without remembering on awaking at any rate *that* I have been dreaming. And very often I can remember in considerable detail *what* I have been dreaming. I am also quite familiar with the experience of considering, in a dream, whether I am dreaming or awake, and of sometimes deciding correctly that I am dreaming and sometimes deciding wrongly that I am awake. As is usual, the Presidential Address was later published in the S.P.R. *Proceedings*. It is to be found in Vol. 52, Part 188, Feb. 1959, (pp. 53–78).

Not long before this, the S.P.R. had had to move from the very attractive house at 31 Tavistock Square, which it had occupied for many years. With great difficulty, alternative accommodation had been secured at Adam and Eve Mews, a small turning off Kensington High Street, beside the 'Adam and Eve' public house. This was then thought by many to be only a temporary resting place, but the moving tent of the S.P.R. has now been pitched there for quite a long time. From then till now many attempts have been made to get possession of more commodious premises with a better address. So far all of them have failed, and it looks as if the S.P.R. were now fixed indefinitely at its present humble quarters, and were lucky to have secured them when it did.

The S.P.R. Council generally meets once a month throughout the year except in July and August. Taking 1959 as typical of my Presidentship, I attended and presided at meetings in each month except July, August, September, and October. Such meetings would start at 6 pm, in order to allow the attendance of members otherwise occupied during the day.

I generally used to travel from and back to Cambridge on each such occasion. I had often a good deal of time to fill in before a meeting, and I did not care to pass it in the restricted area of 1 Adam and Eve Mews. So I got to know that part of Kensington pretty well. In particular, I discovered the beautiful grounds of Holland House, not so very far distant, up a hill off the opposite side of Kensington High Street. There I must have spent many hours in the aggregate, walking about, sitting out, having my tea, and thinking of the past history of the place.

The members present at ordinary Council meetings, beside the President or some ex-President acting for him if he were unavoidably absent, may be divided into the Honorary Officers (Secretary and Treasurer) and the rest. I would like to begin by expressing my very great admiration for the devoted work done by the former, such as W.H. Salter, G.W. Lambert, and Sir George Joy. These very able men have for long periods of their lives spent most of their time and energy in the day-to-day running of the Society. They have done this without any financial reward and in the face of many difficulties of which the average member of the Society knows nothing, and even the average member of the Council knows but little. Sometimes they have had to do what they believed to be right, against the active opposition of this or that member of the Council, who has occasionally gone to great lengths to interfere with their work.

The ordinary Council meetings were not uninteresting, though they tended to last too long and I sometimes had to leave before the end in order to catch my train back to Cambridge. One soon discovered that certain members, individually able and pleasant to deal with, had a deep hatred of each other, and that this was liable to show itself in the course of Council business, often under the most high-minded disguises. Of course one had been prepared for this by experience of the College Council and of college Meetings, and I cannot say that I was particularly surprised to find it in a somewhat exaggerated form in the Council of the S.P.R. I remembered that the Honorary Officers corresponded more or less to our Senior and Junior Bursars. And I noted with amusement that the mutually hostile non-official members, who would yet unite in some unreasonable attack on the actions of the Hon. Sec. were only my Trinity colleagues, Mr X, Dr Y, and Professor Z, slightly larger than life.

So much for ordinary Council Meetings; I pass to Annual General Meetings. For these, I am happy to say, no experience within the College or the

University had prepared me. I do not doubt that many of those who attend are decent, sensible persons. But there are always present a minority of semi-lunatics; of pathologically litigious persons; and of members who, if sane on most matters, have a bee in their bonnet which buzzes on these occasions.

A standard feature at such meetings is a speech by Dr E.J. Dingwall, and he alone of the regular performers deserves individual mention. He, at least, knows very well what he is talking about; and he often brings forward matters which the Council have allowed to sink into oblivion, and which ought not to be just silently neglected. He was Research Officer of the S.P.R. from 31 January 1922 to 25 March 1927, receiving during that period a smallish annual payment for his part-time services. I take it that he is a man of substantial private means and that this payment was of no serious financial importance to him. He has remained a member of the Society, and has contributed many letters and book reviews to its *Journal*. He has always seemed to me to have a psychologically interesting 'love–hate' relationship to the S.P.R.

Dingwall's knowledge of the history and the literature of what may roughly be called 'occultism' is, I should think, unrivalled. I should attach very great weight to any pronouncement of his about any purely literary, bibliographical, or historical question bearing on the subject. He must also have had an immense amount of personal experience of mediums, whether wholly genuine (if any), or completely fraudulent, or with a combination of genuinely paranormal gifts eked out with occasional or habitual fraud. Two of his books, *Some Human Oddities* and *Very Peculiar People* are classics in their line.

His other main interest is in that branch of anthropology which the unsympathetic might describe as 'high-brow pornography', leading to books which are labelled 'curious' in booksellers' catalogues. Examples of his work in this field are his *Studies in the Sexual Life of Ancient and Mediaeval Peoples* and *The Girdle of Chastity*. I think that this particular interest is liable to influence unduly some of his interpretations of allegedly paranormal phenomena. Few can have a keener nose than Dingwall for the supposed presence of flagellation, or other forms of sadomasochism, in contexts where most of us would hardly have suspected it.

I do not know (and perhaps he himself does not know) whether or not he believes or thinks probable that there is a trace of genuinely paranormal gold mixed up with the mass of dross which is presented to psychical researchers. Particularly in his later writings, he has always been most careful not to commit himself on this question.

What I do notice is this. He seems to have what I should regard as a rather naive respect for the negative pronouncements of many natural scientists on these questions. And he seems to hold (what I should regard as the equally naive belief) that, if only enough money were available and were properly spent in experiment and investigation, the question could be definitely settled, in one way or the other, to the satisfaction of everyone whose opinion is worth consideration.

I now leave the subject of the S.P.R. and pass to more personal matters. Trinity College has a considerable sum in trust, called the 'Perrott-Warrick Fund', the income from which is to be spent on psychical research. Generally, the bulk of each year's income is used in supporting a 'Perrott-Warrick Student'. But the Committee has powers to appoint from time to time, if it should see fit, a 'Perrott-Warrick Lecturer' to give a course of lectures in the University on some topic connected with psychical research. In 1958, the Committee invited me to be Perrott-Warrick Lecturer in 1959. I gave six lectures in the Lent Term of the academic year 1958–1959, beginning the course on 22 January 1959, and then continuing once a week up to and including 26th February. I had good and attentive audiences, both of dons and persons in *statu pupillari*, and I decided to ask permission to give (without further payment) a second course of six lectures in the following academic year. This was granted, and the second course of six lectures began on 28 January 1960 and ended on 3 March.

I made these 12 lectures the basis of a book; modifying them, adding much to them, and rearranging the whole. This book appeared in 1962 under the title *Lectures on Psychical Research* (Routledge & Kegan Paul: pp. xi, 450). I had long wanted to write something systematic on the subject, and this gave me an opportunity and an initiative. Although in no sense 'popular' – it must indeed be pretty stiff reading in places – it has been a modest 'bestseller' of its kind.

It does not deal with anything like the whole area of ostensibly paranormal phenomena. Nothing is said in detail about alleged *physical* phenomena. And among alleged *mental* phenomena, such as clairvoyance and telepathy, the philosophically most puzzling one, viz., that of ostensible *pre-cognition*, is not adequately discussed. Since then I have reflected on the latter to the best of my ability, and have published my findings in the chapter entitled 'The Notion of 'Precognition'' in the collective book *Science and E.S.P.* (1967), edited by Dr J. H. Smythies, and published by Mssrs Routledge & Kegan Paul.

I have taken part personally in very few experiments, and I have been present on still fewer occasions when watch has been kept in an allegedly haunted house. There is, I think, one experience of the latter kind which is amusing enough to be worth recording.

There is an ancient house in Cambridge, on a turning off the Newmarket Road, called 'The Old Abbey'. This has long had a reputation of being haunted, and the evidence, as such things go, is fairly impressive. The late Professor Stratton of Caius (President of the S.P.R. 1953–1955) had made a collection of all the most important documentary evidence still in existence. (This has passed into possession of the S.P.R. after Stratton's death in 1960.) Roundabout the turn of the years 1954–1955, the allegedly haunted part of the house, by then let separately from the rest as flats, fell vacant. Stratton arranged for a party of Cambridge academics, interested in psychical research, to pass some nights in this part of the house, equipped with all the latest available recording instruments, etc. He kindly invited me to be one of the party, and to spend a night there.

I gladly accepted and passed the night of 24 January 1955 in the bedroom in which it was reported that a female apparition had been repeatedly 'seen' by the then occupants (who had been a Fellow of Pembroke and his wife). The room was unfurnished, and the weather was extremely cold. So I arrived armed with a mattress to sleep on, blankets to put over me, and an oil stove. My only companion in the room for the night was a young Mr Naylor, at that time an assistant at one of the University's scientific laboratories. He slept in his own chair, provided, like myself, with some kind of mattress and overlay.

Naylor and I agreed to divide the night into successive watches of two hours, in which one of us would keep awake and the other would sleep. If the one who was awake should notice anything that might seem to him out of the ordinary, he was to awaken the one who was then asleep. We went up to the room at about 11 pm, and it was arranged that Naylor should sleep and I should keep awake during the first two hours.

Naylor was soon asleep, and for about an hour I noticed nothing but his rhythmical breathing and the occasional crackings which happen in an old unfurnished room in very cold weather. It would have been difficult to keep oneself from dozing, if conditions had not been so uncomfortable. Suddenly, however, after about one hour, I was startled into complete wakefulness by Naylor's beginning to howl like a werewolf. This seemed promising.

I thought it might be the prelude to something of psychic interest, so I did not disturb him, but kept my attention fixed on the surroundings. After a few minutes he ceased to howl, suddenly woke up, and asked me: 'Have I been talking in my sleep?' I said: 'Not *talking*, but *howling*'. 'Oh', said he, 'I often do that'. I asked him whether he had been dreaming, and he said that he had had no dreams that he could remember. (I was less surprised by the incident than I should have been if Ulf Hellsten had not told me long before of such 'goings-on' as quite common in his family when he and his younger brothers were boys living at home. I am confident that Dr Dingwall would have his views as to the aetiology of this symptom in young, unmarried males.)

So that was that. The rest of the night passed without either of us experiencing anything unusual. The same is true of the members of the party downstairs with their instruments that night, and nothing was observed on other nights. It is a pretty safe generalisation that: 'A watched ghost never walks'.

I will end this Chapter by summarising (1) my own activities in psychical research and (2) the very tentative conclusions to which I have been led:

(1) As regards my *activities*, I would make the following statements:

(i) I have never taken any active part in planning or in conducting experiments, and I have done nothing worth mentioning in observing spontaneous but recurrent phenomena, for example, cases of ostensible haunting or ostensible poltergeist phenomena. In these matters, I have confined myself to trying to give, lucidly and fairly in my own words, accounts of what seem to me to have been well-conducted experiments with positive results, and of what seem to me to have been well-authenticated observations under suitable conditions.

(ii) I have never put forward testable theories as to the *modus operandi* of those ostensibly paranormal phenomena for which I think that there is good evidence that they really happened, that they were not mere chance-coincidences, and that they were not explicable within the generally accepted framework of natural law. I am altogether lacking in the imaginative fertility and the intellectual ingenuity which would be needed in order to devise such theories.

(iii) What I have tried to do is this: (a) to state clearly the principles of logic and of probability involved in estimating the evidence for and against the *actual occurrence* of allegedly paranormal events, and the evidence for and against *holding them to be paranormal* if they did in fact happen. (b) To draw the necessary distinctions between the various notions covered by such a word as 'telepathy' or 'clairvoyance' or 'precognition', and then to give a careful analysis of each such notion as I have distinguished. (c) Finally, in terms of this, to state exactly where the occurrence of 'telepathy', or 'clairvoyance', or 'precognition', etc., would conflict with one or more of the basic limiting principles which are commonly accepted as constituting the framework of all possible natural phenomena.

(2) As regards my *tentative conclusions*, I would state them as follows:

(i) I have never had an experience which would suggest the presence *in me* of any paranormal powers, mental or physical, active or passive.

(ii) I have no *a priori* objection to the possibility of such powers existing in certain individuals. For I see no reason whatever to think it unlikely that the world, as it really is, may be a much odder place than the ordinary, cocksure, natural scientist will admit to be possible.

(iii) I have known personally quite a number of sensible and apparently trustworthy individuals, of my own social and intellectual background, each of whom claims to have had on one or more occasions certain experiences which seem *prima facie* to suggest at least telepathy or telaesthesia, giving rise in some cases to a veridical *quasi*-sensory hallucination. And I think that the accumulated and well-sifted evidence, contained in such a book as Gurney's *Phantasms of the Living*, regarding certain individuals whom I have not known personally, makes it highly likely that such powers exist and are from time to time in operation.

(iv) I think that certain well-attested cases (mostly mediumistic ones) strongly suggest that a part, at any rate, of the organised system of traces and dispositions which was characteristic of a certain human being when he was alive in the flesh, have persisted, at least for a time, after the death of his body.

(v) Lastly, I think that there is a very small minority of well-attested cases which suggest *prima facie* something more than this. They suggest the continued existence and the occasional operation, at least for a time, of something which conceives and tries to carry out certain *intentions*, which were characteristic of a certain now deceased human being when he or she was still alive in the flesh.

ACTING STEWARDSHIP

My narrative now descends with a bump from the Astral Plane to the College Kitchens.

I see in my diary for 1966 that the trouble began, so far as concerns myself, on 15 March of that year. On that day Bradfield (in his capacity of Senior Bursar) came to see me in my rooms, at his own request, and put the following suggestion to me. He said that the then Kitchen Steward, Gareth Jones, would be spending a year in the United States from October 1966 to September 1967, that he would cease to be Steward on his departure, and would become a Tutor on his return. In the light of their knowledge of this, the Council had some time earlier invited Dr Warren to take on the office of Steward on its being vacated by Gareth Jones. Warren had accepted. Some time later this had come to the knowledge of the Professor under whose supervision Warren was working on a research project. The Professor had cut up very rough and had said that it would be fatal to Warren's academic prospects if the latter were to begin to hold the Stewardship before October 1967. Something must, therefore, be done to fill the gap between 30 September 1966 and 1 October 1967. Bradfield asked me to consider seriously whether I would be willing to act as a temporary Steward for this interim period.

The reasons which he gave for his proposal were these. We were losing our old Kitchen Manager, Mr Buck, who had reached, and indeed passed, retiring age. And he was to be replaced by a much more highly paid and experienced Catering Manager, Mr Eden. Again, to the great satisfaction of everyone, we were getting rid (by means of a golden handshake) of our incompetent and drunken former Manciple, before his retiring age; and replacing him by a new one (Mr Small) who was qualified both personally and professionally to fill the office.

Thus, the two key permanent officials in the Kitchen hierarchy, whom we felt ourselves lucky to have recruited and whom we hoped to retain for long in our service, would be starting their new jobs under the worst possible conditions. Neither of them had had any previous experience of the very special peculiarities of catering for and serving communal meals to, the Fellows and the undergraduates of a College. The former Steward would have just relinquished his post; there would be an interval of 12 months before his appointed successor could begin to function, and the latter, when he should at length become available, would be starting without previous experience either of the work or of the personnel.

Under these circumstances, Bradfield felt that it was vitally important to get *some* Fellow of the College to act as Steward for the period. And he felt that the latter should be one with some relevant experiences; with a certain amount of tact as an intermediary between his colleagues and the undergraduates, on the one hand, and the new Catering Manager and the new Manciple, on the other; and of sufficient age and *pondus* to evoke a certain amount of respect in both parties. Bradfield thought that I would fill the bill, and he doubted whether anyone else who would do so would be able and willing to take on the job.

I, of course, saw the force of Bradfield's contentions. I had some of the qualifications needed, and it seemed very unlikely that any other Fellow who had them would be available. But I resisted very strongly; for the kitchen, Stewardship has always seemed to me to be a loathsome office, and I did not want to sacrifice 12 months of the *otium cum dignitate* which I had acquired (however little I might have earned it) in my old age. I made it quite clear to Bradfield that I would consent to act as Temporary Steward if and only if I were convinced that genuine efforts had been made to get someone younger than I, and that, if I should have to accept, I should regard myself as taking on a particularly loathsome prelude to Purgatory.

I did not, however, seriously expect that any very vigorous efforts to find an alternative victim would be made, or that, if they were, anyone would be fool enough to consent. So on 16th March, I had a long talk with J.F. Davidson about the duties of the office. He had been for a number of years an admirable Steward and had retired only on being appointed to a University teaching post which legally prohibited him from continuing to hold such a College office. By 23rd June, it had become clear that no one suitable had been found able and willing to fill the gap. So I then got Gareth Jones, the existing Steward, to tell me all that he could about his experience of the office, which he had filled excellently since Davidson's retirement.

On 1 July 1966, I received a letter from Bradfield, urging me very strongly to consent to fill the gap. So on 21th July, I wrote to him, stating the conditions under which alone I would consent. They were two: (1) I was not prepared to undertake the seating arrangements at College Feasts and other entertainments, which is an essential part of the normal duties of the Steward. (2) I would under no circumstances (even if Warren should not be then available) continue after 30 September 1967.

I already knew by that time that Sir James Butler had been consulted and that he had expressed his willingness to be responsible for the seating arrangements at Feasts, etc. In this, he showed his customary kindness and helpfulness, and it is hardly necessary to add that he afterwards carried out those duties with that seemingly effortless skill and efficiency which he has displayed in all the many and various tasks which he has undertaken throughout his long life.

Any such proposals would, of course, have to be submitted to the Council, and this would happen at their immediately forthcoming meeting on 27 July 1966. They were in fact submitted by Gareth Jones, who was presenting the Steward's customary Long Vacation report. I thought it wise to write beforehand to Bradfield, as Secretary to the Council, emphasising the risks which the Council would be taking, and to ask him to read to them my enclosed letter before they should come to any decision on the matter. The gist of my letter was as follows:

> ... If the Council should be seriously considering appointing me to perform temporarily an essential part of the duties of the Stewardship, they should bear in mind the following highly relevant facts:
>
> I shall be 79 on 30 Dec. 1966, if I should live so long. At present I am, so far as I am aware, in quite good health for my age. But a person in his 80th. year, even if he should continue to live and to escape serious illness, cannot be expected to be so 'quick in the uptake' or so clear-headed or so energetic as a younger man. And at that age there is always a serious risk of death, or of sudden unexpected incapacitation through a stroke, a heart-attack, or having to undergo a major operation.
>
> It is obvious that the Council, in coming to any decision which may concern me, ought to do so with its eyes open to these unpleasant possibilities. I prefer to point them out to the Council here and now for myself, rather than to have them ignored, or tactfully suppressed, or whispered in corners by my colleagues.

The slogan *"debout les morts"* should not be lightly uttered by a responsible body, like the Council; nor should the policy of assigning important duties to *zombies* be entered into without very serious consideration of the risks which it involves.

The Council decided to take the risks – I suspect that some of its members had no very clear idea as to the alleged nature of *zombies* – and on 27 July 1966, I was appointed Acting Steward, under the limitations which I had insisted on, from 1 September 1966 to 30 September 1967. Jim Butler was appointed at the same time to perform the duty of assigning places at feasts during that period. The stipend for the full duties of Steward was £800 per annum. It was arranged that I should take £500 for the performance of the purely administrative portion of them. I do not know whether Jim Butler ever consented to take the remaining £300 for the share of the duties of which he relieved me. I doubt whether he did.

I had already met the new Manciple on 3 January 1966. Gareth Jones introduced me to Mr Eden, the new Catering Manager, on 21st July of that year. I was to have much to do with him. During the 12 months of my Acting Stewardship, I used to see Eden every day, except for the brief periods when he was away on holiday. I would generally go round to his office each morning in the week except Sunday soon after 10 am, and would then have a talk with him about current affairs in the Kitchens, with each of us raising any point which seemed to be of immediate importance. In particular, I would inform him of any matters in the latest Council minutes which concerned the Kitchens, and he would inform me of any incipient complications concerning staff, finance, kitchen equipment, etc.

We soon got on excellent terms, and, I think, always remained so. One must remember that the Catering Manager at Trinity is a highly paid expert, with much previous experience in his profession, running a very considerable commercial business, which is expected year in and year out to make both ends meet, but is not expected to make any substantial annual profit. No Steward, however able and intelligent he may be, and however much of his time and energy he may devote to the job, can possibly have the special technical qualifications, or perform the daily tasks, for which the Catering Manager is appointed and paid. On the other hand, one must remember that the Kitchen business is, in certain respects, very peculiar, and that there is much in it to which the Catering Manager's previous experience will provide very little analogy. (One obvious example is that a profit can be made only during Full Term; that Full Term occupies only 24 weeks out of the 52; and yet that dinners and lunches for members of the High Table have to be provided throughout the year, and for a number of persons in *statu pupillari* through a great part of it.)

Even a not particularly competent Steward, provided that he has been an undergraduate of the College and has since been for some time a resident Fellow of it, can, if he will take the trouble, be useful as an intermediary between the Catering Manager and his subordinates, on the one hand, and the Council, the rest of the Fellows, and the members of the College in *statu pupillari*, on the other. He will be familiar with the peculiarities of the system in general, and he will know a good deal about the idiosyncrasies of certain particular Fellows who are inclined to throw their weight about. And, on the basis of this, he can help the Catering Manager in matters where the latter's previous professional experience can be of little guidance. All this presupposes tact on both sides and respect for each other's special qualifications. I certainly found those qualities in Mr Eden, and I hope that he to some extent found them in me.

The fact that my tenure of office was strictly temporary was in certain respects a boon to me. There was no need, for example, for me to choose and purchase wine on behalf of the Kitchens during the 12 months in question. This enabled me to decline offers by wine merchants to come and see me, and to refuse their invitations to attend wine tastings. I know nothing worth knowing about wine, and I have long since reached an age when it is no longer necessary for me to pretend to do so. I am well aware that there are a few persons who have genuine expert knowledge on this matter. But I have also learned from experience that to pretend to have such knowledge, and to express strong opinions on the basis of this pretence, is one of the commonest forms of bogosity among dons. And it is one which there is a strong temptation to display when young, in order that one may appear 'grown-up' to oneself and to others.

It is also true that my temporary tenure of office came at a time which was in one respect lucky for me. For it coincided with a period of 'wage-freeze', and therefore one had a complete negative answer to any general attempt on the part of the Kitchen staff to have their wages raised. I should have hated the kind of haggling in which I should otherwise have been involved.

The main duties which fell to me, and which would fall to any Steward, come under the following two headings: (1) those toward the Council and

(2) those toward the members of the High Table in general. I will now say a little under each of these two headings.

(1) It is the business of the Steward, in co-operation with the Catering Manager, to keep an eye on the monthly Kitchen accounts. He is expected to present two Reports in each academic year to the Council, and on each such occasion to attend their meeting, to answer their questions, and to explain and defend any proposals which he may have made in his Report. These two occasions are late in July and early in November. The July Report is prospective. It is supposed to give a reasoned forecast of the probable financial results for the whole 12 months, based on those of the previous six. The November Report is retrospective. The Steward and the Council then have in their hands the Kitchen Auditor's Report for the previous 12 months.

I found this part of the work interesting, and within my competence. I have a fair amount of experience of accounts, not only from running my own affairs and those of several relatives pretty systematically, but also from my experience as Acting Junior Bursar during the Second World War. And, if I have any good intellectual quality, it is an ability to express complicated matters clearly in writing. (In *speaking* I am quite hopeless, unless I have written out the speech beforehand.) In the present case, it was Gareth Jones who made the prospective Report on 27 July 1966. It fell to me to make the retrospective one, based on the audited accounts, on 18th November of that year; and the prospective one on 26 July 1967.

I would not like to conclude this topic without expressing my deep gratitude to two very busy men, who never grudged their valuable time when I consulted them. One is Bradfield, in his capacity of Senior Bursar, who discussed these Reports in draft with me. The other is Mr Adams, or Mssrs Alan Charlesworth & Co. (the Kitchen Auditors), who gave me much friendly and valuable help in matters of detail.

(2) The only matter which I will mention under the second heading is my dealings with the 'High Table Complaints and Suggestions Book'. From time immemorial such a book has lain on table in the Fellows' Parlour, and any Fellow or group of Fellows, with a complaint or a suggestion to make about the materials, the cooking, or the service of lunch or dinner at the High Table, can record it here. It is an essential part of the business

of the Steward to read at regular and fairly short intervals what has been written in this book, and to write, beside any complaint or suggestion which has appeared, his own comments.

In some of the older volumes, there have appeared passages which are worth preserving, either from the eminence of the writer, or from something in the form or the content of his entry, or for both reasons. I will mention only the following, going back to before the first World War. It is by A.E. Housman, and it seems (whether by accident or by design) to be reminiscent in form of Swinburne's 'Dolores':

> The salmon at dinner was tasteless, and the lamb was both tasteless and tough.

Needless to say, most entries are not up to this standard, either in the eminence of their authorship or in the literary associations of their form. Nevertheless, it seemed to me to be an essential part of the duty of the Steward to treat each entry seriously and to extend to the writer the courtesy of a brief reasoned comment. So, at the beginning of each week, I used to go over the entries for the week before, to discuss with the Catering Manager the various questions raised, and then to write in red ink beside each entry my comments and my reasons for them. It does no harm to treat one's colleagues as if they were reasonable beings: many of them, at any rate in their more lucid intervals, in fact, are.

The vast majority of the members of the High Table just take whatever is given to them without making any written complaint or suggestion. (I got the impression that some of them suspected that, if they were to write and complain, this would be marked up against them in the Kitchens, and they would, in some undefined way, be made to suffer in consequence!) There were a few who wrote pretty regularly, sometimes because they were of the complaining sort, and sometimes to show-off in a vein of 'clever-silliness'. But, whenever one got a complaint signed by a fair number of members, including several who rarely wrote in the book, I felt that there had pretty certainly been something seriously amiss, and I acted accordingly.

There was one standard kind of entry against which I reacted rather strongly. It was this. Mr, Dr, or Professor X is served, at lunch or at dinner, with a certain dish Y. He dislikes Y, either whenever it occurs or because he is out-of-sorts on that occasion. He proceeds to write in the book: 'Let us never have Y again'. I declined, on principle, ever to comply with any such negative suggestion as this, unless the two following conditions were fulfilled. The complainant must produce a fair number of signatories (say eight to ten) in support of his wish to have Y banished for the future. And this must *not* call forth several signatures in support of continuing to serve Y occasionally. I think that a little reflexion will convince any reasonable reader that this principle is sound.

One thing that I have learned by long experience, in connexion with the laying-out of the High Tables and the service of meals, was this. Some highly sensible improvement might be instituted, either by the Steward on his own authority or by the High Table Meals Committee acting through the Steward. For a short while, it would be carried into practice. But within a few weeks, these instructions would be deliberately or unwittingly ignored, and we should be back in the old situation which they were designed to improve. There can be few matters in which the saying: 'The price of freedom is perpetual vigilance' is better illustrated than in the details of the service of meals in Hall.

My 12 months of acting Stewardship wore on without any incident worth recording here, except perhaps the following. Late in 1966 two Trinity undergraduates hired the Private Supply Room for a dinner at which they and some friends from London were to be present. The occasion had some ostensible connexion with Ulster Protestant history and principles. Whatever the pretext may have been, the party was an extremely wild one. As the Scots say: 'The malt was above the meal', and, as a result, the interior of the Private Supply Room was very badly damaged. This naturally called forth immediate reactions from the relevant authorities. The two undergraduates who had hired the room had uncomfortable interviews with their Tutor and with me as Steward. They were gated by the former, and on 23 December 1966, I sent in a bill of £100 on behalf of the Kitchens for the cost of repairs and redecorations. On 10 January 1967, I received a cheque for the amount, to which no doubt all those who had been present had contributed.

It was no great shock to me to be reminded of the fact (which any Tutor will acknowledge with tears in his eyes) that even the scions of the *haute bourgeoisie*, as these young men were, are liable to their occasional 'oikish' moments. I found the two undergraduates, when clothed and in their right minds, very nice boys. When matters had been amicably settled, I had them to dinner in my rooms, and later on, they returned my hospitality by giving me a very enjoyable dinner at the Pitt Club.

On 27 September 1967, the large metal cabinet, containing files connected with the Kitchen business, was removed from my bedroom to be handed over to Warren. It had been obtrusively cumbering the room for the previous 12 months, and I saw it go with a sigh of relief. The Stewardship may in future be described (without prejudice) as 'Dr Warren's Profession'.

On the following day, I left Cambridge for Ipswich, to begin the three weeks' holiday which ended, as I have recorded above at Lewes with the beginning of a severe and long-lasting attack of giddiness.

The holding of the Acting Stewardship had made it impossible for me in 1966 and 1967 to make my usual late summer and early autumn visit to Sweden. I had, of course, explained the situation to those most concerned, viz., the Bergs and Ulf Hellsten. But it gave me the opportunity of doing what I had been seriously considering for some time, viz., putting a permanent end to such visits.

My motives were no doubt mixed, as one's motives nearly always are; but the following was certainly the predominant one of which I was clearly conscious. At my age one is liable to be suddenly stricken with some serious illness. I know very well that, if this should have happened while I was in Sweden, I should have been treated with the utmost kindness, and should have enjoyed absolutely first-class medical attention. But I should hate to be seriously ill away from home, both for itself and for the inconvenience which it must cause to one's kind friends. So I decided never to go again, and I wrote accordingly to the Bergs and to Ulf. Henceforth my travels will be confined within easy hearse drive of Cambridge.

---

80 TO 81

I will now say something of what happened to me from and including my 80th, birthday up to the end of 1968. I will begin with my 80th birthday.

December 30th., 1967 naturally began with showers of congratulatory letters and telegrams, and with some gifts. Among these, I will single out for mention a telegram from Bertrand Russell, a card of good wishes from the Kitchen Staff, and the gift of a beautiful silver penknife from Dr Husband.

At 4.20 pm, Bradfield fetched me in his car to his home, where I had tea with him and his wife and his son ('The Nord'). There was a superb cake with 80 candles, all of which I managed to blow out with one breath. (The practice of emitting hot air, of which philosophy so largely consists, had no doubt been a good training for me.) Bradfield brought me back to my rooms at about 5.45, and I rested there until dinner time.

In Hall, I sat next to the Vice-Master at dinner. (The Master was away from Cambridge at that period.) Immediately afterwards we went up to dessert in the Combination Room. The end of December is a time when many of the Fellows are away on holiday, or, if not, are giving or receiving private hospitality. Nevertheless, there was a good attendance. The main table was full, and there was a supplementary half-table. I sat at dessert between the Vice-Master, who presided, and Adrian, one of my oldest and best friends since the days when we were both undergraduates.

The Vice-Master proposed my health in a felicitous and friendly speech; the Fellows present drank it, and then I made a short speech of thanks in reply. This I had already written out some days before. I will confine myself here to quoting the penultimate paragraph:

> It is high time for me to sit down. I will end with just two remarks to the youngest of my colleagues. The first is this. As you grow older, you will illustrate in yourselves, or observe with amusement in your contemporaries, that slow progress from the forward-looking young married research-student in the Arbury Road, all Viet Nam and Comprehensive Schools, to the cynical ex-Bursar in his luxurious flat in *Highsett* or *Applecourt*, with his cigar between his lips, his glass of whisky by his side, and his nose buried in the financial columns of The Times. Secondly and lastly, do bear in mind, some 55 or 60 years on, to resign from committees of which you are an old and valued member, before you get too ga-ga to realise just how ga-ga you have got.

The proceedings ended by about 9.45 pm, and I was in bed by about 10.30. I shall never have another 80th birthday unless I should have the bad luck to be reincarnated as a human being, and to live so long. One never knows!

The rest of this chapter revolves around Adrian's accession to the Chancellorship of the University.

The death of the previous Chancellor, Lord Tedder, was announced on 3 June 1967, and Adrian was chosen as his successor on 29 November of that year. The choice naturally gave great pleasure to all of us at Trinity. He had been Master of the College from October 1951 till June 1965. His scientific achievements have been such as to make him outstanding even among that galaxy of Trinity men which includes Newton and Maxwell. But he has not merely been an extremely eminent natural scientist. He has turned his hand to many other matters (including the Presidency of the Royal Society), and it can truly be said of him: *Nihil tetigit quod non ornavit*. His speeches, on the most varied occasions, have been a delight to listen to. They are always felicitous in form, and their content always reveals how much solid work must have lain behind their humour and their happy appearance of spontaneity. Moreover, just by being what he is, and without any attempt to angle for popularity, he has made himself beloved and respected by all his colleagues, old and young.

The Chancellors for a great many years before Adrian have been non-residents; they have been men distinguished in various ways in the great world outside (such as Tedder, Smuts, and Baldwin), but appearing in Cambridge only on rare ceremonial occasions. Adrian is the first resident Chancellor for some hundreds of years. And, owing to the lamented death of Hester, he is living, not merely in the city of Cambridge, but here in our midst in rooms in College. He knows, from his own first-hand experience, the inner workings of our complex and peculiar system of University and Colleges, and, while he was Master of Trinity, he learned what it is to be a Vice-Chancellor of the University.

On 25 January 1968, the College gave a dinner to Adrian in honour of his becoming Chancellor. Thereafter, nothing notable happened in this connexion until 5 June 1968. On that night, the University gave a dinner at the University Centre in honour of Adrian's forthcoming installation as Chancellor, and I was present as one of the forthcoming honorary graduates.

A very pleasant, and quite unique, incident happened before the dinner. Some of the prominent Trinity rowing undergraduates had had the bright idea that it would be fun to row a boat up the River from Trinity to just outside the University Centre, taking Adrian with them as cox. They put the idea to him some days earlier, and he readily consented. They then made preliminary experiments, in order to ascertain whether a boat designed for racing could get under the various bridges which span the River between Trinity and the Mill Pool. It was found that this would be just possible if due precautions were taken. When the time came, Adrian, who had sent his dress clothes beforehand to the University Centre to await him, coxed the boat, appropriately clothed for that purpose, with his usual efficiency.

I have, among my most treasured possessions, a photograph of him sitting at the stern of the boat as cox on that occasion. The oarsmen afterwards came to the dinner as guests of the University, and, I hope, got some return for the pleasure which their brilliant idea and its successful realisation had given.

We had an excellent dinner, followed by a speech by the Vice-Chancellor (Sir Eric Ashby, Master of Clare), and replied to in a felicitous speech by Adrian. At the dinner, I sat between fru Zotterman (wife of one of the honorary graduands from Sweden) and the newly wedded wife of Adrian's son, Richard.

Before passing to describe the events of the following day (6 June 1968), I will say something about the honorary graduands:

It had been decided to mark the occasion of Adrian's installation as Chancellor by giving honorary doctorates to eight persons of distinction in their several subjects. I imagine that Adrian himself had a good deal to say in the choice of these. One of them, who thoroughly deserved the honour of Sc.D. on the merits of his contributions to physiology, was Adrian's old friend and former pupil, Professor Yngve Zotterman of the University of Stockholm. And another, who had no genuine claims to the honour of that degree, and must therefore have owed his selection simply to his continuous friendship with Adrian since undergraduate days, was myself.

Thursday, 6 June 1968, was the day of Adrian's installation as Chancellor, and of his subsequent conferment of honorary doctorates. It was a damp, threatening morning. At 10.45 am, I went along to the Senate House, and with Heads of Houses, other doctors, honorary graduands, etc., made up a procession in the arcade. Eventually, we marched around and entered the Senate House by its southern door. Outside the railings, in the street, was a great crowd. This contained a certain number of silly undergraduates, shouting in chorus: 'Student Power!' When we were all seated in the Senate House, Adrian went into a room at the side to be robed.

While we were sitting quietly, awaiting his re-entry, a young man in the gallery at the eastern end got up and began to make some protest. He was quickly set upon, and carried out, and there was no further disturbance. (I gathered later that the protester had come up from London for the occasion, and that he was not conspicuously sane at the best of times.)

Soon afterwards Adrian returned, in his magnificent robes, which were held up by an elegant Clare undergraduate, dressed in a page's costume and provided with a sword. The Vice-Chancellor made a speech welcoming Adrian. To this Adrian made a short reply, and then formally dissolved the Congregation. After this, he, and many others, went into the University Church to hear 'The Chancellor's Music.' I walked back to Trinity with Patrick Duff.

At about 12.45, I went along to Clare in my Litt.D. gown, but with no hood. After a while, we went into the Hall of Clare, and were entertained to lunch there by that College, as being the one whose Master was Vice-Chancellor at the time. At the luncheon, I sat between Lady Sutherland (wife of the Master of Emmanuel) and Mrs Deer (wife of the Master of Trinity Hall). After an excellent, though inevitably somewhat hurried, lunch, Sir Eric Ashby made a speech, welcoming the honorary graduands. One of the latter, Lord MacDermott of Belmont, Lord Chief Justice of Northern Ireland, replied on behalf of himself and the others. The honorary graduands then went into the Clare Master's Lodge, signed their names in a book, and were robed. Eventually, they went into the Senate House in procession, with Adrian, his page, and the Vice-Chancellor at the head.

When we had arrived at the Senate House Adrian took his seat, facing east, with the page standing behind his chair. The eight graduands, of whom I was No. 4, took their assigned seats, four on the northern side and four on the southern, immediately below the dais on which Adrian was seated.

Each of the graduands was called up in turn and presented to Adrian, whilst the Public Orator made a speech in Latin appropriate to each individual. Immediately after this, the graduand was presented to Adrian, who took him by the right hand, and formally admitted him. After that one took the place on the dais which had been allotted to one. Finally, Adrian formally dismissed the assembly. I am glad to say that there was no further nonsense of student demonstrations in the afternoon.

We then made our way to Trinity, where the College was giving a garden party in Nevile's Court. By that time the weather, which had been rather threatening at times, was fine and sunny. I got hold of the Page, who was accompanied by his parents. He was a medical student in his second year, named Quintin Pink, and his home was in Belfast. After tea, I took the Pinks on tour around the College, showing them the Hall, Combination Room, Bowling Green, and Chapel. Finally, they came to my rooms and sat there for a while, leaving at about 5.45.

So ended a unique and exciting day in my life. After having been for many years a quite *genuine* Litt.D. of the University, I had now become in addition a *bogus* Sc.D. It was the apogee, and we had better leave the rest of my life at that!

CONCLUDING REFLEXIONS

In conclusion, I would like to record certain reflexions, for what they may be worth, I will begin with quite general ones and then pass to some which have been occasioned by certain changes which have taken place during the period under review and which seem likely to go further in future.

(A) *General Reflexions*

(1) *Original Sin*. It seems to me that the doctrine of Original Sin is based on genuine and fundamental facts about human nature. These facts, and their consequences, are what they are, whether or not we accept Christian theological theories as to their causes and their implications. The plain fact is that there is something radically wrong with human beings, as contrasted with non-human animals; that this begins to show itself in the quite early infancy of the human individual, and that it is not something contingent, but is bound up with the specifically human nature and situation.

Fundamentally, what is wrong is a tendency towards hatred and conflict between human individuals, and between one class of them and another, ostensibly justifying itself on ideological grounds which are largely absurd when judged objectively, and issuing often in acts of deliberate cruelty and occasionally in large-scale mutual destruction, Now this is, no doubt, bound up with the specifically human powers of speaking, writing, and thinking of what is absent and of what is merely possible, and with the possession of emotions and desires which could exist only in those who have and who exercise those powers. And this is, of course, *also* a necessary condition of all specifically human positive achievements, for example, of science and technology, of artistic production and appreciation, of heroic unselfish action on religious or moral motives, and so on.

Another important point, which must have contributed to the doctrine of Original Sin, is this. These innate human defects show themselves very early, and of course in a specially naive and uninhibited way, in the life of each individual. Seeing quite young children, I have often been struck by their almost frenzied self-assertion, and by their outbursts of almost maniacal and fiendish ill-temper and attempted violence when not allowed to have their own quite unreasonable way. No doubt, this too is more or less explicable on the following lines.

A peculiarity of the human race, as contrasted with other animals, is this. Each individual has a long period of childhood and of adolescence, during which he must, largely against his will and for reasons which he cannot possibly understand at the time, learn to control his natural functions and to behave properly at table, to check the immediate expressions of his natural egotism and to adapt himself at least outwardly to life as a member of his family and of other and wider societies. And during the later stages, he must learn to speak, to read, and to write, and in a certain measure to think. The stress of all this must be enormous. It is not surprising that a certain number break down altogether in the course of it, and that almost all are left with subconscious tensions which emerge from time to time in adult life as half-crazy beliefs, emotions, desires, and actions.

Yet all this, so far as I can see, is ineradicably bound up with all that makes human beings specifically human, and with the essential conditions for all characteristically human achievements, intellectual, moral, and aesthetic.

(2) *Death.* One thing that I have noticed more and more as I have grown old is a change in the relative importance which the thought of one's own future death occupies in one's total field of consciousness. Until late middle age, I very rarely thought about my own death. It would hardly be an exaggeration to say that, for all practical purposes, I thought of death (except occurring through accident) as something which happens only to other people and of course, particularly to the 'old', i.e., to those in at least the next decade above one's own. As I have grown older and older I have found the thought of my own death occupying more and more of my conscious awareness.

It would not, I think, be true to say that this thought has so far been toned with any particularly unpleasant feeling. I do not, up to the present, feel any dislike of being dead, provided that I really shall be *thoroughly* dead. This world becomes daily nastier and more dangerous, so that one feels that there would be much to be said for being out of it before it is too late. I do intensely dislike and dread the possibility that I may have to start living all over again, whether as a re-incarnated human being or in some non-earthly kind of existence. And, not being like most of my fellow highbrows contemptuously ignorant of certain relevant mediumistic and other data, I am obliged to regard this as a possibility.

I, of course, expect that the *process of dying* may be pretty unpleasant. I dread a long and painful last illness. And perhaps I dread still more the prospect of being kept alive for years in a state of helplessness and second childhood, a burden to myself and to others. The last mentioned possibility seems to me to be one of the most unfortunate results of recent advances in medical technology.

In conclusion, I would add one further reflexion here. My feelings, up to date, accompanying the thought of my own death, have been attached only to the *abstract* knowledge that it *must* happen in the fairly near future. Suppose, however, that a time should come when I know that I have a disease which will certainly be fatal. Or suppose again that I should be, through accident, placed in a situation in which it is obvious that my death must happen in a very short time. I should imagine that in such circumstances I might have a very different feeling towards the prospect of my own death than that which I have so far experienced. And I simply cannot conjecture at present how I should feel then.

(3) *'Liberty, Equality, and Fraternity.'* I like a stratified society, in which I am located in one of the intermediate strata, with those above me to whom I can socially look up, and those below me on whom I can socially look down and by whom I am treated with outward respect. Naturally, I am not such a fool as to ascribe any specially valuable individual qualities to a person, merely because I regard him as my social superior. Nor do I ascribe special individual defects to a person merely because I regard him as socially beneath me. But I do get a certain amount of pleasure from associating with (and perhaps

more from being known to associate with) the former; whilst a social inferior would have to have some, for me, specially attractive personal quality (such as youth and good looks) for me to enjoy associating with him.

I rather like to be on the edge of what is called, by those who are never likely to be members of it, 'the Establishment' or more simply 'them'. I like to know fairly well some of its members, and to be familiar with their policies and activities. But I do not wish to be a member of any 'Establishment' because that would entail duties, and in particular, responsibilities and the incurring and facing of unpopularity, which I should dislike and have always managed to evade. 'Thank God (if there be one)', I would say, for 'the Establishment', and for 'them', who are able and willing to run things (on the whole so efficiently) for 'us'.

Of the three slogans of the French Revolution – 'Liberty, Equality, and Fraternity' – I would say this. The word 'Fraternity', and the ideas associated with it, make me feel slightly sick. 'Equality' I regard as a chimera, and I find it an unattractive one at that. As to 'Liberty', I like to be able to do and say as I please, so far as this is compatible with not causing serious inconvenience or annoyance to others whom my action or inaction may affect. That privilege I have been able largely to enjoy, thanks to the peculiarly favourable position of a Fellow of Trinity, to the tolerance of my colleagues, to the narrow limitation of my own desires, and to the possession after my earlier years of an increasingly adequate private income.

I cannot doubt, however, that the conditions under which alone I have been able to enjoy these freedoms are highly precarious, and that I shall be lucky indeed if they should last for the rest of my lifetime. That they will persist for long after I shall be dead seems to me most unlikely. As population increases, and as the business of producing and distributing wealth becomes more and more complex, the kind of liberty which I have enjoyed will inevitably become more and more restricted in scope and available to a smaller and smaller proportion of my countrymen.

This leads me to one further and sore general remark in conclusion. It seems to me that, as scientific and social technology progresses further, the kind of institutions which it creates for the production and the distribution of wealth will become more and more distasteful to those who have to work in them. The situation of being a mere cog in an elaborate industrial mechanism, which one had no band in designing, which one has no hope of understanding, and which one can contribute nothing to modifying, seems likely to become so unattractive that the following two consequences will follow. A certain proportion will opt out altogether. And those who do not opt out will tend to be sullen and un-cooperative, so that there will be constant friction and not infrequent conflicts and stoppages. So long as those who opt out remain a comparatively small minority, they will be carried on the backs of those who remain, however discontentedly and reluctantly, within the system. But it seems to me that these two consequences, which already reduce the efficiency which the system would theoretically possess if it did not inevitably produce them as by-products, might eventually cause it to grind to a standstill.

(B) *Reflexions on Some Recent Changes*

In conclusion, I will make some remarks on certain changes which have become noticeable during the period under discussion. Some of these had begun already, but had not gone so far as they have since done, Others began during the period in question, and are still going on. As the feelings which I shall express towards most of these changes will be unfavourable, the reader will do well to bear in mind that well-known feature of old age expressed in Horace's lines:

Dificilis, querulus, laudator temporis acti, se puero.[18]

I will begin with a certain general change, viz., increase in population, and will then consider in detail certain changes which have affected Cambridge in general and/or Trinity College in particular.

(1) *Increase in Population.* The crowding of town and country, which has become greater and greater in recent years, depends on a combination of two factors, viz., (i) an increase in the number of individual inhabitants and (ii) the more rapid circulation of the existing population. The latter is due to a change in habits, and this has been rendered possible by the growth of motorised transport in the forms of private cars and of public conveyances, such as tourist or 'sight-seeing' omnibuses. In many of

its effects, an increase in the rapidity of circulation of human beings is equivalent, as in the case of bank notes, to an increase in total numbers. It follows that the optimal maximum number of inhabitants in a country tends to be smaller as the average rate of circulation increases.

I do not know what the optimal maximum population of England would be, and perhaps the very notion is too indefinite to be worth discussing in detail. I will content myself with saying that the actual population has for long been far too large either for comfort or amenity in times of peace or for safety in times of war. In my view, no town should be so large that a person in good health and of normal activity could not easily walk into the country in any direction from its centre. And towns should not be so numerous that there are not large tracts of country between any two of them.

I suppose that one might fairly say that one difference which one would notice between a medieval and a contemporary English town would be the filthy stink of human and animal excrement in the former and the deafening noise of traffic in the latter. But it would be fair to add that a modern town has its own pervasive *inorganic* stink of petrol-fumes; and that it was at any rate easy to get away from the *organic* stench of a medieval town into the pure air of the surrounding country.

In former times, when methods of birth control were little known and still less used, it was common to produce enormous numbers of children. But it was usual for a very large proportion of these to die in infancy or early childhood from one disease or another. Still earlier, in many societies, it was customary to expose unwanted children, so that they died of cold or hunger or were killed by wild animals which were then numerous. One or another of these causes, or both of them together, tended to keep the population from increasing at all rapidly. (The example of Romulus and Remus shows us, however, that even she-wolves could not always be relied upon. But that was admittedly a rare exception.)

The situation nowadays in more or less civilised countries is this. Medical science and technology have largely eliminated the former source of infant mortality, whilst religious and humanitarian considerations have made infanticide on any large scale practically impossible under normal conditions. But the desire for frequent sexual intercourse, which is inherited from primitive, and indeed pre-human, conditions, and which is stimulated by much that is peculiar to contemporary society, is at least as strong and as widely spread as it ever was. Therefore the only way left to check an inordinate increase of population is the deliberate and regular use of methods of birth control.

Now I suppose that in this country practically everyone likely to be concerned is acquainted with various forms of birth control and that the relevant appliances could be obtained without difficulty. No doubt, there is and will be a large minority too stupid or ignorant or indifferent to consider practicing any form of birth control. I would like to see such persons deprived for good and all, in some painless way, of the possibility of having children. But with more or less intelligent and responsible persons (other than Roman Catholics) the question of taking or not taking precautions against the possibility of each particular act of sexual intercourse producing a child must surely be envisaged and decided one way or the other more or less deliberately.

Now there is no doubt that the average size of the family produced by those who know about and practise birth control has increased quite appreciably in recent years. It must therefore be supposed that there has been a fairly widespread desire among married couples to have families of more than one or two children. No doubt this is largely a matter of fashion; and fashions, in this as in other matters, may change quite quickly. All that I can usefully say about it here is this.

I quite understand (though I do not share) the desire to have *some* children, and I think that there are several good reasons, other things being equal, for having *more than one*, if one has any. But I do not understand what motive there can be for having a family of more than two or at most three. It seems to me that, under the conditions which now hold and are likely to continue for the foreseeable future, there might be expected to be a strong motive against doing so. It is this:

In Victorian times, and even in late Edwardian ones, married couples above the poverty line dwelled in fairly roomy houses, and there were available to them at a cheap rate plenty of servants who would live in. It was therefore easy to be free of one's children most of the time. One kept them generally in a special room, the nursery, and in adjoining bedrooms; and they were looked after there and elsewhere by one or more nurse-maids. All this has now utterly changed even for those who are relatively prosperous. Modern houses have few rooms, and those which they have are poky. The housewife has to do most of the cooking and much of the cleaning herself, and there can be no question of getting a resident nurse-maid to relieve her of the constant presence and burden of her children. It seems to me that the wives of my colleagues who have young children have the latter perpetually on their hands and under their feet, and are almost literally throughout most of their waking hours the slaves of their noisy and irrational offspring. I should have thought that this would be a very strong motive indeed against having a prolonged sequence of children.

However that may be, a good deal of contemporary legislation and of collegiate financial policy certainly tends to counteract certain motives against having a large family which would otherwise exist, and which in the past operated strongly on responsible persons. The motives in question were economic and prudential, viz., a consideration of the added cost of feeding, clothing, and educating each additional child. These have now been deliberately nullified or considerably reduced by public legislation and by special College ordinances. No doubt the motive for such legislation is certain obvious advantages which it *immediately* secures or certain obvious disadvantages which it *immediately* diminishes. But it is relevant to point out, what it is very easy to ignore, viz., its *indirect* ill effects in largely nullifying a motive which would otherwise exist and operate against having large families.

So far I have been considering only increase of population due to more children than of yore of English parentage being born and surviving. I cannot leave the subject without referring to a matter which is partly, but not wholly or mainly, quantitative. During the period under review, there has been, for the first time in history, a very considerable immigration of persons who are not even from other parts of Europe, but are completely alien in race, colour, and social traditions; they are particularly numerous in certain occupations, such as service on the railways and in the omnibuses; and in certain areas, they form a majority of the population.

The permission of such immigration seems to me to have been a most flagrant example of culpable unforeseeing negligence on the part of those authorities which permitted it. That such a situation would result in severe internal tensions could have been foreseen by any reasonable person who had paused to reflect and who had considered what had happened and is continuing to happen in the United States; and those in authority who failed to foresee this, or, if they did, nevertheless permitted the kind of immigration which would inevitably lead to it, seem to me to be deserving of the most severe censure.

(2) *Changes affecting Cambridge in General or Trinity College in Particular.*

    (i) *Increase of Motor Traffic in the Streets.* The number of motor vehicles driven in and through Cambridge has vastly increased during the period under review. No doubt there has been a close parallel to this in other places, but here I shall consider it only as it has affected Cambridge.

    The main streets of the city are mostly fairly narrow. The increase in motor traffic has rendered them intolerably noisy, smelly with petrol fumes, and difficult and dangerous to cross during the greater part of most days. This is accentuated by the fact that large vehicles, delivering goods to shops or fetching rubbish away from them, are liable to be standing at places at the side of a street and to be projecting over the adjoining pavement. To crown all, the pavements themselves are crowded with people, many of them pushing perambulators containing the youngest of what Burke would have termed 'the spawn of their disgustful amours', and dragging beside them by the hand the slightly older products of previous exercises in the same process.

    One consequence of the increase of motor traffic in general, and of through-going motor lorry traffic in particular, has been especially detrimental to the amenities formerly enjoyed by those living in Trinity. The Queen's Road, which separates the west side of the Trinity Paddocks from the east side of the Fellows' Garden ('The Roundabout') has become a main thoroughfare, carrying in both directions streams of private cars and of heavy commercial lorries. Just by the part of the road where one would cross from Trinity to the Fellows' Garden, there is a slight curve, which makes it especially difficult to see what is coming. The result is that crossing has become dangerous, not only for age and impotence, but even for the young, the strong, and the virile. More than one Fellow has been run down, though as yet none has been fatally injured. For my own part, I have practically ceased to use the Roundabout and its adjacent inner garden ('Duff's Garden'), of which I was very fond.

In this matter, St. John's College has been much more fortunate than Trinity. All their gardens are on the same side of Queen's Road as the College itself. To the north of their Fellows' Garden (which is, of course, not available to members of other Colleges or of the general public) they have a quiet and most beautiful small garden, which is open to the public at most times, but is not in fact much frequented. It is a haven of peace and beauty, in which I often sit, now that the dangers of getting to and from the Trinity 'Roundabout' have practically excluded me from the latter.

This is only the beginning of the advantages which St. John's now enjoys over Trinity. If one passes through the gate at the north-east corner of the small garden just mentioned and passes straight on, one comes to the magnificent Cripps building. To this Trinity has, and can expect to have, nothing comparable among its existing or its projected new buildings. For any extension of Trinity must either be squashed into holes and corners adjacent to the existing buildings (as, *e.g.*, Angel Court and the new buildings on the site of the old Matthew's Shop on the east of Trinity Street), or be erected somewhere quite remote from the existing College (as, e.g., the proposed extension in Burrell's Field).

Even now I have not come to the end of the advantages enjoyed by St. John's over Trinity. Trinity has, and can have, nothing comparable to the ancient Merton Hall and the Pythagoras Building, between the west end of the Cripps Building and the continuation of the Queen's Road to the traffic lights at the foot of Castle Hill. St. John's has had the good fortune and the foresight to acquire all this, and it is to be congratulated on the magnificent job which it has made of bringing it into external repair and internal habitability without making any essential alteration in its outward appearance.

If, after passing through the small gate which I have mentioned above, one turns first to one's left and then a little later to one's right, one passes behind the back gardens of a couple of houses at the end of Queen's Road. And, a little further on, one comes to a delightful little sunken garden, with a sundial in it, close to the Merton Hall area. Here there is a seat, facing eastwards over the sunken garden, with a view of Merton Hall if one turns one's head a little to the left. It is perfectly quiet and peaceful, as no hole or corner in Trinity now is, and I often sit there of an afternoon and meditate.

There has been in the past a very long ding-dong rivalry between Trinity and St. John's, but now it seems to me that, in amenities, at any rate, the victory has gone decisively and permanently to St. John's:

> O magna Carthago probrosis
> altior Italiae ruinis[19]

(ii) *Increase in Number of Visitors.* A very noticeable change during the period under review has been the enormous increase in the number of persons, not members of the University, wandering about the streets gaping at everything. All Colleges have suffered this influx, but I will confine my attention here to what has happened at Trinity. Here we have them perpetually about the place, strolling in our Courts and walks, visiting the Chapel or the Library, sitting or sprawling by the banks of the River or on the bridge over it, and endlessly taking photographs of the buildings and of each other.

It had always, so far as I am aware, been the custom of the Cambridge Colleges to have their gates open to visitors all day and every day except on one occasion in each year when they were shut so as to prevent the establishment of a right of way. This custom worked very comfortably until fairly recent years. But lately, owing to the general increase in leisure and mobility, it has become a very great nuisance to those living in College. From Easter to late in September the Courts swarm all day with visitors, sometimes in pairs or trios, but more often in large parties. Some of them do not hesitate to walk on the grass plots, and I have even met one man and his wife endeavouring to take their dog with them into the Chapel. Naturally, this nuisance reaches its maximum on fine week-ends and on Bank holidays. Looking out from the windows of my rooms on the first floor in the north-east corner of Great Court, I am often inclined to re-echo Bishop Heber's reflexions on Ceylon and its inhabitants:

> 'Where every prospect pleases, and only Man is vile.'

It would be difficult for the College now to withdraw or seriously to restrict the time-honoured privilege of free entry all day and every day to all and sundry. And it would be almost impossible for one College to do this except as part of a general policy undertaken by it in conjunction with all the others. Yet the present freedom of entry and the present arrangements for exercising control within the precincts of the College were designed for conditions which no longer exist, and are very ill-adapted to those which now prevail. I will give some detailed observations in support of these general statements:

(a) The proprietors of 'sight-seeing' tourist omnibuses find the present situation a perfect godsend to them and exploit it accordingly. They are able to deposit daily masses of their clients in the streets of Cambridge, knowing that the Colleges provide a free entertainment for visitors.

(b) The present structure of the Porters' Lodges, and the nature and number of the staff of Porters, are quite unadapted to a purpose for which they were never intended, viz., the overseeing and controlling large numbers of persons, not subject to University or College discipline, wandering about in the Courts. The Lodges are so constructed that it would be impossible to see from them what is going on outside, and the Porters are pretty fully occupied with duties which keep them most of the time within their Lodges. They cannot be expected to be regularly patrolling the Courts and the Grounds.

(c) I should suppose that the remarks in the immediately preceding paragraph would apply without much modification to other Colleges beside Trinity. But it seems to me that some of the arrangements in Trinity are peculiarly defective as compared with those of most other Colleges. I am thinking in particular of the absence of notices designed explicitly to warn visitors from walking on the grass-plots in the Courts.

Trinity, like other Colleges, has a fairly conspicuous notice at each of its entrances stating the conditions to which visitors are expected to conform. Among these is a clause stating that walking on the grass is not permitted. (Another clause states that no dogs and no perambulators may be brought into College.) It seems certain that a good many visitors, even if arriving singly or in groups of two or three, merely glance in a cursory way at such a notice and do not take in its details. This is true even if their native tongue is English; but in summer many of them are foreigners, some of whom have only a very imperfect knowledge of the language in which the notice is written.

It is, at any rate, quite certain that the notices at the entrances do not prevent the quite frequent introduction of perambulators with their contents, nor the occasional introduction of dogs on leads. And I am pretty sure that the vast majority of cases of failure to observe the regulations exhibited at the entrances arise from negligence or ignorance and not from deliberate disobedience. That the clause in the notices, forbidding visitors to walk on the grass, is ineffective, is still more obvious. From my window, I see this offence continually happening.

Now it seems to me plain that it would at least help to diminish this nuisance if we had in Trinity, as they have in most other Colleges, notices 'Please do not walk on the grass' at *each* of the four sides (or corners) of *each* of the grass-plots. In the summer of 1969, we had no such notices at all. Earlier we had what seemed to me to be a quite idiotic compromise, viz., such notices only on certain plots and not on others, and only on certain sides or corners and not on others of each such plot. If a visitor sees a notice forbidding something in one place, and sees that there is not much notice in another precisely similar place in the same Court, he will not unnaturally tend to assume that where the action is not explicitly forbidden it is permitted.

(iii) *Increase in the Number of Fellows.* The number of Fellows of Trinity (and very likely of other Colleges) has been continually growing. In my opinion, it has long since passed its optimum, and the College has been extremely unwise not to have introduced long ago a change of Statute to make such proliferation impossible or extremely difficult.

If challenged, I should of course decline to state a definite number of Fellows as optimal. But that does not prevent me from feeling quite sure that the present number (well over 100) is far too large. Nor would I hesitate to name *approximate* upper and lower limits. I am sure that over 70 is too many, and that under 40 would be too few.

My main reasons for this opinion are the two following:

(a) The communal apartments of the College, for example, the Hall, the Fellows' Parlour, and the Fellows' Combination Room, have been built so as to provide comfortable and civilised accommodation for about 60 Fellows at any one time. No extension of the Hall is practically possible. An extension of the parlour has recently been completed, at enormous expense. For the moment, it has brought a most welcome relief from the overcrowding which until recently prevailed there, especially after lunch, and to some extent after dinner. But, if the number of Fellows should go on increasing in future at anything like the rate at which it has done in the recent past, this increased space will soon cease to be adequate.

(b) The Fellows form a body of men of various ages and degrees of academic seniority. They range from those under Title A, who have only recently ceased to be in *statu pupillari*, through the middle-aged who are active in teaching and administration, to the elderly and the very old. One of the greatest merits of the system has been that each Fellow, whatever his age or his interests, could be on friendly and familiar terms with all the rest, singling out of course as his special intimates a small selection from the whole body. Now, this depends essentially on the total numbers being kept within strict limits. It is just possible when the maximum is between 60 and 70. It becomes increasingly difficult with any increase beyond 70, and it becomes practically impossible when the aggregate number rises to 100 and over. Nowadays, it would be a matter of special research (which would probably not repay the labour spent) to know all one's colleagues even by name or by sight and to associate correctly in all cases a given name with a given appearance.

One of the commonest and the silliest mistakes which people are liable to make, or to act as if they had made, is to imagine that the qualitative merits characteristic of an institution of a certain limited size can continue when that size is indefinitely increased. I have often thought that the time has come when it would be appropriate to have in the Ante-Chapel a Cenotaph, with an inscription 'To the Unknown Fellow of Trinity'.

(iv) *Spread of Bi-sexuality.* So much for quantitative changes and some of their consequences. It remains to note a qualitative change which began late in the period under consideration, and which is still in progress. This is the growing bi-sexuality of what had always been until quite lately an exclusively male society. At the time of writing this has only reached the point in Trinity at which undergraduates, B.A.s, and Research Students are allowed to bring female guests to lunch and to dinner in Hall. (In the case of undergraduates it is to be hoped and believed that the guests are in general 'girl-friends'; in the case of B.A.s and Research Students it is to be feared that they are in many cases wives.)

(i) It is quite inevitable that certain members of the High Table should argue that similar privileges (if privileges they be) should be extended to members of the High Table. If this claim should be granted, the High Table, and presumably the Combination Room and the Parlour, will become bi-sexual in their composition.

(ii) I will not attempt to argue here a question which is still *sub judice* at the time of writing. Nor is it a question of the kind which I should much care to argue; for it is typically one of those in which 'argument' is mainly the emission of emotional hot-air disguised in intellectual form. So I will end by expressing explicitly my likes and dislikes in such matters. I like the society in which I live and move to be wholly uni-sexual and wholly male, and I like it to have room for and to contain patches of homo-sexuality. So there!

NOTES

1 JW: The speech is also reproduced as Chapter 2.6 in this volume.
2 JW: Hereafter, "S.P.R."
3 JW: Published as "Human Personality, and the Question of the Possibility of its Survival of Bodily Death" pp. 385–430 in Broad, C.D. (1962) *Lectures on Psychical Research* (New York: Humanities Press)

4 JW: Reproduced as Chapter 2.3 in this volume (a paper which was also read *twice* in Helsinki on September 27th and 28th, 1965: see below).
5 JW: Reproduced as Chapter 2.8 in this volume.
6 JW. Reproduced as Chapter 3.3 in this volume.
7 JW: Published as "Dr. Soal's Experiments with Mr. Shackleton and with Mrs. Stewart" pp. 23–43 in Broad, C.D. (1962) *Lectures on Psychical Research* (New York: Humanities Press).
8 JW: Reproduced as Chapter 2.7 in this volume.
9 JW: Published as "Self and Others" pp. 262–282 in Cheney, D. (Ed.) (1971) *Broad's Critical Essays in Moral Philosophy* (New York: Humanities Press).
10 JW: Published in 1958 as "Philosophy" in *Inquiry* 1(2): 99–129, which is presented in two parts, corresponding to the two lectures.
11 JW: Reproduced as Chapter 3.2 of this volume.
12 JW: Published as "The Phenomenology of Mrs. Leonard's Mediumship" pp. 287–314 in Broad, C.D. (1962) *Lectures on Psychical Research* (New York: Humanities Press).
13 JW: i.e., Helsinki.
14 JW: Published as "Obligations, Ultimate and Derived" pp. 351–368 in Cheney, D. (Ed.) (1971) *Broad's Critical Essays in Moral Philosophy* (New York: Humanities Press).
15 JW: Reproduced as Chapter 2.2 in this volume.
16 JW: Reproduced as Chapter 2.3 in this volume.
17 JW: Published as (1961) "Hume's Doctrine of Space" *Proceedings of the British Academy* 47: 161–176.
18 JW: From Horace's *Ars Poetica*. Plausibly translated as: "Morose, complaining, and with tedious praise/Telling the manners of their youthful days."
19 JW: Horace, *Odes*, III, v: "O mighty Carthage, raised higher on Italy's disgraceful ruins."

Part 2

PHILOSOPHERS AND THE HISTORY OF PHILOSOPHY

INTRODUCTION TO PART 2
Joel Walmsley

Broad's most enduring philosophical legacy might fairly be regarded as concerning what we now think of as the *problems* of philosophy, especially in philosophy of mind and science, in the metaphysics of time, and in philosophical theories of ethics. But it should not be forgotten that his body of written work contains many significant contributions to scholarship on philosophers and the history of philosophy as well. Broad's very first publication, in 1906 (aged 18, and the year that he first went up to Cambridge), was an essay comparing the philosophical views of Omar Khayyam and Schopenhauer, and throughout his career he taught and wrote papers on many key historical figures, including Descartes, Berkeley, Locke, and Newton, and posthumously published book-length treatments of Kant and Leibniz.

I suspect that Broad would have found the contemporary distinction between those approaches to philosophy that focus on its history, and those that focus on its problems, to be both artificial and unhelpful. This is because – as is evident in his writing – Broad tends to view historical figures as engaged with tackling the *same* problems with which contemporary philosophy is concerned, and therefore as participants in an ongoing dialogue. The first four essays in this section – on Hegel, Hume, and Bradley – are particularly good examples of this style, which one also finds in his other published work: in each case Broad juxtaposes a careful, painstaking, but *charitable* interpretation and exegesis of the views of those philosophers, with his own views and critical commentary. What we end up with is a sometimes iconoclastic (and, admittedly, sometimes, idiosyncratic) picture of the views of the philosopher in question, but one that *also* gives us a better insight into Broad's own positions concerning the matters at hand.

Of course, this is not to say that Broad avoids an entirely historical mode of writing. The final three essays in this section – on Russell, Bacon, and the development of scientific thought – are focussed primarily on biography and history. But Broad's knack for storytelling here (along with his usual pithy asides) nonetheless makes for a set of compelling narratives; the final paragraph of the *biographical* essay on Bacon included here is just as elegantly composed as the oft-quoted concluding passage from his previously published essay on Bacon's *philosophy*, in which he describes induction as the 'glory of Science [and] the scandal of Philosophy'.[1]

We start with the essay 'Hegel's Views on the Nature of Philosophy', which comes from an undated, handwritten manuscript, and attempts to elucidate the first six chapters of Hegel's *Encyclopedia of the Philosophical Sciences*, focussing on the nature of philosophy itself, and its relations to science, to religion, and to human psychological processes. It is fair to say that Broad was not generally well-disposed to Hegel: in *Five Types of Ethical Theory*, Broad refers to him as 'a disaster', and elsewhere in an essay on McTaggart, he memorably writes:

> If we compare McTaggart with the other commentators on Hegel we must admit that he has at least produced an extremely lively and fascinating rabbit from the Hegelian hat, whilst they have produced nothing but consumptive and gibbering chimeras. And we shall admire his resource and dexterity all the more when we reflect that the rabbit was, in all probability, never inside the hat, whilst the chimeras perhaps were.[2]

The present essay is therefore remarkable for how *charitable* it is towards Hegel in extracting and rendering comprehensible some of the views that are considered. In concluding, Broad writes of Hegel's work that 'Valuable commentaries have been written upon it, but even with their help much remains conjectural or quite unintelligible', but one comes away with the feeling that because of Broad's own contribution, that alleged unintelligibility has been somewhat diminished.

The pair of essays on Hume – 'Hume's Theory of Belief' and 'Hume's Doctrine of the Self' – were originally given as lectures at the University of Helsinki on the evenings of 27 and 28 September 1962 respectively (the latter having also been read at St. Andrews in 1955), and can therefore be profitably read as companions. The former is a detailed analysis and exegesis of Hume's view of belief, its relation to imagination, and the consequences for his accounts of knowledge and causation. The latter supplements this discussion with a focus on Hume's account of the self and personal identity (as it appears in the *Treatise of Human Nature* and the later-published *Appendix*). It is especially interesting insofar as it pays particular attention to how Hume's view is connected to his more general account of substance, and it concludes with a critical discussion of Hume's account of memory. When these two essays are taken in conjunction with Broad's previously published work on Hume's theory of miracles (1917), Hume's doctrine of space (1961), and Hume's ethics (in Chapter 4 of *Five Types of Ethical Theory*), these two essays complete a substantial body of work on some of the most well-known topics discussed by *Le Bon David*.

Broad relates that he had been given a copy of Bradley's *Appearance and Reality* as a Christmas present in 1905 and that he consequently 'arrived in Cambridge in October 1906 in the philosophical condition of an enthusiastic but woolly Idealist'.[3] He soon found that 'The philosophical atmosphere among the younger men was strongly and rather scornfully anti-idealist';[4] indeed, although the two professorships in Cambridge were held by Ward and Sorley at the time, Moore's paper 'The Refutation of Idealism' had been published in 1903, and he, along with Russell 'held the field' in Cambridge. It is therefore interesting to see Broad returning to the views of F.H. Bradley – whom he describes as 'the ablest and the most readable writer of his school' – in the essay reproduced below.

Although Broad had published a lengthy critical notice of Bradley's *Essays on Truth and Reality* in 1914 – when Bradley was still alive – the present essay is taken from a typed manuscript dated 2 June 1955, and provides a much deeper exegesis and analysis of some central themes in Bradley's *Appearance and Reality*. It focuses particularly on Bradley's notion of degrees of truth and reality, and on his theories of judgment, the self, and 'the Absolute', before concluding with some connections between Bradley's version of British Idealism and the subsequent sense-data theories to which Broad himself contributed. Taken alongside Broad's own seminal work on McTaggart, this essay therefore helps to provide a clearer insight into the significant – though often unstated – idealist influences in Broad's own work.

The essay 'Philosophy 1900–1950' is taken from a typed manuscript for a 20-minute talk intended for public broadcast, and dated 5 February 1950.

Broad's handwritten comment on the first page reads 'Written for BBC Europe lecture, but withdrawn by me, as the BBC wanted changes that I was not prepared to make'. What those changes *were* remains unknown. It is a whistle-stop tour of key figures in philosophy in England during the stated period, tracing the relations between Spencer, Ward, Sidgwick, Bradley, Bosanquet, Moore, Russell, Wittgenstein, Ayer, McTaggart, Alexander, and Whitehead. Witty, but also sharply critical in places (especially on Spencer and Wittgenstein), it sits well alongside another of Broad's published essays – the lengthier 1957 'The Local Historical Background of Contemporary British Philosophy' – to demonstrate Broad's deep familiarity with the work of his contemporaries.

The piece on Russell is unusual in that it wasn't so much a *lecture*, as a speech, given on 18 May 1962, to mark the occasion of Russell's 90th birthday. Although Russell was not present on the occasion, it is clear that Broad intended for it to be read again by others since (as recounted in the 'Autobiographical Notes') he deposited a copy in the Trinity College library to be made available for consultation. Although it might be tempting to judge much of the speech's content as somewhat inappropriate for a congratulatory birthday speech – Broad says that Russell's 1918 prosecution and imprisonment was deserved, and criticizes his *A History of Western Philosophy* – perhaps this is more reflective of a combination of Broad's sometimes mischievous character, together with his commitment to candour in all his work, even when dealing with those to whom he owes 'an immense debt'.

The essay on Bacon comes from a typed manuscript dated 8 January 1961 and was given as a lecture at the University of Leeds on 30 January that year, to commemorate the 400th anniversary of Bacon's birth. It is intended as an entirely biographical supplement to Broad's 1926 lecture – published as *The Philosophy of Francis Bacon* – which had been given in Cambridge on the 300th anniversary of Bacon's death. As such, it contains only minor philosophical commentary, but it is a masterful example of Broad's skill in writing history. In the 'Autobiographical Notes' of this volume, Broad writes: 'This address has not yet been published' suggesting that, if this was perhaps his intent, then it has now been fulfilled some 60 years later.

Finally, this section concludes with another largely historical essay on the development of scientific thought, from Pythagoras to Newton. As Broad explains in the 'Autobiographical Notes', this is taken from the manuscript (dated 20 June 1957) for a lecture that was given on 15 July 1957, at Dillington House in Somerset. Unusually, however, the audience was a

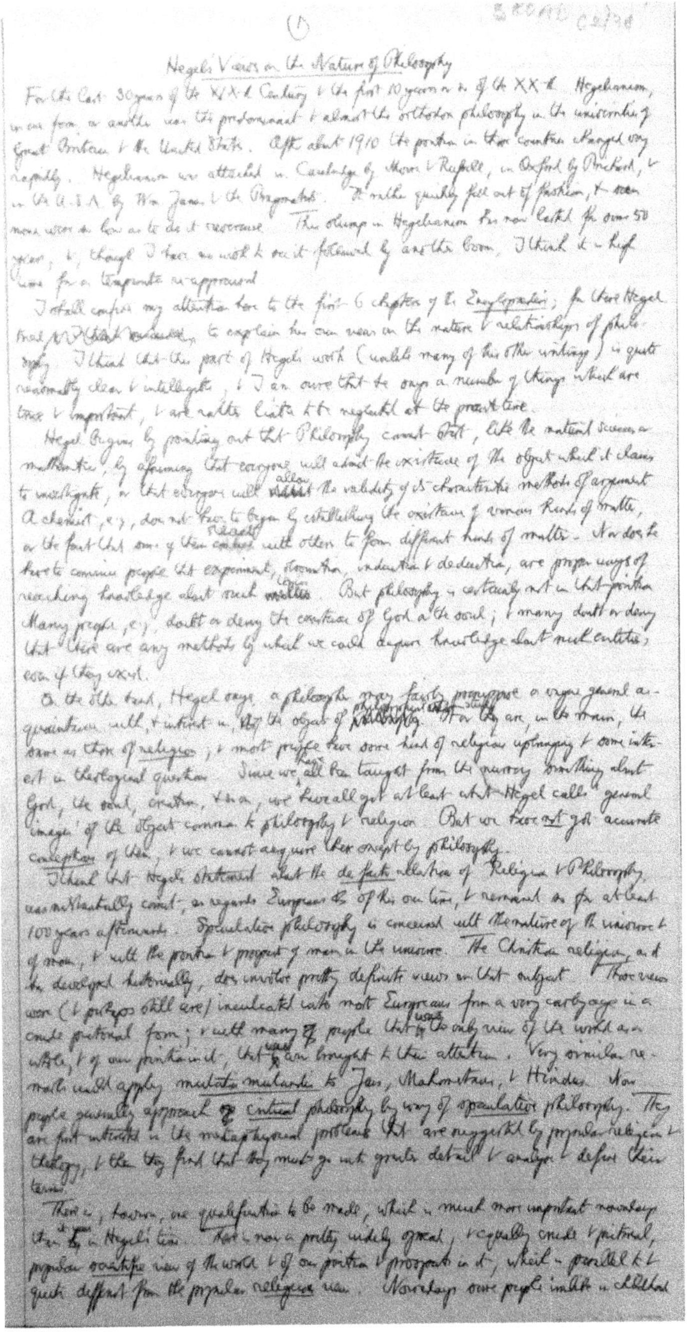

Figure 2.1 Original handwritten manuscript for Chapter 2.1

group of primary school children who were on a week's course there. One can only wonder what his audience must have made of it, for it is particularly concerned with mathematics, astronomy, and dynamics, and it goes into typical Broad-style painstaking detail about some of the ideas that were developing in the period under consideration. It nonetheless also makes for an instructive read for a novice 'grown up', and shows Broad's own training in science – and its history – in context.

NOTES

1 Broad (1926, p. 67).
2 Broad (1952, p. 75).
3 Broad (1967, p. 101).
4 Broad (1959a, p. 50).

2.1

HEGEL'S VIEWS ON THE NATURE OF PHILOSOPHY

For the last 30 years of the XIXth Century, and the first ten years of the XXth, Hegelianism, in one form or another was the predominant and almost the orthodox philosophy in the universities of Great Britain and the United States. After about 1910, the position in those countries changed very rapidly. Hegelianism was attacked in Cambridge by Moore and Russell, in Oxford by Pritchard, and in the United States by William James and the Pragmatists. It rather quickly fell out of fashion, and soon none were so low as to do it reverence. This slump in Hegelianism has now lasted for some 50 years, and, though I have no wish to see it followed by another boom, I think it is high time for a temperate re-appraisal.

I shall confine my attention here to the first six chapters of the *Encyclopaedia*; for there, Hegel tried to explain his own views of the nature and relationships of philosophy. I think that this part of Hegel's work (unlike many of his other writings) is quite reasonably clear and intelligible and I am sure that he says a number of things which are true and important and are rather liable to be neglected at the present time.

Hegel begins by pointing out that Philosophy cannot start, like the natural sciences or mathematics, by assuming that everyone will admit the existence of the objects which it claims to investigate, or that everyone will allow the validity of its characteristic methods of argument. A chemist, for example, does not have to begin by establishing the existence of various kinds of matter or the fact that some of them react with others to form different kinds of matter. Nor does he have to convince people that experiment, observation, induction, and deduction are proper ways of reaching knowledge about such topics. But philosophy is certainly not in that position. Many people, for example, doubt or deny the existence of God or the soul, and many doubt or deny that there are any methods by which we could acquire knowledge about such entities even if they exist.

On the other hand, Hegel says, a philosopher may fairly presuppose a vague general acquaintance with, and interest in, the objects of philosophical study. For they are, in the main, the same as those of *religion*, and most people have some kind of religious upbringing and some interest in theological questions. Since we have all been taught from the nursery something about God, the soul, creation, and such, we have all got at least what Hegel calls 'general images' of the objects common to philosophy and religion. But we have *not* got accurate *conceptions* of them and we cannot acquire them except by philosophy.

I think that Hegel's statement about the *de facto* relation of Religion and Philosophy was substantially correct, as regards Europeans of his own time, and remained so for at least 100 years afterwards. Speculative philosophy is concerned with the nature of the universe and of man, and with the position and prospects of man in the universe. The Christian religion, as it developed historically, does involve pretty definite views on that subject. Those views were (and perhaps still are) inculcated into most Europeans from a very early age in a crude pictorial form, and with many people that was the only view of the world as a whole, and of our position in it, that was ever brought to their attention. Very similar remarks will apply *mutatis mutandis* to Jews, Mahometans, and Hindus. Now people generally approach *critical* philosophy by way of *speculative* philosophy. They are first interested in the metaphysical problems that are suggested by popular religion and theology, and then they find that they must go into greater detail and analyse and define their terms.

There is, however, one qualification to be made which is much more important nowadays than it was in Hegel's time. There is now a pretty widely agreed, and equally crude and pictorial, popular *scientific* view of the world and our position and prospects in it, which is parallel to and quite different from the popular religious view. Nowadays some people imbibe in childhood the former rather than the latter, whilst most of us imbibe a mixture of the two in various proportions. So nowadays I think it would be true to say that the raw material of philosophy is the 'general image' of these two popular views and that the interest in and stimulus to philosophy is often the inconsistency (real or apparent) between the popular scientific and the popular religious views of man and the universe.

The essence of philosophy, according to Hegel, is to move from mere 'general images' to definite *thoughts*. We then find that we are no longer content to take *prima facie* facts merely as given. We want to *prove the existence* of the objects of which we think, and to show the necessity of what we believe about them. This makes it difficult to find a suitable starting point for philosophy. Each of us must in practice begin somewhere; yet any beginning that one may choose seems to be arbitrary. To deal with that difficulty, Hegel points out that there is an ambiguity in the word 'thought.' It is used in a wide and narrower sense. When we say, for example, that 'thinking' is what distinguishes man from the lower animals, we are using 'thought' in the wider sense. When we say (as Hegel does) that philosophy is the 'thinking study of things' we are using it in the narrower sense. Here 'thought' means 'knowledge through *notions*.' Hegel calls thought, in this narrower sense, 'after-thought' or 'reflexion.' He says that thought-products do not at first appear in the form of thought in that sense; they appear as feelings or perceptions or images, and these must be distinguished from thoughts in the strict sense.

I think that the distinction, which Hegel has in mind, is valid and very important, but I am inclined to think that it covers two different cases:

(1) There are innumerable human actions and mental processes, which depend on thought, and could take place only in a thinking being brought up in a society of thinking beings. And yet the actual performance of those processes on any given occasion may not involve thinking, in the strict sense, on that occasion by that individual. When we talk grammatically and naturally, or use properly any system of symbolism, or perform actions which we have been taught in the past, we are carrying out processes of thought in the wider sense. All this presupposes that the agent himself, or someone else, in the past has thought in the strict sense. We might call this '*crystallised* thinking.' If, for example, I now mechanically solve an equation with perfect confidence, by manipulating

the symbols according to rules that I have learnt, I am *not* thinking, in the sense in which I *am* thinking when I analyse a new problem for myself and try to solve it by explicitly comparing and contrasting the factors in it with those with which I am acquainted in other contexts. But *someone* must have thought, in the strict sense, in order to make up the system of symbolism, and to formulate such rules for its operation as will agree with the laws governing the objects to be symbolised. And I must have done some thinking, in the strict sense, when I first convinced myself that the symbolism is appropriate, and that manipulating those symbols according to those rules will solve such problems. Thinking, in this sense, involves having the meanings of one's terms explicitly present to one; analysing them and noting their mutual relations; passing from one to another because you perceive relations which seem to you to justify the transition; and so on. We might call this 'fluid thinking.' In a still wider sense, almost anything that we use properly, as we say 'without thinking', though not 'thoughtlessly', for example, a typewriter, an automobile, etc., may be called a 'crystallised thought.' And, in learning to use them, and still more in mending them when they are out of order, we must to some extent think over again the relevant thought of their inventors. Now *one* thing that Hegel had in mind was this highly important distinction between processes of fluid thinking, on the one hand, and the products of former fluid thinking, crystallised either in mental or in bodily processes which are now more or less habitual, in language, in machines, and so on.

(2) I suspect, however, that he had also another contrast in view. There is an enormous amount going on in human life, which can only be described by saying: 'So-and-so is behaving *as if* he had perceived *a*, had recognised a certain connexion between it and *b*, and had inferred and acted upon a certain proposition about *b*'. And yet the most careful introspection may fail to reveal any trace of such a process. Ordinary sense-perception, for example, is obviously full of this. In order to see a certain thing clearly, for example, one has to converge one's eyes to a certain degree. Now one often behaves just as if one had noted the angle of convergence and had gone through a trigonometrical calculation to determine from it the distance of the object. Actually, there is no direct evidence that one does anything of the kind. But the fact remains that the actual degree of convergence does make one adjust oneself to

the external object, as it would be reasonable to do if one had gone through the process of thought. Now I imagine that this is part of what Hegel had in mind, when he said that 'thought products do not originally appear in the form of a thought, but as a feeling, perception, or mental image'.

Another plausible example would be the contrast between traditional rules of craftsmanship, such as those current among dyers until quite recent times, and the scientific techniques for producing definite dyes at will for particular purposes, and determining the best conditions for applying them. The traditional rules depend on thought, in the sense of rough comparison, proceeding by trial and error, and so on. Animals would not have the thought of dyeing things, and would never have discovered even these crude rules. But the scientific techniques replace them by a deliberate analysis of the whole problem into its essential factors and a deliberate combination of factors with known properties so arranged as to fulfil the assigned conditions. This is genuine fluid thinking.

So thought, in the widest sense, might perhaps be divided, first into *fluid* and *non-fluid* thought. And then non-fluid thought might be subdivided into *crystallised* thought (which represents and depends upon thought that was once fluid) and what I will call *quasi*-thought. I suspect that long continuous processes of fluid thinking hardly exist. In any process of thought, even at a high intellectual level, there are isolated spasms of fluid thinking, interspersed with and overlapped by relevant stretches of crystallised thought and of *quasi*-thought.

There is one other point to be noted before leaving this topic. Hegel seems to identify fluid thought with what he calls 'reflexion'. And by 'reflexion' or 'after-thought' he seems to understand thinking about non-fluid thought and its products. Now, if that be what he really means, I do not think that it is altogether satisfactory. It is, no doubt, true that the materials for fluid thought about all subjects are supplied in the main by non-fluid thought. Ordinary science starts from the crude observations and generalisations of daily life. And logic takes for its raw material men's actual processes of argument, and tries to find why the valid ones are valid and the invalid ones are invalid. In that sense, it is true that all fluid thought is reflexion on non-fluid thought. But it would be safer to express this in the form that all high-grade thinking has for its raw materials the products of lower-grade thinking. We must, at any rate, beware of supposing that all fluid thinking is reflexion on thought-processes. That is plainly not true. It is only logic and certain parts of psychology that could be called 'reflective' in that sense, and fluid thinking is certainly not confined to those subjects.

We can now pass to Hegel's views as to the relations of thought and feeling in *religion*. He considers that failure to distinguish between the wider and the narrower sense of 'thought' has led to two opposite misunderstandings on this point. On the one hand, we find people who insist that religion depends entirely on a specific kind of *feeling* or *emotion* or *intuition*, and that it is perverted and eventually destroyed by thought. This is the type of religious view which is always appealing to the simple piety of the child or the peasant, and contrasting it favourably with the attitude of the scholarly and critical theologian. Hegel particularly disliked that view, and he points out that it rests on identifying thought with what he calls 'reflexion'. His answer is roughly as follows. Religion does, no doubt, involve as an essential factor certain specific emotions and feelings and these themselves are not acts or states of thinking. But they are emotions and feelings of a kind which could exist only in a thinking being. Only such a being could, for example, contemplate the possibility of his existence after death, raise questions about the origin and destiny of the world, and so on. And no one who could not have at least crude and pictorial thoughts of these and similar subjects could possibly feel specifically religious emotion. These characteristically *human* emotions are, as Hegel says, 'moulded and permeated by thought.' But it is quite another matter to reflect on them, analyse them, to reason about them, and to consider their possible ontological implications. That is the business of theology and philosophy.

The opposite mistake is that of those theologians and philosophers who have denied that consciousness of God and true religion can exist except in people who have followed and accepted certain abstract theological arguments and accepted their conclusions. Hegel is here thinking of the view that a person could not, for example, believe in God unless he could follow and accept at least one of the philosophical arguments for God's existence.

These two errors are simply two different consequences of identifying thought with deliberate reflective thinking. In the first case, it leads people to say that religion is altogether independent of, and even antagonistic to thought, merely because its most specific features are certain feelings, emotions, and practices, and because it can obviously exist to a very high degree in quite simple and non-intellectual people. That view forgets that these feelings and emotions are such as could exist only in a thinking being. In the second case, it leads people to say that religion cannot exist except in people who can follow and accept philosophical proofs of religious propositions. That view forgets that a person may accept and act upon many propositions which he could not clearly formulate or prove, and that he may be behaving quite reasonably in doing so.

I consider Hegel's doctrine, about certain factors in human experience being 'permeated and moulded by thought', to be true and very important. It extends far beyond the question of religion and philosophy and it may be worthwhile to discuss it a little more fully.

I think that there are at least two different senses in which certain factors in an experience may be said to be 'permeated and moulded by thought'. (1) As I have said, there are certain emotions which could not exist except in thinking beings, simply because their appropriate objects are such that no one but a thinking being could present such objects to himself even in the crudest form. To take other examples, I do not see how anyone but a thinking being could possibly have a feeling of moral obligation or a feeling of remorse. For those emotions can be felt only towards an object which involves the thought of a *law*, which may or may not be obeyed, or of an *ideal*, which may or may not be realised.

Perhaps, indeed, it might be suggested that precisely the same *emotional attitudes* may exist in certain non-thinking beings, for example, dogs or horses, but that in them it is not directed to these *peculiar objects*, and that we give it a different name, because we name an emotion partly from its characteristic *object*, and not solely from the emotional attitude. Thus, for example, it might be suggested that the two emotions which we call 'fear of a whip' in a dog and 'awe of God' in a man, consist of exactly the *same emotional attitude* directed towards two extremely different objects. If that be so, I shall still say that specifically religious and specifically moral *emotions* can exist only in thinking beings, but I should have to admit that the *emotional attitudes* in those emotions can exist also in non-thinking beings. I should, however, point out that the *emotional attitude* is only an abstract element, hardly capable of existing undirected upon an object real or imaginary. But, for my own part, I should question whether the *emotional attitude* itself could be precisely the same when the objects were utterly different.

(2) This brings me to a second sense in which we may say that certain factors in human experience are 'permeated and moulded by thought'. If we consider ordinary sense-perception, it is obvious that it involves two factors, viz., sensation, and certain beliefs or *quasi*-beliefs which arise, on the occasion of the sensation, from the excitement of traces of past experiences and their associations. But, although we can and must distinguish two factors in sense perception, one of which may be called 'pure sensation' and the other 'thought', it is extremely difficult to separate them. For it certainly seems as if, in many cases, the pre-existing system of beliefs and expectations actually modifies the sensation called forth by the external physical stimulus. Exactly similar external stimuli, acting on a sense-organ of the same person on different occasions, will evoke in him perceptions of objects which actually *look* different or *sound* different or *feel* different, according to differences in his beliefs and expectations at the moment when the stimulus is received. On one such occasion, for example, he may see an object as looking solid, and on another, he may see it as looking flat, or one such occasion as looking convex, and on another as looking concave. This, then, is a second sense in which certain other factors in human experience may be 'permeated and moulded by thought.' They may actually be different in some of their phenomenological qualities from what they would have been if we had not been thinking beings at all, or had had a different set of beliefs and expectations activated at the time. If that happens even to the sensory factor in sense-perception, I feel little doubt that it happens to the affective factor in emotion also.

Hegel now passes to a different, but closely connected, point. He distinguishes between the *content* and the *form* of consciousness. He says that the same content may be present in connexion with many different forms of consciousness, either successively or simultaneously. By different *forms* of consciousness, he seems to mean (a) the different *generic attitudes* which a person may take up towards an object of which he is aware, for example, the cognitive, the conative, the emotional, etc.; and (b) the different *specific forms* of each of these generic attitudes, for example, sense-perception, imagination, discursive cognition, and so on. When Hegel says that the same content may be confronted with many different forms of consciousness, what he has in mind may perhaps be illustrated by the following example. Suppose that at a certain moment I think of James I as the first Scottish King of England, and as a king who was beheaded. Then the proposition that he was beheaded is as much a part of the relevant content of my consciousness as the proposition that he was the first Scottish King of England, though the former is false and the latter is true. On the other hand, the propositions that he wrote against tobacco and against witchcraft might be no part of the relevant content of my consciousness at the time, though they are in fact true. Now, this very same content may be confronted with many different forms of consciousness. I may merely entertain the supposition that he was beheaded, or I may believe it, or I may disbelieve it. Again, if I believe it, I may feel pity towards him on that account, and, if I disbelieve it, I may wish that it had been true. Lastly, any of these various attitudes may be accompanied by more or less imagery, and the imagery may be of the most varied kinds. And in some cases, though not in this particular one, there may also be sense-perception.

Now Hegel says that in ordinary language, the word 'idea' (i.e., the German word 'Vorstellung') means a 'generalised image'. For example, in the example in question one's idea of James, I might consist of vague visual images of a red-haired man with a crown and a sceptre mounting a scaffold. But, Hegel says, in the *proper* sense of 'idea', it means a clear and adequate conception of an object, i.e., a thought of it in terms of its characteristic qualities and relationships. The German word for this is 'Begriff' and it corresponds more or less to the English words 'concept' and 'notion'.

Merely to have images is not to think; though it may be that all thinking starts from picture-thinking, and perhaps it never gets wholly away from imagery of one kind or another. One may have an image of an object without any clear conception of it and conversely one may have a clear conception of an object without being able to call up any images relevant to it. For example, one might have a clear conception of energy, in the technical physical sense, and yet be unable to form any appropriate image of it.

Now Hegel holds that one of the first tasks of philosophy is to substitute clear and adequate *concepts* for more generalised images. He remarks, in this connexion, that people are very liable to think that there must be two utterly different *contents* of consciousness, when really there is one content and two very different *forms* of consciousness confronting it. He uses these considerations to explain the special difficulties that people are likely to find in philosophy. In the first place, they find it very difficult to think of abstract terms, of which they cannot make imitative images. They are always slipping back into concrete instances, which they can imagine. Thus, he says, the singular judgment: 'That leaf is green' presents no difficulty to anyone, though it in fact invokes the categories of existence, of substance, and of quality. But, without considerable practice, it is almost impossible to think of those categories, *as such*, because one cannot form images that imitate them, as the image of a green leaf would resemble an actual green leaf. Secondly, even if people do manage to think of these abstract terms, they tend to feel dissatisfied. For they feel that they *ought* to be able to associate them with familiar images. And, when they find that that is impossible, they feel that they have failed to think.

Hegel sums up his position, so far, by saying that philosophy will have to deal with popular modes of thought, and with the objects of popular religion. It will have to convince the intelligent plain man that there really is a need for knowledge in the philosophical sense and to awaken in him a desire for it. In dealing with religion, philosophy, he says, will have to show that it is 'capable of apprehending the objects of religion from its own resources.' And if and when it diverges from religious conceptions and beliefs, it will have to justify such divergences. I must confess that I do not clearly understand what Hegel means by saying that philosophy is 'capable of apprehending the objects of religion from *its own resources*.' If this means only that, once the data are supplied, theological thinking is of the same kind as philosophical thinking, and must answer to the same tests, I agree. But I do not think that this can be all that it means. If it means that philosophy must be able to reach the same conclusions as religious men accept, *without* any specifically religious data, I do not see that the claim is reasonable or likely to be true. Philosophy does not provide its own data. It takes them from elsewhere, sifts and criticises them, and then synthesises them. I should have thought that this is as obviously true with regard to religion as with regard to physics or anthropology.

So much for the *form* of thinking which is characteristic of philosophy. What about its characteristic *content*? Hegel says that its content is *Actuality* (in German '*Wirklichkeit*'). I take this to mean *what really exists*. We first become acquainted with what is actual through *experience*, of one kind or another, including under this both sense-perception and awareness of what goes on in one's own mind. But, even at the pre-philosophical level, we begin to draw a distinction between appearance and reality, shadow and substance, fiction and fact, transitory and permanent, and so on. And we confine the name 'actual' to the *second* members of such pairs of opposites. The business of

Philosophy is to draw that distinction still more accurately. And the doctrines of Philosophy must harmonise with the actual facts given in experience, after the inessential and the illusory factors in the data of experience have been cleared away.

Now a famous dictum of Hegel's, which he made explicitly in the preface to the *Philosophy of Law*, is that the *Actual* and the *Rational* coincide. This is a startling assertion, and we must now consider what he meant by it and how he defends it. He begins by drawing a distinction between the *existent* and the *actual*. Mistaken beliefs, delusive appearances, evil, and freaks of nature (such as babies with two heads or six fingers) certainly *exist*. But Hegel calls them 'degenerate, transitory, and fortuitous existents'. He says that he means by a 'fortuitous existent' one 'which has no greater value than if it had not in fact existed, but had been merely possible.' He refuses to call such existents 'actual'. So far, all this seems to me to be merely a combination of (a) a statement about how he intends to use certain terms, and (b) certain value judgments which would, no doubt, be widely accepted.

He proceeds to contrast his view, that the actual and the rational coincide, with two views opposed to it and to each other. The first is that what we call 'ideals', and what Kant calls 'Ideas' (with a capital 'I'), are mere chimeras, having no basis in reality, and that philosophy so far as it takes this seriously, is a mere system of moonshine. The second is that these ideals or Ideas, inhabit a kind of superior realm of their own, but are either too refined or too important to be realised in the actual world. Hegel's comment on these two views is summed up in the following words: 'The object of philosophy is the Idea: and the Idea is not so impotent as merely to have a *right* or an *obligation* to exist without actually existing.' He admits that at any given moment there are particular persons, customs, institutions, actions, and so on, which one is quite justified in condemning as not being what they should be. But he maintains that the subjects of such judgments do not belong to philosophy. These imperfect existents are transitory manifestations of something which is permanent, and which is *both* actual and ideal. It is this permanent substratum which is the proper subject of Philosophy. He adds that Reflexion, which is the characteristic mental activity of the philosopher, seeks to discover the *universal* in the particular, the *normal* in the variable, and the *necessary* in the contingent.

In order to appraise these statements of Hegel's we must, I think, begin by distinguishing the following three pairs of opposites: (1) the real and the merely apparent or delusive, (2) the type or ideal and the imperfect instance, and (3) the valuable and the worthless. Let us consider Hegel's doctrine in the light of these distinctions.

(1) A dream or waking hallucination does in some sense exist, but we should refuse to call the scenery or the actors in a dream 'actual' or 'real' things or persons. No doubt the particular interpretation which one will put on this distinction, within the existent, between 'the merely apparent' and 'the actual', will vary with one's particular theories about the nature of the external world and of our perception of it. But the distinction has to be drawn in *some* form by everyone. Now, if by 'rational' we mean 'subject to ascertainable laws and capable of being an object of scientific knowledge', it is quite plausible to say that the 'actual', in this sense, and the 'rational' coincide. Dreams, hallucinations, etc., are private and personal, and disconnected with each other even when they occur in the same person. It seems hardly conceivable that dream objects could be reduced to law, except perhaps indirectly through finding laws connecting the occurrence of such and such dreams with such and such events in the neutral world of brains and nervous systems. So far one can agree with Hegel.

Moreover, it is true that this division between the merely apparent and the actual or real corresponds in at least two respects to a division between the relatively worthless and the relatively valuable. (i) The real, in this sense, is of much greater intellectual interest, since it obeys ascertainable laws and is relatively stable and public. And (ii) it is of much greater *practical importance*, since we have to adjust ourselves to it if we are to carry out our intentions and avoid disaster.

(2) It is also undoubtedly true that science finds it necessary to pass at a very early stage from considering imperfect particular instances, with all their complications and irrelevancies, to considering ideal limiting cases. Thus, for example, theoretical physics finds it necessary to consider the properties of *frictionless fluids*, *perfect gases*, etc. Biologists find it necessary to consider *typical* men or dogs or lions, etc. And so on. But there are several comments to be made on this fact:

(i) The distinction between the ideal limit and the actual imperfect instances is quite different from the distinction between the actual or real and the merely apparent or delusive. Imperfect gases and deformed men are not merely apparent or delusive, as the pink rats of delirium are. The only point in which they resemble the latter is that it is very difficult to bring them under laws.

(ii) This concern with idealised types is not the ultimate end of science, and it has a fairly obvious methodological explanation. The crude undoctored phenomena of the world are so complicated that it would be impossible to deal with them scientifically unless the problem were at first lightened by judicious simplifications. But it is not the object of science to remain at the level of these idealised types. Its business is gradually to deal with more and more complicated phenomena, until it can approximate to explaining concrete particular things and events with all their oddities. I therefore do not admit that philosophy or science (and at present Hegel has not strongly distinguished them) can take the haughty line which he suggests towards 'degenerate, transitory, and fortuitous existences'.

(3) So far, then, I do not agree that the idealised types, with which science and philosophy are admittedly largely concerned, are any more real than their imperfect instances. I agree, of course, that they are also not just arbitrary fictions. They bear a definite relation to the imperfect instances, since they are constructed by idealisation from them, and are indispensable in order to give us scientific knowledge and control of them. In that sense, they are *as real* as their imperfect instances. But is there any *other* sense in which they can be called 'real' or 'actual'? And is there any sense in which they can be called '*more* real' than the imperfect instances?

(i) I am sure that Hegel sometimes uses 'real' as an expression of positive evaluation. Now, in an aesthetic sense, it is true that the world of scientific and philosophic ideal objects is more *beautiful* than the existent world. It has a neatness and tidiness, in comparison with which that world is an ugly muddle. Hence, if by 'more real' you mean 'more aesthetically satisfying to an intellectual observer', we may agree that the ideal is more real that the world of 'degenerate, transitory, and fortuitous existences'.

(ii) I feel pretty certain, however, that this is not all that Hegel had in mind. I think that he considered the various ideal types to be in some sense *actors* in the world, and constantly tending to organise more or less alien and refractory materials. This kind of view got its strongest support from the phenomena of crystal-growth, and the reproduction, self-adjustment, and self-repair of plants and animals. There you do seem to find natural objects automatically striving to reach certain ideal forms, and, though hampered by external accidents and the refractoriness of materials, succeeding more or less, for a time at least. In such cases, one does get the impression that the ideal types do not merely subsist in the world of universals, but are actual forces operating in the world of concrete existents. There they have to cope more or less successfully with accidental circumstances, with all the imperfections of alien material, which tends of itself to fall back into a state of relative disorganisation. I think that it is when ideal types are viewed in that light that Hegel is led to say that 'the Idea is not so impotent as merely to have a *right* or an *obligation* to exist without actually existing.' The sort of facts which I have been mentioning are genuine and important. But it would be safer, if less exciting, to express them by saying that there are in nature spontaneous tendencies to realise and to maintain those ideal types which form the subject matter of certain sciences and of certain branches of philosophy.

So far, Hegel has drawn no sharp distinction between Philosophy and the more general of the sciences. He now proceeds to discuss the relations between the two. He admits that, in a wide sense, any organised body of theoretical knowledge may be called 'philosophy' as, for example, in England, theoretical physics used to be called 'natural philosophy'.

In the first place, he says, science *cannot* be distinguished from philosophy by saying that the former does, and the latter does not, get its data from *experience*. In *every* kind of knowledge, the data must come from direct acquaintance, of one kind or another, with concrete facts. The main differences between Philosophy and empirical science, according to Hegel, are the following:

(1) Science excludes from its province certain *infinite* objects, for example, Spirit, Freedom, God. These are not excluded because our knowledge of them is independent of experience, for it certainly is not so. They are excluded because they are *infinite* objects, and empirical science deals only with finite ones. I do not think that Hegel makes this point at all

clear. 'Infinite' for him generally means *intrinsically unique*, i.e., such that, from the nature of the case, there could not be more than one of the kind. In that sense, I suppose, God or the Universe would be infinite, though I am not clear whether Freedom would be so. I think it is true that the empirical sciences are concerned with *classes* or *species* of things, with events that may occur in *various places* and recur at *various times*, and so on. All such objects would be *finite* in Hegel's sense.

(2) The second point of difference is this. Empirical science has two defects, from the point of view of an ideal system of knowledge. (i) The connexions between the species or kinds in science and the particulars that fall into them are loose and vague. I suspect that Hegel has two things in mind here. (a) The same thing may often with equal propriety be classed in several different ways, for example, as a metal and as a chemical element. (b) From the nature of a natural kind you cannot infer what species will fall under it. You cannot see any necessity, for example, that there should be such animals as cats and dogs, or any impossibility in there being such animals as centaurs. This may be contrasted with certain cases in geometry, for example. From the definition of the generic term 'regular solid' and the axioms of Euclid you can infer that there must be a certain five, and that there can be *only* those five, species of regular solid, viz., the regular tetrahedron, the cube, the regular octahedron, the regular dodecahedron, and the regular icosahedron. (ii) In a scientific theory, the fundamental data are either mere brute facts or mere postulates. Thus, the fundamental defect of empirical sciences *is lack of necessity*. When we try to get *necessary* truth about the really existent, we pass from science to philosophy. There is indeed genuine reflective thought in every advanced science, just as there is in philosophy. But philosophical thought has certain categories of its own, in addition to those of merely scientific thought. (These are the categories which Hegel claims to deal with in the third division of the *Logic*, viz., the categories of the Notion.) Philosophy takes over and transforms all the general results of the sciences, and in doing so, brings them under its own special categories.

Hegel realises that Philosophy, as he understands it, makes very large pretensions. For it claims to discover truths which are *necessary* about objects which are *infinite*, in his special sense of that word. But, he says, these claims can neither be substantiated nor refuted by any *preliminary* investigation. They must be judged at the end of the undertaking, and not before it is begun. This, of course, brings Hegel into head-on conflict with Locke, Kant, and all those philosophers who have held that, before starting on ontology, one should make a preliminary epistemological enquiry into the nature and limitations of the human intellect. Hegel therefore deals explicitly with this contention.

He says that it is very plausible, when put in the form that the human intellect is an *instrument*, like a telescope or microscope, and that it is only reasonable to investigate whether it is fit to perform a certain kind of work before you start to use it for that purpose. He points out, quite fairly, that the analogy is faulty. When you test a physical instrument, you examine it by means of some other physical instrument, which you take as your standard. But when you examine your mind to see whether it is fit to do certain things, your mind is at once the object to be tested, the standard by which the test is made, and the agent who applies the test. To insist on testing the range and powers of the intellect before beginning to use it is, Hegel says, like refusing to go into the water until one can swim.

I agree in the main with Hegel's conclusion, and with his contention that the metaphor of testing an instrument is on the whole misleading. But I think that there are defects in his own statements. (1) After all, what Locke and Kant proposed to test was not the capacity of the intellect to reach truth of *any* kind, but its capacity to reach truth on *certain subjects*, viz., the traditional problems of metaphysics and speculative theology. Now there is no contradiction in supposing that the mind might be perfectly competent to investigate its capacities in that *particular field*, and yet incompetent to come to any reasonable conclusions about the *subjects that fall within that field*, for example, God, Freedom, and Immortality. (2) Hegel's own metaphor, about not going into the water until one had learnt to swim, is itself defective, and is unfair to Locke and to Kant. They might have answered that the appropriate metaphor is that you should not go into the deep end of the bath till you have tried in the shallow end whether you can swim or not. And that does not sound unreasonable.

Nevertheless, I think that Hegel is essentially right here, and that the point can be made without using metaphors and counter-metaphors. The real objections to the epistemologists are these. (i) There is no antecedent likelihood that the mind is any better fitted to investigate its own powers than to investigate the traditional problems of metaphysics. Kant's practical ground for suspending metaphysicians from their occupation, until the capacity of the mind for investigating such subjects should have been tested, was that, after so many centuries and so much devoted work by so many eminent men, no kind of agreement had been reached on the problems of metaphysics. But we can now add that, after an almost equal amount of work by equally eminent men, no kind of agreement has been reached on the problems of epistemology. The practical moral would seem to be either to suspend *both* parties alike from their several occupations, or to let *both* continue to exercise themselves in them.

(ii) There is, I think, a real inconsistency in claiming that epistemology should be preliminary to ontology. Certainly, there is no objection to the mind investigating itself from a purely *psychological* point of view, i.e., trying to determine as accurately as possible what kinds of process are in fact going on, when a person professes to be thinking about certain subjects, for example, about God or about Freedom. But if we are to enquire whether these processes are likely to supply *certain or probable knowledge* on these topics, something else, and something quite different, is needed. We shall have to *presuppose* a great deal of knowledge about the nature and structure of the non-human world, of man, and of the relationships of the latter to the former. Both Locke and Kant quite reasonably do this. But there are among those *ontological* questions, about which the metaphysician was to be forbidden to pronounce any opinion until the epistemologist should have completed his task.

I pass, finally, to Hegel's positive account of the origin and course of development of Philosophy. A philosophically inclined person is one who has a natural craving for a clear, consistent, and comprehensive view of the universe as a whole. But, in the course of trying to think out such a view, one inevitably begins by getting into difficulties and contradictions. The reason for this is that we begin by drawing sharp distinctions, and then treating each term which has been distinguished as internally self-sufficient and as independent and exclusive of other terms which are opposite to it. According to Hegel, that is an *indispensable stage*. It is of vital importance to draw distinctions and to get terms clearly defined. That part of the work of the mind he ascribes to a department of it which he calls *Understanding*.

The defect of Understanding is that, under its influence, we tend to assume that because these terms which we have distinguished and defined are *distinct*, and are in many cases *opposed* in various ways to each other; therefore, they are *independent and mutually exclusive*. The fact that this is a mistake is shown by the contradictions in which one lands when one has reached the level of Understanding and not passed beyond it. The main lesson of *Logic*, Hegel says, is to bring out these contradictions in detail and to show why they arise.

Now at that stage, two possibilities are open. We may simply give up the game, and say that the intellect has shown that the intellect is faulty. In that case, we may either remain contented sceptics, like Hume, or we may deliberately decide to swallow the things that satisfied us in our nurseries and that satisfy plain men in their daily occupations. Extremely few people can remain contented sceptics, and a great many find it neither comfortable nor respectable to give up thinking or to confine it within the bounds set out by ordinary common sense or by traditional religion. For such people, according to Hegel, there is a second alternative. The defects of thought, as mere *Understanding*, can be overcome by thought as *Reason*. The philosopher who passes to the level of *Reason*, in this technical sense, recognises the source of the contradictions into which one falls at the level of mere Understanding, and is able to provide positive solutions. In its purely destructive aspect, Hegel calls it *Negative Reason* and in its constructive aspect *Positive Reason*.

The essence of the solution is always the same. It is to recognise that the terms, which the Understanding has distinguished and defined and has seen to be opposed to each other, are neither self-sufficient nor radically incompatible. They are complementary aspects of more complex and concrete terms, in which they are so combined as not to conflict with each other. The discovery by Positive Reason of the reconciling synthesis at each stage is what Hegel calls 'negating the negation' or 'the return of the original term into itself.' Of course, he does not regard 'Understanding', 'Negative Reason', and 'Positive Reason' as three mutually independent intellectual faculties. They are simply an ascending hierarchy of activities of the faculty of rational thinking. *Understanding* is the characteristic activity of the intellect in ordinary science, critical historiography, and so on. *Negative Reason* is the characteristic activity of the sceptical philosopher, such as Hume or Descartes in his purely negative phases. *Positive Reason* is the characteristic activity of constructive metaphysicians, on Hegel's view.

Now the only conclusive evidence that this can be done is that someone should do it in detail, and that others, who have time, capacity, and interest to study his work, should find it on the whole illuminating and cogent. The very least that can be said of Hegel is that he was not content to formulate and recommend a programme. He did follow his own prescription in the most elaborate detail in his *Logic*, and he did apply his principles, in various special works, to the data of natural science, of history, of law, and so on.

Unfortunately, Hegel's *Logic*, which is the kernel of his philosophy, and by which the rest must stand or fall, is one of the most obscure and difficult works which any obviously sane and intelligent European has written. It is in many places almost impossible to follow, and therefore to appraise fairly. Valuable commentaries have been written upon it, but even with their help, much remains conjectural or quite unintelligible.

I will conclude with two remarks, one on the bad, and the other on the good, aspects of Hegelianism:

(1) I think that Hegel had, in one respect at least, a most unfortunate influence on many of his followers. Instead of trying to define their terms, and to clear up ambiguities, so as to avoid contractions, they tended, under his influence, to welcome the most superficial appearance of contradiction. They said: 'That is just what you would expect in a finite category', and left the matter at that. I do not think that Hegel himself is open to the accusation of solving all difficulties with a single vague formula. On the contrary, he works through the various categories up to the Absolute Idea very gradually and with immense detail and elaboration. One may not accept his general method of argument, or follow many of his particular steps, but at any rate, one cannot fairly say of him, as one might of many of his followers, that he is content to provide a single cheap and easy solution of all the contradictions that he professes to find.

(2) On the other hand, it must be said that Hegel himself, and the best of his English and American admirers, such as Bosanquet and Bradley and Royce, were men of immensely wide and deep general culture. When they speak of history or art or politics or religion, one feels the presence of a most impressive background of personal experience and assimilated knowledge. Now, I think that those qualities are most decidedly lacking in most of the philosophies which have succeeded Hegelianism in England and the United States. They give the impression of being clear, but flat and rather shallow, discussions of very limited topics, by specialists with very limited general culture and personal experience. Of course, as long as they confine themselves to those special topics, no great harm is done, except that they are excluding from their purview most of what makes philosophy of interest to anyone but a few technical experts. But, when they venture to express opinions about more concrete matters such as history or politics or religion, the barrenness of the land becomes terribly obvious.

2.2

HUME'S THEORY OF BELIEF

Hume's theory of belief is to be found in the following places in his works, viz., *Treatise*, Vol. I, Part III, §§ VII–X, both inclusive, the *Appendix*, and *Enquiry*, Sect. V, Part II. What Hume is concerned with here is the difference between actually *believing* and merely *imagining* the existence of some thing or state of affairs or the occurrence of some event, which one is not at the moment actually perceiving or experiencing or remembering.

He says that the case of believing (or rather *knowing*) a *necessary* truth, whether by direct inspection or as a result of a demonstrative argument from intuitively certain premisses, is quite different. In that case one cannot clearly conceive any alternative, for any alternative would involve a contradiction. But in regard to matters of fact, one can, and often does, conceive with equal clearness a number of mutually exclusive alternatives. Those which one disbelieves are as readily conceivable as that (if any) which one believes. The question comes, therefore, to this: What is the difference between actually believing a proposition, which is one of a number of equally conceivable mutually exclusive alternatives, and merely contemplating or imagining it?

There is one comment which I will make at this point, though I do not intend to develop it here. It seems to me quite clear that, even in the case of *necessary* truths, one can in some sense contemplate what I might call the 'impossible alternatives' to them. In any proof by *reductio ad absurdum* in pure mathematics one is contemplating what turns out to be an impossible alternative, drawing determinate consequences from it, and by means of the obvious absurdity of these consequences demonstrating that the alternative in question is impossible. So I am not prepared to accept the sharp distinction which Hume draws between belief in necessary truths and belief in matters of fact. Having made this protest, however, I will confine my attention, as Hume does, to contingent propositions.

I do not think it is possible to give a coherent account of Hume's theory without drawing certain distinctions which he did not explicitly draw. I think it is fairly plain that he had at the back of his mind, especially in the later parts of the *Treatise*, ideas corresponding to the different notions which I am about to distinguish. But I doubt whether the explicit epistemological principles, which he laid down at the beginning and never explicitly modified, leave room for these distinctions.

Suppose that at a certain moment a person is thinking of the proposition which would be correctly expressed by the English sentence: 'There is a biscuit in that box'. I am assuming that the box is opaque and is shut, so that he cannot at the time see or feel or smell its contents, if any. I am also assuming that he is not remembering that there was a biscuit in it when he last saw it open, and just taking for granted that the biscuit is still there. Now, the person in question may very well have before his mind a *visual image*, which is more or less like the visual sensum which he would sense if the box were open and he were looking into it and seeing a biscuit there. It is by no means *necessary* that he should have such a visual image before his mind in order to think of the proposition in question. But perhaps he must have *some* kind of imagery, visual or non-visual, imitative or symbolic, in order to think of the proposition. Conversely, he might have such a visual image before his mind, but it might not be an element in an experience of thinking of the proposition that there is a biscuit in the box. The image might just float before his mind without his thinking of *any* proposition to which it is even remotely relevant. Or, again, it might be an element, for example, in a thought of some proposition about the town of Reading, which is famous in England as a centre of biscuit manufacture.

We must, therefore, distinguish, in connexion with any thought, the following two items, viz., (i) its *presentational* content and (ii) its *propositional* content. The presentational content is any image or sense-datum, visual or auditory, or of some other kind, verbal or non-verbal, imitative or symbolic, that may be before the subject's mind at the time, as a psychological factor enabling him then to think of a certain proposition. The propositional content is the proposition or set of propositions which he is thinking of at the time by means of the presentational content.

Now the propositional content will generally involve a description of some possible thing or person or event or state of affairs. The proposition may merely be to the effect that there is something answering to a certain description, for example, a biscuit in that box. Or it may go further, and assign various qualities and relations to that something. It may, for example, be to the effect that there is a biscuit in that box and that it is square and sweet. We will call the possible existent, which the propositional content describes, and perhaps further specifies, the *referent* of the thought. It is important to notice that the referent of thought is *always* different from its presentational content. The presentational content of a thought, if it is to be the referent of a thought at all, can be the referent only of *another* thought, with its own representational content and propositional content. It might, for example, be the referent of a later thought in the same person, when he was introspecting reminiscently. Or it might be the referent of thought in another person, for example, a psychologist or an epistemologist.

In terms of these distinctions, we can state Hume's question as follows. To *believe* a proposition p evidently involves having a thought whose propositional content is p. Equally plainly it involves something *more*, since one can think of p without believing it. The question is: What is this something more?

Hume considers and rejects the suggestion that the difference consists in *some additional item* in either the propositional or the presentational content. This is quite obvious as regards the propositional content. You are thinking of precisely the same proposition whether you believe that there is a biscuit in the box or merely contemplate the possibility of there being a biscuit in it without believing that there is.

His argument against there being some additional item in the presentational content in the case of belief, as opposed to mere imagination, is twofold. In the first place, if you inspect carefully, you do not seem to find it. There seems to be no special bit of imagery, added to the rest, when you *believe* that there is a biscuit in the box. Secondly, belief or non-belief cannot be created or annihilated by one's volitions at the time. In that respect, belief may be compared to an emotion, such as anger or fear, which arises automatically, in accordance with one's innate or acquired dispositions, when and only when certain occurrent psychological or physiological conditions are fulfilled. Now within wide limits one can call up and banish images at will and can adjoin them to or separate them from other images, So, if the suggestion under discussion were true, one would expect to be able, within wide limits, to believe or not to believe at will any proposition which one can think of. This is notoriously not the case.

The next alternative which might be suggested is this. The difference might consist, not in the presence or absence of any particular *item* in the presentational content, but in a characteristic difference in the *degree* of some quality which belongs to the presentation *as a whole*. I think that Hume toyed with this view, and often talks as if he held it, but later gave it up as unsatisfactory. In Part III, Section VII[1] of the *Treatise* he says that the only possible difference is in what he there calls 'degree of force and vivacity'. Now, this might mean the kind of qualitative difference which there is, for example, between any visual or auditory *sense-datum*, on the one hand, and any visual or auditory *image* (no matter how much like it), on the other. But in the last line of the *Appendix*, he remarks that it would be much nearer the truth to say that 'two ideas of the same object can only be different by their different *feeling*'.

In the discussion at the beginning of the *Appendix*, he describes the difference as 'nothing but a peculiar feeling', and he raises the question whether it is or is not 'analogous to any other sentiment of the human mind'. He asks 'whether this feeling be anything but a firmer conception or a faster hold that we take of the object'. In the Enquiry Concerning Human Understanding (Sect V, Part II) he says that this sentiment is perhaps indefinable, like sensible coldness or angry feeling, but everyone is familiar with it in his own experience. Nevertheless, various descriptions of it are useful. One which he gives is this: 'Belief is nothing but a more vivid, lively, forcible, firm, steady, conception of an object than what the imagination is ever able to attain'. Lastly, in Part III, Sect. VII of the *Treatise* he says that all these various terms are 'intended only to express that act of the mind which renders realities more present to us than fictions, causes them to weigh more in the thought, and gives them a superior influence on the passions and the imagination'. It will be noted that nearly all these descriptions are in fact metaphors from seeing and from handling things.

It seems to me fairly clear that Hume's final view was somewhat as follows. The difference between merely *thinking of* an object as existing and having certain properties, and *believing* that such an object exists and has such properties, is simply this. In the latter case, the thought of this possible object and its alleged properties calls forth an emotion of a certain characteristic kind, which tinges it, and which is absent in the former case. The quality of this emotion is unique, and it is therefore indefinable, though familiar to all of us. But, when the thought of a possible object is tinged with that kind of emotion, it can be described by such metaphorical expressions as 'vivid', 'lively', 'forcible', and 'steady'. It can also be described by reference to some of the characteristic *effects* which it has or tends to have. Thoughts which have this peculiar kind of emotional tone are treated by the thinker more seriously than those which lack it, have more influence over his emotions and actions, and so on. They can also be kept more steadily at the focus of attention for considerable periods on end. Let us for the future call this supposed emotion 'the emotion of credence'.

We come now to the analogy, which Hume thought there was, between this emotion of credence, which tinges certain thoughts and makes them into beliefs, and certain other psychological facts. Hume holds that this emotion is present in its strongest form in *sense-perception* and in *memory*. Here, again, I shall have to state the case, as I understand it, in terms of the distinction which I have drawn.

In ostensible sense-perception one is sensing a sense-datum of a characteristic kind, and one cannot help believing with complete conviction that one is in presence of a certain physical thing or event, for example, a chair or flash of lightning. In the case of visual or tactual perception, the plain man does not as a rule distinguish between the visual or tactual sense-datum which he is sensing and a certain part of the surface of the body which he takes himself to be seeing or touching. But he does regard that body as something more than that small part of its surface. He regards it as a three-dimensional object, with many parts, qualities, and causal properties which are not at the moment being presented to his senses. Thus, even here, we can distinguish two factors, corresponding respectively to the presentational content and to the propositional content of the thought of a possible thing or state of affairs or event which is *not* present to the senses.

The *sense-datum* in the perception corresponds to the imagery which is the *presentational* content of the thought. The propositions, which the percipient instinctively and automatically takes for granted, as to his being in presence of a body of such and such a kind, correspond to the *propositional* content of the thought. Of course, the connexion between the presentational and the propositional content of a perception is quite unique. It is far more intimate than the connexion between those two factors in a *thought*. For the percipient takes the sense-datum, which is the presentational content of his visual or tactual perception, to be part of the surface of the body which is the ostensible object of his perception, and what he instinctively takes for granted about that body is intimately correlated in detail with the details of the sense-datum. Moreover, the propositions which the percipient instinctively takes for granted, on the occasion of sensing such and such a sense-datum, are not explicitly formulated. It would be more correct to say that he automatically adjusts his body as it would be appropriate for him to do *if* he had formulated and were believing certain propositions about the foreign body.

Allowing for these very important differences, we can say that the emotion of credence is at its maximum possible strength when a person is having an actual visual or tactual sensation and thereupon instinctively takes himself to be in presence of a thing or event of a certain kind. According to Hume, it is the same kind of emotion, in a much weaker degree, which tinges the thought of a certain possible object, when the presentational content is only *imagery*, and when the thinker *believes* that object to exist or to have existed or to be about to exist, though he is not actually perceiving it or remembering it. And it is the presence of this emotion, tingeing his thought, which makes the thought a *belief*.

Ostensibly *recollecting* a past event, or a thing as it was in the past, is intermediate in this respect between actually perceiving a thing or event, on the one hand, and believing (without perceiving it or ostensibly recollecting it) that such and such an object now exists or has existed or will exist. It resembles the latter, in that the presentational content is an image and not a sense-datum, and that one has no tendency to identify the image (which is obviously *present*) with the ostensibly recollected object (which is presented as *past*). It resembles the former, in that the emotion of credence in ostensible recollection approaches in strength to that which it has in sense-perception.

It is worth noting that this part of Hume's theory cannot even be intelligibly stated without drawing the distinction between presentational and propositional content, and without realising that the referent of belief is *not* the presentational content, but is the object which is described and further specified by the propositional content. The existence of the presentational content is completely certain in all cases, whether that content be the *sense-datum* which is sensed when one is ostensibly perceiving a certain object or the *image* which is before one's mind in the other kinds of cognitive experience which we have been considering. And the existence of the image is equally certain, whether it functions as the presentational content in an ostensible *recollection*, or in a *belief* in the present or past existence of such and such an object, which one is *not* ostensibly perceiving or recollecting, or in the *mere imagination* of such an object, without belief or with positive disbelief in its existence. That which is believed with complete uncritical conviction in sense-perception, and which may very well be untrue in particular cases, is the proposition that such and such a *body* now exists or that such and such a *physical event* is now happening, and that that body or event is present to one's senses. Similarly, in mere thinking, what is thought of, either with belief or with disbelief or without either, is the proposition that such and such a body has existed or is existing or will exist, or that such and such a physical event has happened or is happening or will happen, outside the range of one's present sense-perception or recollection.

That Hume was quite well aware of all this comes out clearly in an incidental remark which he makes in the last paragraph but two of Sect. VIII of Part III of *Treatise*, Vol. I. He there distinguishes between an image 'considered as the representation of an absent object' and considered as 'a real perception of the mind, of which we are intimately conscious'. When an image functions in the former way, i.e., as part of the presentational content of the thought of an absent object, there is no question about belief in *its* existence. It is the *absent object*, which is believed or disbelieved or merely imagined to exist. But when a person considers one of his own images introspectively, simply as an occurrent in his own stream of consciousness, he has the same complete conviction of its present existence as he would have of the present existence of one of his sense-data, if he were to consider it from the same point of view.

It must be admitted that Hume has never given or attempted seriously to give any account of what is involved in thinking of a proposition. He talks here of an image as 'the representative of an absent object', and in sense-perception he would no doubt say that the impression or sense-datum is in some sense the 'representative' of a present object. But he makes no serious attempt to deal with this representative function. As regards images, he contents himself with the completely irrelevant principle that every image is a causal descendant of a sense-datum which was sensed earlier in the same person's mental history and which in fact resembled it in quality. As regards sense-data, he simply hands the question over to anatomists and physiologists. This, again, is wholly irrelevant.

It should be noted that Hume gives no account of the *temporal* differences in various propositions concerning things and events not present to the senses or to the memory. Yet these are of vital importance. Sometimes a lively and forcible thought of a possible thing or event is a belief that it *has* existed or happened, sometimes that it is *now* existing or happening, and sometimes that it has not yet done so but *will* do so. Then, again, he gives no account of the fact that some such thoughts are beliefs in *singular* propositions, for example, that the cat is in the next room now, and that others are beliefs in *particular* propositions, for example, that dodos used to exist but that there are none now. There seem to be essential differences in the propositional content in such cases. Are there any characteristic differences in the *details of the* presentational content, or in its *quality as a whole*, or in the *nature or strength of the emotion*, which tinges the thought of the object described in the propositional content? Hume considers none of these questions.

We can now pass on to consider Hume's theory of the *causes* which may invest a thought with special force and liveliness, and thus convert it into a belief. As regards one's instinctive taking for granted, when one has a visual or tactual sensation, that one is in presence of a body or a physical event of a certain kind, Hume has nothing further to say. Some psychological facts must be taken as ultimate, and he might fairly regard this as one of them.

As regards beliefs about things and events not present to the senses or the memory, his theory is as follows. The following general principle can, he thinks, be established empirically. Suppose that an association has been set up in a person's mind between the idea of X and the idea of Y. Then, if he should either think of or actually perceive an instance of X, the thought of Y will tend to arise in his mind. If the occasion which excites the association should be merely a renewed *thought* of an X, the thought of Y which is called up will not be specially forcible and lively, and will not amount to a *belief* in the existence of a Y. But suppose that the occasion which excites the association is an actual *perception* of an X. Then the force and liveliness of that perception induces a corresponding, though inferior, force and liveliness in the thought of Y which it evokes. And so that thought tends to be a *belief* in the existence of Y. I suppose that the same kind of result might be expected, though to a lesser degree, if the evoking occasion were an experience of *believing* in the existence of an X without actually perceiving one. Hume, however, confines himself to the case where an X is actually perceived, i.e., where the presentational content of the evoking experience is a sense-datum and not a mere image. In

Part III, Sect. VII of the *Treatise* he says: 'An opinion... or belief may be most accurately defined as *a lively idea related to or associated with a present impression*'.

It seems to me that this general principle, like most general principles in psychology, at best expresses a *tendency*, which is quite often inhibited or reversed by other tendencies. When a perception or a belief is toned with certain kinds of strong emotion (other than the alleged emotion of credence), for example, jealousy or fear, it often does convert into beliefs certain associated ideas which it arouses. But I doubt whether perception or belief not toned with one or other of these strong emotions has much tendency to do this. And, even when it is toned with strong emotion, such as jealousy, it does not convert into beliefs *all* the associated ideas which it arouses. It does this only or mainly to such ideas as might seem to *justify* the emotion if they were true, for example, thoughts of acts of unfaithfulness on the part of the person towards whom one feels jealousy.

We come now to Hume's application of his general principles to the particular case of *causal* beliefs. It may be put as follows. The belief that a particular X-like event, now being perceived by a person, will be immediately followed by a Y-like event, does not arise in him unless he has observed a *considerable number* of X-like events and has observed *each of them to be immediately followed by a Y-like event*. Now, this is precisely the condition under which the idea of an X-like event occurring will become associated with the idea of a Y-like event immediately following. Suppose, then, that this association of ideas has been formed in this way in a person's mind. If, now, a *mere thought* of an X-like event occurring should be brought to his mind, a *mere thought* of a Y-like event immediately following will be aroused in him by association. But in that case, it will remain a mere thought, and will not amount to a *belief*. Suppose, however, that he actually *perceives* an X-like event happening. The associative trace will be stirred as before, and a thought of a Y-like event immediately following will be aroused. But now that thought will have derived a special degree of force and liveliness from the force and liveliness of the actual perception of X which evoked it. So it will be a *belief*, i.e., an *expectation* that a Y-like event will immediately follow.

This is the essence of Hume's psychological theory on this topic. But he makes two additional points, which it is important to note if the theory is to be judged fairly.

(1) In order that this psychological machinery may work, it is not in the least necessary that the person, on perceiving X, should *call to mind* the fact that he has often observed an X-like event and that in each case he has observed

it to be immediately followed by a Y-like event. Still, less is it necessary that he should recollect all or any of these past occasions. The mere *de facto* repetition of such sequences in his past experience suffices to establish the persistent associative trace. And, once this has been established, the mere occurrence in him of a thought or a perception of an X-like event suffices to excite it and to call up the idea of a Y-like event following immediately.

Hume makes this fact a further argument against the suggestion that a person's causal beliefs are reached by any process of *inference* from facts of observational regularity in his past experience. For, where the person straightway expects Y on perceiving X, without calling to mind the corresponding observational regularity in his past experience, he plainly cannot be using the fact of that regularity as a premiss from which he infers his expectation. Hume makes this point in Part III, Sect. VIII, of the *Treatise*, Vol. I.

(2) Hume admits that there are cases where a person comes to believe that X causes Y, although he has *not* often observed instances of X-like events and found each to be immediately followed by a Y-like event. He admits that such a belief may arise 'merely by one experiment, provided it be made with judgment and after a careful removal of all foreign and superfluous circumstances'. (*Treatise*, Vol. I, Part III, Sect. VIII) He says that this can be explained consistently with his general principles in the following way. Although the person in question has not observed previous instances of X-like events followed by Y-like events, he has at the back of his mind traces of a vast number of other observational regularities. These together have produced in him the expectation that like events, in conditions which are alike in all relevant respects, will be followed by like immediate sequents. The production of this *general* expectation has taken place in accordance with the psychological machinery which Hume has described. The *particular* expectation that X will be followed by Y, which may arise as the result of a single carefully designed experiment, is simply an application of this general expectation to a particular case which seems to fall under it.

I have now stated and explained Hume's theory of the generation of causal beliefs, as I understand it, and I will proceed to make some comments on it:

(1) It is important to distinguish between (i) having a sequence of experiences and (ii) having an experience of a sequence. Presumably, the latter

could not occur without the former, but it is quite clear that the former could occur without the latter.

It is easy to imagine a simple kind of creature, for example, an oyster, in which various sensations *in fact* follow from each other, and in which *in fact* a sensation of a certain kind has always been immediately followed by one of a certain other kind. And yet such a creature might never perceive one event *as following on another*, and therefore have no *idea of a sequence* as distinct from having a mere *sequence of ideas*. Suppose that in such a creature X-like sensations occur fairly often and that on every occasion an X-like sensation has been immediately followed by a Y-like sensation. Suppose further that this has given rise to an association in its mind. If the creature now has an X-like sensation, the utmost that can happen through the association being stimulated is that this sensation will be immediately followed by a Y-like image. But merely to have a Y-like image immediately after having an X-like sensation is *not* the same as to have an idea of Y-as-immediately-following-X. Such a creature could have no such *idea*, on Hume's principles, for it has never had such an *impression*. It has had many X-like sensations, and immediately afterwards on each occasion a Y-like sensation, but it has never had an experience which could properly be described as 'perceiving X-as-followed-immediately-by-Y'.

So the first thing to be clear about is this. It is not enough for Hume's purpose that, when the association is aroused by perceiving an X, the idea of a Y should immediately afterwards arise. What is needed is that there should arise the idea of *Y-as-immediate-sequent*. And this requires, according to Hume's general principles, that the original experiences which gave rise to the association should have been, not mere repeated *sequences of perceptions*, but repeated *perceptions of sequence*.

(2) In all matters where temporal conditions are involved there are at least three different questions to be considered. They are (i) temporal *order*, i.e., which event comes before and which after; (ii) temporal *distance*, i.e., whether the events were immediately successive or were separated by a greater or less temporal gap; and (iii) temporal *position*, i.e., whether the sequence is located wholly in the past, or wholly in the future, or with the earlier event present and the later one future.

Now Hume's theory explicitly mentions the two features of temporal order and temporal distance. The X-like sensation is supposed on each occasion to have been followed, and to have been followed *immediately* by a Y-like sensation, and the idea that arises is that of a Y-like event as immediately following an X-like event. But it seems to me that the question of temporal location needs much more explicit consideration than Hume gives to it. He seems to take for granted that the lively idea of a Y-like event as immediately following an X-like event (which, according to the theory, arises whenever an X-like event is perceived after the relevant association has been formed) always takes the form of an *expectation* that the present X-like event will be followed in the *immediate future* by a Y-like event. But why should the belief always, or indeed ever, take that form? Why should it not take, instead, the form of believing that X-like events always have been followed immediately by Y-like events in the *past*, without any reference to the immediate or the remoter future? It seems to me that the fact that the belief takes the form of an *expectation* as to the immediate future must either be accepted as an additional ultimate psychological fact or be given some special explanation. Perhaps the following addition to Hume's theory might be suggested in this connexion.

It seems conceivable that there might be intelligent creatures, who can perceive sequences as such and form the idea of a sequence, but have only the powers of perception and retrospection and no trace of expectation. But neither men nor any known animals are like this. So, as a matter of fact, X-like events have often been perceived when the percipient was in a state of *prospective attention* as to what would come next, and the Y-like events which immediately followed them were then taken as the answer to the unspoken question: 'What next?' Suppose that this person is again in this state of prospective attention at the time when he perceives an X-like event and when it arouses by association the idea of a Y-like event as an immediate sequent. Then his belief will take the form of *expecting* a Y-like event to follow at once. But suppose, instead, that he is in a reminiscent state at the time. Then his lively idea of X-as-immediately-followed-by-Y may take, instead, the form of a memory belief that X-like events *have* always been immediately followed by Y-like events *in his experience*. Or it might take the more general form of a belief that X-like events *always have been* followed immediately by Y-like events in the past history of the world.

(3) Hume treated causation and our beliefs in causal propositions before he treated the external world and our ostensible perceptions of bodies and

of physical events. He neither refers forward in the former to the latter nor does he reconsider in the latter what he has said in the former. But the two notions of causation, on the one hand, and substance (material or mental), on the other, are in fact inextricably bound up with each other.

In the first place, we do not ascribe causal action to our sense impressions, as such, but to the *bodies* and the *physical events* which we take ourselves to be perceiving by means of our sensations.

Suppose, for example, that I see a moving stone approaching a window and coming in contact with it, and then see and hear the splintering of the glass which immediately follows. I have no tendency to believe that the *visual sensations*, which I have when I see the stone moving up to the window, cause the *visual and auditory sensations* which I have when I see and hear the glass splintering and the fragments falling. What I believe is that the *physical process* in the stone, which I perceive by means of the former sensations, causes the *physical changes* in the glass, which I perceive by means of the latter sensations.

Secondly, our notion of a substance is very largely the notion of something with persistent *powers* or *causal properties* of characteristic kinds, which are sometimes in action and often in abeyance. Its actual history is thought of as the particular way in which its powers have manifested themselves in the particular circumstances in which it has been placed. This is as true of a mind, considered as a substance, as it is of bodies.

It is, therefore, hopeless to offer an analysis of causal propositions, or an analysis of physical-process and material-substance propositions, or an analysis of mental-substance propositions, in isolation from each other. Since one cannot do everything at once, and still more obviously cannot state everything at once in speech or writing, one will have to treat these topics successively. But there ought to be constant references forwards and backwards, and an attempt at a final synthesis. Hume made gallant attempts at each of these several tasks, but it seems to me that he kept them too much in water-tight compartments. It was a great merit of Kant, whether or not one agrees with his attempted solutions of these problems, to see that they are all inter-connected aspects of a single complex problem.

(4) Hume may be said to have had this point in mind in Part III, Sect. IX, of Vol. I of the *Treatise*, where he refers to what he calls the two interconnected

'systems' of realities, which we all come to recognise. One of these 'systems' consists of all that a person is *perceiving* at any moment, and all that he is then *remembering* to have experienced or to have perceived. All these items are thought of with special force and liveliness, and are therefore believed to exist now or to have existed, as the case may be. The other 'system' consists in part of all the bodies and the physical events which a person is neither perceiving nor remembering at a given moment, but which he believes to exist or to have existed. It includes also certain experiences, which he is not recollecting and perhaps cannot recollect, but which he believes himself to have had. And it also includes experiences which he believes that other people are having or have had.

Now, according to Hume, all a person's beliefs in the existence of the various items in the second system are generated by his causal beliefs, together with his perceptions and memories of the items in the first system. This applies, not only to beliefs reached by an explicit process of inference, in which beliefs in casual laws are used as premisses. It applies equally to everything that is accepted on the basis of spoken or written testimony. The words heard or read are items in the first system. The beliefs which arise automatically on hearing or reading sentences in a familiar language are beliefs in things or events or states of affairs in the second system. The *thoughts* of these objects arise from the *perceptions* of the words or signs through association, and they acquire the force and liveliness which makes them into *beliefs*, in accordance with the general principles laid down by Hume.

The first system is thus, in one sense, epistemologically prior to the second. But in the end, the second becomes at least as important epistemologically. We come to test particular ostensible sense perceptions and memories by noting whether the items ostensibly perceived or remembered do or do not fit into the second system. If they do not, we tend to dismiss the experiences as delusions or hallucinations.

In conclusion, I would make the following remarks. The central and most characteristic part of Hume's theory of belief is this. To believe in the present existence of a certain thing or state of affairs, which one is neither perceiving nor remembering at the time, is to have an image resembling what one would sense if one were perceiving such an object, and for that image to be invested with a peculiar feeling-tone, which is not present when one is merely thinking of such an object. It seems fairly plain that Hume holds that this kind of feeling-tone is present in its maximal possible degree in experiences of actual perception; that it is present in a somewhat lower degree in experiences of actual recollecting; and that it approximates to, but always falls short of this intrinsic maximal value when one is believing in the present existence of something which one is neither perceiving nor recollecting. The theory might be briefly, and perhaps a little unfairly, summarised as follows. To believe in the present existence of so-and-so, which one is not actually perceiving, is to have an image of so-and-so, which strikes one with such force and liveliness as to be half-way to being an hallucinatory *quasi*-perception.

Now it seems to me that there is extremely little introspective evidence for this. Suppose, for example, that I am looking at a closed biscuit tin, and am believing that it contains a round sweet brown biscuit. I do not find on introspection that I have a visual image resembling the visual sensum which I should be sensing if I were seeing such a biscuit in the tin, accompanied by imagings resembling the tactual and gustatory sensation which I should be having if I were holding and eating such a biscuit. I cannot but suspect that Hume, like many of his English contemporaries and predecessors in philosophy, enormously over-estimated the frequency and the epistemological importance of imitative imagery in ordinary thinking.

It seems to me that Hume's speculations as to the *causation* of certain kinds of belief are of much more interest and importance than his account of the *psychological nature* of such beliefs. Here, as elsewhere in the *Treatise*, Hume's acuteness and good sense, and wide knowledge and interest often break through the limitations imposed by the extremely narrow and quite untenable general principles from which he explicitly starts and which he never explicitly abandons. The whole is a mixture of some extremely good and some pretty bad parts, and it may be doubted whether these can be combined into a single self-consistent system. Perhaps Hume, in his capacity of professional sceptic, would welcome this as grist to his mill.

2.3

HUME'S DOCTRINE OF THE SELF

Hume's doctrine of the Self is closely connected with his general doctrine of Substance. It will therefore be necessary to begin by giving a brief account of the latter. In order to do this, I shall first distinguish two senses of the word 'substance', which I will call the *empirical* and the *metaphysical* sense. I shall substitute the word 'substratum' for 'substance' when used in the latter sense.

A chair or a stone is a substance in the empirical sense; a wave or a flash of lightning or a dance is not. Again, a human mind is a substance in the empirical sense, whilst a feeling of toothache or a process of reasoning or of introspecting is not. Such existents as waves, dances, feelings of toothache, etc., are what Hume would call 'modes'.

We feel it appropriate to use the word 'substance', in the empirical sense, when and only when all the following conditions are fulfilled. (1) Certain *simultaneous* occurrents are associated in one or other of certain specially intimate ways. For example, an occurrence of brownness, an occurrence of coldness, and an occurrence of hardness all occupy simultaneously a single definite area. Or, again, a feeling of toothache and various other experiences co-exist in what we may call the same field of consciousness. Let us call any such specially close combination of a number of simultaneous occurrents an 'outstanding unified phase'. (2) Certain outstanding unified phases, which follow each other in time, are combined with each other in certain specially intimate ways. For example, they may all occupy the same region, and the qualities of the various occurrents may be exactly alike in each successive phase or they may vary continuously. Or, again, the regions which the successive phases occupy may all be different, but they may form a sequence varying continuously in position or in shape or in size, or in any combination of those features. Any such sequence of specially interconnected outstanding unified phases may be called an 'outstanding unified strand'. (3) An outstanding unified strand has further to be subject to laws of the following kind. If any phase in it had been different in such and such respects, then there would have been such and such differences in the phases which preceded it and which followed it in that strand. Such laws generally involve a reference to the phases in certain other outstanding strands which are contemporary with this phase in this strand. They generally involve, for example, certain spatial relations, e.g., adjunction or separation, between the regions occupied by these other contemporary phases and the region occupied by this phase.

When and only when conditions of all these three kinds are fulfilled, we talk of such an outstanding unified strand as the history of a certain empirical substance of a certain kind, for example, of a certain bit of copper or of a certain human mind. We then describe any phase in such a strand as the total state of that empirical substance at a certain moment, for example, as Charles I's total state of mind just before his head was cut off. And we describe any outstanding occurrent in such a phase as a momentary event in that substance, for example, as Charles I's feeling of coldness just before the axe fell.

Now, reference to a *substratum*, i.e., to a 'substance' in the metaphysical sense, occurs when people begin to reflect on the nature of empirical substances. It is suggested that there is, in connexion with each unified strand which counts as the history of an empirical substance, a particular existent entity of a quite peculiar kind. This is held to be at each moment a complete *undifferentiated unit*, as contrasted with the plurality of simultaneous occurrents in any total state of an empirical substance. Again, it is held to persist without the slightest *variation* throughout all the variegated sequence of successive total states which make up the history of an empirical substance. It is supposed to stand in a one-many asymmetrical relation of a unique kind to every total state of the empirical substance and to every occurrent in any such total state. This is expressed by saying that it 'supports' each of them and that they 'inhere in' it. To talk of such a supposed entity is to talk of a *substratum*, i.e., of a 'substance' in the metaphysical sense. It is commonly held that there is a different substratum for each different empirical substance. In the case of those empirical substances which are human minds the supposed substrata are often called 'pure egos'.

It is worth noting that there is really a threefold ambiguity in the word 'substance'. Sometimes it is used in the purely empirical sense and sometimes in the purely metaphysical sense. But people who accept the metaphysical theory often use it in a mixed sense. They think of a 'substance' as a whole consisting of (a) a *substratum*, and (b) the complex of simultaneous occurrents and successive total phases which inhere in that *substratum* and make up the history of an empirical substance.

We can now state Hume's view on the general question quite briefly. (1) He accepted the notion of substance, in the purely empirical sense, as both intelligible and useful. He did so both as regards bodies and as regards minds. He considers what he calls 'the principle of union', i.e., the laws of co-existence and sequence of occurrents characteristic of any empirical substance, as the most important factor in the notion. (2) He rejected the notion of substance in the purely metaphysical sense, and therefore also in the mixed sense. He held that there are no clear intelligible thoughts corresponding to the words and phrases in which this metaphysical theory is formulated. (3) He put forward an elaborate theory of the causes which have led so many philosophers to use what he regards as the meaningless verbiage of 'substrata' and 'accidents' and to believe that it expresses something intelligible and true. In this theory, he deals in turn with the simplicity and the invariableness which have been ascribed to *substrata*. (4) Those who talk in terms of *substrata* and accidents commonly regard the following sentences as expressing necessary truths:

No occurrent could possibly have existed except as an accident in a certain one *substratum* at a certain one moment. On the other hand, a *substratum* could have existed without having been inhered in by those particular occurrents which in fact inhered in it.

Naturally, Hume regards these sentences as meaningless verbiage. He tries to state the facts which have caused such sentences to seem to so many eminent philosophers to be intelligible and to express a necessary truth.

(5) Suppose we were to drop the reference to *substrata* and to inherence, and to confine ourselves to substances in the empirical sense. Then we could translate the above allegedly meaningless sentences into the following intelligible one:

It is self-evidently impossible that any occurrence of temperature or of colour or of toothache, etc., should exist except as an item in such a bundle of interconnected occurrents of various kinds as would constitute the history of some one empirical substance.

This is intelligible, but Hume explicitly rejects it as false. According to him, the so-called impossibility is nothing more than the practical difficulty which we have in overcoming a very strong association due to certain *de facto* peculiarities of our perceptual and our reflexive experience.

I think that this is a fair account, in my own language, of Hume's doctrine of substance in general. We can now pass to the case of human minds or selves. I propose to make the transition in the following way.

In order to show that sentences containing the words '*substratum*' and '*inherence*', as used by Scholastic philosophers, are meaningless, it is necessary and sufficient on Hume's principles to establish the following proposition. It is necessary and sufficient, on his principles, to show that no one has ever been acquainted with anything which presented itself to him as a *substratum* in the way in which, for example, something presents itself to him as *yellow* when he looks at the sun, or the way in which, for example, certain of his experience present themselves to him as feelings of *anger* when he has them. Suppose you were to object that, even without ever having been acquainted with anything that presented itself to him as a *substratum*, a person might be able to think of a *substratum* as an entity answering to a certain description (cf., e.g., the fact that a man who had never seen a certain shade of red might be able to think of it descriptively as the shade which comes between two shades of red which he has seen). Then I think that Hume, on his general principles, might answer as follows. The only available description of a *substratum* would be some such phrase as 'that completely unitary and completely unvarying entity in which all the simultaneous occurrents at each moment and the successive total states at different moments of an empirical substance *inhere*'. But a person could not understand that description unless he could think of the relation which the word 'inherence' purports to name. Now he could not do this unless he had been acquainted with an instance of two terms which presented themselves as standing in that relation to each other, as, for example, a man's nose presents itself as being in the middle of his face to a person who looks at him from the front-view. But it has already been argued that *one* of the terms, viz., that in which the simultaneous occurrents and the successive total states are alleged to inhere, never is presented as such to a person's acquaintance. So, on Hume's principles, a person could not understand a description of a *substratum* in terms of the relation of 'inherence' unless he had already been acquainted with something which presented itself to him as a *substratum*.

On his own principles, then, Hume had only to show that no one is ever acquainted with anything which presents itself to him as a *substratum*. Now he thought it obvious that there are two and only two forms of acquaintance with particulars, viz., sense-perception and what I will call 'reflexive awareness'. But, even on the most naively realistic view of it, sense-perception presents us only with *occurrences* of colour, *occurrences* of temperature, etc., located in certain regions outside our bodies. It does not make us acquainted with entities which present themselves as completely unitary and completely invariant *substrata*, in one of which all the various occurrents and total phases which form the history of any one empirical substance inhere. If we now turn to reflexive awareness, no one would suggest that it could make anyone acquainted with the *substrata* either of material things or of other selves. There is in fact one and only one case in which is it at all plausible to suggest that a person is ever acquainted with an entity which presents itself to him as a *substratum*. It might be held, and it has in fact been held, that each of us is from time to time acquainted by reflexive awareness with *his own pure ego*. So, if and only if he can refute this claim, Hume will have shown, on his own principles and assumptions, that no one can have a thought answering to the word 'substance' as used by Scholastic philosophers.

Hume introduces this topic in the early paragraphs of Bk. I, Part IV, Sect. V of the *Treatise*. He discusses it more fully in the next section, and he reverts to it in the *Appendix* which he added when he first published Book III of the *Treatise*. I shall now consider these three passages in turn.

Part IV., Sect V. After repeating his general arguments against the notion of 'substance' in the metaphysical sense, Hume challenges anyone to tell him what the experience is that is supposed to give to a person the idea of the substratum in which all his various experiences inhere. He challenges anyone to classify and describe this experience, to say whether it is persistent or recurrent, and so on. He assumes, of course, that these challenges cannot be met.

There are two other main points in this Section. The first is this. A common definition of a substance, as opposed to an event or process, is that it is something that might conceivably exist by itself. Hume asserts that this criterion applies just as much to any particular experience as to the pure ego, which is supposed to be the undifferentiated and unvarying substratum in which all a person's experiences inhere. His actual words are as follows: 'Since all our perceptions are different from each other and from everything else in the universe, they are also distinct and separable, and may be considered as separately existent, and may exist separately...' Now Hume uses 'perception' to cover all the kinds of experience which he admits to occur. He is therefore asserting *inter alia* that the very same twinge of pain and spasm of anger, which Jones felt on a certain occasion when Smith trod on his toe, might conceivably have existed in complete isolation from all the rest of Jones's contemporary, earlier, and later experiences. It might conceivably have existed 'all by itself', i.e., not as an experience of any person. Or it might conceivably have existed in such intimate relations with a different set of inter-related experiences that it would have been *Robinson's* twinge of pain, or *Robinson's* spasm of anger, instead of *Jones's*. Hume would, no doubt, hold that all these suggestions are *causally* impossible. But for him, this can mean only that they conflict with very strong habits of belief, due to associations formed by regularities of co-existence and sequence in our past experience.

The second main point in this Section is the following. Hume commits himself to the following assertions:

We have no perfect idea of anything but a perception. A substance is entirely different from a perception. We have therefore no idea of a substance. Inhesion is something supposed to be requisite to support the existence of our perceptions. Nothing appears requisite to support the existence of a perception. We have therefore no idea of inhesion....

If this were taken quite literally, it would imply that we have no idea of a substance even in the empirical sense. For a penny or a person is a substance in that sense. Now neither a penny nor a person is either a sense-datum or an image or an emotion or a bodily feeling or a faint revival of one. And what Hume calls a 'perception' is one or another of these. But it is quite plain in other passages that Hume did not deny that we have an idea both of material and mental substances in the empirical sense. He was concerned only to deny that we have an idea of substance in the metaphysical sense of *substratum*.

Part IV., Sect. VI. We can now pass to the Section which Hume entitles *Personal Identity*. After repeating the arguments and assertions which we have already noted, Hume makes the following definite statement: A human mind is 'nothing but a bundle or collection of different perceptions which succeed each other with inconceivable rapidity and are in perpetual flux and movement'. He also compares a mind to a 'kind of theatre, where several perceptions successively make their appearance'. But he is careful to point out that the analogy must not be pressed. He says that it is 'the successive perceptions only that constitute the mind; nor have we the most distant notion of the places where these scenes are represented, or of the materials of which it is composed'. So the question that arises for Hume may fairly be put as follows: What makes a person think, or rather talk as if he thought, that his mind is, or contains as an essential factor, something which is completely simple and undifferentiated at each moment and which persists without any variation from moment to moment throughout the course of his life?

The answer is on the following general lines. Sometimes a person has under continuous observation for a period an existent which presents no qualitative variation during that period. An example would be hearing continuously an unvarying sound, such as the roar of a waterfall. This kind of experience is the basis of the thought of identity through time in its only strict and proper sense. Sometimes, again, a person has the experience of observing on successive isolated occasions the successive items in a sequence of inter-related existents. An example would be hearing at intervals fragments of a conversation going on in a neighbouring room, for example, on occasions when the door was opened for someone to go in or come out. Here there is certainly *not* identity through time in the strict sense. Now Hume undoubtedly takes these two kinds of experience, and their resemblances, as the basis of his argument. The argument is clear enough in its outline, but I do not find it altogether clear in detail. I shall therefore state in my own way what I take him to have had in mind.

Consider first the experience of hearing continuously an unvarying sound. At any intermediate moment, the phase of actual sensation must be accompanied by a vivid memory of the adjoined stretch of past precisely similar sensation. It will probably be accompanied also by a lively anticipation of adjoined future similar sensation. Next, consider the experience of hearing on successive isolated occasions fragments of a conversation. Suppose that the items are so inter-related that they are strongly associated in one's mind. (In the present example, there might be close resemblance of accent and intonation, a common theme, and so on.) Then each actual sensation will tend here too to be accompanied by memories of the previous items in that particular sequence and by anticipations of later items in it. There is thus a marked resemblance between (a) the experience of continuously observing a single unvarying existent, and (b) the experience of observing, on a sequence of isolated occasions, existents which are so inter-related as to be strongly associated in one's mind. Now Hume's contention appears to be that this marked resemblance between the two kinds of experience tends to make us ignore the fundamental difference between them. It tends to make us think that in the second case too, we have had a single unvarying existent under continuous observation. But this tendency is so glaringly in conflict with the known facts that it cannot manifest itself in its naked absurdity. Instead, we postulate the existence of something in principle *unobservable*, which persists without variation during the intervals, and which presents itself to us on each of the isolated occasions now in one guise and now in another.

Similar remarks apply to the notion of simplicity at each moment, though Hume does not discuss this so fully. Sometimes one is aware at a given moment of an object in which one can distinguish no differentiations. An example would be the visual sense-datum which presents itself to one when one looks up into a cloudless blue sky. Perhaps a better one would be the isolated almost punctiform sense-datum which presents itself to one if one sees a single star on a pitch-dark night. Such experiences as these are the basis of the thought of simplicity in its only strict and proper sense. On certain other occasions, however, one is aware at a given moment of an object which is differentiated, but where the differentiations form a familiar pattern and are strongly associated with each other in one's mind. An example would be the visual and tactual sense-data, which present themselves to one when one holds one's watch in one's hand and looks at the face. Hume's view seems to be that the two kinds of experience are so alike in character that we tend to ignore the fundamental difference between them. We tend to think that in the second case we are observing a simple undifferentiated object. Here again, however, the tendency is nipped in the bud by its conflict with obvious facts. So we compromise by postulating the existence of something in principle *unobservable*, which is itself absolutely simple, but presents itself to us in a plurality of simultaneous inter-connected guises.

Hume claims to confirm the existence and the operation of this principle by pointing to the circumstances under which we talk of 'the same so-and-so' in reference to objects, such as ships, plants, animals, etc., which have obviously undergone more or less considerable changes in course of time. He argues that in all such cases the various parts of an object, or the various successive phases in its history, or both these, are from one cause or another very strongly associated in the mind of any observer.

Hume insists that when we talk of 'identity' or 'sameness' in such cases we are not merely making a legitimate and harmless extension of the meaning of a word.

> ...When we attribute identity, in an improper sense, to variable and interrupted objects, our mistake is not confined to the expression, but is commonly attended with a fiction, either of something invariable and uninterrupted or of something mysterious and inexplicable, or at least with a propensity to such fictions.

I have said that Hume did not question the fact that a human mind is a substance *in the empirical sense*. But I must confess that he sometimes uses expressions which, if taken at their face value, seem to be much more radically sceptical. The following is an example.

> ... That identity is nothing really belonging to these different perceptions and uniting them together, but is merely a quality which we attribute to them because of the union of their ideas in the imagination when we reflect upon them.

It should be noted, however, that immediately after this Hume proceeds to enquire what are the relations between such perceptions which give rise to this association between our ideas of them.

I think that the obvious explanation is the following. He does not mean to deny that there *are* certain perfectly genuine and characteristic relations between the experiences which make up the stream of consciousness of a person. But these relations are not the relation of *identity*, in the strict sense, nor the relation of *common ownership* by something which is *not* an experience but *is* self-identical in the strict sense. They are such relations as contiguity in time and causation. And they are not relations which hold *of necessity* between their terms. The very same experiences, or experiences exactly like them, could conceivably have existed without standing in these relations to each other. It is these genuine, but quite contingent, relations between a person's experiences which cause his ideas of those experiences to become strongly associated with each other when he reflects on them. And it is these strong associations which generate the fiction of a simple unvarying continuous entity, in which all these experiences inhere, and apart from which none of them could have existed.

Now it is a general principle with Hume that the only relations among terms which can give rise to associations between the ideas of those terms are resemblance, contiguity in space or time, and causation. He thinks that contiguity has little influence in the present case, so we can confine our attention to what he says about resemblance and causation.

Under the head of 'resemblance', he brings in *memory*, which obviously plays an important part in the notion of personal identity. I do not find Hume's statements on this topic very clear, but it seems certain that he wishes to make at least the following assertions. Memory functions in two different ways, one direct and the other indirect, in generating the fiction of a persistent unvarying owner of the successive experiences which constitute a person's mental history. Hume describes the first of them by saying that 'memory not only discovers the identity but also contributes to its production.' He describes the second of them by saying that 'memory does not so much *produce* as *discover* personal identity'. We must now consider these two functions which he ascribes to memory.

The direct function seems to be this. A memory-experience, according to Hume, consists of a vivid image occurring later in a certain stream of consciousness and *resembling* an experience which occurred earlier in the same stream of consciousness. Thus, in so far as a person has memories, there occur in the later stages of his mental history experiences which *resemble* certain experiences in the earlier stages of it. But resemblance is one of the relations between terms which tend to produce an association between a person's ideas of those terms. And a strong association between one's ideas of one's own experiences tends to generate the fiction of a persistent unvarying owner of them. This appears to be the sense in which memory 'contributes to the production' of personal identity. Hume must presumably mean 'contributes to producing the fiction of a pure ego which is identical with itself in the strict sense'.

In order to understand the indirect function of memory, we must first consider the part which the relation of *causation* is supposed by Hume to play in connexion with personal identity. Here he makes the following remark: '...The true idea of the human mind is to consider it as a system of different perceptions... which are linked together by the relation of cause and effect and mutually produce, destroy, influence, and modify each other'.

I think that what he must have in mind is the following. Two successive total fields of consciousness belong to the mental history of the same person (he might allege) if and only if either (a) the earlier immediately precedes the later and directly influences it, or (b) the temporal gap between the two is filled by an intermediate sequence of fields of consciousness, each of which is directly influenced by its immediate predecessor and directly influences its immediate successor. This *causal* continuity leads to a strong association, in anyone who observes it and reflects upon it, between his ideas of the various phases in it, whether adjacent or remote. This association tends to generate in him the fiction of something simple, persistent, and unvarying, lying behind all the successive phases.

This brings us to the indirect function of memory. Unless a person had memory, he could have no idea of causation, and therefore no idea of the causal continuity which is the most characteristic mark of a sequence of total fields of consciousness which make up the mental history of a person. But, once he has got the idea of causation by the possession and use of memory, it enables him to fill in, by reference to causal laws, the very numerous gaps between the comparatively few and rather scattered experiences which he actually remembers at any time. He uses it also to extend the series backwards beyond the earliest experiences which he can now remember.

<u>Appendix</u>. Hume came to feel profoundly dissatisfied with his doctrine of the self and self-consciousness. But his premises still seemed to him to be true and his reasoning from them to be valid. So he confesses that he is reduced to a state of complete bewilderment. His account of what he finds unsatisfactory in his theory and of why he feels dissatisfied are highly obscure,

and I am not at all sure that I understand them. I will begin by quoting the three main passages:

(1) 'If perceptions are distinct existences, they form a whole only by being connected together. But no connexions among distinct existences are ever discoverable by human understanding. We only *feel* a connexion or determination of the thought to pass from one object to another. It follows therefore that the thought alone finds personal identity when, reflecting on the train of past perceptions which compose a mind, the ideas of them are felt to be connected together and naturally introduce each other... But all my hopes vanish, when I come to explain the principles, that unite our successive perceptions in our thought or consciousness'. (2) 'In short there are two principles, which I cannot render consistent, nor is it in my power to renounce either of them, viz., (i) *That all our distinct perceptions are distinct existences*, and (ii) *That the mind never perceives any real connexion among distinct existences*'. (3) 'Did our perceptions either inhere in something simple and individual, or did the mind perceive some real connexion among them, there would be no difficulty in the case'.

What are we to say of these passages? It is the second of them which seems to me so puzzling. I cannot see the least conflict between the two principles which Hume says he can neither give up nor reconcile and so I cannot believe that this can be a correct statement of the difficulty which Hume felt. The third passage seems perfectly clear and explicit, and it follows immediately upon the one which I find so obscure. It seems plain that what Hume means by the third passage is this. There would be no insuperable difficulty in accounting for the consciousness of one's identity through time if *either* (a) all of one's experiences were in fact accidents in a simple unvarying *substratum*, of which one was directly aware, or (b) if one could intuit what he calls 'real', i.e., necessary and intrinsic, connexions between the various experiences which make up one's mental history. But the first alternative is contrary to fact, and is not really intelligible according to Hume's previous arguments. And the latter alternative is inconsistent with the principles which he formulates in quotation (2), and which he there carelessly and misleadingly suggests to be inconsistent with *each other*. It is the second alternative which Hume explicitly refers to and rejects in the first passage quoted.

I think that the difficulty, which Hume feels, arises when one tries to combine his account of the inter-connexion of the experiences which constitute the mental history of a person with his account of causation. We are inclined to accept as more or less plausible his view that the various experiences which are counted as belonging to the mental history of a single person are those which stand to each other in very much more direct and intimate *causal* relations than do experiences which are assigned to the mental histories of two or more persons. But suppose we then ask: What is the cash value of this statement on Hume's theory of causation?

Let us take the question quite generally at first, and then apply the answer to our particular case. In general, what is meant, on Hume's analysis of causation, by saying of the particular event X that it causes the particular event Y? We must take this question in two stages, viz., (a) leaving out all reference to a human observer, and (b) bringing in that reference.

(a) If we leave out all reference to an observer, the statement that X caused Y comes down to the joint assertion of the following propositions: (i) X was immediately followed by Y. (ii) X was an event of a certain kind K_1 and Y was an event of a certain kind K_2. (iii) Every event of the former kind has been or will be immediately followed by an event of the latter kind. Now it is plain that this asserts *no* direct relation between the two particular events X and Y except that of *immediate sequence*. (b) Suppose we now introduce a reference to an observer who has actually observed a number of events of the kind K_1 and has observed each of them to be immediately followed by an event of the kind K_2. According to Hume, this will have set up in his mind a strong association between the idea of an event of the former kind happening and the idea of an event of the latter kind immediately following. Suppose that at any time after this he should actually *observe* an event of the kind K_1 happening. Then the idea of an event of the kind K_2 to follow immediately will be aroused in his mind with such vividness as to amount to an actual *expectation* that such an event will follow immediately. Moreover, Hume says, the expectation thus aroused will be toned with a peculiar kind of *feeling-tone*. Such an observer will be inclined to use such phrases as 'X compels Y to happen' or 'X causally necessitates Y' or 'X generates Y'. But, according to Hume, though the grammatical form of these phrases suggests that some peculiar kind of objective relation exists between X and Y, they are in that respect quite misleading. All that they really do is to express the peculiar feeling in the observer which accompanies his expectation of Y when this is evoked by his actual perception of X and by the association of ideas which has been established in his mind.

It is no wonder that Hume felt 'all his hopes vanish'. If we omit the observer, the specially intimate causal connexions, which were to be the characteristic mark of experiences that fall within the mental history of a single person, reduce to nothing but *de facto* relations of immediate sequence. If we introduce the observer, they reduce to nothing but these, together with certain feelings in him which he expresses in language that misleadingly suggests an objective relation of necessitation or generation among the experiences he observes.

Moreover, Hume still has on his hands the self as reflexive observer of its own non-reflexive experiences. He has in fact two problems, viz., (i) the *internal* unity of the self as reflexive observer, and (ii) the unity *between* the self as reflexive observer, on the one hand, and the mass of non-reflexive experiences, on the other, which it reflexively observes and about which it spins unintelligible fictions. For, after all, the experiences reflexively observable and the experiences of reflexively observing them are experiences belonging to *the same person*. Naturally, Hume will not want to introduce a pure ego at the second level after laboriously eliminating it at the first. But, if he is to avoid this, his only alternative is to admit, among experiences at the reflexive level, real specific relations, such as he has denied to hold among those at the non-reflexive level.

Some Comments on Hume's Doctrine. Having now expounded Hume's doctrine to the best of my ability, I shall conclude my paper with some comments upon it.

(1) Suppose we were to drop Hume's analysis of causal sentences and were to allow that, if X and Y are two particular events, the sentence 'X caused Y' asserts a specific kind of relation between them, quite independent of any observer and his feelings. Even so, it is quite plain that the two relations of similarity and causation are not sufficient to mark out a group of experiences as constituting the mental history of a single person.

Hume has told us nothing about the relations between a number of *simultaneous* experiences which mark them out as items in the total mental state of a single person at a given moment, as opposed to being contemporary experiences of several different persons. At a certain moment, Smith has a twinge of Toothache T_s and a feeling of nausea N_s. At the same moment, we will suppose, Jones has also a twinge of toothache T_j and a feeling of nausea N_j. Of these four experiences, *all are simultaneous*. T_s resembles T_j, and is *unlike* N_s, and N_s *resembles* N_j and is *unlike* T_s. Obviously, T_s and N_s stand to each other in a certain symmetrical relation R, in which neither of them stands to T_j or N_j. And T_j and N_j stand to each other in the same kind of symmetrical relation R and do not stand in that relation to T_s or N_s. It seems to me that this symmetrical relation R, which unites *all* the simultaneous experiences of any *one* person and *none* of the simultaneous experiences of any *two* persons, is quite unique and peculiar, and that Hume has altogether ignored it.

(2) Passing from what we might call the 'transverse' to what we might call the 'longitudinal' unity of a personal stream of consciousness, I would make the following remarks.

Undoubtedly there are certain familiar experiences which present themselves to a person who has them as states of non-inferential awareness of certain *earlier* experiences, had by *himself*, or of the objects of such experiences. We may describe these as 'ostensible rememberings'. An ostensible remembering may be either veridical or delusive, and there are various tests for deciding this. It seems also to be a fact that, under normal conditions, *all* experiences which present themselves to a person as states of non-inferential retro-cognition present themselves to him as cognitions of experiences formerly had by *himself* or of the objects of such experiences. That there are ostensible rememberings; that some of them are veridical and some delusive; and that all ostensible non-inferential retro-cognitions occurring under normal conditions are ostensible rememberings; these are three *empirical facts*. But it is an *analytical* proposition that, if an ostensible remembering be *veridical*, then the earlier experience to which it refers occurred in the *same* personal stream of consciousness as itself. That this conditional proposition is merely analytical is liable to be described by the following linguistic circumstance. The word 'remember' is commonly used in such a way that it would be ridiculous to say 'He remembered so-and-so, but in fact, he never had such an experience or witnessed such an event'. It is thus used, not in a purely descriptive psychological way, but as equivalent to what I have called *'veridical ostensible remembering'*. If this is forgotten, the sentence 'A memory and the experience to which it refers always occur at different stages of *the same* stream of personal consciousness' seems to state something which is both certain and synthetic, and to provide an empirical criterion for deciding whether two non-simultaneous experiences belong to the same or to different personal streams of consciousness. For the reasons given this seems to me to be a mistake.

Reverting to Hume, I would say that his attempt to analyse memory in terms of similarity and causal ancestry is quite hopeless. Obviously, a later experience of Smith's may *resemble* and be a *causal descendent* of an earlier experience of Jones's just as well as it may resemble and be a causal descendent of an earlier experience of his own. To have an ostensible remembering, whether veridical or not, of a certain past experience or of the object of a certain past experience, quite obviously does *not* just consist in having a present vivid image which in fact resembles that past experience or its object and is in fact a causal descendent of it. One could quite well conceive a being, who had any number of vivid images which in fact resembled and were causally descended from his earlier experiences, but who never remembered a single one of his experiences or their objects. For ostensibly to remember involves actually making or being able to make a *judgment* to the effect: 'I had such and such an experience, or witnessed such and such an event or thing'. And a being who had all the images in question might be completely incapable of entertaining *any* proposition at all, or any proposition about the *past*, or any proposition about *himself*. The plain fact is that Hume has never given any account of the experience of entertaining a proposition. At most he has attempted to give an account of what makes the difference between *merely* entertaining one and *believing* one.

(3) Hume's contention that any experience, which in fact occurred as an item in a certain total phase of the mental history of a certain person, might conceivably have occurred all by itself or as an item in the mental history of some other person, seems to me very hard to swallow. I am sure that the suggestion strikes most people as *absurd*, like the suggestion of the smile of a Cheshire cat without the cat (or a smile without a face), and not merely *startlingly unfamiliar*, like the suggestion of a talking cat. I suspect that anyone who persuaded himself that it is not really absurd would be the victim of a false analogy. I suspect that he is thinking of a person's total field of consciousness at any moment

HUME'S DOCTRINE OF THE SELF   161

as like a momentary arrangement of the bits of coloured glass in a kaleidoscope and that he is thinking of a person's mental history as like the successive arrangements of such bits of glass which would arise if the kaleidoscope were continuously shaken. Certainly, any of these bits of glass might have existed in a different kaleidoscope or in no kaleidoscope at all. All analogies between something so completely unique as a personal mental history and anything material are necessarily misleading. But it would be hard to imagine a more misleading analogy than this.

(4) When Hume discusses the circumstances under which we tend to call a material thing of a certain kind, for example, a ship or an animal organism, 'the same so-and-so', in spite of profound changes in it, we must note the following fact. In all this part of his discussion, he talks in popular terms of independent material *things* and of a *person* keeping such a thing under *observation*. The principles which he here puts forward to explain how we come to apply the words 'identical', 'same', etc., might look much less plausible when the results of his analysis were applied to the 'persons' who make the observations, to the 'things' which they observe, and to the process described as 'observing'. This is of course a criticism which holds generally of Hume's philosophy. Many of the parts of it are quite plausible when considered severally. But if we try to view them collectively, which he never did except in the *Appendix*, the whole is utterly incoherent.

(5) In conclusion, I want to touch on the challenge which Hume issues to anyone to classify and describe the experiences on which he bases his alleged idea of a pure ego and his alleged conviction that all his experiences inhere in one such entity. What weight, if any, should one attach to such challenges and to failure to meet them?

What Hume is demanding is in effect this. His opponent is to mention and describe a particular kind of experience which is related to his alleged idea of a pure ego in the kind of way in which his visual experience when he looks at the sun or at a bit of gold is related to his idea of a yellow object, or in the kind of way in which his feeling when someone treads on his toe or insults him is related to his idea of an angry emotion.

Such a demand presupposes acceptance of the general negative principle that a person cannot have a thought which does not arise in this way from a sensation or an emotion of a specific kind which he has already had. The only ground that Hume offers for this principle is a combination of the following two propositions. (i) An empirical generalisation in psychology to the effect that every image which a person has is a causal descendent of a sensation or emotion which that person has already had and which exactly resembled the image in quality. (ii) The tacit assumption that to have a thought of X either consists in or at any rate involves having an X-like image. Now the psychological generalisation is admitted even by Hume to be uncertain in marginal cases. Moreover, it obviously *presupposes* the notion of personal identity, since the original impression must have occurred in the mental history of the person in whom the image afterwards occurs. And, finally, it is difficult to see what evidence there could be for it on Hume's general principles and his analysis of remembering. As to the tacit assumption, I can only characterise it as palpably false and quite inconsistent with much of Hume's own philosophy, for example, his doctrine of our ideas of space and time. Lastly, if we consider the principle on its own merits, and apart from the reasons which Hume gives for it, it seems to me to have no kind of plausibility. It is plausible as regards specific sensal and emotional qualities and relations, such as yellowness, anger, spatial adjunction, temporal sequence, and so on. It has no plausibility as regards our thought of the structural feature or categories in terms of which we interpret our experience as a whole. Where Hume criticises any particular alleged category, or any alleged *a priori* principle which involves that category, on specific grounds, he is always worth serious attention. But in so far as he merely issues general challenges on the basis of unexamined restrictive principles he can safely be ignored.

2.4

THE PHILOSOPHY OF F.H. BRADLEY

Francis Herbert Bradley was born in 1846 and died in 1924. His long life was spent in Oxford and devoted to philosophical thinking and writing, and it would generally be admitted that he was the most eminent and influential English philosopher of his time. Since his death, the kind of philosophy which he taught has become outmoded, and I suppose that few present-day philosophers in England or America make a serious study of his writings. Fashion plays a very great part in philosophy, and it is a subject in which fashions change very quickly. For my own part, I expect the eclipse of the Bradleian type of philosophy to be only temporary, and, as Bradley was the ablest and the most readable writer of his school, any revival of interest in Absolute Idealism is almost certain to centre upon him and his work.

When Bradley was a young man the orthodox philosophy in England was empiricism in epistemology and logic, and utilitarianism in ethics. The prophet was J.S. Mill, and Herbert Spencer was still a name to conjure with. But the fashion was beginning to change, and Bradley played an important part in changing it. His first book, *Ethical Studies* (1876), was a brilliant and devastating attack both on hedonistic utilitarianism and on Kantian ethics, and an eloquent plea for the notion of 'self-realisation' as the key to moral theory. His second book, *Principles of Logic* (1883), was on its critical side an attack all along the line on Mill's logic, and, on its constructive side, an attempt to defend and develop the 'coherence' theory of judgment and inference. Bradley had made an intensive study of German idealism, and he acknowledged a great debt to Kant and to Hegel, but he was not an uncritical follower of any philosopher.

By 1893, when Bradley published his most important book, *Appearance and Reality*, the battle had been for the time won. Some form of Absolute Idealism, deriving from Hegel, and from Kant interpreted in a Hegelian manner, had become the orthodox philosophy in England and the United States, and it remained so until about 1910. But Bradley's intellect was essentially critical and sceptical. He was highly dissatisfied with some of the characteristic doctrines of his fellow Absolute Idealists. *Appearance and Reality* is at once a criticism of those aspects of Idealism and an attempt to construct a more satisfactory and a much more modest and sceptical form of that philosophy. The book at once became the centre of philosophical discussion, both for other idealists and for those then youthful philosophers, such as Moore and Russell, who were beginning to react against idealism. In connexion with these controversies, Bradley wrote many important articles in philosophical journals. These were collected and published in book form in 1914 under the title *Essays on Truth and Reality*. This contains Bradley's maturest thoughts on the subject to which he had devoted his life-work. It should be added that Bradley, unlike most of the philosophers of his school, was much interested in *empirical* (though not in *experimental*) psychology, and published a number of articles on psychological topics.

It is plainly impossible in an hour's lecture to do justice to so many-sided a thinker as Bradley. I shall confine my attention to *Appearance and Reality*. Even here a severe selection must be made, and I shall consider only a certain few doctrines which are specially characteristic of Bradley's philosophy and are fundamental to it. Those which I shall choose for consideration are his doctrine of *Degrees of Truth and Reality*, his theory of *Judgment*, his doctrine of the *Self*, and his positive account of the nature of the *Universe as a collective whole*. All these topics are intimately interconnected for Bradley, and the order in which one takes them is to some extent arbitrary.

(1) *Degrees of Truth and Reality*. Bradley draws a distinction between existence and reality. On his view, all appearances exist; all have some degree of reality; some have more reality than others, and none are completely

real. I think that the whole matter can be made considerably clearer if we draw certain preliminary distinctions.

We will begin with the term *Appearance*. The notion of an appearance or manifestation involves two distinct but inseparable factors, viz. (a) a certain something which appears or manifests itself to someone, and (b) a certain characteristic, simple or complex, which it appears to have or presents itself as having. Let us call these two factors respective the *Manifesting Term* and the *Ostensible Nature*. In ordinary sense-perception, for example, the manifested term is something which one is presented with by sight or touch or hearing, etc. And the ostensible nature is some characteristic, such as redness, coldness, squeakiness, etc., which it sensibly presents itself to one as having. Now when Bradley says that every appearance certainly exists, I take him to mean at least that in every instance of appearing some *term* or other really is manifesting itself. I think that he may mean in addition that we cannot reasonably raise the question whether such and such an *ostensible nature* is being presented in a particular instance of appearing. For this forms the description of the appearance under consideration. The only sensible question which can be raised is as to the *real* nature of the term which is undoubtedly presenting itself with such and such an *ostensible* nature. For example, in sense-perception, there is no doubt whatever that *something* is manifesting itself to the percipient, and there is no doubt whatever that it presents itself as extended, coloured, cold, squeaky, and so on. The only question here that can reasonably be raised is: 'Is this term, which presents itself here and now as extended, coloured, etc., really so? Could any term really have such characteristics as this term and many others present themselves to our senses as having?' The same would apply, *mutatis mutandis* to any kind of appearance.

It is now fairly easy to see what is meant by the notion of Degrees of Reality. If it is admitted that a term may present itself as being of a nature which differs from its actual nature, then it is plain that the ostensible nature may diverge less or more from the real nature and so be a less or a more misleading indication of the latter. Now an appearance can be described only by stating the ostensible nature of the term which is manifested in it. We might therefore say quite intelligibly that an appearance has a less or a higher degree of reality according as the ostensible nature which is presented in it diverges more or less from the real nature of the term which is manifesting itself in that appearance. This gives a meaning to the phrase 'Degrees of Reality' which is largely independent of any of Bradley's special views on other questions in metaphysics or logic.

Even without taking these into account, we could admit, I think, that no appearance could fail to have *some* degree of reality. And that is asserted by Bradley. For to deny this would be to say that in some cases the manifested nature is divergent in *every* respect from the actual nature of the manifesting term. There seems no reason to admit this even in the case of the wildest dream or waking hallucination. But Bradley also asserts that no appearance has *complete* reality. I do not think that this is obviously true unless we accept certain special doctrines of Bradley's on other questions. I will now develop this statement.

To say that a certain appearance was completely real would be to say that there was no discordance between the ostensible nature which the manifesting term presents and the nature which it actually has. Of course, one might admit that no term could manifest its *whole* nature in any one appearance or in any finite set of appearances to a finite being. But, apart from certain special doctrines of Bradley's, there seems no reason why there must be in every possible appearance a *positive discordance* (as distinct from a mere *inadequacy*) between the ostensible and the actual nature of the manifested term. There are, however, two characteristic doctrines of Bradley's which ensure that *every* appearance, as such, is to some extent unreal.

(i) According to Bradley the distinction between a term itself and the nature of that term involves contradiction and cannot be ultimately real. Yet that distinction is involved in every appearance as such, for in every appearance there is a *term* which presents itself as having such and such *characteristics*, for example, redness, coldness, etc., distinct from itself. (ii) Moreover, according to Bradley, there is no real plurality of existent terms or substantives. There is only one genuine substantive, viz., the universe as a single unique all-embracing individual, i.e., what Bradley calls 'the Absolute'. So in every appearance, the manifesting term is really one and the same, viz., this one all-embracing individual. But it is quite certain that in every appearance the manifesting term presents itself, not as the Absolute, but as this or that finite substantive, for example, this table, that man, and so on. To that extent, then, you must say that in every appearance that which is manifesting itself does so in a misleading way. So it does follow from our definition of 'appearance' together with these two doctrines of Bradley that every appearance has *some* degree of reality and that no appearance can be completely real. And that is exactly what Bradley asserts.

I shall consider these two doctrines of Bradley's in more detail under the heading of this theory of Judgment. In the meanwhile, I will mention the two criteria which Bradley gives for estimating the degree of reality of any appearance. They are *comprehensiveness* and *internal coherence*. He regards these two features as intimately interconnected, but he admits that for us they may diverge considerably.

Bradley does not tell us a great deal in detail about the results of applying these two tests. But the following point is worth noticing. If a characteristic is such that it can be manifested in particular places and for particular durations, then the more extensively it is manifested in space and time the higher the degree of reality which we may assign to the appearances in which it is manifested. By that criterion, for example, appearances of mass will have a higher degree of reality than appearances of colour. But, on the other hand, the very fact that a characteristic can be manifested indifferently in any region however small and for any period however short is a sign that it is pretty poor in content, like mass or colour or temperature. The richer and more concrete kinds of characteristic, such as a musical theme or the pattern of a picture or an historical trend, cannot be manifested at all except as pervading a whole long stretch of time or a whole considerable region of space or both. And there is much in them that cannot be manifested to the *senses* alone.

I will conclude and sum up what I have to say about Bradley's doctrine of Degrees of Truth and Reality as follows. On his view, there is not really a plurality of existent substantives; there is one and only one genuine individual, viz., the Absolute. Again, there is not really a plurality of mutually independent characteristics. And, lastly, the very distinction between a substantive, which has characteristics, and characteristics which belong to a substantive, is ultimately untenable. Yet all these ultimately unsatisfactory notions are involved in the very essence of an appearance as such. So *every* appearance will necessarily fall short of complete reality by misrepresenting what it manifests in at least these three respects. But, granting this, we can still raise the question: 'What kind of appearance will *least* misrepresent that which every appearance really manifests, viz. the Absolute?' It seems clear that on Bradley's premises, the inevitable misrepresentation will be reduced to a minimum if the following two conditions are fulfilled. (i) If the manifesting term is presented, not as a finite substantive capable of existing in isolation at a particular place and date, but as the universe as a single individual, or at any rate as something which could exist only as dependent upon and specifically contributing to that one individual. (ii) If the ostensible nature consists, not of a single simple characteristic, like colour or extension, but of something, like the theme of a musical composition, in which many features can be distinguished by analysis but in which all are fused together into a single coherent unity. I think that this is, roughly, what Bradley's two criteria amount to.

(2) *Theory of Judgment.* I have already had to refer to certain features in Bradley's theory of judgment, and I will now consider that theory in more detail. Our intellects work by making judgments and by drawing inferences which depend on the logical relations between judgments. Now to make a judgment consists either in ascribing a certain adjective to a certain substantive or class of substantives or in asserting that one substantive or class of substantives stands in a certain relation to another substantive or class of substantives. Examples of the former kinds of judgment are: 'This object is round' or 'All pennies are round'. Examples of the latter are: 'York is north of London' or 'Cats eat mice'. Judgments of the first kind presuppose the notion of a substantive which possesses a number of different qualities, but is fundamentally different from each of its qualities severally and from all of them collectively. Judgments of the second kind presuppose the notion of a plurality of substantives, each possessing a nature of its own and in principle capable of existing without the others, and of relations between two or more of them. The notions of quality and of relation are distinct, but they are closely bound up with each other. The various qualities which belong to a single substantive are, for that very reason, interrelated in a specially intimate way which might be

called 'co-inherence'. Moreover, many attributes which seem at first sight to be pure qualities are found on closer inspection to involve relations, for example, attributes like 'large', 'strong', etc. Again, a given kind of relation, for example, 'louder than', can relate only substantives having certain qualities, for example, sounds.

Now Bradley argues that, although we cannot help thinking in terms of this scheme of substantives, each with its own set of qualities, and each related to others by various relations, we can see on reflexion that it involves insuperable intellectual difficulties.

I shall not attempt to state or criticise his detailed arguments, but it is easy to see in outline the nature of the difficulties. As regards the notion of a substantive and its attributes, the point may be put as follows. It is an essential part of the very notion of a substantive that it is something which *has* qualities and *stands* in relations. This seems to imply that it is other than the sum total of its qualities and its relationships. But any description of what a substantive is must take the form of a judgment about it, and any judgment about it can only ascribe some quality or relationship to it. So we seem to be in the position of knowing that a substantive *must* be something other than its qualities and relationships taken either severally or collectively, and yet from the nature of the case being debarred from saying or thinking anything positive and specific as to what a substantive in its own essence could be. Locke summed this up in the phrase that substance seems to be 'a something I know not what.'

Similar difficulties, for what they are worth, could be raised in regard to the notion of a plurality of substances standing in relation to each other. Bradley also has special arguments of his own which I shall not here discuss. I propose instead to consider one simple alleged fact, which Bradley regards as quite fundamental, and which I believe lies at the back of his objection to the whole notion of a plurality of inter-related substantives.

The alleged fact is that there is something logically and psychologically prior to both substantives and relations between them. This something may be called 'unities'. Both terms and relations are abstractions, which we make at a certain level of our mental development from unities. Unities are presented, as such, in sense-awareness and in feeling. They are, and are felt to be, complex and highly differentiated. When we start thinking about such a unity, we substitute for it a diagrammatic schema of independent substantives and relations between them. We cannot help doing this, and it is an essential condition of intellectual progress to do so. But we are mistaken if we identify this schema with the original unity of which it professes to be the analysis. So the notion of terms, which could exist independently of each other and of the wholes in which they are parts, and which could by coming into relations with each other constitute such wholes, is a complete perversion of the real order. Any term less than the whole is an abstraction, and a partly misleading abstraction, from a unity which does *not*, in fact, consist of a number of mutually independent interrelated terms.

The kind of fact which Bradley had in mind is quite well illustrated if we consider a visual field as it is presented, say, to a baby. It may contain, for example, one outstanding patch of colour which a grown person would take as the surface of a table, another which he would take as the surface of the floor, and so on. But let us take the field simply as it exists for the baby and as it exists for the grown man apart from the interpretation which he automatically puts upon it when he is fully awake and attentive. Then it would certainly seem quite absurd to regard it as a whole built up out of various visual sense-data in various mutual relations, each of which might have existed in isolation from the field as a unit, and which might have been differently arranged, like the bits of glass in a kaleidoscope. Here, at any rate, it seems much more reasonable to regard the total visual field as the natural unit, and to regard the various visual sense-data as so many outstanding features in it.

Now Bradley takes this as typical. He holds that in the case of all genuine unities, and therefore *a fortiori* in the case of that all-embracing unity which is the universe as it really is, the whole is logically prior to what we take to be the various substantives which together make it up, and logically prior to what we take to be the various relations which combine and order these substantives. The analogy of pre-existing bricks, which are brought together in certain relations in which they need not have stood to each other, and so together constitute a house, is fundamentally misleading according to Bradley. But in our thinking about unities we cannot help using this kind of intellectual schema. It is a useful, and indeed indispensable, device, but reflexion shows us that it cannot do justice to the nature of any genuine unity.

We can now understand why Bradley gives a much humbler position to thought and reason than many other Absolute Idealists have done. We may put the case as follows.

If the ideal of thought be to know anything completely, then we can recognise, by thinking out its implications, that this is an ideal which from the nature of the case is unattainable. To know a thing completely, from the point of view of discursive thinking, would be to know all the propositions which are true of it or all the facts about it. But that is a mere phrase, for there is no such collection. The ideal of thought is completed knowledge, but a little thought shows that this is an ideal that discursive thinking could never conceivably attain. No doubt, beside thinking *about* terms we can also be *directly acquainted* with certain terms. Human beings, for example, are directly acquainted with certain colour expanses, sounds, smells, aches, etc., when suitable conditions are fulfilled. Since a person can make judgments, for example, 'This is red', 'This red expanse is beside that blue one', about terms with which he is directly acquainted, we can compare and contrast the two kinds of cognition, viz., being *directly acquainted with* a term and making a *judgment about* a term. When we do so we notice the following three facts. (i) However many qualities we may distinguish in a term, and however many relations we may note between it and other terms, there always remains an inexhaustible residue to be distinguished and noted and asserted in judgments. There is no conceivable resting place in that direction. (ii) Even if *per impossibile* that endless series could be completed, the set of qualities and relationships would still not *be* the term to which they are ascribed in our judgments. And to know the infinite series of facts *about* it would still be utterly different from being directly acquainted *with* it, as when one actually hears a tune or sees a pattern of colours. (iii) Yet *mere* direct acquaintance in itself is a very poor thing, hardly worth calling knowledge, and any advance on it requires the recognition and distinction of qualities and relations and the making of judgments.

So, Bradley concludes, our experience, with its two inseparable aspects of direct acquaintance and discursive thinking, and with its striving by piling up judgments to reach an end which we can see to be unattainable by such means, suggests to us a different kind of experience. It suggests a kind of ideal experience which would combine

(i) the directness of feeling or sensation and its power of grasping a unity as such, with (ii) a simultaneous complete knowledge of detail, which we now strive to reach by piling up analysis on analysis and distinction on distinction and judgment on judgment. This ideal kind of experience, which is certainly not possessed by any ordinary human being in his normal state of consciousness, seems to be very much what Spinoza had in mind when he spoke of the 'Third Kind of Knowledge'. We shall return to it when we consider Bradley's positive account of the nature of the Absolute.

(3) *The Self.* Bradley devotes two long and important chapters to the notion of a Self. The first is mainly analytical. In it, he tries to show that the word 'self' is highly ambiguous, and he tries to distinguish various senses in which it is used. The second chapter is critical. He tries to show in it that the notion of a 'self' in each of these senses of the word is incoherent and intellectually unsatisfactory.

The general difficulty may be stated as follows. We want to find something in connexion with the stream of consciousness of an individual, which we can properly describe as his essential self, and which we can distinguish in some consistent and practically applicable way from the various experiences which come and go without affecting his personal identity. Now it is doubtful whether you can find any persistent unvarying *experience* or *group of experiences* which will provide a criterion of personal identity. The most plausible candidate would be the background of organic sensation connected with a person's body and its organic processes. But, although this generally changes but slowly in character, it does alter profoundly between infancy and old age. Moreover, it changes fairly quickly at the age of puberty, and it may do so suddenly and profoundly as a result of accident, illness, or shock. Yet personal identity may be maintained. Suppose that, in spite of these facts, we insist that there must be some experience or group of experiences which goes on continuously and without qualitative change from the cradle to the grave, throughout sleeping and waking, and so on. Then we must admit that it is so fragmentary and poor in content that it would be absurd to *identify* it with a person's self or regard it as *sufficient* to constitute personal identity. If we go more into detail about the criteria of personal identity we note the following facts. (i) Identity of body is plainly insufficient. For there are cases where the body remains one and the same, but there are several distinct personalities, either alternating or simultaneous with each other. (ii) Psychical continuity, in the sense of there being no temporal gaps completely void of experiences, is neither necessary nor sufficient. In dreamless sleep, for all that we know to the contrary, there are such gaps, and yet personal identity is preserved. In cases of alternating personality, there may be no such gaps, and yet the personal identity is broken. (iii) The capacity to remember is neither a necessary nor a sufficient condition. It is plainly not necessary, since everyone admits that he has had experiences which he cannot now remember, and the range of a person's power of remembering varies both in length and in width from one moment in his life to another. Nor is it sufficient. There are ostensible memories, i.e., experiences in which a person seems to himself to be directly aware of a past experience or of the object of a past experience of his own, which are certainly delusive. In general, ostensible memory has to be tested by reference to other criteria, for example, the testimony of others, written records such as diaries and letters, and so on. No single criterion of personal identity is sufficient, and the precise degree to which the various corroborative tests must be fulfilled cannot be fixed on any rational principle.

In view of this, some philosophers have taken a person's self to be something of a unique and peculiar kind, which is absolutely simple and unchanging, and somehow *owns* all his experiences but is not itself either an experience or the object of any experience. This may be called *Pure Ego*. To this Bradley's reaction is the following. If you had already got a consistent account of the empirical self and its characteristic unity and identity, you might offer the theory of a Pure Ego as a metaphysical explanation of these empirical facts. It would indeed, on his view, be a hopelessly bad explanation. The Pure Ego would be a typical 'something, I know not what', and the connexion between its alleged internal simplicity and unchanging identity, on the one hand, and the complexity and the constant change in the content of the Empirical Self, on the other, would raise insoluble difficulties. But really the Pure Ego theory is not even a bad explanation of empirical facts which can be clearly and coherently stated. Having failed to give any consistent account of the characteristic unity and identity of a person as empirical facts, the supporters of this theory simply change the subject and offer this unobservable, simple, unchanging entity as what is *meant* by a Self. To this Bradley answers that a Pure Ego may be a very fine thing, but it is plainly not what anyone understands by his self.

Bradley's own account of the Self and of self-consciousness is by no means easy to understand or to state briefly and clearly. An essential preliminary is to distinguish between a *Self* and what he calls a *Psychical Individual*. Every self is a psychical individual, or at any rate, the contents of any self are part of the contents of a psychical individual. But a psychical individual need not be a self, and no part of its contents need be the contents of a self.

The following example will illustrate the distinction. Consider the case of a very simple and lowly creature, such as an oyster. One assumes that there is a certain stream of experience, of a very elementary kind, in connexion with the life of any one oyster. One assumes that any two experiences, simultaneous or successive, in the life of one and the same oyster would be interconnected in some more intimate way than would the experiences in the lives of two different oysters. We can express this by saying that experiences which arise in connexion with the life of any one oyster are the experiences of one *psychical individual*, whilst those that arise in connexion with the life of any other oyster are the experiences of another *psychical individual*. But no one would care to call such a stream of experiences the experiences of a *self*.

The next point to notice is the distinction between what I will call *mere feelings* and *directed experiences*. In describing a mere feeling the only sensible question that can be raised is as to its *quality as an experience*. Is it a feeling of warmth or of coldness, of tickling, of nausea, and so on? But in describing a directed experience it is always sensible to raise, not only this question, but also one of a fundamentally different kind, viz., What is its ostensible *object*? Examples of directed experience are ostensible perceptions (whether veridical or hallucinatory), ostensible memories (whether veridical or delusive), emotions like fear, jealousy, etc. (whether directed to a real or to a mistakenly believed or to a merely imagined state of affairs); and so on. You cannot ostensibly perceive, or ostensibly remember, or feel such an emotion as fear, without ostensibly perceiving some *thing*, or ostensibly remembering some *event*, or feeling fear of some *person* or *thing* which you know or believe to exist and which you take to be dangerous. The last example shows clearly that a directed experience can be *also* a feeling, though not of course a *mere* feeling. Fear and anger, for example, differ in their quality as experiences, just as the mere feelings of coldness and of nausea do, but, unlike these mere feelings, they also are of their very nature directed to ostensible objects, whether real or delusive, for example, snakes, ghosts, etc. Bradley holds that *every* kind of directed experience, for example, an ostensible perception, an ostensible memory, and so on, is also a feeling.

In terms of these distinctions Bradley's view, as I understand it, may be stated as follows. It is intelligible to talk of a *Self* in connexion with a psychical individual, if and only if some of the experiences in its stream of consciousness become objects to other experiences in that stream. So far as I can see, Bradley takes the notion of *becoming an object* as primary, and says very little positive about the correlative notion of *being directed upon* an object. At any moment in the history of any psychical individual, in connexion with which one can properly talk of a self, certain of the experiences in its stream of consciousness are differentiated as objects. It seems that, on Bradley's view, what is directed upon them is the residue of the contents of that psychical individual which at the time is not so differentiated. Both the former and the latter are and remain feelings. But each is now something more than a feeling; one being not only a feeling but also an object of cognition, volition, emotion, etc., and the other being not only a feeling but also a state of cognising, willing, etc.

Bradley holds that there is no part of the content of a psychical individual which is in principle incapable of becoming an object to the rest of its content, and no part which is in principle bound to be an object and incapable of falling into the unobjectified residue. The contents of such a psychical individual as a human being is always divided up in this way at every moment of his waking life, but the line between the objectified and the subjective part of this content is continually shifting. In drowsy states, for example just before going to sleep and just after waking up, the objectified part of the total content may be evanescent. Since the residue is *subjective* only in relations to a part which is *object to* it, this means that human consciousness is reduced for the moment almost to that state of pure feeling which is presumably the permanent condition of psychical individuals, such as oysters, which cannot properly be called 'selves'.

Bradley thinks that the word 'self' is used with the following systematic ambiguity. Sometimes it is used in such a way that the contents of a self at any moment are to include *only* that part of the contents of a psychical individual which are at the time *not objectified*, and to exclude that part which is objectified relatively to the former. Sometimes it is used in such a way that the contents of a self at any moment include *both* these parts of the content of a psychic individual. Suppose, for example, that a person were feeling toothache and at the same time wishing that it would stop. Then on the narrower interpretation, only the experience of wishing the toothache to stop would count as part of the content of his self; the toothache itself, being the object of that experience, would not. On the wider interpretation both the experience of toothache and the experience of wishing it to stop would count as parts of the content of his self. One way of describing such a case would be to say that the toothache is part of the content of the *Me*, but not of the *I*, whilst the experience of desiring it to stop is part of the content of the *I*, but not of the *Me*. In that terminology, the ambiguity of the word 'self' may be expressed as follows. In one sense the contents of a self at any moment include *only* the contents of the I, and *not* those of the Me. In the other sense, they include *both* the contents of the I and those of the Me.

For the purpose of Bradley's philosophy, the upshot of this elaborate critical description of the notion of the Self is as follows. Many Idealists have held that each of us is provided, in his own self and his awareness of it, with a special source of insight into reality. Here, it is alleged, everything is perfectly certain and perfectly intelligible. From this, they have often gone further, and have claimed to find a clue to the nature of the universe in what they claimed to know with certainty about themselves. Leibniz, Berkeley, Schopenhauer, and Lotze in several ways are eminent examples of such philosophers. Bradley's contention is that in self-consciousness we have no revelation as to the nature of the self which is coherent and intelligible enough to be used as a clue to understanding the nature of the universe.

Three main claims have been made for self-consciousness as providing a solution to problems which are otherwise insoluble: (i) It is alleged that here and here alone *subject and object are identical*, whereas in all other cases of cognition they are different. It is argued that, since in this case, the subject *is* what it knows, it must *know* what it is. To this Bradley's answer is that to talk in this way misrepresents the facts of self-consciousness. What is known is never identical with what knows it. In self-consciousness, the subject or I at any moment is that part of the total content of the psychical individual which is then *merely* felt. The object or *Me* is a part of the total content which is then not merely felt but also *objectified*.

(ii) It is alleged that awareness of one's own unity and identity enables one to understand the *unity* of a substance against its various contemporary qualities, and the *identity* of a substance against its varying successive states. To this Bradley answers that we have found the notions of personal unity and personal identity to be extremely vague and confused, and have not managed to give any satisfactory analysis of them. Therefore self-knowledge cannot be used to enable us to understand the unity or the identity of anything else.

(iii) It is alleged that in self-consciousness a person is aware of himself as *active*, and that this awareness enables him to understand causation and to give an intelligible account of the essential nature of the actually existent as opposed to the merely apparent or the merely possible. To this Bradley answers as follows. If by 'activity' you mean literal deliberate volition, it is preposterous to pretend to interpret causation in inanimate things or the lower animals, for example chemical attraction or nest-building, in terms of activity. If, on the other hand, you mean something more primitive than this, which is unanalysable, but of which you are directly aware, for example Spinoza's *conatus* or Schopenhauer's *will-to-live* or Bergson's *élan vital*, of what possible use can it be as a principle of intellectual understanding and explanation? You might as well try to explain everything in terms of some simple unanalysable feeling, such as tickling or warmth.

(4) *Bradley's positive account of the Absolute.* I pass now to the last topic which I shall discuss, viz., Bradley's positive account of the Absolute, i.e., the Universe as an individual and the only complete and perfect individual. Several points, which have been touched upon under previous headings, here become highly relevant.

The following are the main features of his doctrine.

(1) The Universe, as it really is, must be an internally coherent whole, excluding every kind of contradiction and inconsistency.
(2) Since all appearances are so many different ways in which the one reality presents itself, all of them must tell us something about its real nature. But *every* appearance presents reality as having characteristics which involve contradictions when we think out their implications, and appearances of *different kinds* present reality as combining characteristics which would be incompatible with each other. So appearances both severally and collectively misrepresent reality. Still, none of them completely misrepresents it; some do so less than others and they can be arranged in a scale in that respect, and we have no other source of information about the detailed nature of reality besides the various kinds of appearance which it presents. For example, one very pervasive appearance which the world presents is that of being composed of a set of material particles distributed in space and interacting in accordance with fairly simple mathematical laws. Another very pervasive appearance which it presents is that of containing biological organisms evolving in interaction with an environment. Another is that of containing more or less rational persons, and societies composed of such persons. Now each of these appearances must correspond to some important feature of the universe as it really is. According to Bradley, none of these ostensible features could belong as such and without modification to reality. It would involve contradiction to describe the universe as literally a set of interacting particles, or as literally an organism or set of organisms, or as literally a person or a society of persons. And it would still more obviously involve contradictions to describe the universe without qualification simultaneously in *all* these ways. But any account of the universe which omitted the fact that it appears under *each* of three guises, and under *all* of them together, would be defective. Nor need we remain at that point and treat them all as on a level. According to Bradley, for example, it would be considerably less misleading to regard the universe as a person or as a society of inter-related persons than to regard it simply as a set of material particles interacting according to mechanical laws. There must be some *real* feature of the universe at the back of every *apparent*

feature however incoherent; the universe must combine all these real features in some coherent way, in spite of the inconsistencies between their several manifestations; and some of the appearances misrepresent the real nature of the universe much less or represent it much more adequately than do others.

(3) The universe is not a whole composed of a set of substantial parts in mutual relations. It is differentiated, indeed, and is not just a blank unity, but none of its differentiations could conceivably exist apart from it and apart from any of its other differentiations. If we talk in terms of substance, it is less misleading to say that there is only one substance and that this is the universe, than to say that there are many substances and that the universe is composed of them. But the notions of substance and attribute and state are ultimately unsatisfactory, and so it is in the end misleading to think of the universe as the one substance and to think of everything else as a state or attribute of it.

(4) The next point in Bradley's doctrine is that all the contents of the universe, as it really is, are of the nature of *experience*. I will quote two characteristic assertions of his on this topic. (i) 'To be real, or even barely to exist, must be to fall within sentience'. (ii) 'Feeling, thought, and volition... are *all* the material of existence, and there is no other material actual or possible'.

These statements must be taken along with the account which we have already given of Bradley's view of the self. He says explicitly that he does *not* mean that egos or subjects exist in their own right and that everything else is merely a state of a subject or dependent upon being an object to a subject. As we have seen, he holds that both cognising subject and cognised object are secondary. They arise through a certain kind of division in the content of a psychical individual, and that content was originally pure feeling and neither cognitive experience nor cognised object. The subject, if and when it develops within a psychical individual, is the part of its content which continues to be *mere* feeling. The object, if and when it develops, is the part which continues indeed to be felt but also begins to function in certain other ways.

Perhaps the following example will help us to understand what Bradley has in mind. Suppose I have a very faint organic sensation. At first, on his view, there is no question here of subject or cognitive act or cognised object. You can only say that the whole mass of my experience becomes coloured or toned in a certain way. Suppose now that I begin to attend. Then I may recognise this as a pain of a certain kind localised in a certain place in my total field of bodily feeling. It has not thereby ceased to be felt, but in addition to being felt, it has become the object of a state of attention and perhaps of a state of aversion. I may then go on to judge: 'There is something wrong in my stomach'. Here the feeling is not merely itself an object of attention and aversion; it has also become a *sign* by means of which I judge about something other than itself, viz., a part of my body.

Now Bradley holds that all the special sense-data, i.e., visual, auditory, tactual, etc., are of the nature of feelings, just as much as aches, tickles, etc. Now a feeling need not be *an object* of cognition, desire, or emotion to any subject; for there are feelings before there is any division of the contents of a psychical individual into subject and object. Nor need a feeling *fall within* a subject as part of its content. For not only are there feelings before any division into subject and object has taken place, but also, when such a division has taken place, the contents of the *object* remain feelings whatever else they may become.

Bradley would hold, then, that the sense-data of the special senses are mental in one and only one sense, viz., that they are of the nature of feelings. They are not mental in the sense that they must be part of the content of some cognising or willing *subject*. And they are not mind-dependent in the sense that they can exist only as *objects* to such a subject. When the content of a psychical individual divides into a subjective and an objectified part, certain items in the latter become the immediate objects of the former. And in that form, they are used as signs, and enable the subject to make judgments and to have thoughts which refer beyond the psychical individual in whom that subject and these immediate objects are and remain feelings. Let us call the objects of such thoughts and judgments 'mediate objects'. Now these mediate objects are not as a rule *prima facie* feelings or experiences of any kind; they include, for example, such objects as chairs, trees, human and animal bodies, atoms, light waves, and so on. But Bradley's contention seems to be that in the end mediate objects can be thought of only in terms of such entities as can be immediate objects, i.e. sense-data, images, etc., which are the contents of some psychical individual or other.

(5) All the contents of any psychical individuals are *ipso facto* contents of the Absolute, and all the contents of the Absolute are of the same intrinsic nature as the contents of a psychical individual, i.e., they are of the nature of feelings. Whether the whole content of the Absolute is completely exhausted by the contents of the various psychical individuals, sub-human, non-human, and super-human, or whether there is a part of the content of the Absolute which is not contained in any finite psychical individual, Bradley does not profess to be able to decide for certain.

(6) Lastly, he holds that the content of the Absolute forms a unity more complete and intimate than that of the contents of any of the finite individuals among whom it is distributed. We can guess at the nature of this unity only by analogy with that which we find in the experience of the most perfect psychical individuals known to us in their most exalted moments. We know that it cannot take the form of discursive thought, judgment, and reasoning, because this necessarily operates within the framework of substance and attribute, terms and relations, which we can see to be ultimately unsatisfactory. It must somehow grasp, in a single timeless synoptic intuition, all and more than all that our intellects distinguish by analysis and piece together by successive sets of judgment and inference. We cannot conceive or imagine what such an experience will be like, but, as Bradley is never tired of telling us, 'what may be and must be certainly is'.

2.5

PHILOSOPHY 1900–1950[2]

Anyone who attempts to describe in a talk of 20 minutes' duration so vast a subject as the developments in philosophy since 1900 must deliberately limit his field in some way. I shall do this by taking as my main theme that with which I am best acquainted, viz., the changes which have happened in *English* philosophy in that period. I shall refer to Continental and American philosophers only in so far as they had an important influence on the thought of their English colleagues.

Looking back to 1900, we may begin by noting one ironic fact, which should serve as a skeleton at the feast of any philosopher who might be tempted to deem his work immortal. This is the death, apparently without hope of resurrection, of a system of philosophy which had seemed not many years before to be enormously important and the last word in enlightenment. I allude to the so-called 'Synthetic Philosophy' of Herbert Spencer. His system, at the time when he was building it, had fitted like a glove the social and intellectual conditions of England. But that doctrinaire individualist and incorrigible optimist had survived into a world which was becoming steadily more collectivist and militant and emotional. When he died in 1903 in his 83rd year he was a venerated relic from an earlier age, and when his *Autobiography* appeared in 1904 admiration for his lifelong devotion to truth, as he saw it, was mingled with amusement at his queer crotchets and his child-like self-centredness.

For the professional experts, Spencer's metaphysics had received its *coup de grace* in 1899 in Ward's Gifford Lectures, *Naturalism and Agnosticism*. The relevant chapters in Sidgwick's *Lectures on the Ethics of Green, Spencer, and Martineau*, published in 1902, completed with dry humour the demolition of his ethical doctrines.

By the turn of the century the predominant – one might almost say the orthodox – philosophy in England, Scotland, and the United States had become absolute idealism in one form or another. Outside Cambridge, almost every important philosophical chair was held by a Kantian or a Hegelian. The serious influence of German idealism on English academic philosophy goes back to the publication in 1865 of Hutchison Stirling's *Secret of Hegel*. Highly important in its development had been the Oxford philosophers T.H. Green, Wm. Wallace, and Edward Caird. But the two greatest names in our period, and the culminating points in this line of thought in England, were F.H. Bradley and Bernard Bosanquet.

Bradley was a man of genius, who never held a teaching post, but whose influence was enormous. He combined a devastating gift for destructive criticism with very wide interests, a deep emotional life, and a remarkable power of constructive synthesis. He was master of a highly individual epigrammatic style. He could and did transfix opposed doctrines and their advocates with barbed phrases, which perhaps made them seem more ridiculous than they really were, but which certainly render his writings most exciting and entertaining. Bosanquet was a man of a very different type. Immensely cultivated and learned, highly virtuous and public-spirited, he was (though to say so may seem like brawling in a church) just a shade too Olympian. His literary style had been infected by his studies in Hegel, and can only be described as resembling glue thickened with sawdust.

Bradley's first work, *Ethical Studies*, had been published as far back as 1876. His *Logic* appeared in 1883, and his metaphysical masterpiece *Appearance and Reality* in 1893. Much of the philosophical discussion in England from then until 1914 was concerned with the doctrines of *Appearance and Reality*. Bradley himself was at the height of his powers and contributed frequent important articles to *Mind*. Many of these are collected in his *Essays on Truth and Reality* (1914), which contains the most mature expression of his views. Bosanquet's vast treatise on *Logic* had appeared in 1888, and his extremely Hegelian (and to English liberals highly shocking) *Philosophical Theory of the State* in 1899. His two series of Gifford Lectures, published in 1913 and 1914 under the titles *The Principle of Individuality and Value* and *The Value and Destiny of the Individual* may be described as the swansong of English absolute idealism.

Much of the development of English philosophy since 1900 can be summarised under the title 'The Decline and Fall of Absolute Idealism'. I will now try to describe some of the main chapters in that history.

The most important single influence has certainly been that of Professor G.E, Moore. I shall ignore for the present his work in Ethics, and consider only his contributions to metaphysics and epistemology. His influence has acted both directly, through his published writings, and at second hand through its effect upon other highly gifted and original thinkers, of whom the most important is Lord Russell. Moore's long series of meticulously careful essays on absolutely fundamental points began in 1903 with his *Refutation of Idealism*. Most of his papers up to 1922 were collected and published in that year under the title *Philosophical Essays*. Since then his most influential published work has been his essay *A Defence of Common Sense*, which appeared in 1925.

The other most important factor has been the work of Lord Russell. This has been concentrated on different topics at different periods. It began with work of fundamental importance on pure logic and the foundations of mathematics. In this, the main external influences came from the Italian logician Peano and the German Frege. The fruits of this period were *Principles of Mathematics* (1903) and the three vast volumes of *Principia Mathematica*, written in collaboration with Whitehead and published from 1910 to 1913. In his middle period Russell made most original and stimulating contributions to the philosophy of matter, of mind, and their mutual relations, developing a theory of neutral monism. The main results of this phase are contained in *Analysis of Mind* (1921) and *Analysis of Matter* (1927). Russell, unlike Moore, has always been interested, not only in matter as known to common sense through perception, but also in matter as conceived by the mathematical physicist. This topic is already treated elaborately in the *Analysis of Matter*, whilst Russell's latest work, *Human Knowledge, its Scope and Limits* (1948), is largely concerned with the problem of the justification of scientific theories.

Each of the topics which I have mentioned in connexion with Moore or with Russell has been developed by other important writers. The so-called 'sense-datum' or 'sensum' theory of perception received what is perhaps its final treatment in 1932 in Professor H.H. Price's book *Perception*. The connexion between the refined concepts of mathematical physics and the crude data of perception was worked out by Whitehead, with special reference to the theory of relativity, in three masterly books, The Principles of Natural Knowledge, The Concept of Nature, and The Principle of Relativity, which appeared from 1919 to 1922. The philosophy of induction was treated, in close connexion with that of probability, by Lord Keynes in his Treatise on Probability (1921), and by two men of brilliant gifts who died young, the Frenchman Nicod and the Englishman Ramsey. Mention must also be made here of W.E. Johnson, a philosopher whose influence is by no means adequately represented by his published work. The three volumes of his Logic (1921 to 1924) contain not only an elaborate treatment of the methods of demonstrative induction but also important contributions to general philosophical logic and to the analysis of the notions of cause and substance as used in physics and in psychology. Johnson's work on probability and problematic induction was to have formed the subject of a fourth volume, but age and illness prevented him from completing it. It was of great originality and first-rate importance, and Lord Keynes generously and justly acknowledged his indebtedness to it.

I suspect that some of the most important developments in inductive logic are embedded in the work of the mathematical statisticians, such as Professor R.A. Fisher. What is needed now is that they should be disentangled and analysed by a philosopher familiar enough with mathematics to understand it and when necessary to treat it with contempt. We may perhaps hope that Mr Kneale of Oxford, whose admirable work Probability and Induction (1949) shows him to have the necessary qualifications, may undertake this task. Ramsey, who could have done this admirably, devoted much of his short life to certain questions of pure logic, involved in the foundations of mathematics, which had first been raised by Russell. His contributions to philosophy were collected after his untimely death and published in 1931 under the title The Foundations of Mathematics.

In 1922 there appeared a book which has been the main source in England of a stream in philosophy which is still flowing strongly and has received tributaries from many other sources. This was Tractatus Logico-Philosophicus by the Viennese philosopher Wittgenstein, who settled in Cambridge in the middle twenties of the century and held the chair of philosophy from 1939 to 1947. He has exerted an enormous influence by his lectures, his classes, and his personality; indeed, there has been a tendency among a few of the weaker brethren and sisters who always surround a great man to convert his philosophy into a kind of mystery-religion with a cultus of the deified Founder. Other tributaries to this have come from members of the so-called 'Vienna Circle', such as Schlick and Carnap, differing in many important respects from Wittgenstein. But the general trend of the movement, which is called 'logical positivism', is to deny in principle the possibility and indeed the significance of all constructive metaphysics. It holds, further, that what appear to be moral judgments are really mere expressions or evokers of emotion or are disguised commands or admonitions. Perhaps the clearest statement and defence of the general positivist position is to be found in Professor Ayer's *Language, Truth, and Logic* (1936) and his *Foundations of Empirical Knowledge* (1940). The best account of the application to ethics is contained in *Ethics and Language* (1940) by an American writer, Mr. Stevenson. I think it may fairly be said that logical positivism is as much the predominant school of thought at the end of our period as was Spencer's philosophy of evolution in the 1880s and absolute idealism in the early 1900s.

Although the main current in philosophy during the period has been away from constructive metaphysics, and although that tendency has been quickened and supplied with a theoretical basis in recent times in the so-called 'verification-principle', the last 25 years have witnessed at least three speculative systems on the grand scale in England. Their authors are McTaggart, Alexander, and Whitehead.

McTaggart started as a professed Hegelian, and three of the first four of his published works are interpretations of Hegel or developments of certain philosophical problems on what he regarded as Hegelian lines. But, in his exquisitely lucid and concise style and his fondness for sharp distinctions and clear-cut alternatives, McTaggart was as un-Hegelian as any man could be. When he came to construct his own system he abandoned Hegelian concepts and the dialectical method and used ordinary straight-forward deduction. His *Nature of Existence* (Vol. I published in 1921 and Vol. II posthumously in 1927) seems to me to owe much more to Leibniz than to Hegel. It is certainly a work of genius of the most original and imposing kind, leading by sustained flights of deductive argument from extremely abstract premisses to highly startling and concrete conclusions. As a piece of pure virtuosity, it is unique, but its arguments have produced no conviction and I believe them to be capable of complete refutation.

Both Alexander and Whitehead have been greatly influenced in certain respects by the French philosopher Bergson, whose *Évolution Créatrice* appeared in 1907. Neither of them attempted to proceed by way of deduction, but both claimed to provide a synoptic view of reality as a whole. Alexander's *Space, Time, and Deity* is a most impressive book, which strives to combine an ultra-realistic view of cognition with a thorough-going application of the notion of emergent evolution. It attracted and deserved great attention when it appeared in 1920. Since then it seems to have fallen into an oblivion from which I hope it will someday emergently evolve. Of Whitehead's *Process and Reality* (1929), I can only say that persons whose opinion I respect regard it as an epoch-making book, that from what I know of Whitehead himself and his other works I think that they may well be right, but that for my part I must confess that much of it is unintelligible to me.

Before drawing to a close I must revert for a moment to one subject, viz., ethics, which I have already touched upon in connexion with logical positivism. At the beginning of our period in 1903, Moore published his *Principia Ethica* which became and long remained the centre of ethical discussion. Thereafter the torch passed from Cambridge to Oxford. The two most important works in later years have been *The Right and the Good* (1930) and *Foundations of Ethics* (1939). In them, Sir David Ross has stated and defended with great ability an improved form of intuitionism.

It is time for me to bring my talk to an end. To make prophecies about the future developments of philosophy would at any time be a gratuitous piece of folly. It would be more than usually so at a time when a few well-directed atomic bombs may at no distant date eliminate urban civilisation in this country, or the setting up of a communist or fascist régime may drive free critical thought underground for centuries. All that I will venture to say is that, if I know anything of human nature, the present eclipse of speculative metaphysics is a purely temporary phenomenon. I suspect that the urge to philosophical speculation is innate in the human mind, and that, however much you may expel it with a positivist fork, it will return. I should hardly expect, however, to see further attempts at purely or mainly deductive systems, such as Spinoza's or McTaggart's, for any properly trained logician now knows too much about the nature of a deductive system to imagine that success along those lines is possible. On the other hand, I should not be surprised to see a revival, in some modified form, of absolute idealism. I believe that it expresses *one* of the fundamental ways in which men's minds work. And I am sure that the works of Kant and of Bradley, for example, contain much of permanent value which is now ignored or misunderstood simply because it is clothed in a dress which has become unfashionable.

2.6

BERTRAND RUSSELL'S 90TH BIRTHDAY

Unfortunately, both the Master and the Vice-Master are unavoidably absent tonight, and so I have been asked to propose the toast of Bertrand Russell on the occasion of his 90th Birthday. I am very glad to have the honour of doing this, however much I may regret that the talk has not fallen into abler hands. I owe a great deal to Russell and feel deeply grateful to him both for his personal kindness to me when I was a young man and for the immense profit which I have gained from his teaching and from his writings on logic and philosophy. It may not be out of place to say a few words about this personal debt before passing to the wider aspects of Russell's life and achievements.

Russell's book *The Principles of Mathematics, Vol. I* was published in 1903, while I was at school. It happened that my mathematical master at Dulwich, the late Mr. F.W. Russell (of this College), had bought and read it. Knowing that I was beginning to be interested in philosophy, he gave me his copy in 1905, and I then tried to read it. Much of it was of course wholly beyond me at the time, but, when I came up to Trinity in October 1906, I found that it was being eagerly discussed by many of the younger fellows. It is an extraordinarily exciting book, dealing *inter alia* with some topics which Russell hardly touched upon in his later works, and, when I came to read it carefully and with understanding, I derived immense stimulation and enlightenment from it.

Russell himself was away from Cambridge during my time as an undergraduate (1906–1909). He had gained a Fellowship under the then title (α) in the election of 1895. That Fellowship expired in 1901 after the normal period of six years. It required neither residence nor research, and Russell had left Cambridge and had embarked on the first stage of what was to prove a long and variegated matrimonial career. But in 1910, a special Lectureship in Logic and Philosophy was created for him in the College, and he returned in the October of that year to Trinity as Lecturer and member of the High Table and with the right to rooms in College, though without a Fellowship. I was then working on my Fellowship dissertation. I attended Russell's lectures, saw a good deal of him, and received constant help and stimulation from him in my work. I believe (though I am not quite certain) that he was one of the examiners of my thesis in the election of 1911, when I first became a Fellow of the College. He had rooms on the north side of Nevile's Court, and I have spent many delightful hours there, fascinated by his conversation, with its wit and humour and its wide range of topics.

I had already left Cambridge to take up a minor post in St. Andrews at the time when I was elected to my Fellowship, and I did not return into residence. But I used to spend six weeks or so in Trinity during each Long Vacation until the outbreak of war in 1914, and during those periods I saw much of Russell. I can well remember the Long Vacation of 1914 in this connexion. Maynard Keynes had by then got the proofs of his *Treatise on Probability*, and had lent them to Russell for his critical comments. Russell and I used to go over those proofs together in Russell's rooms and to discuss them, and we were doing this up to that fatal and accursed 4th of August, when war was declared. Keynes was reft away to London (if I am not mistaken on the back of A.V. Hill's motor bicycle) to take care of the nation's war finances, and the lights of European civilisation went out. The book on Probability remained in cold storage until 1921.

I pass now from personal reminiscence to the complex theme of Russell's connexions and disconnexions with the College. As I have already mentioned, he had held a Fellowship under Title (α) from 1895 to 1901, and had been appointed in 1910 by the Council to a specially created College Lectureship in Logic and Philosophy of Mathematics, without a Fellowship, for a period of five years. Early in 1915 the Council, in view of the fact that this Lectureship would automatically lapse in October, decided to elect Russell to a Fellowship under the then title (ζ) – corresponding to the present Title B – as from October 1915. This was the prelude to a complicated drama of strife between the College, as represented by its then Council, and Russell. For a most admirably full, clear, and fair account of it, I would refer you to Hardy's brilliant pamphlet, *Bertrand Russell and Trinity*, privately printed in 1942.

Put briefly, the essential facts are these. Russell had publicly taken a very strong line against the war from its beginning. In May 1915, he applied to the Council for leave of absence for the following Michaelmas and Lent terms, i.e. the first two terms of his tenure of the proposed Fellowship. The Council replied that, if he should be elected to the proposed Fellowship under title (ζ), leave of absence would be granted if and only if it were for the purpose of work on the subject for research in which the Fellowship was to be awarded, viz., the systematic study of philosophy and mathematics. Russell, on the other hand, intended to devote the period to political activity in opposition to the war. He therefore wrote to the Council, making a counter-proposal. This was that the decision to elect him to a Fellowship should be rescinded, and that, instead, his Lectureship should be renewed for a further period of five years from October 1915, and that he should be granted leave of absence for the ensuing Michaelmas and Lent Terms. This proposal was accepted by the Council on May 28th, 1915.

So matters stood until June 1916, when Russell was charged at the Mansion House before the Lord Mayor of London with making, in a printed publication, 'statements liable to prejudice the recruiting and discipline of H.M.'s forces'. The statement in question referred to the treatment of a certain Mr. Everett, a conscientious objector. The whole affair appears in retrospect to be a storm in a teacup, but Russell was found guilty and fined £100, and this sentence was confirmed on appeal on 29 June 1916.

The College Council lost no time in going into action. On 11 July, they decided unanimously to deprive Russell of his Lectureship, on the ground that he had been convicted of an offence under the Defence of the Realm Act. Shortly afterwards Russell, in protest, took his name off the books of the College.

There is no question that Council acted within its rights. But most of the younger Fellows, and some of the older ones too – notably James Ward – felt that the grounds for dismissal were quite inadequate, and that the Council's action was discreditable to an institution which should stand up for freedom of thought and speech at all times, and especially when they are threatened, as they always are in time of war. Many of the Fellows were, of course, away on war-service of one kind or another, but no less than 22 out of a total of 58 signed a letter of protest to the Council. Among the signatories who are still Fellows of the College were Littlewood, Hollond, Simpson, Gow, Butler, Adrian, and myself. Dennis Robertson's signature could not be obtained in time, owing to his absence in the East on military service. This memorial was submitted in the autumn of 1916. The signatories, whilst expressing their dissatisfaction with the Council's dismissal of Russell, stated that they did not intend to take any action so long as the war should last.

Unfortunately, in February 1918, Russell committed a blazing indiscretion, which must have seemed to many who had hitherto been sympathetic to him to provide a kind of retrospective justification for the Council's action in 1916. The United States had at long last entered the war on the side of England and her allies, at a time when we were nearly at our last gasp both financially and militarily. Russell signalised the occasion by publishing an extremely offensive sentence to the effect that the American army, whatever its prowess against the enemy might prove to be, would be useful for intimidating strikers in England and France, an occupation to which it was accustomed at home. He was (quite deservedly, in my opinion,) prosecuted and sentenced to 6 months' imprisonment. On appeal this was altered from the second to the first division, and Russell spent a not uncomfortable half-year in Brixton Prison, during which he wrote his *Introduction to Mathematical Philosophy*.

In November 1918, Germany and her allies surrendered unconditionally. The world had been 'made safe for democracy', though it was soon to become apparent that democracy was not safe for the world. By the latter part of 1919, most of the absent Fellows had returned, and action began to be taken on the question of the Council's dismissal of Russell. The form that it eventually took was a long memorial to the Council, asking that Russell should be invited to return to the College. The letter was drawn up with consummate tact, skill, and diplomacy by Hollond, with the object of enabling the Council to retreat without loss of face and of re-establishing so far as possible the shattered unity of the Society. It was signed by 27 of the 58 Fellows, and 5 others, who preferred not to sign, sent personal letters to the Master in support. Of these 32 Fellows, 10 are still with us, viz., Littlewood,

Hollond, Simpson, Butler, Adrian, Dennis Robertson, Burnaby, Taylor, Nicholas, and Southwell. Gow and I, who had signed the original protest, had ceased at the time to be Fellows.

The memorial was considered by the Council on 28 November 1919, and on 12 December, of that year the Council decided by a majority to offer to Russell a lectureship in Logic and the Principles of Mathematics for 5 years from 1 July 1920. On 16 January 1920, the Master was able to announce Russell's acceptance.

One might have hoped that a most disagreeable incident had now closed, with peace restored all round and honour satisfied. But, although there was not and never has been any further quarrel between Russell and the College, a set of unfortunate circumstances prevented this from being made obvious to the world at large. Russell in fact, though his own action, never took up the lectureship which the College had offered and he had accepted. In the first place, in July 1920, just as his tenure was to have begun, he applied for leave of absence for the academic year of 1920–1921. This was granted, and he spent that period travelling and lecturing in China. Then, on 14 January 1921, he resigned the lectureship, and his resignation was accepted. It was motived, not by any difference with the College, but by the fact that he was about to be divorced and to re-marry, and that he feared that this might embarrass his supporters among the Fellows, and arouse new dissensions.

That the breach really had been healed is shown by the fact that in 1925 the Council invited Russell to give the Tarner Lectures, and that he accepted. The substance of those lectures was published in 1927 under the title *The Analysis of Matter*, and forms one of Russell's major contributions to philosophy.

Hardy's pamphlet of 1942 ends with the following sentence: 'All the world knows that there was a quarrel between the College and one of its most famous members: could it not be told, in language which leaves no possibility of misunderstanding, that the quarrel has since been healed?' Hardy's question did not long await a satisfactory answer. On 3 December 1943, the Council unanimously resolved to offer a Fellowship under Title B to Russell. He was informed that neither residence nor lecturing would be required of him, though the College would welcome it if he were inclined to lecture, and would pay a fee to him for so doing. Russell had been in the United States for a long period, which was then ending somewhat stormily, and was planning to return to England in the summer of 1944. He cabled his acceptance, and was duly elected on 14th January, and admitted on 10th October of that year. He was invited by the College to give lectures during the academic years 1944–1945, 1945–1946, and 1946–1947, at a stipend of £300 for each year. He accepted, and his lectures attracted huge audiences. During part of this period, Russell was living in London and travelling to Cambridge, and during part of it, he was living in Cambridge, at one time in his own house and later in College. For a time in 1946, when I was away for some eight months in Sweden, he occupied my rooms, which may thus fairly be described, not only as Newton's, but also as Russell's rooms. It was a great pleasure to all of us to have him here once more, full of vigour, making many new friends among the younger Fellows, and adding enormously by his good company and his brilliant conversation to the pleasure of dining in Hall and frequenting the Parlour.

It should be noted that it was Trevelyan,[3] then master, who was the initiator and forwarder of this complete, final, and public reconciliation. As an undergraduate, he had been a friend and younger contemporary of Russell's at Trinity, and I suppose that he must now be almost the only man living of whom that can be said.

To complete this account of Russell's relations with the College, I need add only that, when the tenure of his Title B Fellowship was about to end in 1948, the Council prolonged it until Michaelmas 1949. When Russell vacated the prolonged Fellowship on 30th September of that year, he entered the haven which all good Fellows of Trinity hope to attain, viz., a Fellowship under title E. It is under that Title that he is now one of us for the rest of his life.

I hope I have not taken up too much time on the topic of Russell and the College. This is a domestic occasion and I believe that some of the older Fellows may like to be reminded, and many of the younger may like to be informed, of the details of a very tangled and much-misunderstood tale. I turn now to the subject of our Toast, and I will try to be reasonably brief.

Being a Fellow of Trinity is a healthy occupation, but not many even of us reach our 90th birthday. In my memory, only two beside Russell have done so, viz., Tennant and Lenox-Conyngham. Mere length of days is not a thing to be wished for; it is too often 'but labour and sorrow'. But it happens that each of these nonagenarian Fellows was in the enjoyment of good health and full of mental vigour at the time of his birthday, and in such cases, we can rejoice, though with trembling.

What an astonishing career Russell has had! And what energy and enthusiasm he has shown and still continues to show! In the purely intellectual sphere, his contributions to logic and the philosophy of mathematics would be admitted by all competent judges to have been epoch-making. His contributions to theory of knowledge and to what (since I am told it is no longer a 'dirty' word) I may call 'metaphysics', for example, his *Analysis of Mind*, his *Analysis of Matter*, and his *Inquiry into Meaning and Truth* are at the moment out of the latest philosophical fashion. They are often referred to somewhat slightingly by what I may describe as the 'Wittgersnappers'. For my own part, I have found them extraordinarily suggestive and stimulating, and I shall be much surprised if many of those scornful young men will have been found to have accomplished in their prime anything comparable in value to some things which Russell has written in his old age. To the critical study of the history of philosophy, Russell made one major contribution quite early in his career, viz., *The Philosophy of Leibniz* (1900). His other contribution, *A History of Western Philosophy* (1944), is an amazingly vigorous and readable work, especially when one remembers that the author was over 70 when he wrote it. Its qualities have made it a 'best-seller', and it has in abundant measure the defects of those qualities. It is full of personal and political prejudice, and is often grossly unfair and misleading in its dealings with philosophers whom Russell dislikes. The accounts, for example, of the philosophy of Aristotle and Kant, I can only describe as disgraceful. But I know of no one else who could have written so good a bad book on the topic.

His philosophical activities have, of course, been only one side of Russell's life. He has been a passionate advocate of causes which have been at the time unpopular, and he has not been content with supporting them in speech and writing, but has never hesitated to descend into the arena of practical agitation. Before 1914, he was an impassioned supporter of women's suffrage; during the war of 1914–1918 he was (as we have seen) vehemently active in opposition to current opinions and sentiments; and since the end of the Second World War, he has devoted himself to the advocacy by speech, writing, and action, of unilateral atomic disarmament on the part of this country.

As to women's suffrage, most people would now agree that he was right. As to our entry into the First World War and its continuance to the bitter end, no one who realises the disastrous consequences to England in particular and Western civilisation in general would care to say with confidence that he was wrong. (On the other hand, since no one can form any reasonable conjecture as to the consequences which would have followed alternative courses of action in the situation which faced us in 1914–1918, it is no less impossible to say with confidence that he was right.) As to the policy which he is now advocating in the desperate situation in which the world now finds itself, the question is too contemporary, too topical, and too tragical to be discussed here and now.

In connexion with these practical concerns, Russell has written many books on social, political, and moral topics. He became deeply interested in the education of children, and for a time ran a school in which the pupils were brought up on the principles which he advocated. I do not know whether they grew up better or worse than, or very much the same as, those trained on more conventional lines. Since most of them must have been the children of non-typical parents and have come from non-typical homes, comparison, even if it were possible, would be uninformative. For my own part, I suspect that educationists enormously exaggerate the differences resulting from different forms of education. Lastly, in 1929, Russell published a famous book entitled *Marriage and Morals*. Of this, it can at least be said that it is based on a wealth of matrimonial experience which few of us can equal, and which only the monarch who founded this College and the fortunes of the Russell family has surpassed.

In his 90 years, Russell has known almost everyone of interest; has travelled very widely, has lived in China and in the United States; and, when over 70, has escaped from a wrecked aeroplane, and, after swimming for some 20 minutes[4] in not very genial waters of Oslo Fjord, was picked up little the worse for the experience. Surely he, if anyone, could re-echo the last words of Lady Mary Wortley Montagu: 'It has all been *most* interesting!'.

I ask you now to drink to the health and happiness of Bertrand, third Earl Russell, one of the greatest of our living contemporaries and one of the most shining ornaments of the College.

2.7

FRANCIS BACON (1561–1626)

On 5 October 1926, the University of Cambridge celebrated the 300th anniversary of the death of Francis Bacon, one of the most distinguished of its sons. It fell to me to deliver the public lecture in the Senate House, which was an item in the programme. I chose then to confine myself to trying to explain and appraise Bacon's contributions to the logic and methodology of scientific discovery and invention, and his prophecies of the technological revolution to which the application of those methods would give rise. What I had to say on that topic is available in print to anyone whom it may interest, and I have seen no reason to modify my published views. Tonight, therefore, when we are commemorating the 400th anniversary of his birth, I shall concentrate on his public life, and only at the end of my lecture shall I make a brief reference to what was in fact his chief claim to count as a mastermind.

Francis Bacon was born on 22 January 1561, at York House near Charing Cross, the official residence of his father Sir Nicholas Bacon, Lord Keeper under Queen Elizabeth I. The Bacons were an East Anglian family who had, like their relations-in-law the Cecils, by their own great abilities, by fortunate marriages, and by skilful hedging in difficult times, risen on the ruin of the monasteries to wealth and influence. The first known member of the family is Robert Bacon of Brickstone, Suffolk, who had been sheep-reeve to the immensely wealthy abbey of Bury St. Edmunds, and had no doubt managed to glean a little wool for himself. He married Isabella Cage, daughter of John Cage of Pakenham. Nicholas Bacon, Francis' father, was their second son.

Nicholas was born in 1509, went up to Corpus Christi College, Cambridge, in 1523, and graduated in 1527. Cambridge was then, and for some time afterwards, the training ground for scions of the Tudor 'establishment'. He then studied law at Gray's Inn, becoming an 'ancient' in 1536. He was plainly a very able man, comparable with his eminent colleague and brother-in-law William Cecil, first Lord Burghley, who had come from similar origins and had undergone similar training. Persons in their position had to tread warily; they might end on the scaffold, but, if they managed to keep their heads both literally and metaphorically, they had many opportunities for profitable pickings in the spoil of the monasteries. Nicholas secured lands in Herts, Norfolk, Wilts, and Hants, which had belonged to the abbeys of St. Albans, Walsingham, and Thetford. In 1550, he bought the estate of Gorhambury, close to St. Albans. He began to build Gorhambury House, which Francis eventually inherited and beautified. It was completed in 1568, and Queen Elizabeth often visited him there. He was a man of great moderation in all things, and the motto which he had written up over the entrance to the hall was *Mediocria firma*. Francis, after his fall, may well have contemplated his father's motto rather wistfully.

Sir Nicholas married twice. He had six children by his first wife. Francis was the younger of the two children (both sons) of his second marriage. Their mother was Ann Cooke, born 1528 and died 1610, second daughter of Sir Anthony Cooke of Gidea Hall in Essex. Cooke was a distinguished scholar and had been tutor to Edward VI. His daughters were brought up to be excellent classical scholars. Lady Bacon could and did correspond in Latin and in Greek with learned men. Her elder and no less accomplished sister Mildred became the second wife of William Cecil, first Lord Burghley. So Burghley was Francis' maternal uncle by marriage, and Burghley's son, Robert Cecil, afterwards first Earl of Salisbury was his first cousin. He thus started life with relatives who were highly influential, but might easily prove (as they did) unwilling to advance a kinsman who might become a serious rival.

Lady Bacon became a formidable old woman in her widowhood. She favoured Puritanism, both in theology and in morals, and she bombarded her two sons with admonitory letters. Both of them were somewhat feckless in money matters, and Francis had a strain of magnificence and carelessness which got him into debt and made him, as a young man, a source of considerable worry and expense to his mother. In the latter part of her life, she became very peculiar indeed, and Goodman says of her that 'she was little better than frantic in her old age'. It is of some interest to note that her elder son, Anthony, was lame from birth and a lifelong invalid, whilst her sister's son, Robert Cecil, was a hunchback. The Cooke genes certainly contributed brains, but one wonders whether they may not also have carried a certain bodily weakness with them.

However that may be, Francis had no obvious bodily defects. He is described by Evelyn as of middling height, with a spacious and open forehead and lively pleasing eyes. Harvey told Aubrey that they reminded him of the eyes of a viper. He lived to the age of 65, his death may fairly be counted as due to a combination of accidents, and he showed throughout life immense powers of work, both professional and purely intellectual. But he was plainly to some extent a valetudinarian. Dr Rawley, his chaplain, who had lived in his household for many years and had known him intimately, tells the following curious story. At every eclipse of the moon Bacon (whether aware of what was happening or not) would be seized with a sudden fit of fainting, which would cease, without leaving any ill effect, as soon as the eclipse ended. Aubrey, too, relates that Bacon once fell down in a swoon while walking in Sir John Danvers' garden at Chelsea, and had to be picked up and revived by Lady Danvers.

Bacon's tastes and inclinations, like those of his master James I, were homosexual. This is explicitly stated by Aubrey. Aubrey, no doubt, was an old gossip. But it is confirmed by Arthur Wilson, who had good opportunities for observation, and it is implied by remarks in letters from their mother to Anthony and to Francis. Just as much of the extravagance and scandal in James I's court was due to the misbehaviour of his male favourites, such as Carr and Villiers, so too did a good many of Bacon's troubles spring from the venality and riotousness of domestics who were also boy-friends, such as the Welshmen 'Jones' and 'Enny', against whom Lady Bacon inveighs in her letters. These physically tough but morally frail young men imitated in their humbler sphere James's magnificent Somersets and Buckinghams.

Anthony and Francis were together entered Trinity College, Cambridge, on 5 April 1573, and were matriculated on 10th June, of that year. Francis was then only 12 and Anthony only 15, but there was nothing unusual in this. They shared rooms in College, and their Tutor was Whitgift, Master of Trinity and later Archbishop of Canterbury. They remained on the books until 1575. But the studies of Cambridge undergraduates then were always liable to be interrupted, as were Newton's later, by outbreaks of plague in the insanitary town. Such an interruption took place from August 1574 to March 1575. So Cambridge in general and Trinity in particular cannot lay claim to any large share in Bacon's education, though he was throughout his life a loyal son of his University and his College.

At the age of 16, Francis was sent by his father to Paris, where he lived at the house of the English ambassador, Sir Amias Paulet. The ambassador was very favourably impressed with him, and during Bacon's residence in Paris sent him over to England with a commission to Queen Elizabeth which needed secrecy and dispatch. He acquitted himself well in this and returned to France to continue his continental travels. He had been known to the Queen since his early boyhood. She used to chat with him and to call him 'her young Lord Keeper'.

Bacon's father died in 1579 at the age of 70 after a short illness, through a chill contracted by falling asleep in a draught from an open window. His valet had been too respectful either to shut the window or to awaken his master. So keeping the servants too much in their place was as fatal to the father as too great familiarity with them was to be to the son. Sir Nicholas had intended to set aside a considerable sum of money to buy an estate for Francis, but his death prevented this. The elder brother Anthony inherited most of the landed property, and Gorhambury was left to Lady Bacon for life. Francis got only a small sum of money and had to set about earning a living.

He had been admitted at his father's Inn of Court, Gray's Inn, in 1576, *de societate magistrorum*. In 1582, he was admitted as an 'utter barrister', and in 1586 as a bencher of that Inn. He set himself to study law and became a highly accomplished lawyer. But his tastes were extravagant and his aims were high, so he very naturally turned to his uncle, William Cecil, Elizabeth's chief minister, in the hope of official patronage.

In his application to Burghley, Bacon stated that his private ambitions were moderate, but he had 'taken all philosophy for his province', and that he wanted some office which would give him leisure and sufficient income to pursue his philosophical studies. All that Burghley did for his nephew was to procure for him in 1589 the reversion to the office of Registrar to the Star Chamber. The salary would be considerable, about £1,600 a year, but it did not in fact come into Bacon's possession until 20 years later. We must remember that Burghley had his own son Robert to provide for; that, quite apart from parental predilections, Robert was a very able man, and that Burghley might well hesitate to introduce a potential cuckoo into the nest in the person of his clever and highly insinuating nephew Francis. Be that as it may, Burghley's lack of forthcomingness was the prelude to that connexion of Francis Bacon with the Earl of Essex, which has done no good to his reputation.

Robert Devereux, second Earl of Essex, was born in 1567. He belonged to the old nobility and had estates in various parts of England and Wales, but he was by no means wealthy for his station in life. Like Bacon, he had been an undergraduate at Trinity College, Cambridge. He was well educated and capable of appreciating the society of learned men, of poets, and of artists. In many ways, he was a most attractive young man, extremely good-looking, heroically courageous in face of personal danger, kindly to his servants and dependents, faithful and assiduous to help his friends, and openly and honourably vehement against his enemies. He was and remained, however, singularly headstrong and imprudently outspoken, with none of those powers of holding his tongue, saying less than he thought, dissimulation, and simulation, which that wise youth Francis so persuasively preached and, up to a point successfully practised. Elizabeth was highly susceptible to such charms as distinguished Essex, and by 1587, when he was 20 and she 53, had completely fallen for him. But she, unlike her cousin and successor James in his later years, never allowed her favourites to dictate her policy, and was extremely resentful of anything on their part which might seem to betray a wish to do so.

Essex had been brought up under Burghley's guardianship. But, in spite of or perhaps because of this, there was between them something more than the tension which is usual between gifted and impatient youth and cautious conservative old-age. Francis Bacon began to turn his eyes on Essex as a possible rival at court to the influence of the Cecils, in the early 1590s when he was himself in his early thirties. To use his own words, he 'applied himself to Essex in a manner which I think happeneth rarely among men'.

At this point, Francis' elder brother Anthony comes on the scene and begins to play an important part. Anthony was some two years older than Francis. If not a universal genius like his younger brother, he was a man of exceptional industry and ability, especially in matters of foreign politics. Late in 1579, when was 21, he had set out, at Burghley's suggestion, on a continental tour in search of political intelligence. At that time he was on good terms with his uncle and was writing affectionate letters to him. As it turned out, he was continuously abroad for the next 12 years.

During that period he lived successively in Paris, in Bourges, in Geneva (where he Lodged with Theodore Beza, whom he induced to hand over the Codex Bezae to Cambridge University), in Bordeaux, in Béarn (where he met Henry of Navarre), and finally in Montauban (where he spent five years in close touch with Henry's Protestant advisers). Both his mother and his brother had disapproved of his long absence, which had involved Lady Bacon in considerable expense. But it had enabled him to make very useful contacts with influential foreign statesmen and their underlings, and had given him an unrivalled first-hand knowledge of foreign affairs. He returned to England, in very poor health, at the end of 1591. In February 1593, he was elected to the House of Commons as a member for Wallingford. Francis had already been an MP since 1586 in successive parliaments as a member for Taunton and for Liverpool. In the Parliament of 1593, he sat for Middlesex.

Anthony, like Francis, sought preferment from his uncle Burghley. He was even less successful, for he did not secure even a reversion, and he was highly indignant with the Cecils. Early in 1593, probably through Francis' influence, Anthony was brought into Essex's service and became a member of his household. At the same time, Francis introduced Phelipps, a skilled intelligence agent and decipherer. The idea was to make Essex and his outfit a serious rival to the Cecils and theirs, as a reliable source of foreign intelligence for the Queen. This scheme worked at first, in as much as Essex was appointed to the Privy Council in 1593 and his opinions on foreign affairs were taken seriously by Elizabeth.

We come now to the tangled affair of the Attorney-Generalship. In 1593, this was about to fall vacant. Francis wanted it, and Essex was willing to back his claims to the utmost with the Queen. His rival for the post was Edward Coke, another old Trinity man. Coke showed himself throughout his long life to be an odious person, a bully (though by no means a coward), and a skinflint, overbearing in prosperity and cringing in adversity. But he was already eminent as a common lawyer and was to become supremely so, and he was eight years older than Bacon. There could be no question that he was professionally much the stronger candidate, and he was backed by the Cecils. On the other hand, Bacon was certainly not a mere speculative windbag unfit for the office, as his cousin Robert took the opportunity to insinuate to the Queen.

Essex pressed Bacon's suit in season and out of season, used very intemperate language to and about the Cecils, and obviously made himself a nuisance and the name of Bacon a bore to the Queen. Just at this time, Bacon got himself into Elizabeth's bad books by a speech which he made in the House of Commons. Parliament had agreed to grant the Queen three subsidies, to pay for national expenditure which could not be met out of the hereditary revenues of the crown. Burghley proposed that this gift should be collected in four years. Bacon made an eloquent speech, in which he alleged that this would inflict great hardships, and proposed a period of six years instead. In the course of his speech, he said: 'The gentlemen must sell their plate, and farmers their brass pots, ere this be paid'. In this matter, the House of Commons decided unanimously against Bacon's proposal, so no harm was in fact done to the Queen's interests. But she was furious with Bacon. There seems no reason to doubt that his action in the matter was conscientious, and, so far as is known, he never apologised to the Queen for it. It wrecked any chance that he might have had of the Attorney-Generalship, and taught Bacon a lesson which he never forgot. To the best of my belief, he never again publicly advocated a measure that was likely to be unpopular with the powers that be.

Eventually, Coke was appointed, and Essex accepted the *fait accompli*. He now badgered the Queen to make Bacon her *Solicitor-General*, and in this, he was supported by the Cecils. That Essex's well-meant importunity was not likely to be helpful with a masterful woman like Elizabeth, is well shown by the fact that on one occasion she interrupted his pleadings for Bacon by boxing his ears and telling him to go to bed till he could find something else to talk about. She then adopted her favourite policy of shilly-shallying, and it was not until a year and a half later that she filled the office by appointing Serjeant Fleming. The plain fact is that Essex had made the very name of Bacon a weariness to the Queen, that Bacon had personally offended her by his speech in Parliament, and that on grounds of general policy she was averse to being surrounded with servants who might be Essex's creatures.

Essex himself was well aware that Bacon had suffered in the Queen's eyes by his attempted advocacy. With very great generosity he compensated Bacon by the gift of an estate, viz., Twickenham Park and its garden of Paradise. Years afterwards Bacon sold this for £1,800, and that was considered to be a low price. So it was a handsome gift. In view of what was soon to happen, the terms of Bacon's acceptance are well worth noting. He wrote that he accepted the estate subject to the old feudal proviso 'with a saving of faith to the King and his other lords'. And in another letter, he said: 'I reckon myself as a common; and so much as is *lawful to be enclosed* of a common, so much your lordship shall be sure to have'. Essex thus had fair warning that Bacon was not his for better or for worse and that Bacon would have no hesitation in abandoning him if he were to engage in courses that were or appeared to be disloyal.

In the autumn of 1596, Essex returned to London in triumph from a brilliant victory over the Spaniards at Cadiz. He was then at the height of his career. He became and remained for the rest of his life, the darling of the London mob, and he was for the moment on his best behaviour with the Queen. Bacon took the opportunity to write to him an elaborate letter, containing a most acute diagnosis of the main dangers of his position and extremely wise advice as to how he should behave towards Elizabeth. He pointed out that nothing could be more alarming to her than the thought of Essex as a hero with the populace, dependent on his reputation as a soldier, and in financially embarrassed circumstances which he might be suspected of aiming to mend by ambitious military schemes. Essex, while *in fact* keeping his favour with the mob, should (Bacon advised) take every opportunity to inveigh against popularity when talking to the Queen. He should keep the *substance* of his control over military affairs, but should avoid all appearance of it by ceasing to ask for military offices and instead taking remunerative civil ones. Bacon accompanied this general advice with a good deal of characteristically Baconian detail about the particular arts, tricks, and subterfuges which Essex should employ in his conversations with Elizabeth.

All this was excellent advice in its way and might have been useful if only Essex had been a man more or less like Bacon. As things were, there was no hope of Essex consistently acting on it, for it was in some respects above his head and in others beneath his honour.

In the spring of 1597, Bacon, always short of money, was seeking the hand of a wealthy widow, Lady Hatton. He offered at that time to do a deal with Egerton, the Lord Keeper. Bacon proposed to give up, to Egerton's son, his reversion to the Clerkship of the Star Chamber, if Egerton would secure for Bacon the Mastership of the Rolls. Nothing came of this. And, although Essex did everything in his power to secure Lady Hatton for Bacon, she chose to marry his rival Coke instead. This was a lucky escape for Bacon, for, as Macaulay puts it, 'she made Coke as unhappy as he deserved to be'. But it left him in his financial straits, and in the autumn of 1598, he was actually arrested for debt, though he was not long detained.

By this time Essex was nearing the end of his tether. He had ignored Bacon's warnings and neglected his advice, and he was now to pay the penalty. In 1595, an extremely dangerous rebellion had broken out in Ireland under the Earl of Tyrone. Four years later, after many quarrels and reconciliations with Elizabeth, Essex was sent as commander of an English army to crush the rising. Though personally as brave as a lion, he was utterly incompetent as a strategist, as an administrator, and as a statesman. After wasting much time and manpower and money in futile marchings and counter-marchings, he had a meeting with Tyrone; made on his own authority a ludicrous truce with him, and then suddenly returned against orders to England. The Queen was, most justifiably, furious with him, and he was put under arrest and subjected to an informal trial at which Bacon appeared against him as Queen's counsel. On 20 July 1600, shortly after this, Bacon wrote to Essex as follows: '...Though I confess that I love some *things*—as the Queen's service,..., her honour, her favour, the good of my country, and the like—' (better), 'yet I love few *persons* better than yourself, both for gratitude's sake and for your own virtues, which cannot hurt but by accident or abuse'.

Shortly before this a characteristically Baconian bit of over-clever mystification had occurred. At his brother Anthony's suggestion, Francis drew up a *pretended* correspondence between Essex and Anthony, writing letters in the character and style of each, addressed to the other. Here the fictitious 'Anthony' bids Essex not to despair but to await patiently a change of fortune, while the fictitious 'Essex' acclaims Anthony as the most devoted of his friends. This bogus correspondence was to be laid before the Queen as genuine.

The end of Essex's tragi-comedy came in 1601. Elizabeth had granted to him for a term of years the monopoly of the sale of sweet wines, and this was an important source of income to him. The grant now expired. Essex sued for its renewal, Elizabeth procrastinated and at length declined. The topic of monopolies in general had become a very delicate one, and Parliament had petitioned the Queen against the abuses of them. Essex was in despair, and he was surrounded by hot-livered and bone-headed military comrades. In 1601, they made, with his connivance, a futile attempt to rouse the city mob, with the intention of seizing control of the Queen's person and getting rid of her present advisers and in particular Robert Cecil, who had succeeded to his father's office on the latter's death in 1598. The attempt was a fiasco, and Essex was arrested and arraigned for high treason.

The trial was conducted by Coke, as Attorney-General, with Bacon as Queen's counsel. Coke was, as usual, scurrilous and brutal to the accused, whilst Bacon was polite and moderate in tone. But, if he avoided the bludgeon, he plied the stiletto very effectively and did all that he could to emphasise Essex's offence. There was in fact no doubt of his guilt, and no one can blame Elizabeth for at length and with great reluctance ordering his execution. But he had been and he remained so popular, and there had been so much sentiment about him, that the government decided to defend their action in a public pronouncement. Bacon was requested or commanded to draw up this document, but it was subjected to many alterations by others, and it is impossible to say how much of it in its final form was written by him. It appeared in 1601 under the title: 'A declaration of the Practices and Treasons... by Robert, late Earl of Essex'. Naturally, no punches were pulled in it.

Bacon's part in the authorship of this manifesto made him unpopular at the time, and, in view of his personal obligations to Essex, the whole incident has left a rather sour taste in the mouth of posterity. In 1604, he published an elaborate apology for his conduct, entitled: 'Sir Francis Bacon, his Apology in certain Imputations concerning the late Earl of Essex', which puts as good a face on his conduct as a skilled advocate and a master of English prose can do.

The angel of death was busy at the turn of the century in Bacon's circle. Anthony died in 1601, and his property passed to Francis, who now for the first time became possessed of substantial independent means. Burghley had died three years before. In 1603, Elizabeth died, and, through the careful preparatory manipulations of Robert Cecil, James VI of Scotland came to the throne as James I of England without trouble.

What the translators of the Authorised Version describe as 'the appearance of Your Majesty as of the Sun in his strength... upon the setting of that bright Occidental Star, Queen Elizabeth of happy memory' was the occasion for 'agonizing re-appraisals' on Bacon's part. Essex, like many English politicians, had had dealings with James in Elizabeth's last years, and James took a favourable view of him and would therefore not be initially well disposed towards Bacon. However, Bacon early applied to James for favour and managed to overcome any prejudices against him that the King may have felt. He was knighted in 1603; though that was little to boast of, for James was almost as prodigal with honours on his accession as was Lloyd George at the end of the first World War. Robert Cecil continued, as long as he dared, to oppose Bacon's advancement, but Bacon was soon firmly fixed in the King's favour.

After writing many servile letters of application to Cecil (now Earl of Salisbury), to Lord Chancellor Egerton, and to the King, Bacon was appointed Solicitor-General in 1607. Coke had by then ceased to be Attorney General, having been appointed Chief Justice of the Common Pleas in the previous year. In the following year the long-awaited Clerkship to the Star Chamber, with its salary of £1600 p.a., at length fell vacant. In 1610, old Lady Bacon died, and Francis became the sole owner of Gorhambury.

Bacon was now definitely on the way up, and already in 1606 had married Alice Barnham, daughter of a former Sheriff of London. Her mother is ominously described by a contemporary writer as 'a little violent lady'. The marriage, which was no doubt entered into by Bacon for financial reasons, was childless and unhappy. Bacon, in a codicil to his will, revoked, for what he described 'just and grave causes', the bequests which he had made to his wife in the body of the testament. From what Arthur Wilson relates in his *Life and Reign of King James I* one can infer what had happened. Bacon had neglected his wife for his male servants, and she had consoled herself with hers. As Wilson puts it: 'Seldom doth the husband deviate one way, but the wife goeth another'. Shortly after Bacon's death, his widow married her gentleman usher, Sir Thomas Underhill. If Aubrey's remark that she 'made him deaf and blind with too much Venus' be anywhere near the truth, she may fairly be said to have done her best to make up for lost time.

Meanwhile, Bacon had sat continuously as a member of the House of Commons. There were constant quarrels between James I and his successive parliaments, largely about money. James's favourite text was 'Blessed are the peacemakers', and he liked to imagine himself in the role of reconciler of the religious differences and the political rivalries of Europe. It was not an unworthy ideal, but it made no appeal to the House of Commons, who wanted a spirited anti-Spanish and anti-Roman-Catholic policy. On the other hand, James was grossly extravagant, and so the country squires who mainly composed the House of Commons and would in any case have objected to paying the taxes which a spirited foreign policy would have required, could excuse their inconsistency and their parsimony by the legitimate plea that James could be trusted to waste on his favourites any money that might be granted to him. In these contrary winds and choppy seas, Bacon managed to steer a remarkably even course. Without losing favour with the King, he gained the approval of the House. In 1604, he was repeatedly chosen as their spokesman in conferences with the House of Lords, and in 1609 he was in the delicate position of spokesman for presenting a petition of grievances to the King.

One very sensible measure which James was anxious to carry through was a union of his two kingdoms of Scotland and England. Bacon thoroughly approved of this idea, and he played an important part as a Commissioner in drawing up the detailed proposals which were finally put before Parliament. He advocated and defended them in a great speech in the House of Commons on 17 February 1607. But the narrow-minded anti-Scottish feeling of the House was too strong for him, and the proposals were rejected.

His cousin, Robert Cecil, Earl of Salisbury, died on 24 May 1612. Shortly afterwards Bacon published a new edition of his *Essays*. To this, he added an essay on *Deformity*. It was widely believed that this was his last tribute to the deceased statesman, who had been, it will be remembered, a hunchback. The way was now open for Bacon's rapid political advancement. A week after Salisbury's death he wrote an elaborate letter to the King, offering his political services. He declared himself (sincerely, I think) to be a convinced royalist, but pointed out (quite truly) that he had never been out of favour with Parliament. In a somewhat later letter, he offered to abandon law altogether for the Council. At about the same time he applied, unsuccessfully, for the office of Master of the Rolls, vacant through Salisbury's death.

In the following year, 1613, Bacon attained, at the age of 52, the office of Attorney-General, which he had vainly sought from Elizabeth in his younger days. His rival Coke became in the same year Chief Justice of the King's Bench, They were soon to be busy with a famous society scandal which nearly touched the King.

In 1617, after much coming and going, James's favourite, Robert Carr, Earl of Somerset, and his odious wife Frances Howard, were at length brought to trial by their peers on the charge of having secured, by the administration of a clyster containing arsenic, the murder of Carr's former friend and counsellor Sir Thomas Overbury, while he was a prisoner in the Tower of London. Frances Howard, who had already dabbled in necromancy and the administration of potions, in order to secure the nullity of her first marriage and to get Carr as her second husband, was almost certainly guilty. Carr was most likely sincere in asserting and maintaining his innocence. The earlier stages of the investigation had been conducted by Coke, but the prosecution in the trial before the House of Lords was entrusted to Bacon. He, on taking over, describes the case as 'of good thread, but needing to be well strung together', and he alleged that Coke had bungled the preliminary investigation by following untrustworthy rumours and discovering mare's nests.

There was in fact a great deal going on behind the scenes, and all Bacon's skill and subtlety were needed in personal dealings with Somerset on the King's behalf. The scandal had become so notorious that it would have been almost impossible to avoid bringing the pair to trial. It was important for the prestige of the Crown that the verdict should not be in the nature of an acquittal for either of the accused, and it was even more important that Somerset should not have a motive and an opportunity to divulge in public extremely delicate matters concerning the King. What James wanted was that both parties should plead guilty and be publicly condemned, and that he should then exercise the royal prerogative of mercy on their behalf. He had, indeed, fallen out of love with Somerset, whose temper had become intolerable, and had taken up a new favourite. But he had no wish to proceed to extremes with persons in the social position in which Frances Howard had been born and to which he had raised her husband. On the other hand, it would have been contrary both to etiquette and to prudence for the King to promise clemency beforehand on condition of a subsequent avowal of guilt at the trial.

Bacon had thus an extremely awkward hand to play. Somerset was an obstinate and headstrong young man. He was naturally disinclined to plead guilty, with no guarantee of pardon, to a murder of which he was in fact innocent. He insisted at times that he would not attend the trial unless forcibly dragged thither, and at other times he threatened to make very damaging revelations in court, which James no doubt knew that he was in a position to do. Through Bacon's skill, it all ended happily, but it was touch and go to the last moment. Somerset never pleaded guilty, but he made no indiscreet revelations. James must have been indeed thankful to Bacon when the case ended with the court finding both parties guilty and condemning both to death, and with the King thereupon pardoning them and letting them retire into indecent obscurity with a pension of £4,000 p.a. to Somerset.

Whilst Carr's sun was setting in these murky clouds, that of George Villiers, his successor in James's affections, was rising with extraordinary rapidity. Starting in 1614 at the age of 22, when he was first brought to James's notice by persons anxious to undermine Carr, he had risen by 1618, entirely by good looks, good manners, and gentlemanly accomplishments, from being the second son of an impoverished Leicestershire squire of good lineage to be Marquis of Buckingham and the second richest nobleman in England. Buckingham has had, and has probably on the whole deserved, a 'bad press' with the historians. But there must have been something remarkable in a man who both won the doting affection of the half-senile and rather disreputable James and became and remained an object of hero-worship to James's eminently respectable and highly fastidious son Charles.

As might be expected, Bacon was quick to jump onto the Villiers bandwagon. It must have seemed to him to be a case of Essex over again, with enormously increased opportunities on his side. The favourite was now a callow youth, of no exalted birth and with no experience of courts, instead of being a great nobleman in his own right. Bacon himself was no longer just a clever ambitious young man with his way to make, but had become a lawyer, a politician, and a philosopher of acknowledged eminence. And James, unlike Elizabeth, might be expected to become dominated by his favourite and to be influenced by him in matters of public policy. So Bacon hoped to mould Villiers and to imbue him with his own far-sighted political ideas, and then through him to induce the King to put those ideas into practice.

Just as Bacon had written an admirable letter of advice to Essex, so in 1616 he wrote a famous letter to Villiers, which appears in his works under the title: 'A Letter of Advice by Sir Francis Bacon to the Duke of Buckingham when he became Favourite to King James'. The matter and the style could hardly be better. Villiers is told that he should now refer all his actions chiefly to the good of his sovereign and his country. He is reminded that 'it is the life of an ox or a beast always to eat and never to exercize', but 'men are born (and especially *Christian* men) not to cram in their fortunes, but to exercize their virtues'. In another letter of about the same date, Bacon added a warning, which reads somewhat ironically in view of what was soon to befall himself at Villiers' hands: 'By no means be you persuaded to interfere… by word or letters in any cause depending, or like to be depending, in any court of justice'.

At first, Villiers looked up to Bacon with respect and gratitude, and Bacon himself acted as steward on his behalf for an estate which the King had granted to the favourite. But it could not possibly last, and a person of Bacon's intelligence ought to have foreseen this. The head of a young man would need to be much stronger than was that of Villiers, if it were not to be turned by the favours of a king who likened him to St. Stephen, who said publicly of him 'Christ had his John and I have my George', and who loaded him and his relatives with estates and offices. Buckingham soon grew too big for his boots, flouted Bacon's advice, and treated him with upstart insolence.

Bacon had a humiliating lesson, in connexion with his hated rival Coke and the latter's daughter by Lady Hatton. Buckingham's elder brother, Sir John Villiers, wanted to marry this daughter, who would be very wealthy. Coke, who was Chief Justice of the King's Bench at the time when Sir John first made these proposals, had arrogantly flouted them. But in 1616, Coke had fallen into disgrace and had been suspended from his office for one of the few fine actions of his life, viz., his refusal to give to the King an assurance of how he would give judgment in hypothetical future cases which might touch on the royal prerogative. Coke now approached Buckingham to intercede for him with the King and offered his daughter to Sir John on any terms that the Villiers clan might care to make. Bacon took fright, fearing the influence that Coke might gain through an alliance with the family. He proceeded to write letters to the King and to Buckingham, who were in Scotland at the time, alleging all sorts of objections to the marriage on high public grounds.

The only result of this intervention was that Bacon received a severe snub from the King and offended the all-powerful Villiers connexion. He at once changed front, and offered unsolicited to use his interest with the girl's mother to promote the match. The mother, it will be remembered, was the Lady who had declined to be his wife and had married Coke in Queen Elizabeth's days.

Cordiality with Buckingham, though now on a footing of subservience by Bacon, was soon restored. On March 7th., 1617, largely through Buckingham's influence, he was appointed Lord Keeper. In the following year, he became Lord Chancellor, and was raised to the peerage as Baron Verulam of Verulam. It was an eventful year. Villiers was raised to the Marquisate, Sir Walter Raleigh was executed, and the 30 Years' War began.

Bacon held very definite and enlightened views to the purely judicial and the political functions of the Chancellorship, and he developed these in a brilliant memorandum to James when applying for the office. In every respect but one, his performance of his duties as Lord Chancellor was admirable. Within three months of his appointment, he had cleared off all the arrears in the Court. The historian S.R. Gardiner, who is by no means prejudiced in his favour, pays him this high compliment: 'As far as we know, his justice was... as exemplary as his energy... In later years, when every man's mouth was against him, no successful attempts were made to reverse his decisions'.

Bacon reached the zenith of his public career in 1620, when he was created Viscount St. Albans. There is a famous ode to him on his 60th birthday by Ben Jonson, describing the feast at York House, and addressing Bacon as:

> England's High Chancellor: the destined heir,
> In his soft cradle to his father's chair:
> Whose even thread the Fates spin round and full
> Out of their choicest and their whitest wool.

But the Fates belong to that sex which has been described as *varium et mutabile semper*, and Bacon's luck was to turn against him in less than 12 months.

There were two different kinds of irregularity which Bacon had committed in his capacity of Lord Chancellor. One was in connexion with the granting of patents for various kinds of monopolies to various individuals. This involved Buckingham and his relatives and hangers-on. The other was the taking of gifts by Bacon and by his servants from suitors in the Court of Chancery whose cases were or were about to be submitted to the Lord Chancellor for judgment.

The House of Commons which met in January 1621 contained among its most prominent members Bacon's enemy Coke and that very able business 'tycoon' Lionel Cranfield, afterwards Earl of Middlesex. At their instigation, the House set up an enquiry into the monopolies which had been granted in the preceding seven years. There were two that seemed particularly scandalous. One concerned the granting to certain individuals of what we should now describe as the monopoly for issuing licenses for starting new inns and ale-houses and for carrying on from year to year those already in existence. The other was a monopoly for the manufacture and sale of gold and silver lace, which had been granted to two rascals, Mompesson and Michel, who had fraudulently used copper and other base metals as counterfeits.

Having investigated and severely censured these and certain other monopolies, the House proceeded to the delicate questions: How had they been secured? And, in particular, how had they happened to pass the scruting of the official referees, of whom Bacon was one, and to receive the royal seal? They had, in fact, been procured in many cases by the applicants greasing the palms of Buckingham or his mother or others of his relatives, and by Bacon automatically passing without comment any application for a patent which came before him with Buckingham's *imprimatur*. In particular, Buckingham's half-brother, Sir Edward Villiers, had been hand-in-glove with Mompesson and Michel, though his name was discreetly absent from the patent granted to them.

Bacon might conceivably have surmounted this hurdle, if it had stood alone. For James could not allow a scandal which so nearly concerned the Villiers gang to be probed too deeply. On the advice of the new Lord Keeper, Williams, Dean of Westminster, the King came to the House of Lords on March 26th, 1621, inveighed against the patents in question, and gave up to justice all the lesser criminals. The Lords professed to be satisfied. Buckingham escaped censure and punishment, and Bacon might well have escaped with him.

But already on March 14th, Coke and Cranfield had complained in the House of Commons of the protection afforded by the Court of Chancery to insolvent debtors. Before anything could be done about this allegations were received, first from Christopher Aubrey and then from Edward Egerton, two unsuccessful litigants in that Court, of the direct acceptance of bribes from them by Bacon. On March 17th, the Commons, without committing themselves, referred the question for investigation to the House of Lords. Next day Bacon was, or pretended to be, too ill to leave his house, and asked for time to reply. Further accusations were brought by another unsuccessful litigant, Lady Wharton, who stated that she had personally handed money to Bacon while her case was *sub judice*. The custom of the time did indeed allow of presents being taken by judges from suitors, but *not* while a suit was pending.

Bacon soon realised that there was no escape for him. In the middle of April, he delivered to the Lords, by the hands of Prince Charles, a letter of *general* confession. In this he renounced all justification for himself, and, in his own words, asked only 'that his penitent submission might be his sentence, and the loss of the seals his punishment'. The House was not satisfied with this. They drew up a detailed accusation in 28 articles. The last of these should be noted. It accused him of having 'given way to great exactions of his servants, both in respect of private seals, and otherwise for sealing injunctions'. It is said that one day during this agonising crisis in his life Bacon happened to pass through a room in which several of his servants were sitting. They respectfully rose in his presence. He exclaimed: 'Sit down, my masters; your rise hath been my fall'.

The Lords ordered Bacon to make a particular answer to each of the 28 charges. On 21st May, he replied, admitting every charge and throwing himself on the mercy of his judges. Their sentence was crushing, probably the more so because they had very good reason to believe that most of it would be remitted by the King. Bacon was condemned to pay the fantastic fine of £40,000 – at least £400,000 in present-day terms – to be imprisoned in the Tower during the King's pleasure; to be forever incapable of any public office or employment, and never again to sit in Parliament or to come within the verge the Court.

Except for the public ignominy, which Bacon felt very deeply, and for the loss of the salary and emoluments of office, which he could ill afford, the sentence was largely nugatory. After brief confinement in the Tower, the King set him free and forgave him his fine. He had to suffer a further humiliation before the rest of his sentence was remitted. He had hoped to keep York House, the place of his birth, as a London residence. But Buckingham wanted it, and, through his influence, the pardon was held up until Bacon had consented to part with the house to Cranfield, who was at that time a creature of Buckingham's. At length, on Bacon's personal appeal to James, the last restriction, that of banishment from the verge of the Court, was annulled. He was, in fact, summoned as a Peer to the opening of Charles I's reign.

Bacon had five more years to live. He should have been comfortably off. He had a pension of £1,800 p.a. and his own inherited property, which was estimated to bring in a further £600 p.a. But he had saved nothing, his debts were enormous, and the payment of his pension was irregular. He was not a man who could easily retrench and live simply. He was often in difficulties, and in 1623, he applied unsuccessfully for the Provostship of Eton College. He never received any further preferment after his fall.

He lived now mainly at Gorhambury, engaged in literary, historical, and philosophical work. During those years he met the philosopher Hobbes, then only in his early 30s. Hobbes told Aubrey years later of how Bacon would walk up and down meditating, in the gardens which he loved and had formed and beautified, and of how Hobbes would accompany him and take down in writing any idea that occurred to Bacon and which he wished recorded. Bacon praised Hobbes, in contrast with others who performed this office for him, saying that he could always recognise his own ideas again in Hobbes's notes because he (unlike the others) had the wit to understand what Bacon had in mind.

It is to Hobbes, as reported by Aubrey, that we owe the best account of the circumstances of Bacon's death. Bacon, in the early spring of 1626, was taking the air near Highgate in a coach with Dr Witherborne, a Scottish physician to James I. There was snow on the ground, and the idea struck Bacon that meat might be preserved in snow as well as in salt. To try the experiment they alighted at a poor woman's cottage at the foot of Highgate Hill and got her to kill one of her hens and gut it. They then stuffed the body with snow, Bacon helping in the operation. He became chilled, and he felt so unwell that he could not return to his lodging in Gray's Inn. So they went to the Earl of Arundel's house in Highgate. The family were away, but Bacon was hospitably received by the servants and put into a good bed, which they warmed with a warming pan. But it had not been slept in for a year and was thoroughly damp. Bacon grew worse, and within a few days he died, according to Hobbes, of 'suffocation'. The last letter that he dictated (for he could no longer write) was to Arundel. In it, he compares himself to Pliny, who lost his life in investigating too incautiously the eruption of Vesuvius which destroyed Pompeii. The date of his death was April 9th, 1626. The cold-storage industry might well take Francis Bacon, if not as its patron saint, at least as its martyr-founder.

Bacon was buried, by his own directions, in St. Michael's church, St. Alban's, where his mother's bones already lay. After his death, the manor of Gorhambury passed into the ownership of Thomas Meautys, who had been secretary to Bacon as Lord Chancellor, had served him faithfully throughout his later troubles, and became in due course Secretary to the Council and a knight. Meautys, it is pleasant to record, caused a monument to be raised in the church to his old master. Later in the century, Gorhambury passed, by purchase from Sir Thomas's heirs, into the hands of Sir

Harbottle Grimstone, who was Master of the Rolls from 1680 to his death in 1685. Aubrey asserts (with what truth I do not know) that Sir Harbottle in 1681 had Bacon's coffin removed in order to make room, when the need should arise, for his own.

The second paragraph of Bacon's will begins with the famous sentence: 'For my name and memory, I leave it to men's charitable speeches, and to foreign nations, and the next ages'. We should not be celebrating the 400th, anniversary of Bacon's birth, if he had been only or mainly such a man as I have described in this lecture – a very able lawyer and far-sighted statesman, too clever by half, who accepted rather too easily and played rather too self-consciously upon the ruling passions of the real holders of power, and who ended by blundering, with his head in the air, into a dirty puddle which a less intellectual but shrewder worldling might have instinctively avoided. That he was something incomparably greater than this was recognised, not only by 'foreign nations and distant ages', but by some of his own countrymen and contemporaries. Shortly after his fall, when there was nothing to be gained by flattery, Ben Jonson wrote of him:

> My conceit of his powers was never increased... by his place or honours. But I have and do reverence him for his greatness, that was only proper to himself, in that he seemed to me ever, by his works, one of the greatest men and most worthy of admiration that had been in many ages. In his adversity I ever prayed that God would give him *strength*, for *greatness* he could not want...

Bacon had reacted against the current academic philosophy in general, and the current Aristotelian logic and physics in particular, ever since he was first subjected to them as an undergraduate at Cambridge. By the age of 25, he had composed a philosophical work which, to quote the phrase that he used 40 years later, 'with great confidence and a magnificent title I named *The Greatest Work of Time*'. The background of all his public work, and the occupation of every moment of his leisure, was reading, reflecting, and writing in order to formulate, illustrate, propagate, and ensure the supply of materials for a *new method*, which should give to mankind a well-founded theoretical understanding of nature, leading to deliberately planned and executed technical control over it. He described the entire undertaking as *Instauratio magna*

Imperii Humani in Universum, i.e., the *restoration* of the empire of man over the universe; a dominion which he believed, or professed for literary purposes to believe, to have existed before the Fall and to have been lost through the sin of our first parents.

Bacon was fully convinced that the ignorance of how nature works, and the consequent lack of control over it, which had prevailed from the earliest times up to his own day, were by no means inevitable. They sprang, not from any fundamental imperfections in the human senses or the human intellect, nor from lawlessness or inextricable complexity in nature, but simply and solely from failure to proceed methodically at all or still worse from the use of a mistaken method. Bacon valued science both as an end in itself and for the limitless power over nature which he believed it could give. He thought that the failure of the Aristotelian physics to lead to any useful practical applications was a sure sign that it was on the wrong track. But he was no less convinced that it is fatal for scientists to work short-sightedly at the solution of this or that particular technical problem. If and only if they concentrate primarily on discovering, by suitably designed experiments and careful observation and appropriate reasoning, the fundamental laws and the minute mechanisms of nature, they will be able to suggest and initiate innumerable fruitful practical applications.

Bacon justly accused the academic natural philosophers of his time of accepting, on the authority of Aristotle, sweeping general principles which Aristotle himself had reached by hasty and uncritical generalisation from a few rather superficial observations, and then wrangling with each other about the conclusions which might be drawn by syllogistic reasoning from them. He saw that what was needed was a method by which we could slowly and cautiously rise from observed facts to wider and deeper generalisations, testing every such generalisation at each stage by deliberately looking for possible exceptions to it, and rejecting or modifying it if such exceptions should be found. This is what may be called 'inductive reasoning'. Men had of course always been practising it to a certain extent in an unwitting and unsystematic way. It may fairly be said that Bacon did for it, or at any rate for one essential part of it, what Aristotle had done for the arguments current in the law courts and in political life. He abstracted and exhibited the principles and some of the presuppositions of such reasoning, so that in future men might perform it wittingly, with a full awareness of what they were doing and of what was required of them if they were to do it effectively.

Bacon realised that every man inherits or acquires certain mental kinks, of which he is generally quite unaware. These tend to lead us astray in our thinking, and we need to be put on our guard against them. Bacon calls them 'Idols', and he distinguishes the most important of these insidious sources of fallacy as Idols of 'the Theatre', of 'the Tribe', of 'the Market-place', and of 'the Cave'.

Had I been lecturing on Bacon a hundred years ago, I could have concluded with a paean, not only on his insight and foresight in proclaiming and preparing the way for the Great Instauration, but also on the results of that revolution. To-day that string needs to be greatly muted. Man's control over inanimate nature and other living beings is now so complete as to give to humanity the capacity of swarming like mites in a cheese or maggots in a dung-heap, and the complementary power of almost destroying itself in the present, of corrupting the genetic make-up of the survivors, and of polluting for an indefinite future that part of the universe which is its birthplace, its home, and its store-house. The powers which science bestows are in the hands of individuals and societies whose emotional and volitional equipment is for the most part infantile or anachronistic, and whom a sensible parent would hesitate to entrust with a pop-gun. Contemporary men and women are not fundamentally different in their motivations and their emotional reactions from Essex and Buckingham, from Elizabeth and Frances Howard, and from the conspirators in the Gunpowder Plot. But, thanks to the Great Instauration, they are far more capable of actively initiating or passively permitting or incoherently blundering into irreparable damage on a worldwide scale. Bacon's swans, as we have seen, had a way of turning out to be geese. And it would not be out of character, if humanity were to let him down badly as did Essex and Buckingham, and if, before the next 100th anniversary of his birth (or indeed of his death), the Great Instauration should only too literally have ended in smoke.

2.8

THE HISTORICAL DEVELOPMENT OF SCIENTIFIC THOUGHT (FROM PYTHAGORAS TO NEWTON)

A complete account of the development of scientific thought would have to deal, not only with the history of mathematics and the physical sciences, but also with the growth of the biological sciences, and with those which are specially concerned with man, such as psychology and anthropology. To present such a picture would require a whole course of lectures, and the lecturer would need to have at his command a range of varied knowledge which very few possess. I must therefore make a selection, and I am going to leave out altogether the *biological* sciences and those which are specially concerned with *man*. Even after that big omission, I shall have to make a further selection. I shall say little, if anything, about *chemistry* or about the various *special branches* of physics, such as optics, acoustics, heat, electricity, etc. What I shall be mainly concerned with today is the development of mathematics, astronomy, dynamics, and *general* physics.

These subjects have grown up in very close connexion, and in constant interaction, with each other. And they are the most fundamental of all the sciences. For *all* things, whether living or non-living, men or animals or vegetables or minerals, have shape, size, and relative position in space, and they or their parts can be measured and numbered. Now, these are the properties with which geometry and algebra, and arithmetic are concerned. Then, again, all things, whether living or non-living, have mass; they are all sometimes at rest and sometimes in motion; and they influence each other's movements by friction, attraction, repulsion, and so on. Now motion and rest, and the laws according to which one body affects the movements of another, are the subject matter of dynamics. Lastly, the place in which we live, and from which we make all our observations, is the earth; and all that we can observe or act upon or be acted upon by is either in the earth or in the heavenly bodies or in the spaces between them. Now astronomy (in which I include for the present purpose the elements of geography) is the science of the shapes, sizes, positions, and motions of the earth and the heavenly bodies. So, although what I am going to talk about is only a small selection from a much greater whole, it does include the most fundamental and all-pervasive of the sciences.

I will begin with geometry. The ancient Egyptians had much need of mensuration, both for measuring fields flooded each year by the Nile and for erecting temples and other great buildings. They had discovered certain practical rules, which they used in mensuration. They knew, for example, the particular fact that a triangle, whose sides are in the proportion 3:4:5, has a right angle opposite its longest side. They used this fact for marking off right-angles in surveying and building. But they seem to have had no idea of the general proposition about right-angled triangles, of which this is just one particular instance.

The first people in the world, so far as we know, to discover geometry, in the sense of general propositions about all figures of a given kind, rigidly proved and logically interconnected, were the Greeks. And one of the first propositions about which we can say with fair confidence that it was originally proved in a certain place and at a certain date is the one that I have just mentioned, viz., that in any right-angled triangle the sum of the squares on the sides which enclose the right-angle is equal to the square on the side opposite it. This is still known as the *Pythagorean* Theorem. Pythagoras was born in the island of Samos around about 550 B.C. He migrated first to southern Italy and later to Sicily, in both of which places there were at the time important Greek colonies. He was a mixture of what we should now call philosopher, mathematician, and religious mystic. He founded a kind of monastic institution, where he and his followers lived an ascetic life of meditation and scientific speculation. The Pythagoreans laid particular stress on the notion of pattern, harmony, and symmetry in nature, and they held that it consisted in characteristic relations between *numbers*. They discovered, and attached great significance to, the fact that there are simple *numerical* relations between the lengths of strings which, when plucked, give rise to sounds which harmonise with each other.

There is every reason to believe that either Pythagoras himself or one of his early disciples discovered the general theorem about right-angled triangles, and invented the proof of it which still appears in all school books on geometry. It is also said, though that is perhaps more doubtful, that it was one of the Pythagoreans who first discovered that some lengths, for example, that of the *diagonal* of the square, are intrinsically incommensurable with some others, for example, that of the *side* of the same square. However that may be, this fundamentally important fact was recognised quite early by the Greek mathematicians, and many of them wrestled with it and its implications.

The next Greek to be noted is *Plato*. He was born at Athens in 420 B.C. and died there in 348 B.C., but spent an important part of his 80 years' life in Sicily. Plato was a man of universal genius, and one of the world's greatest metaphysicians, moralists, and political thinkers. But what is of special interest to us is that he had been deeply influenced by the Pythagoreans, and regarded mathematics in general and geometry in particular as the type of and the key to all truth. I do not know of any particular proposition in mathematics associated with Plato's name. But we certainly owe to him and to his immediate disciples the whole idea of rigid proof, starting from clearly defined notions, simple and self-evident axioms, and a few postulates which everyone would be inclined to grant, and proceeding deductively from these to the demonstration of theorems and the solution of problems. It is hardly possible to over-estimate the importance and the novelty of this process of making absolutely clear and explicit, at the outset of one's argument, all the ideas which are to be used and the assumptions which are to be made in the course of it, and of not surreptitiously introducing, as one goes on, any different ideas or additional assumptions. It is difficult for us, who are used to the notion of rigid proof in mathematics, to appreciate fairly the achievement of those who first conceived it and first practised it.

In about 387 B.C., Plato founded an institution in Athens, called the *Academy*, which played an immensely important part in the development of mathematics in general and astronomy in particular. The Academy in some ways resembled a college in Oxford or Cambridge. It was a place where a group of scholars and research workers lived in close co-operation under a head chosen by themselves. It lasted until 529 A.D., i.e., for about 920 years, considerably longer than any college in Oxford or Cambridge has yet done. Even then it did not die a natural death, but was murdered. For it was shut down by the emperor Justinian in A.D. 529 in the supposed interests of Christian orthodoxy.

The members of the Academy in its earlier years made immense contributions to mathematics in general and to astronomy in particular. But from about 300 B.C. the centre of Greek activity in these subjects was the university founded in *Alexandria* by *Ptolemy Soter*, the first Greek king of Egypt. It was at Alexandria, round about 300 B.C., that *Euclid* published the world's most famous and influential treatise on mathematics, entitled the *Elements*. This is a compendium of all the main results reached by Greek mathematicians in the 250 years odd which had elapsed since Pythagoras was in full activity. But it is much more than a mere compendium of results. The propositions are rigidly proved and arranged in a systematic order, in accordance with the ideals of logical rigour which had been initiated by Plato and developed by his followers in the Academy.

The *Elements* is divided into 13 books. Books I to IV deal with the plane geometry of the straight line, the triangle, the rectangle, and the circle. Book V deals with the general notion of proportion, and Book VI applies this to triangles and other plane figures. Book X is concerned with the notion of incommensurables, which is the geometrical equivalent to the notion of irrational numbers. Books XI to XIII deal with the geometry of solids, and in particular the regular polyhedra. The treatment of proportion in Book V is taken over from *Eudoxus*, who lived from 408 to 355 B.C., and studied at the Academy under Plato. Euclid's *Elements* eventually found its way back into Western Europe after the dark ages by way of translations from Arabic, and it remained the standard textbook on elementary geometry until the beginning of the present century.

An important branch of geometry which was developed at Alexandria, was the theory of *conic sections*, i.e., of the ellipse, the hyperbola, and the parabola. About 75 years after the publication of Euclid's *Elements* there appeared another great geometrical compendium, dealing exhaustively with this subject. This is the *Conic Sections* of *Apollonius of Perga*, who lived from 260 to 200 B.C. approximately, and studied and taught in Alexandria. This too became a standard work, and was for the next 2000 years the textbook for students of geometry who wished to proceed beyond Euclid's *Elements*.

Apollonius introduced most of the notions and technical terms now used in treatises on conic sections, and he investigated most of the properties which are still treated in such works. All the great mathematicians, astronomers, and physicists of the XVIth and XVIIth centuries, such as Galileo, Kepler, Descartes, and Newton, were steeped in Euclid and Apollonius from their school days, and they probably had a greater skill in treating problems by the classical geometrical methods than any mathematician could claim to-day.

I must now go back a little in time from Apollonius to another distinguished Alexandrian, viz., *Archimedes*. He was born at Syracuse in Sicily in 287 B.C., but studied at Alexandria, returning to Sicily in course of time and dying there in 212 B.C. Here again, we have a man whose writings remained standard works for nearly 2000 years. I must omit any account of his famous and fundamental contributions to hydrostatics and mechanics, and will concentrate here on his achievements in geometry. He devoted himself largely to determining the lengths of curved lines, the areas enclosed by plane curves, and the areas and volumes of curved surfaces. Most of the standard elementary results in this field were obtained and proved by him. He showed, among other things, that the ratio of the circumference to the diameter of a circle must lie between $3^1/_7$ and $3^{10}/_{71}$.

In dealing with such problems, he used a general method called the *Method of Exhaustions*. This had been invented by the early Academician Eudoxus, whom I have already mentioned as the founder of the purely geometrical theory of proportion and of incommensurables. The method consists in showing that the magnitude which we wish to evaluate lies between two others, which we can evaluate, and then showing that the difference between these two can be made less than any assigned quality, however small. An example would be that the area of a circle lies between the area of any regular polygon *inscribed in it* and that of the regular polygon with the same number of sides *described about* it, and that the difference between these two areas can be made less than any quantity that we choose to assign, by making N, the number of sides in the two polygons, sufficiently great. The Method of Exhaustions was an ancestor of the *Integral Calculus*, invented in the XVIIth century by Newton and independently by Leibniz. By ingenious applications of this method, Archimedes and other Greek geometers managed to solve many problems which we should now attack by integration.

The genius of the Greek mathematicians lay rather in pure geometry than in arithmetic or algebra. But we must realise that they often proved, as *geometrical* propositions, the equivalents of well-known formulae in elementary algebra. Thus, for example, the earlier propositions in Book II of Euclid's *Elements* are the geometrical equivalents of such algebraic formulae as $(a + b)^2 = a^2 + 2ab + b^2$ and $(a + b)(a - b) = (a^2 - b^2)$, and so on. Then, again, they discovered extremely ingenious geometrical constructions which are equivalent to solving the general quadratic equation $ax^2 + bx + c = 0$, in the case where the roots are real. Propositions 27, 28, and 29 of Book VI of Euclid's *Elements* set forth these constructions.

However, as time went on certain members of the Alexandrian school treated what we should now call *algebra* for its own sake and independently of geometry. The first treatise on algebra was written at Alexandria towards the end of the IIIrd century A.D. under the title of *Arithmetica*. Its author was Diophantus, one of the last of the great Greek mathematicians. He introduced the use of a special symbol to denote the unknown quantity which is to be determined by solving an equation in which it occurs. He had general methods for solving any equation of the first or second degree, and he managed to solve at least one particular equation of the third degree.

Alexandria, after a long period of decline, was finally occupied by the Arabs in 642 A.D. Fortunately, there were able Arabian scholars interested in mathematics. They translated into Arabic most of the chief works of the Alexandrian mathematicians, and in that way, these were preserved while Western Europe was in a state of chaos and barbarism, and were eventually made available in Latin translations.

The study of algebra began to revive in the West in the XVIth century A.D. The greatest mathematician of that period was the Frenchman, François Viète (commonly known as Vieta), who lived from 1540 to 1603. He managed to give general solutions for equations of all degrees up to and including the 4th. Algebra assumes the form in which we know it at the hands of another great Frenchman, Descartes (1596–1650). He introduced the convention of using letters near the end of the alphabet (*e.g.*, x and y) to represent unknown quantities, and letters near the beginning (*e.g.*, a, b, and c) to represent known ones. He also introduced the index notation for powers, for example, x^2, y^3, z^n, etc. Apart from introducing these valuable notations, he made extremely important contributions to the general theory of equations of any degree.

But Descartes' most revolutionary and fruitful contribution to mathematics was not in algebra but in his discovery of *analytical geometry*, a device whereby any geometrical problem becomes in principle soluble by algebra, and any geometrical relation can in principle be represented by a geometrical figure. He effected this by taking three arbitrary planes, intersecting each other at right-angles, and assigning to any point three numbers, called *co-ordinates*, which express its perpendicular distances from each of these planes. This system of assigning numbers to points is still known as the *Cartesian* system of co-ordinates, in honour of Descartes, whose name was Latinised to *Cartesius*. This epoch-making idea was first published by him in 1637 in a book entitled *Géometrie*.

It remains to say a word about ordinary arithmetic and numerical calculation. I think that few of us realise how wonderful an invention was the familiar way of representing numbers which we were all taught to use in early childhood. We commonly take it for granted and ask no questions about it. The essential point of it is this. By means of ten arbitrary symbols, viz., the figures '0', '1', ... '9', we can construct, in accordance with a simple general rule, the symbol for any integer whatever above 9. It is not until one has such a system that one can formulate general rules for adding, subtracting, multiplying, and dividing any integers whatever. For what the rules do is to enable us to write down the symbol for the sum or the difference or the product or the quotient (as the case may be) of any two integers, when the symbols of these integers are given. Most of us learn these rules by rote in childhood, and ever afterwards use them mechanically without knowing the reasons for them. But of course, there *are* reasons for them, and these are bound up with the principles of this particular way of symbolising numbers.

It is not known who invented this system. It seems certain, however, that it originated in *India*. An essential feature of it is, of course, the recognition of *nought* as one number among others, and the provision of a special symbol for it. This was a feat of genius. From India, the system passed to the Arabs about the middle of the VIIIth century A.D. Early in the IXth century an Arabian mathematician, *Al Khwarizmi*, wrote a treatise on it. From the Arabs, it spread to the West in the XIIth century, and thereafter there was a rapid development of arithmetic in Europe. It is commonly called the *Arabic System* of notation, though this does less than justice to the Hindoos. The extension of the system to express, by means of decimals, any *fraction* as well as any integer, comes fairly late. Decimals were first systematically treated by the Dutch mathematician and physicist, *Stevinus*, born in 1548 and died in 1620. The notation we now use for decimals was first introduced by the Scottish mathematician *Napier* (1550–1617). It was he too who greatly facilitated numerical calculation with large numbers by the invention of *logarithms*. He published the first table of them in 1614. These were calculated to the base e. Logarithms to the base 10, which are what we commonly use nowadays, were introduced in 1624 by *Henry Briggs*, who was a professor of geometry at Oxford, and died at the age of 70 in 1630.

I have now taken you on a rather headlong and breathless gallop through the odd 2,200 years of the history of mathematics from Pythagoras in 550 B.C. to the death of Descartes in 1650 A.D. It is now high time to retrace our steps and to consider the development of astronomy.

The natives of Babylonia, Egypt, Asia Minor, and Greece had ample opportunities for observing the heavenly bodies, for the skies there are seldom clouded, as they so often are in our part of the world. They had strong practical motives, partly sound and partly superstitious, for doing so. The sound motive was for purposes of navigation and time-reckoning. The superstitious one was the almost universal belief that the heavenly bodies influence the fate of individuals and of nations, and that there are lucky and unlucky configurations of the heavenly bodies. In the course of thousands of years these peoples, and particularly their priests, had accumulated a mass of astronomical observations.

Now, if the positions of the heavenly bodies are observed from the same place on the earth night after night over a long period, it becomes plain that these objects fall into two classes. The vast majority of them appear simply to make a complete revolution about the earth between any two successive midnights on an axis through one of them, called the *Pole Star*. These are called *stars*. But there are seven easily observable and identifiable heavenly bodies, viz., the sun and the moon, and Saturn, Jupiter, Mars, Venus, and Mercury, which appear to move in complicated closed curves with variable speeds and each with its own characteristic period. The Greeks distinguished these seven as *planets*. (The word πλανῆτες in Greek means 'wandering'.) The fact that the earth itself is a *spherical* body (which is by no means obvious, or even plausible, at first sight) was recognised quite early by Greek thinkers, and was generally accepted by 387 B.C., the approximate date at which Plato founded his Academy.

By that time a great mass of fairly accurate observations as to the apparent movements of the various heavenly bodies, as seen from the earth, had accumulated. Plato set to the Academy the following problem: To describe, on a single general scheme, all the observed motions of all the known heavenly bodies, so that the position of each at any assigned past or future date can be inferred. This problem was set under the following three conditions: (1) The earth is to be taken as fixed, and all the other bodies as revolving around it. (2) The only fundamental celestial motions are to be assumed to be *circular*. (3) Every such circular motion is to be assumed to take place at *uniform speed*.

The first person to provide an approximate solution to that problem on those assumptions was Plato's pupil *Eudoxus* (about 408 to 355 B.C.), whom we have already met with as the inventor of the Method of Exhaustions in geometry. The next important contributor was *Hipparchus* (180 to 125 B.C.). He was the first systematic astronomer, and, considering the means available to him, one of the greatest on record. He did most of his work at the observatory which he had built for him on the island of Rhodes. He discovered that the apparent annual motion of the sun about the earth is *not* exactly centred on the latter. He also discovered the *precession of the equinoxes*, i.e., the fact that the axis about which the stars appear to rotate round the earth every 24 hours is not really fixed in direction, but itself rotates very slowly (like the axis of a spinning top), completing its revolution in about 26,000 years. As a geographer, Hipparchus was the first person to use the notions of latitude and longitude for assigning positions to places on the earth's surface.

The final outcome of the labours of a whole series of Greek astronomers on the problem posed by Plato was set forth systematically by the Alexandrian astronomer and geographer *Ptolemy* (A.D. 90–168). The problem was solved by Hipparchus and Ptolemy by means of a combination of two devices, viz., the *Theory of Excentrics* and the *Theory of Epicycles*. According to the former theory, it is not the earth itself, but a point at some distance from it and fixed relatively to it, which is the common centre of all the ultimate uniform circular motions. According to the theory of excentrics, each member of the solar system circulates uniformly about a centre peculiar to it. But this centre itself is not, in general, at rest. It circulates in turn uniformly about another centre, which may in its turn be circulating uniformly about another, and so on. Such a series always ends, however, after a finite number of terms, with a centre which circulates uniformly about the fixed centre of the universe. The ultimate circles, with this common fixed centre, were called *Deferents*. The other circles in such a series were called *Epicycles*. By providing each heavenly body with enough epicycles, and by suitably choosing the rates of circulation in its deferent and in each of its epicycles, all the long-term appearances of the sun, the moon, and the other planets, as seen from the earth, can be accounted for to any degree of approximation. Finally, the short-term appearances, i.e., those that repeat themselves once every 24 hours, were explained by supposing that the whole system of planets, luminaries, and fixed stars rotates as a rigid whole about an axis through the Pole Star in that period.

In itself, this scheme is simply a mathematical solution of a mathematical problem. As such, it is a wonderful achievement, and it can be criticised only on the ground that equally effective and much simpler alternative schemes can be devised, if we drop or modify the three basic assumptions on which it rests. But unfortunately, it was treated as a *physical* theory by Aristotle and his successors, and the Aristotelian way of thinking became predominant in Western Europe. The fixed stars were regarded as attached to the inside of a rotating spherical shell, which encloses the rest of the universe. The deferent of each luminary and of each planet was associated with a special concentric spherical shell, rotating on an axis whose axle-boxes were attached to the inside of the starry sphere. And so on. For reasons which we need not consider here, two additional spheres, called the *Crystalline Sphere* and the *Primum Mobile* were assumed to surround the sphere of the fixed stars. And for most purposes, the theory of excentrics (which is essential in order to account accurately for the appearances) was ignored, and the centre of the universe was identified with the centre of the earth.

Now this theory of the structure of the universe was associated in Aristotelian physics with a certain theory of the materials of which it is composed. This is the theory of the *Four Elements and the Quintessence*. This may be stated as follows.

Going outwards from the earth, the first rotating sphere which we come to is that associated with the moon's deferent. This divides the universe into a sublunary and a celestial region. It was held that there is a profound difference between sublunary substances and their changes, on the one hand, and celestial substances and their changes, on the other. The heavenly bodies and their spheres are composed of a superior kind of substance called the Fifth Element or Quintessence. This is not subject to generation or decay or changes of quality. The only kind of change of which it is susceptible is perpetual uniform circular motion. But everything in the sublunary world, i.e., the earth and its atmosphere as far as the sphere of the moon, is ultimately composed of four elements, to which the names *Earth*, *Air*, *Fire*, and *Water* were given. In each of these four elements, we can distinguish in thought two correlated factors, viz., *substratum* and *quality*.

The substratum of all four is the same, and is called *materia prima*. This is ingenerable and incorruptible, and it occupies continuously the whole of the sublunary sphere. (It might be compared with the *ether*, as conceived by XIXth century physicists, and it is probably the ancestor of that idea.) The characteristic *quality* of each element was conceived as follows. There are two fundamental pairs of opposite qualities, viz., *Hot-Cold* and *Moist-Dry*. Of these *Hot* is considered positive as compared with *Cold*, and *Moist* as compared with *Dry*. (This opinion was probably based on the fact that germination and growth are fostered by warmth and moisture and checked by cold and drought.) Now there are four possible combinations of these qualities taken in pairs, viz., C&D, C&M, H&M, and H&D. Each element consists of *materia prima* characterised by one of these combinations. *Earth* is cold and dry, *Water* cold and moist, *Air* hot and moist, and *Fire* hot and dry. These elements are capable of two kinds of change. In the first place, a portion of *materia prima* can lose one such pair of qualities and gain another instead, so that one element is transformed into another. Secondly, each of the four elements has a certain *natural place* in the sublunary sphere. When it is there it rests, or moves quietly. When it is out of its place it tends automatically to move into it, and such motions are *violent*. The proper place of *Fire* is at the circumference, and so it tends to move upwards from the earth. The proper place of *Earth* is at the centre, and so earthy things tend to move downwards. The proper places of *Air* and *Water* are intermediate, that of *Air* being immediately below that of *Fire*, and that of *Water* immediately above that of *Earth*.

As I have said, this theory of the structure and contents of the universe is due to *Aristotle*. He was born in 384 B.C. and was perhaps the most distinguished all-round member of Plato's Academy. His interests and his immense abilities lay more in logic and biology and metaphysics than in mathematics and astronomy. He left the Academy on Plato's death in 348 B.C. After a period, during which he was away from Athens, he returned in 335 B.C., and founded there his own school, called the *Lyceum*. He was head of it until 323 B.C., when he finally left Athens. He died in the following year. The theory which I have just outlined was expounded in his work entitled *Physics*.

During the breakdown of Western civilisation, following on the barbarian invasions, Aristotle's *Physics* and some of his other works were eagerly studied and commented upon by Arabian scholars, and it was through them that Aristotle's physical theories first became known again in the West. By the middle of the XIIIth century, Latin translations direct from Greek manuscripts became available. In that century St. Thomas Aquinas (1225–1274) made a deep study of Aristotle, and constructed a synthesis of the Aristotelian and the Catholic Christian views of the universe. St. Thomas was a man of genius, with immense powers of work, who had mastered all the knowledge available at his time. After a certain amount of opposition, the theory of the universe which he had constructed, incorporating the Ptolemaic astronomy and Aristotle's doctrine of the elements, swept the board. It became for the next 300 years the accepted picture of the world. It is the framework, for example, of Dante's *Divine Comedy* and of Milton's *Paradise Lost*. It has even contributed to ordinary speech such phrases as 'to be in one's element' and 'to be above one's sphere', which most of us use without the least suspicion of their origin. I shall devote the rest of my lecture to the revolution in thought which took place in the XVIth and XVIIth centuries, and which substituted for this Aristotelian-Ptolemaic conception of the universe that of Copernicus and Newton, in which we were all brought up.

As more accurate and detailed knowledge of the movements of the heavenly bodies accumulated, the Ptolemaic scheme had to be made more and more complicated in order to cope with the facts in terms of the three fundamental assumptions of a fixed earth and heavenly rotations which are all circular and all uniform in speed. So it naturally occurred to a few astronomers of outstanding originality and boldness to question these assumptions. Could not all the observed facts be accounted for equally well or better, and much more simply, in a scheme which started with different initial assumptions? At least one eminent astronomer of the Alexandrian school, *Aristarchus of Samos* (about 310–250 B.C.), had suggested that the earth moves round the sun, and that the stars are immeasurably further from it than the sun is. But the idea was not followed up until nearly 1,800 years later.

The first astronomer to take this suggestion seriously was *Copernicus*, a Polish astronomer born in 1473. The book in which he stated and worked out his theory in detail is entitled *De Revolutionibus Orbium Coelestium*. It seems to have been completed by 1517, but it was not published until 1543, when Copernicus lay on his death-bed. Copernicus ascribed to the earth both a daily rotation about its axis and an annual revolution about the sun. He assumed that the planets also revolve about the sun and not about the earth. But he retained the old assumptions that all the revolutions are circular and uniform in speed. He was therefore unable to do without excentrics and epicycles, though he was able to do with far fewer than were needed in the old geocentric scheme.

The next astronomer in the series is *Tycho Brahe*, a Danish nobleman who worked for many years at his own observatory on the little island of Ven, in the Sound. He was born in 1546 and died in 1601. His astronomical instruments were far more accurate than those of his predecessors, and his observations much more systematic. He rejected the Ptolemaic system, but he also rejected (for quite plausible reasons) that of Copernicus. According to him, the earth is at the centre of the universe, and the sun and the moon revolve around it, as in the Ptolemaic system. But all the other planets revolve about the sun, and are carried round the earth with the sun in its annual revolution. As before, all the motions are assumed to be circular and of uniform speed.

The last step was to get rid of these assumptions. This was taken by *Kepler*. He was a German, born in 1571. After being for a while professor of mathematics in Graz, he went in 1600 to Prague as assistant to Tycho Brahe, who had been appointed to a post there by the emperor Rudolf II when things had become too hot at home in Denmark. On Brahe's death in 1601 Kepler succeeded him as a mathematician to the emperor. He was very poorly paid and had to keep his head above water by practising astrology for wealthy patrons, of whom the most famous was Wallenstein. He died in 1630.

The essential points which Kepler established are these. (1) He agrees with Copernicus that the sun is at rest, and that the earth rotates daily on its own axis and revolves annually around the sun. (2) The paths of these bodies about the sun are *not* circular. They are *ellipses* of various degrees of excentricity. (3) The sun is *not* at the common centre, but at the common *focus* of all these ellipses. (4) The speed with which any of these bodies describes its elliptical path around the sun is *not* uniform. It varies from point to point in the path, though it is the same on every occasion when the planet again passes through the same point.

But Kepler did very much more than establish these four points. He had a mystical Pythagorean conviction that the motions of all the planets must constitute a single pattern, expressible in simple and elegant numerical relationships. Inspired and sustained by a kind of burning religious faith in this idea, he put forward one hypothesis after another, and carried through the grinding labour of testing each against masses of relevant astronomical observations. In the end, three and only three suggested relationships stood up to the tests. These are known as Kepler's *Laws of Planetary Motion*. The first of them I have already mentioned, viz., that the curves described by all the planets are *ellipses* with the sun as their *common focus*. The second is that, for each planet, the line joining its centre to that of the sun revolves at such a rate that it always sweeps out *equal areas in space in equal lapses of time*. The third is that, for any two planets, *the squares of the times* taken by each to make a complete circuit round the sun are to each other as the *cubes of their mean distances* from the sun.

The stage was now set for the transformation by *Newton* of purely descriptive and predictive astronomy into *dynamical* astronomy, i.e., a system in which all the facts, including Kepler's three laws, are traced back to the action of the sun on the planets and the interaction of the planets with each other, in accordance with the laws of motion and the law of gravitation. This he accomplished in his *Principia*, published in 1687.

But an essential pre-requisite of Newton's achievement was the work of the great Italian scientist Galileo, born at Pisa in 1564 and died near Florence in 1642. He was a man of extraordinary genius, both practical and theoretical. He invented the telescope and made valuable observations with it. He discovered that a pendulum takes the same time to complete each successive swing, and thus provides a means of constructing accurate time measurers. But for our purpose, his most important achievements are his work on the time taken by bodies to fall through given heights, and his proof that the path taken by a projectile shot out at an angle to the earth's surface is a parabola.

Galileo showed, by a masterly combination of experiment and mathematical reasoning, that, when the effects of the buoyancy and resistance of the surrounding air are eliminated, all bodies fall at the same rate, independently of their shape, size, density, and composition. He showed that, under these conditions, any body falling in the neighbourhood of the earth's surface does so with a velocity which increases *proportionally to the time* which has elapsed since it began to fall. He deduced correctly from this that the velocity attained by such a body would be proportional to the *square root of the distance fallen*. In the case of a projectile, he showed that its actual motion is compounded out of two different tendencies to move, which co-exist in it independently of each other. One of these is its tendency to go on moving parallel to the earth's surface with the velocity with which it was initially projected in that direction. This remains *unaltered* from the beginning to the end of its course. The other is its tendency to go on moving at right angles to the earth's surface with the velocity with which it was initially projected in *that* direction. This varies from moment to moment, exactly as it would if the projectile had simply been projected vertically upwards, gradually losing speed, and eventually falling vertically, gradually gaining speed, in accordance with the laws already discovered by Galileo for falling bodies.

The upshot of this work of Galileo's is the following. The fundamental kind of motion is *not* circular, as the Greeks had thought, but *rectilinear*. Again, rectilinear motion, once begun, does *not* tend to die away of itself. It does not need to be kept up by something external acting on the moving body. On the contrary, any body already moving in a given straight line with a given velocity will automatically *go on* moving in the same direction with the same speed, unless something from outside it acts on it and alters its direction or its speed or both. This is known as the *Law of Inertia*. It is implicit in Galileo's results, and he explicitly recognised certain important special cases of it, but the first person to formulate it accurately and generally was Descartes.

Sir Isaac Newton (1642–1727) formulated this law in his *Principia* as the First Law of Motion. His *Second Law of Motion* may be stated as follows. Suppose that a force from outside is acting on a moving body at any moment, and thus causing a change in the velocity with which it is then moving. Then the *rate* at which the velocity will be changing at that moment is *directly* proportional to the *force*, and *inversely* proportional to the *mass* of the body on which it is acting. Thus the notion that turns out to be fundamental in dynamics is the rather unfamiliar one of the *rate of change of a velocity at an instant*. This is what is called *acceleration*. To complete the foundations of dynamics one other law is needed. This states that, if a body *A* acts dynamically on a body B, then B always simultaneously reacts dynamically on *A*. And the force exerted by B on *A* is always equal in intensity and opposite in direction to that exerted by *A* on B. This is Newton's *Third Law* of Motion.

Newton now tried the following hypothesis. Let us suppose that the sun attracts each of the planets with a force which is *directly* proportional to the product of its mass by that of the planet, which is *inversely* proportional to the square of the distance between the centres of the two, and which is *directed* at any moment along the line joining their centres at that moment. He then worked out mathematically how the planets would have to move, in accordance with the three laws of motion, if that hypothesis were true. He showed that, if and only if it were true, the planets would revolve about the sun in accordance with precisely those three laws which Kepler had shown that they do in fact obey.

The next question was this. Can the force with which the sun attracts the planets be identified with any force with which we are already familiar on earth? We know that the moon revolves around the earth very much as the earth and the other planets revolve round the sun. Moreover, Galileo's telescope had revealed that the planet Jupiter has satellites which revolve about it very much as the moon revolves about the earth. It therefore seemed plausible to suppose that the attractive force which the sun exerts on the earth and the planets is not something *peculiar to the sun*, but is something *common to all bodies whatever*. So Newton tried the hypothesis that *every* particle of matter attracts *every other* particle with a force directly proportional to the product of the masses of the two and inversely proportional to the square of the distance between them. He was able to show that, if and only if this hypothesis were true, then the attraction exerted by a solid homogeneous spherical body at any point outside its surface would be exactly the same as if all its mass were *concentrated in single particle at its centre*.

Now the earth is very nearly a sphere, so we can apply this theorem to it. It follows that the attractive force which it would exert on any body close to its surface is *directly* proportional to the product of the earth's mass by the mass of that body, and *inversely* proportional to the square of the earth's radius. Now, according to the Second Law of Motion, the acceleration produced in any body by any force is *directly* proportional to the force and *inversely* proportional to the body's mass. It follows that all bodies near the earth's surface will fall with the same acceleration, regardless of their mass. And that is what Galileo had already established experimentally. So this hypothesis of Newton's accounts very well for the known *terrestrial* facts. It therefore begins to seem reasonable to think that the force which keeps the planets in their elliptical orbits round the sun, and the force which accelerates falling bodies near the earth, are just two different manifestations of a single fundamental force which acts between *any* two material particles.

Newton clinched the argument by considering the intermediate case of the moon. This is a nearly spherical body, which revolves about the earth in a path which is very nearly an ellipse with the earth at its focus. We know its mean distance from the earth (about 239,000 miles), and we know the radius of the earth (about 3,900 miles). We also know the acceleration which the earth's attraction produces in bodies falling near its surface (about 32 feet per second per second). From these data, we can calculate the attractive force which the earth would exert on a body at the moon's distance from it. Now suppose that this is the force which keeps the moon in its orbit round the earth. Then we can calculate, in accordance with the three Laws of Motion, the *time* which the moon should take to make a complete circuit round the earth. When Newton at length had the correct measurement of the earth's radius at his disposal, he calculated the period of the moon on this hypothesis as 27 days. The actual value is 27.3 days. So the agreement is good enough to make his hypothesis practically certain.

The theory of universal gravitation was now firmly established, and Newton devoted himself henceforth to explaining, by means of it, detailed terrestrial and celestial phenomena, such as the tides and the precession of the equinoxes. His achievement was all the more remarkable in that he had had to develop a new branch of mathematics, the Differential Calculus, in order to deal with velocities which vary in magnitude and in direction from instant to instant and from point to point. Another form of the same calculus was invented independently at much the same time by the great German philosopher and mathematician Leibniz (1646–1716), and there was an unedifying squabble as to priority between the two great men and between their lesser followers.

It was no exaggeration when Pope wrote the lines:

> Nature and Nature's laws lay hid in night;
> God said: 'Let Newton Be!', and all was light.

Newton set the pattern in which all physical thinking was moulded for the next 200 years, and it was only then that another poet had to add the couplet:

> It could not last. The Devil, crying 'Ho!
> Let Einstein be!', restored the *status quo*.

But that is another story, which cannot be told now.

NOTES

1. JW: Vol. 1.
2. CDB: Written for BBC Europe lecture, but withdrawn by me, as the BBC wanted changes that I was not prepared to make.
3. CDB, 8/vi/1964: I have since learned that it was Hollond, and not Trevelyan, who initiated the proposal.
4. CDB, 27/v/1969: No. It was quite a short swim to an adjacent boat. See Russell's 'Autobiography', Vol. III, p. 45–46.

Part 3

SCIENCE AND METAPHYSICS

INTRODUCTION TO PART 3
Joel Walmsley

For the first two years of his undergraduate studies in Cambridge, Broad was enrolled in Part I of the Natural Sciences Tripos, with his major subjects being physics and chemistry, and minor subjects mineralogy and botany. It is therefore perhaps unsurprising that when he switched to the 'Moral Sciences' Tripos for Part II of his degree, his philosophical interests continued to include (and to be informed by) the sciences. Broad's first book, *Perception, Physics, and Reality* (1914), features detailed mathematical discussions of the laws of mechanics, and of optics, and his (1923) *Scientific Thought* was originally delivered as a set of lectures to science students (including Paul Dirac) in Bristol in 1920–1921. Throughout his published work, Broad treats the concepts and developments of science with the same historical and technical exhaustiveness as he does the philosophical discussion to which he applies them.

The papers in this section straddle the boundary between these scientific and philosophical aspects of Broad's background. We start where the last section ended, taken from an undated and type-written manuscript, and a more historical treatment, this time examining the way in which science came to acquire the specific *quantitative* methods that we now take to be characteristic of it. Broad focuses here on physics in general, and in dynamics and gravitation in particular, looking at the developments introduced by Galileo and Newton (the latter being, of course, a one-time occupant of Broad's rooms in Trinity College), and also explored by Descartes and Leibniz. Although Broad has written separately on these figures elsewhere, it is particularly interesting to see his treatment of them in juxtaposition, and the manuscript

DOI: 10.4324/9781003081135-16

is somewhat unusual – for Broad, at least – in that it contains a diagram (illustrating Galileo's experiments with pendula); Broad's hand-drawn illustration is reproduced here as Figure 3.1.1.

One of Broad's lasting and famous contributions to 20th century philosophy is, of course, his work on Philosophy of Time, both in its own right, and in his commentaries on the work of McTaggart (see Thomas, 2019; Oaklander, 2020). Although the archives of Broad's previously unpublished work do not contain further material on his treatment of time *per se*, the remaining three papers in this section may be fruitfully taken as companion pieces – to each other, and to Broad's work in Philosophy of Time – insofar as they concern the temporal phenomena of causation, change, continuity, and discontinuity.

The manuscript 'Notes on Causation' was, according to the 'Autobiographical Notes', given as a lecture to the Philosophy Society at the University of Oslo on 24 March 1955. Although the opening paragraphs bear some similarity to a much older publication – 'Mechanical and Teleological Causation' from 1935 – the remainder of the paper takes the discussion in a different direction by focusing on causal topics that Broad thinks have been neglected in philosophical discussion, especially *singular* propositions of causal connection, and more general principles *about* causation. Interestingly, Broad's contention here seems to be that a philosophical theory of causation ought to pay much more attention to the experiences and resultant perceptual knowledge (and especially our own sense of *agency*), that give rise to a common-sense understanding of causation, and he proceeds to give such an account in his typical analytic style.

Relatedly, in 'Some Remarks on Change, Continuity and Discontinuity' (given as the John Scott lecture to the Royal Society of Edinburgh on 10 November 1957) Broad tackles the questions of what we mean when we talk about sequences of events, and how that is connected to views about the continuity (or discontinuity) of space and time. It is, in characteristic Broad style, exhaustive (perhaps even *exhausting*) in its treatment, but it allows Broad to tease out the consequences even of views which he himself finds doubtful (e.g., that space, or time, may be discontinuous). Again, unusually for Broad, the manuscript contains some very small marginal diagrams, which I have re-created here for illustration.

Finally, we have a short and fascinating paper in which Broad proposes, develops, and elaborates a logical formalism for the analysis of change (and of 'quiescence'), before going on to show how certain logical consequences of these axioms we nonetheless rule out as *ontologically impossible*. The logical proofs here are developed using the notation of Whitehead and Russell's *Principia Mathematica*, in keeping with what Broad later wrote (1967, pp. 103–104) about the influence of Russell on his own work:

> Undoubtedly the most concrete debt which I owe to attending Russell's lectures at that period is familiarity with the notation and methods of *Principia Mathematica*, and a certain facility in handling them. Of course one was somewhat inclined at the time to over-estimate the importance for philosophy of putting questions and arguments into symbolic form. That was inevitable with young men newly furnished with a fascinating gadget and anxious to 'show off' with it, as one might with a new sports-model. But I have repeatedly found this technique extremely useful in analysing and formulating philosophical problems, and in freeing one from the hopeless ambiguity and muddle of ordinary language when used for anything but the everyday practical purposes in subservience to which it has evolved.

Broad's paper here is an excellent example of this: he starts by noting his dissatisfaction at the lack of an adequate ordinary language treatment of the notion of change, but by using Whitehead and Russell's notation and methods, he is able to formulate and derive some instructive and interesting consequences.

3.1

INTRODUCTION OF QUANTITATIVE METHODS

The medieval physics, founded mainly upon Aristotle, was essentially qualitative and not quantitative. The conceptions with which it worked were drawn from biological and psychological facts and were not susceptible of quantitative formulation or mathematical deduction. The profound change in physics which took place in the XVIth and XVIIth centuries was bound up with a transformation from a purely qualitative to a mainly quantitative standpoint.

In this lecture, I propose to confine myself to an account of the development of the concepts and laws of dynamics including gravitational theory. This was the first natural science to assume a strictly quantitative form, and it was long regarded as the model for other branches of physics and as the basis of them all. Moreover, it was developed, not only by persons whom we think of primarily as great scientists, such as Galileo and Newton, but also by professional philosophers, such as Descartes and Leibniz. Both of the latter were very much concerned with dynamics and its supposed philosophical implications.

I shall now give an account of the development of dynamics at hands of Galileo and Newton, who were primarily scientists and not philosophers in the modern sense of those words. I shall then say something about Leibniz's treatment of the subject and his criticism of Descartes' dynamics. Leibniz and Descartes are men whom we should now regard primarily as philosophers and not as scientists. We must remember, however, that the distinction was not then nearly so sharp as it has become since. Galileo, for example, was a realist of the Platonic or Pythagorean type. He held that mathematical reasoning makes us aware, little by little, of selections from an infinite system of inter-connected pre-existing truths which God sees intuitively as a single whole. Newton, again, continually touches on metaphysics and theology, as, for example, in his notions of Absolute Space and Time and his theory that the former of these is the sensorium of God. On the other hand, neither Descartes nor Leibniz was a mere speculative metaphysician or a mere analytical philosopher. Each was a mathematician of genius; the former being the inventor of analytical geometry, and the latter sharing equally and independently with Newton in the glory of discovering the Differential Calculus.

From these preliminary remarks, I pass to the work of Galileo on falling bodies and on the motion of projectiles. It is a well-known fact that when a body falls from rest its velocity increases as it descends. Galileo did not ask himself 'Why do bodies fall?' but 'In accordance with what quantitative law do they fall?' He sought to determine what circumstances are, and what are not, relevant to the fall of bodies, and he sought to discover a mathematical formula connecting the velocity attained, either with the time which has elapsed or with the distance which has been traversed since the body began to fall. This was a revolutionary change in the method of approach to a physical problem.

As we now know, the situation is complicated by the fact that falling bodies are surrounded with air and are subject to an upward thrust equal to the weight of the air which they displace. They are also subject to a resistance which increases with their velocity. The effects of these causes, though negligible in the case of falling bodies of high density and spherical shape, such as a bullet, are very considerable in the case of a specifically light laminated body, such as a leaf or a bit of thistle-down. It was therefore commonly, and quite reasonably, held that the time taken by a body to fall through a given height is less for denser than for rarer bodies. Galileo tried the experiment of dropping bodies of various weights from the leaning tower of Pisa. He satisfied himself that, if the effect of the surrounding air is allowed for, the time of descent of a body through a given height is independent of its density.

His next step was to put forward certain alternative hypotheses about the law in accordance with which the velocity of a body increases as it falls. He considered two and only two alternatives, viz., the two simplest that he could think of. One is that the velocity attained is proportional to the *distance* through which the body has fallen. The other is that it is proportional to the *time* that has elapsed since it began to fall. Before attempting to test these hypotheses by experiment he tried to deduce by mathematical reasoning certain consequences which would follow according to whether the first or the second of them was true.

By such reasoning, he persuaded himself that the hypothesis that the velocity attained is proportional to the *distance* fallen leads to impossible consequences. His argument is in fact fallacious. Perhaps the best argument which could have been used before the invention of the Integral Calculus would have been the following. If the velocity be proportional to the distance fallen, a body starting from rest will not have acquired *any* velocity until it has fallen *some* distance. But, on the other hand, until it has acquired *some* velocity, it cannot have fallen *any* distance. Therefore, if this hypothesis were true, no body starting from rest would fall through a finite distance in any finite time. Since this is plainly contrary to experience, the hypothesis which leads to it may be rejected. Let us present Galileo with this argument, for what it is worth, in exchange for his own which is worthless.

Galileo now felt justified in confining his attention to the hypothesis that the velocity attained is proportional to the *time* which has elapsed. He proceeds to infer, quite correctly, that on this hypothesis the distance fallen should be proportional to the *square* of the time which has elapsed. This deduction involved the performance by a graphical method of a very simple integration.

Now it is much easier to measure distances and lapses of time than to measure velocities directly. So this consequence can be tested experimentally, whilst it would not be at all easy to test directly the hypothesis from which it was deduced. Nevertheless, two considerable experimental difficulties had to be overcome. (1) There was no instrument available to Galileo for accurately measuring short lapses of time. Pendulum clocks did not exist, for the isochronism of the pendulum was discovered and theoretically established later by Galileo himself, and applied by him to the construction of clocks, as a result of his work on the laws of falling bodies. Accordingly, he had to devise a method of measuring short lapses of time. For that purpose, he took a wide cylindrical vessel with a small hole in the bottom which he could open and shut at will with his finger. He filled the vessel with water, opened the hole when the body began to move, and shut it again when the body had traversed a given distance. Since the level of the water does not vary appreciably during the short time taken by a single experiment, he assumed that the quantity of water discharged would be proportional to the time which has elapsed.

(2) The second practical difficulty is that falling bodies move so quickly that no accurate measurement can be made by this means of the times which they take to traverse reasonably short distances. Galileo therefore turned his attention to the case of bodies rolling down inclined planes. Here, by making the slope of the plane gentle enough, he could make the time of descent long enough to be measured accurately. He found that in such cases his observations fully confirmed his deduction that the distance traversed should be proportional to the square of the time taken.

The next step is to pass back from the case of a body moving down an inclined plane to the original problem of a body falling freely. Galileo made the transition by way of the following proposition, viz., that the velocity which a body acquires by rolling down an inclined plane depends only on the height through which it has descended and is independent of the slope of the plane. He established this proposition in two ways, one deductive and the other experimental.

The deductive method consists in showing that, if the velocity attained in falling through a given height varied with the slope of the plane, it would be possible to arrange a system of inclined planes by means of which a body could raise itself above its starting-point simply by the momentum which it has acquired in rolling down from that point. This is plainly contrary to universal experience.

The direct experimental proof was as follows, Galileo hung a small weight on a long thin thread from a nail in a vertical board, and let the weight swing freely as a pendulum. In the vertical line below the point of suspension and above the point from which the bob of the pendulum starts to swing he drove another nail at various heights in various experiments (see Figure 3.1.1).[1] Suppose now that the pendulum is descending from right to left. When the thread becomes vertical it will touch the nail, and the part of it between the point of suspension and the nail will remain vertical. The rest of the thread, with the weight attached to it, will continue to rotate to the

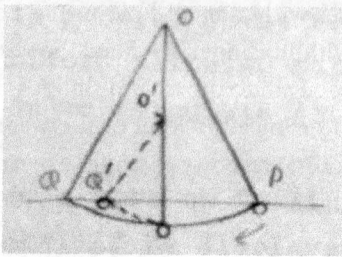

Figure 3.1.1 Scan of Broad's own illustration.

left about the nail as a fixed centre. Galileo found, as he had expected, that no matter at what height he fixed the nail the height reached by the weight was always the same, viz., that from which it had started to swing downwards from the right.

Now in each experiment, the weight starts to ascend with the same velocity, viz., that which it has acquired by swinging back to the vertical from its starting-point on the right. The experiment shows that this is always just sufficient to carry it up to the same height on the left, no matter whether its course of ascent after the thread has touched the nail is steep or gentle. Conversely, when it swings back again from left to right, it always reaches the level from which it originally started when it swung from right to left, no matter where the nail may have been inserted in the vertical line. It is interesting to notice that in all this Galileo is formulating an important particular case of the Conservation of Energy.

Having established the proposition that the velocity acquired depends only on the height descended and not on the slope of the plane, Galileo can at once transfer the results which he has established for bodies rolling down inclined planes to the case of a body falling freely. To do this, he has only to apply the Principle of Continuity. For a freely falling body is simply the limiting case of a body falling down an inclined plane which makes an angle of 90 degrees to the horizontal.

Galileo made another appeal to the Principle of Continuity in considering the other limiting case, viz., a plane which makes an angle of 0 degrees with the horizontal. Imagine a body which has rolled down an inclined plane and has acquired a certain velocity in doing so. Let it then start to roll up another inclined plane. Apart from air resistance and friction, it will travel upwards, gradually losing speed, until it stops at the height from which it originally started. Now imagine the slope of the second inclined plane made gradually less and less until in the limiting case it becomes zero. The body will travel further and further and will lose speed more and more slowly as the slope is diminished. Therefore in the limiting case, it will lose no speed but will continue to travel onwards forever with its original velocity. Thus Galileo arrives at a particular case of the Law of Inertia. He never formulated the law in its general form; he seems to have thought mistakenly that it applied to uniform circular motions as well as to rectilinear motions. The first person to formulate it generally and correctly seems to have been Descartes.

Before leaving Galileo's work on falling bodies there is one remark which I would like to make. If he displayed the genius of an angel, he also had the Devil's own luck. Of all the innumerable alternative hypotheses which might have been true, he considered only the two simplest. He rejected the one that happened to be false by a fallacious argument, and so saved himself the trouble of testing it. The other happened to be the true one. Kepler, seeking for laws connecting the periodic times of the planets with their distances from the sun, had no such luck. He had to try hypothesis after hypothesis until he hit on the by no means simple ones which fitted the facts.

We can now consider Galileo's application of his work on falling bodies to the then unsolved problem of the path of a projectile. We will suppose that the body is projected upwards at an angle to the vertical. Galileo solved the problem by a flash of insight of the highest order. He saw that the actual motion of the projectile at any moment can be regarded as compounded vectorially of two motions, one horizontal and the other vertical. The horizontal component continues throughout to be the same in velocity in accordance with the Law of Inertia. The vertical component follows exactly the same law as if the body had been thrown straight upwards, and, after gradually losing its initial velocity, had then momentarily come to rest and started to fall straight downwards with gradually increasing speed. The law of this increase and decrease of velocity had already been ascertained in the way which I have described above. Now the properties of conic sections had been well known since Greek times. Galileo was able to show by geometrical reasoning that a body endowed simultaneously with such horizontal and vertical motions would describe a parabola. And he was able to determine the precise nature of the parabola in terms of the magnitude and direction of the velocity of projection and the earth's gravitational attraction.

Here again, Galileo recognised a particular case of a fundamentally important general principle in dynamics, viz., that a motion with given speed in a given direction can be resolved into components at right angles to each other, and that each component is causally determined quite independently of the others.

I pass now to the work of Newton. Newton's system was built on foundations which had been laid by Galileo in dynamics and by Kepler in astronomy. His contributions to the science of dynamics may fairly be described as a generalisation of the results which Galileo had reached in dealing with the special cases of bodies falling and projectiles moving near the earth's surface.

Looking backwards, and expressing ourselves in terms of ideas which we owe largely to Newton, we may say that Galileo was dealing with dynamical transactions subject to certain special simplifying conditions. These conditions are the following. (1) The processes studied took place in a field of force of a single kind, viz., a gravitational field, (2) The force under consideration was practically uniform because all the experiments were done on bodies close to the earth's surface. (3) The force itself was of a very peculiar kind and was not fitted to disclose the distinction between mass and weight. For, since the *gravitational* force on a body is directly proportional to its mass, whilst the acceleration produced in a body by *any* kind of force is inversely proportional to its mass, bodies of all masses will fall with the same acceleration in the same gravitational field. (4) The fact that the earth was rotating daily on its axis and at the same time revolving annually around the sun with Galileo and the bodies on which he was working was of negligible importance in these experiments. Newton's great achievement was to formulate a set of concepts and principles which apply to all motions whatever, no matter what may be the causes which initiate, accelerate, or decelerate them, or modify their direction.

The first need was to clear up certain points about space, time, and motion which had been left vague by Galileo. A body which is moving in a straight line with uniform velocity relative to the surface of the earth will be describing a very complicated path with variable speed relative to the sun. Again, a body whose velocity is uniform when lapse of time is measured by one method will be moving with variable speed when it is measured by certain other methods. Now it is usual to state the Law of Inertia in the form that a body, if unaffected by external causes, will continue to rest or to move with uniform velocity in a straight line. It now appears that this statement is indefinite until we specify the axes to which we refer the motion and the chronometer by which we measure lapses of time.

Newton recognised this difficulty, though the expedient which he adopted is generally recognised to be wholly unsatisfactory. He postulated two entities, which he called *Absolute Space* and *Absolute Time*, and he formulated the laws of motion in terms of motions which describe equal distances along straight lines in Absolute Space during equal lapses of Absolute Time. This device is neither theoretically satisfactory nor practically applicable. It is the recognition of a problem, not the solution of it. It was severely and justly criticised by Leibniz, though Leibniz's alternative treatment of the problem must be pronounced to be equally unsatisfactory in my opinion.

Assuming, for the sake of argument, that the Law of Inertia can be stated in a form which is neither indefinite nor tautological nor in principle unverifiable, the term *Force*, as used in dynamics, can be defined or described as follows. A body is said to be acted on at a certain moment by a force if and only if there is at that moment either a change in it from rest to motion or a change in the magnitude or the direction of its velocity. The direction of the force will be the direction of this instantaneous change of velocity. The magnitude of the force will be directly proportional to the instantaneous acceleration. Whether this account of force is applicable without great artificiality to statics is a question which I shall not discuss here.

The next important advance is the introduction of the concept of *Mass* and the clear distinction of it from weight. Galileo, for reasons which have been suggested above, did not grasp this distinction. We may put the point as follows. (1) All bodies have a property in virtue of which they offer resistance to any agent tending to alter their state of rest or uniform motion in a straight line. Different kinds of body of the same size and shape offer different degrees of resistance to precisely similar changes in their state of rest or uniform motion in a straight line. These facts are the basis for ascribing to bodies a certain measurable property which may be called *Inertial Mass*. (2) All bodies have a property in virtue of which they attract each other. Different kinds of body of the same size and shape at the same distance apart attract each other to different degrees. This is the ground for ascribing to bodies a certain measurable property which may be called *Gravitational Mass*. (3) It is an empirical fact that the gravitational and the inertial mass of a body in all cases bear the same proportion to each other, so that with a suitable choice of units they are always equal.

The distinction between mass and weight is easily grasped if we consider the case of a horizontal flywheel pivoted on bearings which are as nearly frictionless as possible. Everyone knows that a considerable effort is needed to set such a wheel rotating if it is at rest or to stop it if it is in motion. Everyone knows that the effort is greater *ceteris paribus* if the wheel is made of heavy material, such as lead, than if it is made of light material, such as plywood. Yet there is here no question of raising a weight against the attraction of the earth, since the wheel remains horizontal and every part of it remains at the same height. Therefore it is plain that we are concerned here with a property of matter which, though connected with weight, is different from weight. The facts may be summed up by saying that every body has mass, that different bodies have in general different masses even if they are geometrically exactly alike, that the same body keeps the same mass in all its dynamical transactions, and that the acceleration produced in any body by a force is inversely proportional to its mass.

Now Galileo had shown that bodies of different mass at the same place on the earth fall with the same acceleration if the effects of the surrounding medium are eliminated. It follows that the gravitational attraction of the earth on any body at a given place is directly proportional to the mass of that body. Hence at any given place weight is proportional to mass, and therefore masses can be compared by the simple device of weighing them. For weighing just consists in balancing the gravitational attractions of the earth on the bodies in the two adjacent scale-pans.

No further primary concepts are needed in formulating the laws of dynamics. But one further principle is needed, and this was recognised and stated by Newton in his *Third Law of Motion*. Suppose that a body A exerts force on a body B. Newton asserts that this is always one side of a mutual transaction. The body B must exert simultaneously on A a force which is equal in magnitude and opposite in direction to that which A is exerting on B. That this principle, though true, is neither obvious nor trivial may be realised by anyone who asks himself what answer he would make to the following question from an intelligent child: 'If the trucks are pulling the engine back with the same force with which the engine is pulling them forward, how does the train as a whole ever move?'

We are now in a position to describe Newton's discovery of the law of universal gravitation and his application of it to explain a whole series of celestial and terrestrial phenomena, not only in qualitative outline, but also in quantitative detail. This was the first, and it remains the most spectacular, large-scale triumph of the quantitative method in science. It produced, quite rightly, an immense impression on contemporary and subsequent thought.

The basis here is Kepler's work on the motions of the planets. Kepler had shown that the apparent daily and yearly motions of the stars, the sun, and the planets could be accounted for most simply and to a very high degree of accuracy by supposing that the earth rotates on its axis once in every 24 hours and that it and the planets describe ellipses of various excentricities and with various periods about the sun as a common focus. The latter part of this proposition constitutes Kepler's First Law of Planetary Motion.

Now Kepler was a Platonic or Pythagorean number-mystic possessed of infinite patience in computation. His number-mysticism gave him an intense conviction that there *must* be quantitative regularities covering all the planetary motions, and his infinite patience in computation sustained him in calculating the results of one hypothesis after another and comparing them with the observed positions of the planets night after night. Eventually, his faith and his works were rewarded by verifying two extremely odd quantitative laws which proved in Newton's hands to be of the utmost importance. The first is that the line joining a given planet to the sun sweeps out equal *areas* in equal lapses of time, no matter where the planet may be in its course at the beginning of such a period. The area swept out in a given time varies from planet to planet but is constant for any given planet. This is Kepler's Second Law. The other regularity connects the periodic times of different planets. Kepler found that for any two planets the *squares* of the times which they take to make a complete revolution about the sun are to each other as the *cubes* of their mean distances from the sun. This is Kepler's Third Law.

It is worthwhile to remark how very odd these laws appear before one knows the reason for them, and how far from simple they are. Kepler tried numerous hypotheses and just went on trying less and less obvious ones and stolidly computing their consequences until he hit on the three which fitted the observations. By Newton's time, these three empirical laws were generally accepted and it was felt that there must be some explanation of them, but no one knew what the explanation might be.

To these laws must be added one other astronomical fact which had been established by Newton's time. Galileo had invented and constructed the first telescope and with it, he had discovered that the planet Jupiter has several moons which revolve about it as our moon does about the earth. It was found that the periodic times of Jupiter's moons in their revolutions about Jupiter obey a law of the same form as Kepler's Third Law, i.e., that the squares of the times which they take to revolve about the planet are to each other as the cubes of their mean distances from it.

Now, since the planets move round the sun, our moon moves round the earth, and Jupiter's moons move around Jupiter, there must in each case be a force which continually acts on these moving bodies and prevents them from flying off tangentially in straight lines with uniform velocity in accordance with the Law of Inertia. It is very easy to show that Kepler's Second Law, i.e., the description of equal areas in equal times by the same planet, will be satisfied if and only if the force acts along the line joining the moving body to the body about which it revolves. Three questions at once present themselves. (1) Is it the same kind of force in each case? (2) If so, how does that force vary with the distance between the moving body and the central body? (3) Can this celestial force be identified with any with which we are already familiar in terrestrial phenomena?

Now the fact that Kepler's Laws are obeyed by Jupiter's moons in their revolutions about Jupiter as well as by the planets in their revolutions about the sun at once suggests that the same kind of force is acting in both cases. Again, although the planets move in ellipses about the sun as their common focus, and not in circles about the sun as their common centre, it happens that the ellipses are very nearly circular and therefore that the focus is very nearly central. And, although the velocity of any planet is not exactly the same at every point in its orbit, it is approximately so. Lastly, although the sun and the planets are not mere points but are large bodies, still their distances apart are so great in comparison with their radii that we can begin by treating them simply as massive points.

So, as a first approximation, we can suppose that the sun and the planets are massive *particles*, and that each planet moves in a *circle* about the sun with a characteristic *constant* velocity. Now, on these three simplifying assumptions, it is easy to show that the periodic times of the planets will be connected with their distances from the sun in the peculiar way stated in Kepler's Third Law if and only if the force which attracts each planet to the sun is directly proportional to the mass of the planet and of the sun and inversely proportional to the square of the distance between them. Obviously, then, this suggested law of attraction is worth further investigation.

The next step is as follows. Might not the force which keeps the planets in their orbits about the sun and keeps Jupiter's moons in their orbits about Jupiter and keeps our moon in its orbit about the earth be identical with the force with which we are familiar at the earth's surface as gravitation? Newton proceeded to test this suggestion by working out its consequences in the case of the moon. On this supposition, if the earth can be treated as a particle with all its mass concentrated at its centre, the gravitational force at the earth's surface will be directly proportional to the earth's mass and inversely proportional to the square of its radius. The gravitational force due to the earth at the moon will be directly proportional to the earth's mass and inversely proportional to the square of the distance between the centres of the earth and the moon. Now the gravitational force at the earth's surface is known, and so are the earth's radius and its distance from the moon. Therefore, we can at once calculate what force the earth would exert on the moon on the hypothesis which is being tested. From this, we can calculate what should be the period in which the moon revolves round the earth, on the simplifying assumption that it moves uniformly in a circle about the earth as centre, which is a rough first approximation to the truth. Suppose that the calculated period of the moon should agree very closely with its actual period. Then the hypothesis on which the calculation is based will be confirmed. In that case, we could tentatively identify the force which keeps the moon and the planets in their orbits with the force which makes unsupported bodies near the earth fall to the ground.

Newton worked out the whole of this argument at the age of 23. With the numerical data available to him at the time, the calculated period of a complete revolution of the moon about the earth would be about 23.3 days. The actual period is about 27.3 days. So the discrepancy was considerable. Much later he repeated his calculations with more accurate data about the earth's radius. The calculated period of the moon's revolution now came out to 27 days, a discrepancy of little more than 1% from the actual period. Evidently the hypothesis that the force which keeps the moon and the planets in their orbits is the force which we experience on earth as gravitation had become extremely plausible.

But it will be remembered that the calculations had been made on a number of simplifying assumptions. The hardest part of Newton's work remained to be done. He had now to remove the preliminary simplifications and see whether as good or better results would follow. He had to take into account the fact that the sun, the planets, the moon, and the earth are not really mathematical points but are finite spheroids. He had also to allow for the fact that the planets really move in ellipses with variable velocities about the sun as focus and not in circles with constant velocities about the sun as centre.

First, he succeeded in proving the very beautiful theorem that the attraction produced by a solid sphere composed of matter which attracts in accordance with the inverse-square law is exactly the same at any external point as if all its mass were concentrated at its centre. Thus, the first simplifying assumption turns out to be, not an approximation at all in so far as the bodies concerned are accurately spherical, but a true account of the facts.

Next, he managed to prove that a body moving round a point to which it is attracted in accordance with the inverse-square law will describe an ellipse about that point as focus and that the area swept out by the line joining the two will be proportional to the time elapsed. He also proved that, if there be several bodies moving at different distances round a common point of attraction, their distances and their periods of revolution will be connected by Kepler's Third Law.

Kepler's Laws were now completely explained, and Newton's hypothesis that every particle attracts every other with a force directly proportional to the product of their masses and inversely proportional to the square of the distance between them was firmly established. The rest of Newton's work on gravitation was twofold. He applied his principles to explain certain terrestrial phenomena due to the gravitational influence of the heavenly bodies upon the earth, for example, the tides. Secondly, he applied it to explain the precession of the equinoxes and certain minor anomalies in the motions of the planets, and more especially of the moon, which arise from the fact that each body is attracted to some extent by all the other bodies in the solar system.

It remains to consider a very important theoretical point in connexion with Newton's work which links up with his discovery of the Differential Calculus but is also of much wider significance.

Let us first consider what Newton had to do in order to calculate the gravitational force exerted by a solid sphere at a point outside it. He had to treat the sphere as composed of a very large number of particles each so small that it could be regarded as approximating to a point with a very small mass. He had then to compound together the very small attractions which each of these particles would exert at the external point in question. Finally, he had to determine the limit to which this total force would approach as each particle was made smaller and smaller whilst their number was made greater and greater. This is what we should now call a problem in integration.

Let us next consider the problem of determining the path of a particle projected with a certain tangential velocity and then left to move under the gravitational attraction of a centre of force. The dynamical principles required are precisely the same as those which Galileo used in dealing with the path of a projectile. But the problem is far more complex and it involves mathematical concepts and principles which were not needed by Galileo. In Galileo's problem, the force acting on the particle was constant in magnitude and direction throughout the transaction. In Newton's problem, the force is continually altering in magnitude, since it depends at each instance on the distance of the particle from the attracting centre, and this is constantly changing. Again, the force is continually altering in direction and making different angles to the instantaneous direction of the planet's motion. So, Newton had to deal with velocities which varied both in magnitude and in direction, and moreover with the variations of their variations from moment to moment. In every dynamical problem, we have to deal with the notions of instantaneous direction, instantaneous velocity, and instantaneous acceleration. And in the problem of the attraction of the solid sphere, we need the concept of the density of a body at a point.

Such concepts are now so familiar that we are inclined to forget how difficult, and sophisticated, and paradoxical they are. If we confine our attention literally to a single moment and a single position the particle is not moving at all, for motion involves at least two positions, however near together, and at least two instants. If, on the other hand, we consider the history of the particle throughout any interval, no matter how short, there is in general no one magnitude and no one direction that can be ascribed to its velocity. Again, density is the ratio of the mass of a bit of matter to its volume. If we confine ourselves literally to a single point, it has no mass and no volume, and the ratio is meaningless. If, on the other hand, we take any finite volume, however small, the ratio may vary with the size of the volume chosen, since the density of the body may vary continuously from point to point within it. Therefore all such concepts need to be carefully defined, the definitions need to be justified, and the principles involved in manipulating such concepts mathematically need to be established. This is the work which Newton accomplished, imperfectly indeed in respect of logical rigour but adequately for the purposes of applied mathematics, in his Theory of Fluxions.

Particular problems in integration had been solved long before Newton's time by special devices. This had been done in connexion with determining the lengths of certain curved lines, the areas enclosed by certain plain curves, and the volumes enclosed by certain curved surfaces. But each problem had been solved by some special trick, whose discovery depended on the insight or the luck of some individual mathematician. The nearest approach to a general method of differentiation which existed had been developed by Newton's teacher, Barrow, in his *Geometrical Lectures*. Barrow had given geometrical methods of doing what we should now describe as finding the first differential coefficient of many of the commonest mathematical functions.

Still, the following assertion is roughly true. The general conception of the rate of change of one variable magnitude with respect to another for any given value of the latter hardly existed; still less did the conception of rates of rates of change. No general method existed by which such quantities could be calculated as soon as the functional relation between the two magnitudes was given. And it was not recognised that the problem of integration is the converse of the problem of determining rates of change. All this we owe to Newton, and independently to Leibniz. Newton approaches the problem from a geometrical standpoint; Leibniz, so far as I can make out, from that of the Calculus of Finite Differences. Neither of them succeeded in putting the Infinitesimal Calculus on a satisfactory logical basis, and the logic of Newton's theory of Fluxions was severely and justly criticised soon after his death by the Philosopher Berkeley in his *Analyst* and his *Defence of Free Thinking in Mathematics*. Nevertheless, physicists and applied mathematicians rightly felt that they had been presented with concepts and methods of incomparable power and fertility. They very sensibly decided to use them for all that they were worth, and to leave to professional logicians and pure mathematicians the task of tidying up the theoretical foundations if and when they could. This task was not completed until the latter part of the XIXth century, when it was accomplished largely through the work of Weierstrass.

I shall conclude my lecture by saying something about the work of Descartes and Leibniz, the two great professional philosophers who concerned themselves with dynamics as an integral part of their philosophy.

Descartes made one contribution of the utmost importance to the development of quantitative methods, viz., the invention of analytical geometry. He insisted that all geometrical facts can be represented by numbers and their arithmetical relations, and that all relations between correlated variables can be represented geometrically by curves, surfaces, etc. His contributions to physics in general and to dynamics in particular are also important, but they are mixed with so much error that they cannot be praised without considerable reservations.

We must always remember that Descartes was engaged in a struggle, both in his own mind and with external opponents, against the Scholastic physics in which he had been brought up at La Flèche. He thought, quite rightly, that the great defect of that system was to provide purely verbal explanations of phenomena by postulating crowds of special faculties, powers, dispositions, substantial forms, and so on, in matter. These postulated entities were wholly unfruitful; nothing new could be inferred from them which might suggest new experiments by which they might be tested, verified, refuted, or modified. Moreover, Descartes was convinced that the ideas of such powers and faculties were fundamentally and irremediably confused; that they arose through failure to distinguish clearly between matter and mind; and that they involved ascribing to matter properties which can occur only in connexion with embodied minds. The only feature in our notion of matter which seemed to Descartes to be clear, distinct, and fruitful in consequences is its purely geometrical and kinematic properties of shape, size, position, and motion. He therefore insisted that nothing but these properties should be admitted in physics in general and in dynamics in particular.

Now the fact is that, whilst this doctrine of Descartes is most valuable in getting rid of a whole mass of rubbish, it makes too clean a sweep. This was pointed out very clearly by Leibniz in his criticisms of the Cartesian dynamics. Matter has at least two properties, essential to dynamics, which cannot be deduced from or identified with its purely geometrical and kinematic properties. One of them is *impenetrability*. This must not be confused with hardness. It is the fact that no region of space can be occupied throughout by two bodies, whether hard or soft, at the same time. This is of course quite compatible with the fact that a region can be occupied throughout by an intimate mixture of two kinds of matter, A and B, so interspersed that every sub-region which is empty of A is filled with B and every sub-region which is empty of B is filled with A.

The other non-geometrical and non-kinematic property of matter is *inertia*. This involves, as Leibniz pointed out, two aspects, one negative and the other positive. The negative aspect is that a body is incapable of altering its own state of rest or of uniform rectilinear motion, as the case may be. The positive aspect is that a body resists any other body which influences its own state of rest or of uniform rectilinear motion. It has a positive tendency to continue to rest or to continue to move uniformly in a straight line, and it will slow down or divert any body which interferes with this tendency. The phenomena of impact exhibit the two properties of impenetrability and inertia in the most obvious way.

Now Descartes was, of course, aware of these facts and indeed insisted on them. But they do not fit into his purely geometrical and kinematic system, and his attempts to insert them into it lead to embarrassment in principle and mistakes in detail. Descartes was, I believe, the first person to state the Law of Inertia completely and correctly. It is summed up by his first two laws of motion. The first law is that every body opposes any external cause which tends to change its state of motion or of rest. The second is that every moving body continues to move with the same velocity and in the same direction which it is moving at a given instant unless it is then affected by an external cause. Descartes professed to deduce these laws from the immutability of God. It is an empirical fact that God has created a world in which there is motion, although it is logically possible that he might have created a world in which everything was at rest. But, granted this lapse, we must postulate the minimum of variation in a world created by an immutable Being. Therefore we must assume that the total quantity of motion in the world will always be the same though it will be differently distributed at different moments. And we must assume that all changes in the distribution of motion will take place in accordance with unchanging laws of the simplest kind.

This brings us to an important mistake of detail which Descartes made and Leibniz pointed out. By the 'quantity of motion' in a body at any moment Descartes seems to have meant the product of the mass of that body by its velocity at that moment, no account being taken of the direction of the motion but only of its speed. Now Leibniz pointed out that quantity of motion, so defined, is *not* conserved in dynamical transactions. He also showed that something else *is* conserved, viz., the total momentum in any given straight line. This is the product of the mass of a body by its velocity in a given straight line, the velocity being reckoned positive if the body is moving in one direction in the line, for example, from east to west, and negative if it is moving in the opposite direction in the same line, for example, from west to east.

The difference between Leibniz's true law of the Conservation of *Momentum* in a given straight line and Descartes' false law of the Conservation of *Motion* without regard to direction can easily be seen in the following elementary example. Imagine two equally massive, imperfectly elastic spheres moving with equal speed in opposite directions in the same straight line and coming into a head-on collision. After the collision, they will rebound. Their velocities will still be equal in speed and opposite in direction, but, since the bodies are imperfectly elastic, the speed of rebound will be less than the speed just before collision. Let the speed of collision be u and the speed of rebound be v for each body. The quantity of motion, in Descartes' sense, before the collision is 2mu, where m is the mass of each body. After the collision it is 2mv. This is smaller than 2mu, since v is less than u. So the quantity of motion has not been conserved. Now consider the total momentum in a given direction, for example, from left to right, in the straight line in which the bodies are moving. Before the collision, it was mu − mu, i.e., zero. After the collision, it is mv − mv, i.e., zero. So the momentum in a given direction *has* been conserved, whilst the quantity of motion without regard to direction has not. The two laws are different and incompatible with each other, and Leibniz's is the one which is true.

Descartes' mistake about this general principle led him into mistakes of detail. He professed to deduce from his principle seven laws about the motions of bodies after collision with each other under various conditions of relative mass, velocity, and direction. These laws are all seriously wrong. The correct laws of impact were established by Wren, Huyghens, and Newton. What is needed here is one correct general principle, viz., the Conservation of Momentum, and one special empirical law. The latter was discovered experimentally by Newton. It may be stated as follows. Suppose that two bodies moving in the same straight line collide, either head-on or by overtaking each other. Then their relative velocity in a given direction after the collision bears to their relative velocity in the opposite direction before the collision a positive ratio which is (a) constant for bodies of a given material, (b) different for bodies of different material, and (c) not greater than unity. This ratio is called the 'coefficient of elasticity' or of 'restitution' for the material in question. It reaches its upper bound of unity in the case of perfectly elastic bodies.

Now, this brings us back to Leibniz. On metaphysical grounds, which I shall not discuss here, Leibniz asserted another conservation-principle in addition to the Conservation of Momentum. This is the Conservation of *Vis Viva*. The *vis viva* of a moving body at any moment is the product of its mass by the *square* of its speed at that moment. It is in fact twice the quantity which we now call *Kinetic Energy*. Leibniz held that in all dynamical transactions the total amount of *vis viva* in the interacting bodies must remain unaltered, though there would be changes in its distribution. Now it is very easy to prove that, in the case of bodies which interact by collision, the *vis viva* in the system remains constant if and only if the bodies are perfectly elastic. If they are imperfectly elastic there is a loss of *vis viva* after the collision which increases with the divergence from perfect elasticity. Leibniz was fully aware of this fact. But, as a metaphysician with an *a priori* principle to defend, he was not the man to let such an empirical fact trouble him. His solution was to say that the *vis viva* which disappears from two imperfectly elastic bodies as wholes after collision is balanced by an increase in the *vis viva* of the minute parts of these bodies. The latter are set in motion by the collision, and the *vis viva* which they thus gain ceases to be measurable but keeps the conservation-principle intact.

If we should be inclined to smile in a superior way at this device of Leibniz's, we shall do well to remember that his Conservation of *Vis Viva* is the first adumbration of the Conservation of Energy, and that the latter principle has to be saved by precisely the same means as the former. We should say nowadays that the kinetic energy lost by imperfectly elastic bodies when they collide is balanced by the heat, sound, and other kinds of energy which are generated by the collision. And it is usual to hold that these kinds of energy are the outward manifestations of vibrations and other motions in the minute particles of the colliding bodies and the surrounding medium. We have considerably better detailed empirical evidence for such statements than Leibniz had for his, but it may fairly be said that he anticipated on *a priori* grounds an important general principle of conservation which for us is based on a judicious mixture of experimental fact and conventional 'cooking'.

This brings me to the last topic that I shall mention, viz., the long and famous controversy between the Leibnitians and the Cartesians on the correct measure of what they called the 'living force' of a body. The living force of a body is its power of producing mechanical effects by its motion, for example, by impact, by raising a weight to a certain height, by compressing a spring, and so on. This was contrasted with the 'dead force' of a body, which is its power of producing effects while at rest by mere static pressure. The Cartesians alleged that the true measure of the living force of a moving body is the product of its mass by its velocity, i.e., what we should call its *momentum*; the Leibnitians asserted that the true measure is the product of its mass by the square of its velocity, i.e., what we should call twice its *kinetic energy*.

Many very famous men took part in this controversy. The first published work of the great philosopher Kant is a very acute and learned treatise on the subject which appeared in 1747 under the title *Gedanken von der wahren Schätzung der lebendigen Kräfte*. D'Alembert is generally credited with being the first person to dissolve the controversy by showing that each party was right in what it asserted and wrong in what it denied.

The essential point of d'Alembert's solution may be put as follows. Suppose that a body of mass m is moving at a certain instant with a velocity v in a certain straight line; for example, the body might be a trolley projected along a straight level railway track. Suppose that at that instant a force begins to act in the opposite direction to its motion, and that thereafter this force remains constant in magnitude and direction until it brings the body to rest. In our example, such a force might arise through the brake being applied and then kept on at constant pressure.

Now we can raise two alternative questions. (1) For how long a *time* will the body continue to move until this constant force brings it to rest? And (2) for how long a *distance* will the body travel before this same constant force brings it to rest? It is obvious that either the time taken or the distance traversed by the body before being brought to rest by a given constant resistance might equally reasonably be taken as the measure of its living force. There is no room for argument here, it is just a matter of taste.

Now the answer to the first question is that the *time taken* is proportional to the *momentum*, i.e., the product of the mass by the velocity, and the answer to the second question is that the *distance traversed* is proportional to the *vis viva*, i.e., to the product of the mass by the square of the velocity. Nor are these two answers logically independent of each other. The first follows immediately from Newton's law that the force is equal to the rate of change of momentum. And the second follows from the first by a mere mathematical transformation, viz., the fact that the rate of change of a velocity with respect to time is equal to the rate of change of half the square of that velocity with respect to distance. Thus, the Cartesian and the Leibnitian each made a tacit assumption, and each gave the right answer on his own assumption. The controversy arose and continued because the assumptions of the two parties were never made explicit; and, when they are made explicit, it becomes plain that there is no rational ground for preferring one to the other.

3.2

NOTES ON CAUSATION

In surveying the various topics which ought to be discussed under the head of Causation it is useful to begin by distinguishing two kinds of causal propositions, viz., *Propositions of Causal Connexion* and *Principles about Causation*. The former assert or deny of something that it is causally connected with something. They may be singular, for example, 'I am opening my umbrella' or completely general, for example, 'Rise of temperature makes metals expand'. General propositions of causal connexion are called *Causal Laws*. A principle about causation is a universal proposition about causal connexion in general, for example, 'Every event is causally determined', 'The complete cause of any event is continuous in time with it', and so on.

About propositions of all these kinds, two sorts of questions may be raised, viz., analytical and epistemological, thus giving rise to six kinds of question in all. The former are concerned with the *analysis* of singular propositions of causal connexion, of causal laws, and of the various principles about causation which have been widely accepted. They are also concerned with the distinction and definition of various terms, such as 'necessary condition', 'sufficient condition', and so on, which emerge when we try to enunciate the various kinds of causal propositions accurately. As examples of *epistemological* problems about causation, we may adduce the following question: Do we *know* any facts of causal connexion? If we have no knowledge in this department, have we at any rate *rational beliefs*, or are all our beliefs here simply the products of non-rational causes, such as retentiveness and association? Again, if we have rational cognition on these matters, what is the nature of our evidence, and in what way does it give us knowledge or justify our beliefs? All these questions can be raised about each kind of causal proposition which we have distinguished, and there is no reason to expect that the same kind of answer will hold in each case. For example, it might well turn out that we *know* some principles about causation, but do not strictly know any proposition of causal connexion. Or, again, it might turn out that we *know* some singular propositions of causal connexion, but do not strictly know any causal laws.

Although it is essential to distinguish the various kinds of causal propositions and the two kinds of questions which can be asked about each, it is to be expected that the nature of one's answers to some of these problems would have an important bearing on the answers which it would be reasonable to give to others of them. Suppose, for example, that you analyse propositions of causal connexion in the way proposed by the regularity theory. Then the principle that every event is causally determined may lose all plausibility. On the other hand, if you think that you have *a priori* knowledge of this principle, that may cause you to doubt the regularity theory. And so on.

Here, as elsewhere in philosophy, each part of the subject is interconnected in the most complex way with all the other parts; and this makes it extremely difficult to know where to begin and quite impossible to feel much confidence in what one says about any one part until one has treated the whole. Nor do the problems of causation, which I have distinguished, form a closed system. For causation connects *events* in *substances* with other events in the same or different substances. So complete discussion of causation would involve a discussion of the notions of substance and event; whilst the notion of substance, in its turn, involves the notion of causal properties and dispositions, and thus refers you back to the problems of causation.

It seems to me that, in England at any rate, many philosophers since Hume's time who have discussed causation have tended to take much too narrow a view of the subject. They have tended to confine themselves to propositions of causal connexion, and have almost ignored principles about causation. They have further tended to restrict their attention mainly to causal laws, as distinct from singular propositions of causal connexion. And, even in this doubly restricted field, their interest has been primarily epistemological.

They were in fact almost wholly concerned with the nature and justification of *inductive generalisation*. I should be the last to deny the importance and interest of this problem, but it is only one out of the many problems connected with causation. I propose tonight to ignore it altogether and to consider topics which are less familiar here and now.

Prima facie it would seem reasonable to begin any discussion on causation by considering the simplest kind of singular propositions about causal connexion. If I wanted to discuss perception, I should give as examples the sort of facts which are expressed by such sentences as 'I see the Trinity clock', 'I hear the Trinity clock striking', 'I am feeling my watch in the dark', and so on. None of them contain the word 'perceive', which is abstract and slightly highbrow but each contains a word, for example, 'see', 'hear', 'feel', which expresses a form of perceiving. In the same way, when I want to discuss causation, I shall naturally ask you to consider the sort of facts which are expressed by sentences like 'I am lifting a weight', 'I am chopping a log of wood', 'I am pushing a roller', and so on. None of them contain the word 'cause', which is also abstract and slightly highbrow, but the words 'lifting', 'chopping', 'pushing', which they do contain, all express forms of causing. If you want to make a person think about perception, you must get him to think about such perfectly familiar processes as hearing, seeing, feeling, etc., and, if you want to make him think about causation, you must not start with out-of-the-way and highly abstract notions, like the law of gravitation, but must get him to think about such familiar processes as lifting, chopping, pushing, and so on.

Causing is expressed in ordinary European languages by what grammarians call 'transitive verbs', though not all transitive verbs express causing. For example, the verb 'to love' is transitive; but the sentence 'John loves James' does not, *prima facie*, express a proposition of causal connexion.

Let us consider such a sentence as 'I am lifting a stone', or 'I am pushing a roller'. It marks out a certain causal transaction in the following ways. (i) It mentions or refers to or implies a certain kind of object which is being acted upon. 'Lifting' implies an object which has weight, and pushing implies an object which has inertial mass. (ii) It mentions or implies certain kinds of change in this object as being the immediate outstanding consequences of certain processes in the agent. 'Lifting' implies that a heavy object is being *raised* against gravitational attraction; 'pushing' implies that a massive object is being moved *parallel to the ground* in spite of its own inertia and the frictional resistance of the ground. (iii) It implies that these changes in the object are the immediate consequences of certain specific kinds of change in the agent. This is particularly obvious where the transitive verb implies that the result is produced by means of certain kinds of instrument. Cf., for example, 'chopping', 'sawing', 'cleaving', each of which refers to characteristically different ways of producing the same kind of result, viz., the division of a sensibly continuous and cohesive object into readily separable parts.

Now an essential feature in the experiences which give rise to the notion of causal transaction is that of resistance or reaction. This feature is brought most forcibly to one's notice when one's action fails altogether to produce the intended result. I may try to lift a stone, and, after struggling with it, may be unable to do so because it is too heavy; I may try to rush a roller and fail to move it because it is too massive; and I may try to cleave a bar and fail because it is too hard or too tough. These are limiting cases of a feature which is present in a greater or less degree in all my transactions with external objects. If I succeed in lifting the stone or pushing the roller or severing the bar, it offers more or less resistance to my efforts; I have to take more or less time and exude more or less sweat to complete the operation; I am pushed back or pulled down and my limbs are compressed or strained and stretched to a greater or less extent. There are numberless words like 'hard', 'tough', 'heavy', 'light', and 'soft', which express the characteristic kinds and degrees of reaction of various objects to certain kinds of action upon them. There are, of course, limiting cases at the other end of the scale where the resistance or reaction on the agent is evanescent.

So far I have considered only transactions in which one of the agents is a person and the other is a thing. But these are intermediate between two other cases. In some transactions, which must have been much commoner in earlier times than they now are among civilised people during peacetime, both the interacting terms are persons, and each is aware of himself both as agent and as patient in the same transaction. This happens in wrestling, in hand-to-hand fighting, in playing Rugby football, in tugs-of-war, and so on. Two persons who have been engaged in such a transaction may talk it over afterwards. Then each can testify to the other that he felt himself to be acting upon him and to be reacted upon by him. Thus, the testimony of each confirms the other's conviction that his opponent was an agent in the same sense in which he knows directly that he himself was one.

At the other extreme are interactions between inanimate objects, which we can watch only from the outside, for example, moving stones breaking windows, running water turning a mill-wheel, trees bending and writhing and splitting in a gale, and so on. In some such cases, however, we may be more than mere spectators. While I watch the trees writhing in the gale I may be battling against the wind myself, and, when I watch the stream turning the mill-wheel, though I may not be in the water myself, I may remember trying to row or to swim against a stream in the past. Thus I am able, so to speak, 'to put myself in the place of' the writhing trees and the turning mill-wheel.

Closely connected with this factor of resistance and reaction in causal transactions is the following notion. We think of things as tending to persist in certain quiescent states unless interfered with by some external agent. Again, we think of certain processes in things as following a certain natural course unless some external agent intervenes to modify them. We expect solid bodies to keep their continuity, their size, and their shape, unless they are cut or pounded or pressed or pulled; we expect bodies at rest to remain at rest unless they are pushed or their supports are removed; and we expect moving bodies to continue moving in the same direction, at any rate for a time, unless something is done to stop them or to divert them. All action is conceived as imposing upon things modifications, either of some quiescent state of them, or of processes already going on in them; modifications which would not otherwise have taken place. And the resistance or reaction which the patient exerts on the agent is conceived as a manifestation and a measure of its tendency to persist in that state of quiescence or that course of change on which the agent is imposing a modification. In acting on another thing or person each of us is conscious of persisting with effort in a certain process against the resistance which the patient makes, and he is conscious that his action is continually modified by this resistance. He thinks of the patient as having a tendency and a certain amount of power to persist in its original state of quiescence or its original course of change, as being forced to modify this in consequence of his efforts, and as reacting on him with more or less vigour and enforcing more or less modification on his own processes in proportion as this power of persistence is greater.

The same ideas are applied when we are mere spectators of a transaction between two inanimate objects, for example, the smashing of a window by a moving stone. The window has a tendency to remain in the form of a continuous flat sheet; the tendency would be stronger if it were of steel and weaker if it were of tissue-paper. The stone has a tendency to continue moving in the name direction with undiminished speed; this tendency would be stronger if it were a rifle-bullet and weaker if it were a bit of thistle-down. At the moment of coming in contact these tendencies conflict; the tendency of the stone to continue its rectilinear motion imposes a change of form on the window-pane, and the tendency of the glass to keep its continuity imposes a change on the motion of the stone. Each, as we say, 'forces' the other to start behaving in a way in which it would not otherwise have behaved at the time, and the amount of 'force' exerted by each on the other depends on the strength of its tendency to persist in its previous state of quiescence or its previous course of change.

In this example, we have a sudden and dramatic transaction, but exactly the same principles are involved in a process of continuous interaction. The case of a stone whirling round in a horizontal plane at the end of a string provides a familiar example of the latter. At each moment the stone has a tendency to continue moving in its then direction, i.e., to fly off at a tangent. On the other hand, the string has a tendency to resist being stretched, and (if stretched) to return to its natural unstretched length. At each moment. these two tendencies conflict. The tendency of the string to resist stretching, and to return to its natural length if stretched, imposes a change on the direction of the stone's motion; and at the same time, the tendency of the stone to fly off at a tangent keeps the string from resuming its unstretched natural length.

Lastly, we must notice that common sense recognises the presence of vigorous interaction in many cases where no perceptible process of change is taking place but a quiescent state of equilibrium under stress is being maintained. An obvious example of this in transactions between persons would be a period of deadlock in the course of a wrestling-match. Here the immediate experiences of each wrestler assure him of the profound difference between this state of affairs and the geometrically similar state of affairs which would exist if his body and his opponent's body were merely posed by a photographer in their present positions. An intermediate case is provided by a person holding up a heavy weight for a period, or keeping a strong elastic cord stretched between his widely opened arms. This is utterly different from holding one's arms at the same distance apart with an unstretched bit of string held just taut between them. And so we pass from this intermediate case to cases where all the agents are things and a person is a mere spectator of their interaction. A heavy picture hanging from a hook by a cord attached to two eyes at the back of it is a very simple and familiar example. In a sense nothing is happening and the system may remain unchanged for years, but the picture is interacting with the cord at each of the points of attachment, the cord is interacting with the hook, and the hook is interacting with the picture-rail. And all this becomes manifest in a dramatic way if at any time the cord should perish or the hook or the eyes work loose. A human spectator of such a system 'knows what it is like' to be a member of such a system; for he is a psycho-physical being and, in his double capacity, he has both been subject to such stresses and he has had the peculiar experiences which manifest them to him.

I can now sum up the position as follows. Each of us has two quite different sources of perceptual knowledge of a certain one material object, viz., his own body. The two sources may be called extra-somatic and intra-somatic sensation; the former includes sensations of sight and hearing, the latter consists of what is called 'organic sensation'. Each of us can see and touch and feel other bodies as well as his own, and can discover that there is no essential difference between them and it, so far as extra-somatic perception can show. In addition, each of us has internal perception of processes in his own body and in that alone. Now none of us is wholly or mainly a mere spectator of his own and other bodies; each is constantly an agent and a patient in transactions with other bodies, in which he acts on them and they react on him. And, whenever a person's body is involved in a transaction, he perceives in it, by intra-somatic sensation, strains and pulls and pressures. On such occasions he is consciously trying either to impose some desired change of state on some external thing or to modify the course of some external process; or else he is trying to preserve his own present state or to continue in some course of his own against the action of other things or persons which are tending to alter it. In either case, he cannot but recognise in the other agent in the transaction an entity which resembles himself in having persistent tendencies to go its own characteristic way; tendencies which may conflict, or cooperate with his intentions, so that the actual history of both agents is modified continually throughout the period of their interaction. Now each of us has had plenty of experience which may be arranged in the following series. (i) Interacting with other persons, as in wrestling; (ii) interacting with things, as in pushing a roller; (iii) watching other persons interacting with each other, as in seeing a football match; (iv) watching other persons interacting with things, as in watching a carpenter sawing wood; and (v) watching things interacting with each other, as when we see a stone breaking a window. Moreover, many of the transactions which we see taking place between things are, to all outward appearance, of much the same kind as some in which we have ourselves been involved. Most of us have been knocked down by a person in a hurry, as a ninepin is knocked down by a ball, and most of us have bent and swayed in a gale, as a tree can be seen to do. At the top end of this series, each agent has direct perception of himself as acting and reacting, and can receive from the other direct testimony that he too has acted and reacted in corresponding ways. At the bottom end of the series, neither direct perception nor testimony is possible. But the gap is bridged by the series of intermediate cases and by the obvious similarity between many of the interactions of inanimate objects and many of those of persons. As a result of all of this, when I see or think of two inanimate objects interacting I cannot but ascribe to each of them something analogous to that which manifests itself to me in consciousness as *persistent intention*, and something analogous to that which manifests to me in consciousness as *strain and tension and resistance*. I do not, of course, unless I am a fairly primitive man, ascribe to them *consciousness* of a tendency to persist in a certain state or to change in a certain way. And I do not, of course, ascribe to them *consciousness* of being strained or of offering resistance. Since I do not believe them to be conscious at all, I do not suppose that they are conscious of their own active tendencies or their own states of tension, any more than I suppose that they are conscious of their own shapes and sizes and positions and velocities. What I find myself assuming without question is something of the following kind. That in me, who am a psycho-physical being, the experience of persistently intending a result, and the occurrence of certain organic sensations, are manifestations to consciousness of active tendencies and states of stress and strain which exist also in purely physical things (if such there be) and are involved in their interactions. From the nature of the case, these tendencies to persist in a certain state or to go on changing in a certain way, and those conditions of stress and strain, cannot be manifested as experiences in things which have no consciousness. But, so far as I can see, it is not meaningless to suppose that they *exist* in such things. It is true that, unless I had had the experience of carrying out my intentions against obstacles and unless I had had certain sensations originating in my muscles and joints, I could have formed no idea of the active tendencies and the internal stresses and strains which I now ascribe to inanimate things which I see interacting. It is equally true that, unless I had had certain sensations originating in my eyes, I should have no idea of shape or size or position or colour. But, when I ascribe shape and size and colour and position to inanimate things, I am ascribing to them, not eyes or visual sensations, but certain properties which I become aware of through the visual sensations which I have when my eyes are stimulated. Similarly, when I ascribe active tendencies and states of strain to inanimate objects, I am not ascribing to them muscles and joints or experiences of carrying out intentions or organic sensations. I am ascribing to them certain characteristics which I, as an agent, *possess*, and which I, as a conscious and a self-conscious agent, *become aware of* through my experiences of striving to fulfil my intentions and through the organic sensations which arise when the nerve-endings in my muscles and joints are stimulated.

It is legitimate to raise the question of whether we are justified in regarding these familiar experiences, which we have when we wrestle or lift or push or throw, as revealing certain peculiar features in ourselves which I have called 'active tendencies' and 'states of strain'. If this were answered in the affirmative, it would be legitimate to raise the further question of whether we are justified in ascribing similar features to inanimate objects when we see them in situations somewhat like those in which we have been when we had such experiences. These questions need to be raised and discussed, just like the question of whether we are justified, on the strength of our visual sensations, in ascribing colours, shapes, sizes, and positions to our own bodies and to foreign bodies. But at present, I am concerned only with the *analysis* of singular propositions of causal connexion, and not with the question of whether any of them are true or well-founded. I am concerned at present only with what we have in mind when we say such things as that the wind is bending the tress, that the cord is supporting the picture, and so on. And I am quite sure that what I have in mind on such occasions is something like what I have been trying to describe, even if every such belief that I have ever had should have been baseless or false.

Now how, if at all, does this fit in with the treatment of causation which we find, for example, in Hume and his admirers and in their opponents?

In the first place, we notice that they agree in concentrating their attention on *laws*, i.e., universal propositions, and they hardly discuss singular propositions of causal connexion at all. Their controversies with each other turn on whether laws are assertions of regular co-existence and sequence or are assertions of some kind of entailment of one characteristic by another. I suppose that both parties would agree that *singular* propositions of causal connexion must be analysed in terms of *causal laws*, whether causal laws themselves be assertions of regular sequence or assertions of entailment. But it must be confessed that they hardly ever attempt any careful analysis of singular propositions of causal connexion on these lines. Before considering these matters in any detail, I would make the following superficial preliminary remarks.

(1) *Prima facie* it is extremely odd that *singular* propositions should have to be analysed in terms of *universal* propositions. It is quite the opposite order to what one would have been inclined to expect. (2) The controversy between the regularity analysis and the entailment analysis seems *prima facie* to be concerned with the general fact that causal laws are *universal* propositions rather than with the specific fact that they are propositions about *causation*. For, in considering the analysis of *any* universal proposition, the question naturally arises whether it can be regarded as a conjunction of singular propositions or whether it must be regarded as asserting some kind of necessary connexion between characteristics. So far as I can see, this kind of question would have arisen, and the two opposed kinds of answer to it would have suggested themselves to reflective persons, even if we had never had the kind of experiences which suggest the notion of causation to us. They would have arisen over purely classificatory universal propositions, such as 'All swans are white' and 'All cloven-hooved animals chew the cud'. (3) On the occasions which lead us to enunciate singular propositions of causal connexion, such as 'The wind is bending the tree', 'The cord is supporting the picture', 'I am pushing the roller', and so on, we do *not* seem *prima facie* to be thinking either of regular sequence or entailment. And we most certainly *are* thinking of the quite different factors which I have described in the earlier part of my paper, and which Hume and his followers and most of his opponents altogether ignore. When I read what these writers have written on the subject it seems to me that it might be a record of the observations and reflexions of disembodied spirits who have spent their eternity in idly watching the play of shadows on a screen.

I know that these authors must in fact have lifted weights and pushed rollers and been knocked down at football and buffeted by gales, like lesser men. But, when they philosophise about causation, they ignore just those experiences from which, as it seems to me, the notion of causation and all the other notions which are involved in it are derived. Of course, more elaborate discussion might show that each of these three considerations is either irrelevant or superficial, but I think that *prima facie* they justify a certain feeling of discomfort.

I will next mention two closely connected points where the practice of concentrating all one's attention on causal laws has, in my opinion, put many philosophers on the wrong track. The first is the topic of causal necessity. Both regularity theorists and entailment theorists apparently hold that propositions of causal connexion seem *prima facie* to be necessary propositions. They then dispute about the basis of this alleged appearance of being necessary. The entailment theorists say that such propositions really are necessary, and presumably hold that that is a sufficient explanation of their appearing to be so. The regularity theorists say that such propositions are not really necessary, and they then proceed to account for the delusive appearance of being necessary by referring to associations formed by repeated experience of similar conjunctions or sequences. Now I suspect that both parties are engaged in chasing the same wild goose. Propositions of causal connexion are, in some sense, 'assertions *of necessitation*', but I do not think that they make any claim to be *necessary assertions*. And I suspect that there is little more than an unfortunate verbal likeness between 'necessity', in the sense in which it is opposed to 'contingency' and is predicated of a proposition or a fact as a whole and 'necessitation', in the sense in which it forms part of the content of propositions of causal connexion. I will assume that we know roughly what we mean then we ascribe necessity to a proposition or a fact and when we contrast this with contingency, and I will try to explain what I understand by the 'necessitation', which is part of the content of propositions of causal connexion.

I think that the notion of causal necessitation is bound up with certain features which I emphasised in my discussion of singular propositions of causal connexion. I said that persons and things are regarded as having characteristic tendencies to persist in certain quiescent states and in certain courses of change; that they are thought of as being diverted from their normal states of quiescence and their normal courses of change only by the action of the other things which have active tendencies of their own, and that they are thought to resist such interference and to react on the agents which are disturbing them. We thus contrast the undisturbed course, which the history of a person or thing would pursue if it were left to itself, with the modified course which is imposed on it when other things act on it and when the active tendencies of each have to be accommodated to those of the other. We think of the degree of constraint imposed as indicated by the extent of the modification and the vigour of the patient's reaction to the agent. The notion of causal necessitation is this notion of one thing or person enforcing, by its action, a modification on the state of quiescence or the process of change which another thing or person would pursue if left to itself and which it resists being diverted from.

This notion is really quite familiar to everyone, and anyone who pretends to be puzzled about it may fairly be accused of 'raising a dust and then complaining that he cannot see'. So far as I can tell, it has not the faintest connexion with the notion of entailment, in the sense in which one proposition entails another or the presence of one characteristic entails that of another in the same subject. And propositions which assert necessitation, in this sense, make no claim to be necessary propositions, in the sense in which a valid syllogism or the proposition that shape involves extension is necessary.

It is often extremely difficult to find out what a given thing, or a thing of a given kind, would persist in doing if left to its own devices. A subject, such as dynamics, generally dates its scientific life from the time when this question is settled. It will be worth considering this particular example for a moment. The difficulty which I have mentioned is at its maximum when all things of the given kind are always being interfered with to an appreciable extent by other agents. Now moving bodies on or near the earth's surface are, as we now know, always subject to friction or the resistance of air or water and to the earth's gravitational attraction; whilst heavenly bodies, though nearly free from frictional interference, are constantly attracted by the sun and by each other. It was very natural for persons who concentrated mainly upon the heavenly bodies to suppose that their inherent kinematic tendency was to persist in traversing closed curves, and it was plausible to suppose that these curves would be of the simplest kind, viz., exactly circular, if it were not for perturbations due to other agents. It was equally natural for persons who concentrated mainly on bodies at or near the earth's surface, such as bowls, curling stones, arrows, cannonballs, etc., to take very different view of their inherent kinematic tendency. It would appear *prima facie* here that the inherent tendency is to persist in moving in a straight line. But there were many puzzling complications. There is motion along a plane in the earth's surface, which seems to die away slowly of itself unless an external agent keeps on renewing it; there is motion up and down, which seems to have an inherent tendency to diminish or increase automatically and quite rapidly, and there is the curvilinear motion of projectiles shot off at an angle to the vertical. It needed an extraordinary effort of genius in Galileo to suspect and to verify the fundamental fact that in all cases the inherent kinematic tendency is to persist in *rectilinear* motion with *constant* speed; and that all departures from this course of change are due to the action of other agents on the moving body.

In all that long process of speculation and observation, no one doubted that there was *some* state of quiescence or *some* mode of motion which a body had an inherent tendency to maintain if left to itself, and no one doubted that the actual motion of any body would be some modification of this imposed by other agents which interacted with it. Everyone agreed that a resting body tends to remain at rest and to resist agents which impose motion on it. The questions at issue concerned bodies already in motion. Is the inherent kinematic tendency a tendency to *stop dead* at every instant unless kept going by a further dose of external influence, as a flame would do if not constantly supplied with fresh fuel and air? If not, is it a tendency to go on, but with *ever-diminishing velocity*, as the sound of a stricken bell dies away unless the bell be struck again? Or is it a tendency to go on with *undiminished velocity* in the same direction? Each of these alternatives is logically possible; and the last, which is the correct one, was *prima facie* the least plausible in the light of the crude data of ordinary observation.

The decision between these alternatives had to be made by the methods of experimental science, viz., suggesting hypotheses, deducing observable consequences in assignable conditions, and then imposing those conditions and observing what happens. But the important point for us to notice is this. The whole of this work presupposed the notions of agent and patient, of free motion and motion imposed by external agency, and of inherent tendencies to persist in some state or other of quiescence or of motion. I believe this to be merely a simple and striking example of a general fact. Causal laws are general propositions which formulate detailed answers to the following three kinds of interconnected question: (i) What states of quiescence and what modes of change have such and such agents an inherent tendency to maintain? (ii) Under what conditions do such and such other agents break in upon the privacy of agents of the former kind, stirring them from their quiescence, imposing modification on their inherent processes of change, and suffering modifications themselves through the reactions which are set up? And (iii) what is the nature of the modifications imposed by agents of the second kind on the history of agents of the first kind when the conditions for interaction between them are fulfilled? If we take the simple case of billiard-balls on a table, the answer to the first question is the First Law of Motion; the answer to the second is 'When they come in contact with each other', and the answer to the third is the Laws of Elastic Impact.

I suggested some time ago that the exclusive concentration of their attention upon causal laws had led philosophers astray on two closely connected points. I have now dealt with the first of these, viz., causal necessity. The second is the so-called 'Law' or 'Principle' of Universal Causation. There is a perfunctory discussion of this in Hume's *Treatise* and it is ignored in his *Enquiry*. Mill, in his *Logic*, has a good deal of not very coherent discussion about the 'Principle of the Uniformity of Nature', which is perhaps his version of this principle. I will conclude my paper by a brief consideration of it.

Let us for the present take the principle to assert that every event is causally determined. The first point that emerges is that it is impossible to state the principle accurately without introducing the notion of singular propositions of causal connexion. For what it asserts is that, if Y be any event, then there is another event X which causally determines Y. Therefore the principle cannot be understood unless we understand sentences of the form 'The event X causally determines the event Y'. Now those who take causal laws to be the fundamental kind of proposition of causal connexion, whether they be regularity theorists or entailment-theorists, must analyse singular causal propositions in terms of causal laws. How would this be done?

We are given very little help in answering this question by writers on the subject, so we must attempt an answer for ourselves. I take it that a causal law would be a proposition of the form 'Any manifestation of the characteristic ϕ in circumstances of the kind K would be followed immediately by a manifestation of the characteristic ψ in an adjacent place'. (This would need a good deal of polishing-up before it could pass muster with a critical person, but it will do for the present). Regularity theorists and entailment theorists would quarrel with each other about the right analysis of 'would-be' in such propositions, but they could both agree in accepting them as the fundamental propositions of causal connexion. We can now deal with the singular propositional function 'The event X causally determines the event Y'. It must presumably be analysed somewhat as follows. 'There is a characteristic ϕ and a characteristic ψ and a kind of circumstances K, such that (i) the event X is a manifestation of ϕ in circumstances K, (ii) the event Y is an immediately subsequent manifestation of ψ in an adjacent place, and (iii) any manifestation of ϕ in circumstances of the kind K would be immediately followed by a manifestation of ψ in an adjacent place'.

I pass by the question of whether this is in the least what one has in mind when one says that this caused that and proceed to apply this analysis of singular causal propositions to the Principle of Universal Causation. This principle, on the present interpretation, asserts that, if Y be any event, then there is an event X, a characteristic ϕ, a characteristic ψ, and a kind of circumstances K, such that the three conditions stated above are fulfilled.

Now I do not believe that this extremely complicated proposition is what people had in mind when they said that every event is causally determined and when they professed to find this self-evident. I do not believe that anything involving the notion of *law* was in their minds at all. I suspect that what they had in mind might be expressed roughly as follows. Suppose that a thing has been in a state of quiescence or in a process of uniform change for a finite period. Then either its inherent tendency is to preserve this state of quiescence or this uniform process of change, and it is doing so because it is being left to itself. Or this state of affairs is due to an equilibrium among the forces that are acting within it or upon it. In either case, a change will not occur in the thing in question unless some change occurs in the relation of other agents to it.

3.3

SOME REMARKS ON CHANGE, CONTINUITY, AND DISCONTINUITY

Laws of nature are *prima facie* of two kinds, viz., laws of co-existence of attributes and laws of a sequence of events. An example of the former is the law that any organism which has the power of rational speech has the characteristic bodily form and anatomical structure of a human being. An example of the latter is the law that, when one moving body overtakes and makes contact with another body moving more slowly in the same direction, the velocity of each is altered in certain assignable ways, depending on the masses and the elasticities of the two bodies. I think it will be found that most laws of co-existence presuppose laws of sequence. For the former are generally laws of the co-existence of *dispositional properties*, for example, inertial mass and the power of gravitational attraction. Now, these dispositional properties are defined in terms of certain changes which a substance would undergo or would produce in other substances under assignable conditions, and this, in turn, involves a reference to laws of sequences of events. Both for that reason, and because the subject is of great intrinsic interest and importance, I shall concentrate in this paper on events and their sequences.

Different views have been held, by philosophers of equal eminence, on the correct analysis of laws of sequence. Some, for example Stout, have held that they predicate something analogous to logical entailment; others, for example Hume, have held that they predicate *de facto* regularity of sequence. But there is a question prior to this, which concerns all parties alike. Whatever may be the nature of the relationship which is predicated in such laws, it is agreed that the terms which it relates are *events* or classes of events. It is agreed also that events which are related as cause to effect are in *immediate* sequence to each other. It is true that one might say quite correctly in ordinary speech, for example, that hearing a certain bang now is the effect of a distant explosion which happened some seconds ago. But in all such cases, we should admit that the effect is really a remote *causal descendent* of the so-called 'cause'. We should admit that strictly speaking, the cause of the auditory sensation was something which *immediately* preceded it, for example, a disturbance in the auditory nerve of the hearer; and that, strictly speaking, the effect of the explosion was something that *immediately* followed it, for example, a disturbance in the air surrounding the gun. The prior question, or rather the two inter-connected prior questions may then be put as follows: What exactly do we mean by an *event*? And what exactly do we mean by one event *immediately following another*?

We may begin with the following platitude. An event can be said to happen only if there is a *change* of some kind. Now a change involves a lapse of time, however short. For there to be a change there must be some qualitative or relational dissimilarity between an earlier phase and an adjoined later phase of what I will call 'an identifiable strand of continuously occupied duration'. I use this artificial phrase because I do not want to confine my attention to events in the history of what one would call a 'thing' or 'continuant'. I want to include, *inter alia*, such a strand of continuously occupied duration as a continuous auditory sensation going on for some appreciable time, for example, the sound heard in the neighbourhood of a water-fall or the sound described as a 'singing in the ears'. Undoubtedly a sound, in this sense of the word, can persist unchanged for a period or can change either suddenly or continuously in pitch or in loudness or in both. A strand of continuously occupied duration may, of course, be of such a special kind as to count as part of the history of a certain thing. In that case changes in it are counted as changes in that thing's qualities or relationships.

SOME REMARKS ON CHANGE, CONTINUITY, AND DISCONTINUITY 277

If we take 'invariance' as the contrary opposite of change, it is no less obvious that invariance involves a lapse of time, however short. For there to be invariance there must be complete qualitative or relational likeness (either in one or more assigned respects or in all respects) between an earlier phase and an adjoined later phase of a strand of continuously occupied duration.

It follows at once that to talk either of *instantaneous* change or of *instantaneous* invariance is nonsense, if taken literally. It may be, however, that such phrases are convenient short-hand expressions for notions which are intelligible and useful or even indispensable. I believe this to be the case, and I shall now try to unpack and define these phrases. I think it will be convenient, to begin with the very simple case of a continuous outstanding sound of appreciable duration in someone's auditory field.

I shall begin by presupposing the notion of an instant of time, and by assuming that time is continuous, in the sense that between any two instants, however near together, there is another instant. I start with the notion of an instantaneous cross-section of a sound at a certain instant t, and with the determinate values at that instant of the three inseparable but independently variable features of intensity, pitch, and tone-quality. I take as an undefined (but not necessarily undefinable) notion that which is expressed by such a sentence as: 'The Sound S has the intensity i, the pitch p, and the tone quality q, at the instant t'. A sound can of course be invariant in intensity, for example, while it is changing, for example, in pitch; or it can be invariant in both or changing in both simultaneously. Let us concentrate at present on a single feature, say *intensity*, and ignore the other two.

To say that S's intensity is *invariant* at the value i at the instant t, comes to this. It is to say that there is an instant t_1 earlier than t, and an instant t_2 later than t, such that at *every* instant between these two S has the intensity i (see Figure 3.3.1).

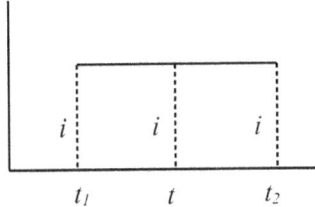

Figure 3.3.1

278 SCIENCE AND METAPHYSICS

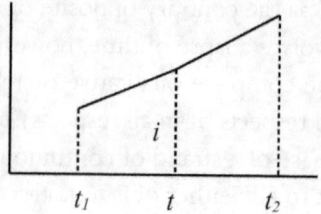

Figure 3.3.2

The notion which is complementary to that of invariance at a given value at a given instant is the notion of *passing continuously through* a given value at a given instant. To say that S's intensity is *passing continuously through* the value i at the instant t is to assert the following three propositions. (i) The intensity of S at t is i. (ii) There is an instant t_1 earlier than t, and an instant t_2 later than t, such that at every different instant between t_1 and t S has a different intensity, and at every different instant between t and t_2 S has a different intensity. (iii) The intensities had by S at the successive instants between t_1 and t form a *continuous* sequence which *converges* to the limit i, and the intensities had by S at the successive instants between t and t_2, form a *continuous* sequence which *diverges* from the limit i (see Figure 3.3.2).

It remains to define the statement that the intensities had by S at the successive instants between t_1 and t converge to the limit i. This is a short-hand expression for the following complicated proposition. For any assigned fractional number ε, however small, there is an instant $t_ε$ between t_1 and t, such that for every instant between $t_ε$ and t the numerical difference between the intensity at that instant and i is less than ε. The statement that the intensities had by S at the successive instants between t and t_2 diverge from the limit i can be defined in the same way *mutatis mutandis*.

We come next to two complementary notions, each of which involves a certain kind of *discontinuity* at the instant t, but neither of which involves a *sudden jump* in the value of the variable at that instant. A sound, for example, might have been changing continuously in intensity up to the instant t, attaining the intensity i at that instant, and it might thereupon become invariant in intensity at the value i for a period (see Figure 3.3.3a). Conversely, a sound might have been invariant at the intensity i for a period up to the instant t, and it might thereupon begin to change continuously from that intensity for a period (see Figure 3.3.3b).

SOME REMARKS ON CHANGE, CONTINUITY, AND DISCONTINUITY 279

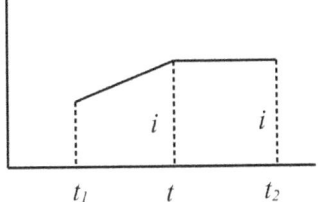

Figure 3.3.3a

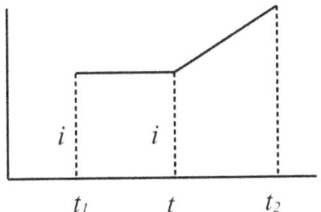

Figure 3.3.3b

It will be enough to define the first of these notions; for, if that is done, the second can be defined *mutatis mutandis*. To say that S was changing continuously in intensity up to the instant t, and that it then became invariant at the intensity i which it had attained at t, is to assert the following three propositions. (i) There is an instant t_1, earlier than t, such that at every different instant between t_1 and t S has a different intensity. (ii) There is an instant t_2 later than t, such that at t and at every instant between it and t_2 S has the *same* intensity i. (iii) The intensities had by S at the successive instants between t_1 and t form a *continuous* sequence converging to the limit i, the intensity which S has at t.

Finally, we come to four notions, all of which involve discontinuity at t in the special sense of a *sudden finite jump* in the value of the variable at that instant. They may be classified as follows.

(1) A sound might have been *invariant* at a certain intensity i up to a certain instant t, and it might thereupon become *invariant* at a definitely different intensity i' (see Figure 3.3.4a). (2.1) A sound might have been *changing continuously* in intensity for a period up to the instant t, attaining the intensity i at that instant, and it might thereupon become *invariant* at a finitely different intensity i' (see Figure 3.3.4b). (2.2) is the complement to this. A sound might have been *invariant* up to the instant t at the intensity i, and it might

280 SCIENCE AND METAPHYSICS

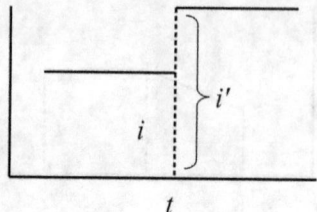

Figure 3.3.4a

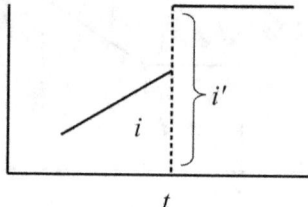

Figure 3.3.4b

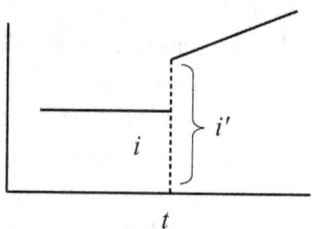

Figure 3.3.4c

thereupon start to *change continuously* from a finitely different intensity i' (see Figure 3.3.4c). (3) A sound might have been changing continuously up to the instant t, attaining the intensity i at that instant. It might also change continuously from the instant t. But the continuous changes which start from t might begin at an intensity i' which is *finitely different* from the intensity i attained in the continuous change which ends by t (see Figure 3.3.4d).

It will be enough to define (1), (2.1), and (3); for (2.2) can easily be defined *mutatis mutandis* from the definition of (2.1).

(1) To say that S is invariant up to the instant t at the value i, and is invariant from the same instant at the different value i', is to assert the following three propositions. (i) There is an instant t_1 earlier than t, such that at every

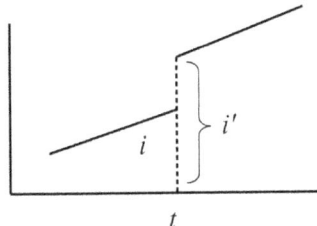

Figure 3.3.4d

instant between t_1 and t S has the same intensity i. (ii) There is an instant t_2 later than t, such that at t and at every instant between t and t_2 S has the same intensity i'. (iii) The intensities i and i' are different. (A *prima facie* instance of this general notion is provided by the pitch of the sound heard when a locomotive, which is discharging steam invariantly through its whistle, passes an observer standing by the side of the line. There is an instantaneous finite lowering of pitch at the instant when the engine ceases to approach and begins to recede from the observer.)

(2.1) To say that S has been changing continuously in intensity up to the instant t, at which it attains the intensity i, and that it thereupon becomes invariant at the different intensity i', is to assert the following five propositions. (i) S has the intensity i at the instant t. (ii) There is an instant t_1 earlier than t, such that at every different instant between t_1 and t S has a different intensity. (iii) These intensities form a continuous sequence which converges on the limit i. (iv) There is an instant t_2 later than t, such that at every instant between t and t_2 S has the same intensity i'. (v) The intensities i and i' are different.

(3) To say that S has been changing continuously up to the instant t, at which it attains the intensity i, and that it thereupon begins to change continuously starting from the different intensity i', is to assert the following six propositions. (i), (ii), and (iii) are the same as those with the corresponding numbers in (2.1) above. The remaining three are as follows. (iv) There is an instant t_2 later than t, such that at every different instant between t and t_2, S has a different intensity. (v) These intensities form a continuous sequence which diverges from the limit i'. (vi) The intensities i and i' are different.

We can now summarise and generalise the results which we have so far reached and re-classify them. Let S be an identifiable strand of continuously occupied duration, and let D be a determinable characteristic which is manifested in one determinate form or another in every instantaneous cross section of it. Consider an instantaneous cross-section at the instant t. Then there are the following possibilities. (1) That S is at that instant in a *state of invariance* at a certain determinate value δ of D. (2) That it is at that instant *passing continuously* through a certain value δ of D. (3) That at that moment there is a *smooth transition*, either (a) from a state of continuous change, in which S has just attained a certain determinate value δ of D, to a state of invariance at the same value, or (b) from a state of invariance at a certain determinate value δ of D to a state of continuous change starting at the same value. (4) That at that instant there is a *discontinuous transition*, which may take any of the following alternative forms. (a) From invariance at a certain value δ of D to invariance at a different value δ' of D. (b) From continuous change, in which S attains a certain value δ of D by t, to continuous change starting from a different value δ' of D. (c) Either (α) from invariance at a certain value δ of D to continuous change starting from a different value δ', or (β) from continuous change, in which a certain value δ of D is attained by t, to invariance at a different value δ'.

Having enumerated and defined all these possibilities, I will now make some remarks about them.

In the first place, they can be adapted at once to the case of rest or motion of a particle in a straight line. The determinable D in that case is the distance from a fixed point O on the line L to a variable point P on it in a given direction. Rest or motion in curvilinear lines or in straight lines having different positions and orientations, involves many complications of detail because the determinable of spatial position then has more than one dimension. But there is no modification in principle. Let us, then, restrict our attention to a particle confined to a single straight line. Possibilities (1) and (2) are respectively those of being at rest at a point and being in motion through a point, at an instant. Possibility (3a) is that of moving into a position with a finite velocity at a certain instant and then stopping dead there for a finite period. Possibility (3b) is that of being at rest at a certain position up to a certain instant and at that instant beginning to move out of it with a finite velocity, as, for example, when a resting billiard-ball is hit by a moving one.

It is important to note that the various logical possibilities covered by the various sub-divisions of (4) are commonly held to be ruled out *a priori* in the case of a moving or resting particle. The reason is this. All the alternatives that fall under this heading involve combining the proposition that the particle

S is at the position P at the instant t with one or other of the following two propositions. Either (a) that there is an instant t_1 earlier than t, such that at *every* instant between t_1 and t (no matter how near to t) S is at a distance from P which is greater than a certain assignable finite distance. Or (b) that there is an instant t_2 later than t, such that at *every* instant between t and t_2 (no matter how near to t) S is at a distance from P which is greater than a certain assignable finite distance. Now we commonly regard the combination of the first proposition with either of the two latter as self-evidently impossible. The reason is obvious. Either of these combinations is what we should express colloquially by saying that one and the same particle would have 'jumped from one position to another without any lapse of time and without having occupied successively a continuous sequence of intermediate positions'. Now our criterion for a strand of occupied duration to count as the history of one particle is such as to rule this out.

As we have seen, the situation is different in the case of a sound and its pitch. A continuous whistling noise, which is at one constant pitch up to an instant t and continues therefrom at a different constant pitch (as when a whistling locomotive passes an observer) counts as one and the same sound, provided that its intensity varies continuously and its tone-quality is practically invariant.

Suppose, however, that there were well-established facts which compelled us to admit the possibilities enumerated under heading (4) above in the ease of certain entities which have commonly been counted as elementary particles, for example, electrons. Then we could deal with the situation in either of the three following ways. (A) We might keep the old criterion for the identity of a particle through time and the old notion that elementary particles are ingenerable and indestructible in the course of nature. We should then say that these so-called 'particles' are not strictly elementary particles, but are like genuine elementary particles in certain assignable respects and unlike them in others. (B) We might keep the old criterion for the identity of a particle through time, but drop the notion that elementary particles are ingenerable and indestructible in the course of nature. We should then say that, in the circumstances assigned, one elementary particle S ceases to exist on reaching the point P at the instant t, whilst another elementary particle S' (resembling S in all or most respects) begins to exist as from the same instant at the different point P'. (C) We might keep the notion that elementary particles are ingenerable and indestructible in the course of nature, but modify our criterion of identity through time, so as to allow us to say, in certain circumstances, that one and the same particle *may* jump from one position to another without any lapse of time and without having occupied successively a continuous sequence of intermediate positions. Each of these alternatives would involve a wrench; but a wrench of some kind is inevitable when new facts are discovered which show that certain features, that have hitherto always been found in intimate conjunction with certain others, can and do occur in separation from the latter.

I pass now to a closely related topic, which will occupy the rest of this chapter. As is well known, certain philosophers, for example, Leibniz and Kant (in his *Anticipations of Perception*), have enunciated allegedly *a priori* principles of continuity in nature. Others, for example, Earl Russell in some of his moods, have tended to go to the other extreme. They have felt that to ascribe continuity to things and processes in nature is to credit that slatternly old lady with an artificial tidiness which is only to be found in the bandboxes of pure mathematics. Let us call the two kinds of philosophers 'Continuitists' and 'Discontinuitists', respectively. I will now say something about each of these positions in turn.

Of the four logical possibilities enumerated in our summary, the continuitist must certainly reject No. 4, which covers the various cases of *discontinuous* transition. He would obviously have no objection to No. 1, viz., a state of invariance at t at a certain value δ of a determinable D; nor to No. 2, viz., continuous passage at t through a certain value δ of D. But what would he say to No. 3, i.e., to cases of *smooth* transition at an instant, either from a state of continuous change to one of invariance at the value δ then attained or from a state of invariance to one of continuous change starting from the value δ which has been invariant up to then? (An illustration from the case of sound would be that of a sound which has been continuously increasing in intensity for a period up to the instant t, and thereupon remains invariant in intensity for a period at the level attained at t. A parallel illustration from the case of motion would be that of a particle which has been moving continuously along a straight line for a period up to the instant t at which it enters the point P, and thereupon stops dead and remains at rest for a period at P.)

I am sure that neither Leibniz nor Kant would accept these at their face value. Take, for example, the case of a transition from motion to rest or from rest to motion. A Continuitist would rule out *a priori* the logically possible case of a moving body literally stopping dead at an instant, and the logically possible case of a resting body literally starting to move at an instant with a finite velocity. He would say that what must be really happening in what looks like the former case is a continuous but extremely rapid slowing down of the velocity to zero. He would say that what must really be happening in what looks like the latter case is a continuous but extremely rapid increase of velocity from zero to the finite value which it seems to have attained instantaneously.

We may generalise this contention as follows. Suppose that there seems to be an instantaneous transition in S at t, from a state of continuous change in respect of a determinable D which attains the value δ at the finite rate ρ at that instant, to a state of invariance at that value. Then (according to the Continuitist) there must in fact be an instant t_1 earlier than t, such that throughout the period from t_1 to t the *rate of change* of D diminishes continuously from ρ to zero at t. Suppose, again, that there *seems* to be an instantaneous transition in S at t, from a state of invariance at the value δ up to that instant, to a state of continuous change in D starting from that value at a finite rate ρ. Then (according to the Continuitist) there must in fact be an instant t_2 later than t, such that throughout the period from t to t_2 the values of D have been changing continuously, and at a *rate* which increases continuously from zero at t to ρ at t_2. We may sum this up as follows. In all apparent cases of *instantaneous* transition at t from change to invariance or from invariance to change the Continuitist sees cases of very rapid *continuous change*, at a *rate which changes continuously* to or from zero at the instant t.

Now, this brings us to a question of definition, which would in any case have to be faced at some point and which may as well be settled now. The phrase 'rate of change at an instant' (or, in particular, 'velocity at an instant') is plainly nonsensical if taken literally. And the phrase 'zero rate of change' (or, in particular, 'zero velocity') is somewhat paradoxical. Each is in fact a convenient shorthand expression for a complicated notion, which involves reference to other instants beside the one in question. I will now unpack these phrases.

It will be convenient to begin, as before, with the concrete case of a prolonged sound. Let the sound S be changing continuously in intensity, and suppose that it passes through the intensity i at the instant t. Consider any instant τ which is earlier than t. Let S's intensity at τ be i_τ. By hypothesis its intensity at t is i. Consider the ratio of the *difference* of these two intensities, i.e., $i - i_\tau$, to the *lapse of time* between the two corresponding instants, i.e.,

$t - \tau$. Let us denote the fraction $(i - i_\tau)/(t - \tau)$ by r_τ. To say that the intensity of S *enters upon* the value i at the instant t at the rate ρ, is to assert the following proposition. Take any magnitude ε, however small. Then there is an instant t_ε, earlier than t, such that for *every* instant τ between t_ε and t the corresponding ratio r_τ differs numerically from ρ by less than ε. The statement that the intensity of S *issues from* the value i at the instant t at the rate ρ', can be defined *mutatis mutandis* in a similar way. Here, of course, we shall have to consider instants *later than* t instead of those earlier than it. If and only if ρ', the rate at which S's intensity issues from the value i at t, is equal to ρ, the rate at which it enters upon that value at that instant, we can say that S's intensity *passes through* the value i at t at the rate ρ.

The definitions just given can at once be generalised. The general notion is that expressed by the sentence: 'In respect of the determinable D the persistent particular S enters upon (or issues from) the determinate value δ at the rate ρ'. In order to define this, we have merely to substitute δ for i and δ_τ for i_τ in our definition for the particular case of a sound which is changing continuously in intensity and passes through the intensity i at the instant t.

The application to rectilinear motion is immediately obvious, and the application to curvilinear motion involves only further complexities of detail. If we confine ourselves to rectilinear motion along a line L, ρ would be the velocity with which a particle S, which is moving continuously on L from a fixed point O on it, *enters* the point P at the instant t, and ρ' would be the velocity with which it *leaves* that point at that instant.

The meaning of the phrase 'zero rate of change' (or, in particular, 'zero velocity') is now obvious. Rate of change at an instant, as we have defined it, is the limit of a sequence of ratios of the form $(\delta - \delta_\tau)/(t - \tau)$ as τ approaches indefinitely to t. That limit may be some number greater than nought or it may happen to be nought. If the latter alternative is fulfilled, we may say that the rate of change into the value δ at the instant t is *zero*.

We can now generalise the Continuitist's contention. Our definition leaves it logically possible that the rate at which S *enters upon* the value δ of the determinable D at the instant t might differ from the rate at which it *issues from* that value at that instant. The Continuitist would reject *a priori* this logical possibility, for it would involve what we might call a 'discontinuity of the second order'. I suppose that a dyed-in-the-wool Continuitist would *a priori* reject discontinuity of *any* order in nature.

A *prima facie* instance of a second-order discontinuity would be provided by a billiard-ball travelling in a certain direction with the velocity u_1 and being overtaken by another travelling in the same direction with the greater velocity u_2. *Prima facie* its velocity is increased *instantaneously* at the instant of collision. It enters the position P (say from the left) with the velocity u_1 at the instant t, and it issues from that position (to the right) at the same instant with the velocity u_2, assuming that the balls are of equal mass and perfectly elastic. The Continuitist would deny that this can really be so, and he would have no difficulty in accounting for the appearance in terms of his principle. He would compare the collision between the two balls, which appears to be a literally instantaneous transaction, with the collision between two trucks provided with spring-buffers, which is plainly a transaction that goes on for a short but appreciable period. During the imperceptibly short period of contact between the billiard-balls the velocity of the overtaker is *continuously* diminished from u_2 to u_1, whilst that of the overtaken is *continuously* increased from u_1, to u_2.

The following point is worth noting. We must carefully distinguish the following two notions, viz., (i) entering upon and issuing from the value δ of the determinable D at the instant t at *zero rate*, and (ii) being *invariant* at the value δ at the instant t. A reference to our definitions shows at once that the two notions are utterly different. The following example from rectilinear motion well illustrates the difference. Consider a body thrown vertically upwards and attaining its maximal height, the position P at the instant t. It does *not rest* at P. But it *does* enter P with zero upward velocity at t, and it *does* leave P with zero downward velocity at the same instant.

Before leaving the Continuitist and passing to the Discontinuitist, it will be worthwhile to consider the following point. A continuous change in respect of a determinable D presupposes that the possible determinates under D form a continuous range. That is obvious from our definitions. Now, it is commonly assumed that this condition is fulfilled, for example, for the intensity and the pitch of sounds, for distance from a fixed point along a straight line, and so on. But there are plenty of determinables for which it plainly is not fulfilled. A geometrical example would be the property of being a regular solid, with its five determinate possibilities of being a regular tetrahedron, a cube, a regular octahedron, a regular dodecahedron, or a regular icosahedron. A physical example would be the determinable called 'phase', with its three determinate forms, solid, liquid, and gaseous. Imagine a body which *could* only have the form of a regular solid of some kind or other, but can change from one shape to another within that range. Suppose it changes its shape at the instant t. Then the change *must* be discontinuous. It must have had someone regular shape, for example, cubical, for a period, however short, up to and including t; and then at every instant between t and some later instant t_2 (however near to t), it must have some other regular shape, for example, icosahedral.

Our other example, viz., 'phase' in its technical scientific sense illustrates a possible combination of continuity with discontinuity. Consider the process of heating up a mass of water to its boiling point, and then continuing to supply heat until a part or the whole of it has evaporated. Let us take the process simply as it appears at the macroscopic level, and ignore all molecular or quantic theories as to what is going on in the ultra-microscopic background. There are four determinables to be considered, viz., quantity of heat supplied, temperature, phase, and mass of water in one phase or another. All but the third of these have *prima facie* a continuous range of possible variation, whilst the third has just the three possible forms, solid, liquid, and gaseous. Now the situation is as follows. (1) Up to the instant at which the whole mass of water reaches the temperature 100°C, there is continuous increase in the quantity of heat absorbed and a correlated continuous rise in temperature, whilst the phase remains *invariant* in the liquid form. (ii) At every instant after this, until all the water has been turned into steam, there is continuous increase in the quantity of heat absorbed, whilst the temperature remains *invariant* at 100°C. As regards phase, the change is in one sense *discontinuous*, viz., from the liquid to the gaseous phase. But it is *continuous* in the following sense. The proportion of the total mass which is in the gaseous phase increases continuously and at a constant rate.

I think that a rigid Continuitist would have to say that this is a particular case of the following general principle, which he would regard as *a priori*. Wherever there is a change in respect of a determinable whose determinates do *not* form a continuous range, there must be some other determinable, associated with the former in a way analogous to that in which mass is associated with phase in our example, whose determinates *do* form a continuous range. And the change must be continuous in respect of this associated determinable.

Let us now consider the position of a Discontinuitist. I think that we can distinguish four alternative forms which this might take. These can be arranged in ascending order of rigour as follows. (1) The Discontinuitist might admit that there are determinables with a continuous range of possible variation, but deny that there can be continuous change even in respect to these. (2) He might deny that there can be any *qualitative* determinables, for example, intensity, pitch, with a continuous range of possible determinates under them, but he might admit that *purely spatial* determinables, for example, distance and angular deviation, and the purely temporal determinable of time lapse, have a continuous range of possible values. He would deny, however, that there can be continuous change even in spatial position or direction. (3) He might deny that either qualitative or spatial determinables have a continuous range of possible determinates under them, but admit the continuity of time. (4) Finally, he might go the whole way and deny even the continuity of time. I will now say something about each of these alternatives.

(1) There would be no difficulty in reconciling the first alternative with all the observable facts. Let D be a determinable, supposed to have a continuous range of possible values, and let us suppose that S appears *prima facie* to change continuously in respect of D throughout a period from t_1 to t_n. I shall assume that the criterion of identity through time for such particulars as S is such that D must be manifested continuously in one form or another throughout any period in which one and the same S would be said to exist. Then the Discontinuitist could reconcile the appearances with his principles in either of the two following ways:

(a) He might allege that what looks like a continuous change of a single persistent particular S with respect to D is really a discontinuous sequence of the following kind. There is a short-lived particular S_1, which exists from and including t_1 to and including t_1', and throughout the whole of that period has D in the value δ_1. Between t_1' and t_2 there is no particular of the S-kind. From and including t_2, up to and including t_2' there is another short-lived particular S_2, which has D throughout the whole of this period in the value δ_2. Between t_2' and t_3 there is again no particular of the S-kind. And so on throughout the period t_1 to t_n. Each of the separated periods during which a particular of the S-kind exists would have to be short compared with the duration of a human specious present. So too would the intervals which separate them, during which there is no particular of the S-kind. Finally, the difference between the values of

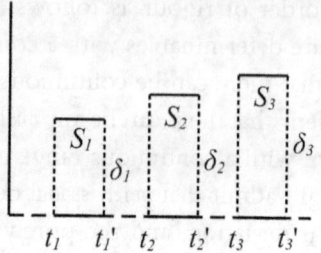

Figure 3.3.5

D which characterise Ss which come next to each other in the series would have to be small compared with the normal human range of discrimination of D (see Figure 3.3.5).

Suppose, for example, that there appears to be a single persistent sound, S, of continuously varying intensity. Then, on this interpretation, there is really a discontinuous sequence of short sounds, S_1, S_2, etc., each of invariant intensity and each of different intensity, separated by short intervals of silence in respect of that kind of sound. The intensities of neighbouring short sounds in the sequence would differ very slightly from each other.

(b) The second possible line which a Discontinuitist of Type (1) might take is this. He might allege that what seems *prima facie* to be a continuous change of S in respect of D is really a sequence of the following kind. From t_1 up to and including t_2, S would have D in the form δ_1; from t_2 up to and including t_3 S would have D in the form δ_2; and so on. The intervals $t_2 - t_1$, $t_3 - t_2$, etc., would all be very short, and the difference between the values of D, for example, δ_1 and δ_2, in any two immediately successive short intervals of the sequence would be very small. This view admits that there really is a single persistent particular S, as opposed to a mere sequence of short-lived particulars, S_1, S_2, etc., separated by short temporal gaps (see Figure 3.3.6).

It should be noted that, on this view, there would be a *last* instant t_2, at which S had D in the form δ_1, a *last* instant t_3, in which S had D in the form δ_2, and so on. But there would be no first instant at which S had D in the form δ_1, no first instant at which S had D in the form δ_2, and so on. For, if time is continuous, there is no first instant after a given

SOME REMARKS ON CHANGE, CONTINUITY, AND DISCONTINUITY

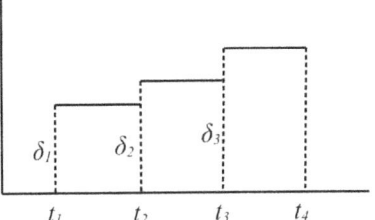

Figure 3.3.6

instant. What we could say, however, is that the last instant at which S has D in the form δ_1 is the lower limit of the sequence of instants at which S has D in the form δ_2, and so on. (Of course, we might equally well have supposed that S has D in the form δ_1 at t_1 and every instant after it up to *but not including* t_2, that it has D in the form δ_2 at t_2 and every instant after it up to *but not including* t_3, and so on. In that case, there would be a first instant in each of the successive periods of invariance, but no *last* instant in any of them. And then the first instant at which S has D in the form δ_1, would be the upper limit of the sequence of instants at which S has D in the form δ_1, and so on. This supposition would be empirically indistinguishable from the one which I have suggested.)

(2) Alternative (2) could be reconciled with all the observable facts, in the case of qualitative determinables, in precisely the same two ways as Alternative (1). In fact, the only difference is the following purely theoretical one. On the first alternative, there is nothing in the nature of qualitative determinables, as such, to rule out the possibility of continuous qualitative change. This logical possibility is just *directly* denied on inspection to be ontologically possible. On the second alternative, it follows from the alleged nature of qualitative determinables that all change in respect of them *must be* by jumps.

Alternatives (1) and (2) admit the continuity of both space and time. Before passing to alternatives (3) and (4), both of which deny the continuity of space, I will say something about the application of alternatives (1) and (2) to the special case of motion. As usual, we will simplify the discussion by confining it to rectilinear motion in a single straight line L. We will take a fixed point O on the line L, and take as our determinable D the distance along L in a given direction from O to a variable point P. Alternatives (1) and (2) assume that the range of determinates under this determinable is *continuous*. What we have to deal with now is the case of *prima facie* continuous motion of a particle S along L.

It is obvious that this could be interpreted in the first of the two ways described above. We should have to say that there is not really one persistent particle S, occupying a sequence of positions, but a sequence of short-lived particles, S_1, S_2, etc., each of which is at rest throughout the whole of its short existence. S_1 exists for the short period from t_1, to t_1', and rests at P_1 throughout that period. At t_2, shortly after t_1', S_2 begins to exist, and continues to do so during the short period up to and including t_2'. S_2 rests at the closely adjacent point P_2 during the whole period of its existence. And so on. There really would be no motion at all, as that phrase is ordinarily understood.

Can we deal with motion, on the present assumptions, in the second of the two ways described above? I think that we should come up against an *a priori* difficulty. What we should have to suppose is the following. From t_1, up to and including the slightly later instant t_2, the particle S occupies a certain position P_1 on the line L. From t_2 up to and including the slightly later instant t_3, S occupies the slightly remoter position P_2 on L. And so on. Now the difficulty here is this. It seems unintelligible to suggest that one and the same particle could occupy one position at one instant and another position at another instant without having occupied each of the intermediate positions at intermediate instants. Now the alternatives which we are at present discussing accept the continuity of space and of time. Therefore, they admit that there *are* positions on L intermediate between any two positions P_1 and P_2 on it, no matter how near together, and they admit that there *are* instants between *any* two instants t_1 and t_2 however near together. Yet they have to maintain that the particle S does *not* occupy any of the positions intermediate between P_1 and P_2 at any of the instants intermediate between t_1 and t_2. For at t_1 it occupies P_1 and at *every* instant after t_1, up to and including t_2, it occupies P_2.

I conclude then that anyone who admits the continuity of both space and time must either admit the continuity of motion or deny the possibility of motion in the ordinarily accepted sense. If he is willing to take the latter course, he can remain a Discontinuitist and save the appearances in the first of the two ways described above.

(3) I pass now to Alternative (3), which denies the continuity of space but accepts that of time. Let us consider how it would deal with apparently

continuous motion confined to a single straight Line L. Since space is now supposed to be discontinuous, the possible distances along L in a given direction from a fixed point O in it will form a *discrete* sequence, OP_1, OP_2, etc. It will be meaningless to talk of a position *between* P_1, and P_2, as it would be, for example, to talk of a phase between solid and liquid or of a kind of regular solid between the regular tetrahedron and the cube.

Now it seems self-evident that a particle at *every* instant of its existence must occupy *some* position or other. Since we are supposing S to be confined to the straight line L, it must at every instant of its existence occupy some position or other on that line. It follows that we cannot intelligibly suppose that a particle S, moving along L, ceases to occupy P_1 at a certain instant t_1 and begins to occupy the next position P_2 at a certain later instant t_2. For, since we are assuming time to be continuous, there *are* instants between t_1 and t_2, however, near together those two instants may be. And, since we are assuming space to be discontinuous, there are *no* positions between P_1 and P_2. Therefore there would be instants, viz., those between t_1 and t_2, at which S would be literally *nowhere*. To avoid this absurdity we shall have to regard the motion of S along L in the following way. We shall have to suppose that S occupies P_1, from a certain instant t_1, up to and including t_2, that it occupies P_2 from t_2 up to and including t_3, and so on. There is a *last* instant at which it occupies each position in the sequence, but there is no first instant at which it occupies any such position. The last instant at which it occupies any point P_n, is the *lower limit* of the continuous sequence of instants at which it occupies the next point P_{n+1}.

In this way, Alternative (3) could deal with the appearance of continuous motion. It is not logically necessary to assume that the intrinsically indivisible distance between each pair of adjacent points is the same. But it seems a reasonable assumption to make. If we do so, what would be called the 'velocity' with which S traverses the line L would depend upon how long S *rests* at successive adjacent points. If it rested for a very short time at each of two adjacent points which it successively occupied, we should say that it is 'moving *fast*' there and then; if it rested for a longer time, we should say that it is 'moving *more slowly*' there and then.

(4) Lastly, I will briefly consider Alternative (4), which denies the continuity of time as well as that of space. On this view, there is a

discrete sequence of instants, t_1, t_2, etc., such that it is meaningless to talk of an instant between any two adjacent ones, t_r and t_{r+1}. There is also a discrete sequence of positions, P_1, P_2, etc., such that it is meaningless to talk of a position intermediate between two adjacent ones, P_s and P_{s+1}.

Now it is easy to prove the following proposition. Let t_r be any instant, and let S occupy the position P_s at that instant. Then at t_{r+1} S must occupy either P_s or the position immediately next to it in one direction or the other, i.e., P_{s+1} or P_{s-1}. The argument runs as follows. At every instant at which S exists it must occupy *some* position on the line L. Now at no instant can it occupy a position *between* P_s and P_{s+1} or *between* P_s and P_{s-1}, for by hypothesis there are no such positions. Suppose then, if possible, that at t_{r+1} it occupies a position, such as P_{s+2} or P_{s-2}, which is *not* immediately next to P_s. Then S would have got to that position *without* having at *any* intermediate instant occupied the intermediate position P_{s+1} or P_{s-1}, as the case may be. For by hypothesis there is *no* instant between t_r and t_{r+1}. But this consequence is commonly held to be self-evidently impossible; so the supposition which leads to it must be rejected.

We see then what rest and motion must consist in, on the present hypothesis. To rest in a position is to occupy it at *two or more* consecutive instants. To move is to occupy a position at a certain instant, and at the next consecutive instant to occupy the next consecutive position on one side or the other. There will be an intrinsic maximal velocity, viz., when S occupies a position at *only one* instant, and occupies the next consecutive position on one side or the other at *only* the next consecutive instant. What appear as lesser velocities would consist really in S occupying each of two consecutive positions at *several* consecutive instants, for example, occupying P_1 at t_1 and t_2 and occupying P_2 at t_3 and t_4 and t_5.

I am by no means sure that any clear idea corresponds to the suggestion that space may be discontinuous. I am still more doubtful whether any clear idea corresponds to the suggestion that time may be discontinuous. But, if these suggestions be thinkable, then the consequences which I have drawn about rest and motion would seem to follow.

3.4

THE LOGICAL ANALYSIS OF CHANGE

In this paper, I propose to give a logical analysis of the notions of Change and Quiescence and certain other notions associated with them. I have not come across any adequate treatment of this topic in the course of my reading, and I have often found myself held up in my attempts to formulate accurately the notions of Causal Law and Singular Causal Proposition by the absence of an analysis of Change and Quiescence. Moreover, it is only when one has accurately defined these terms and has seen what follows from them by mere logical deduction, that one can judge whether there are any general principles about change which might claim to be synthetic *a priori* propositions. For such a principle about change would, I suppose, be one that does *not* follow logically from the definitions and yet *does* appear to be intrinsically necessary on inspection. It is fashionable to deny that there are any such propositions; but, as I have never seen any satisfactory reason for this opinion, I do not attach very much weight to it. For these reasons, I think that the following elementary exercise in formal logic may not be altogether trivial.

In considering qualitative change we are not generally concerned with the appearance or the disappearance of supreme determinable characteristics, such as colour, temperature, mass, etc., in a substance. We are concerned rather with variations in the determinate form of determinables which are present, in some form or another, throughout the whole history of a substance. In this chapter, I shall restrict my attention to this kind of change.

Let P be a determinable quality, p a determinate under it, and s a substance which has P in some form or other throughout its history. I start with the undefined notion expressed by the sentence 's has p at t_1'. I symbolise this by $p(s, t_1)$. An instance would be 'This substance is now in the solid state'.

We can now define two correlated expressions, viz., 's has p continuously through a period which ends by t_1' and 's has p continuously throughout a period which starts from t_1'. (I use the phrase 'ends *by* t_1' and 'starts *from* t_1', as opposed to the phrases 'ends *at* t_1' and 'starts *at* t_1', respectively, in order to express the fact that I wish to exclude t_1 in each case from the period under consideration.)

This being understood, it is plain that the first of these expressions means that s has p at every moment between t_1 and some *earlier* moment. The second means that s has p at every moment between t_1 and some *later* moment. I propose to symbolise them respectively by $p(s, \rightarrow t_1)$ and $p(s, t_1 \rightarrow)$. It is obvious that the formal definitions will be as follows:

$$p(s, \rightarrow t_1) =_{df} (\exists x) :. \ t < t_1 . t \not< t_1 - x :\supset_t p(s,t) \qquad (1.1)$$

$$p(s, t_1 \rightarrow) =_{df} (\exists x) : t > t_1 . t \not> t_1 + x :\supset_t p(s,t) \qquad (1.2)$$

We will now define two correlated expressions closely connected with these, viz., 's lacks p continuously throughout a period which ends by t_1' and 's lacks p continuously throughout a period which starts from t_1'. Since to lack p is formally equivalent to having non-p (i.e., $\bar{p}$), these can be conveniently symbolised by $\bar{p}(s, \rightarrow t_1)$ and $\bar{p}(s, t_1 \rightarrow)$, respectively. (The reader must be careful not to confuse these with the contradictories of 1.1 and 1.2, respectively. These are symbolised $\sim p(s, \rightarrow t_1)$ and $\sim p(s, t_1 \rightarrow)$. We shall consider them in due course.) The formal definitions of $\bar{p}(s, \rightarrow t_1)$ and $\bar{p}(s, t_1 \rightarrow)$ are plainly the following:

$$\bar{p}(s, \rightarrow t_1) =_{df} (\exists x) :. \ t < t_1 . t \not< t_1 - x . \supset_t \sim p(s,t) \qquad (1.11)$$

$$\bar{p}(s, t_1 \rightarrow) =_{df} (\exists x) : t > t_1 . t \not> t_1 + x . \supset_t \sim p(s,t) \qquad (1.21)$$

We are now in a position to define the two correlated expressions 's gets p at t_1' and 's loses p at t_1'. I take the first of them to mean that s has p at t_1 but has

THE LOGICAL ANALYSIS OF CHANGE 297

lacked p continuously throughout *some* period, however short, which ends by t_1. I take the second of them to mean that s has p at t_1 but lacks p continuously throughout *some* period, however short, which starts from t_1. We will symbolise these two notions by $G(s, p, t_1)$ and $L(s, p, t_1)$, respectively. The formal definitions are as follows:

$$G(s,p,t_1) =_{df} p(s,t_1) \cdot \bar{p}(s, \to t_1) \qquad (2.1)$$

$$L(s,p,t_1) =_{df} p(s,t_1) \cdot \bar{p}(s, t_1 \to) \qquad (2.2)$$

It is plain that, with these definitions, each of the propositions is consistent with the other and also with the contradictory of the other. Thus, each of the four combinations permitted by the Laws of Contradiction and Excluded Middle is internally consistent. They may be symbolised as follows:

$$GL(s,p,t_1) =_{df} p(s,t_1) \cdot \bar{p}(s, \to t_1) \cdot \bar{p}(s, t_1 \to) \qquad (3.1)$$

$$G\bar{L}(s,p,t_1) =_{df} p(s,t_1) \cdot \bar{p}(s, \to t_1) \cdot \sim \bar{p}(s, t_1 \to) \qquad (3.2)$$

$$\bar{G}L(s,p,t_1) =_{df} p(s,t_1) \cdot \sim \bar{p}(s, \to t_1) \cdot \bar{p}(s, t_1 \to) \qquad (3.3)$$

$$\bar{G}\bar{L}(s,p,t_1) =_{df} p(s,t_1) \cdot \supset : \sim \bar{p}(s, \to t_1) \cdot \sim \bar{p}(s, t_1 \to) \qquad (3.4)$$

The last of these, as it stands, is not strictly comparable with the other three. But if we combine it with $p(s, t_1)$, we get a proposition which is strictly comparable with them, viz.,

$$p(s,t_1) \cdot \bar{G}\bar{L}(s,p,t_1) := p(s,t_1) \cdot \sim \bar{p}(s, \to t_1) \cdot \sim \bar{p}(s, t_1 \to) \qquad (3.41)$$

Now each of these five formulae, except the first, involves either the expression $\sim \bar{p}(s, \to t_1)$ or the expression $\sim \bar{p}(s, t_1 \to)$. At this stage, it will be well to see exactly what these amount to. In order to do so, we have only to refer back to the definitions 1.11 and 1.21, above. From them, we deduce at once the following pair of equivalences:

$$\sim \bar{p}(s, \to t_1) . \equiv :: (x) :. (\exists t) : t < t_1 . t \not< t_1 - x . p(s,t) \qquad (1.111)$$

$$\sim \bar{p}(s, t_1 \to) . \equiv :: (x) :. (\exists t) : t > t_1 . t \not> t_1 + x . p(s,t) \qquad (1.211)$$

It will be noticed that the expressions on the left of the signs of equivalence, though negative in form, are positive in meaning. For the proposition on the right of the equivalence-sign in 1.111, when put into words, comes to the following: In *every* period, however short, which ends by t_1, there is *at least one* moment at which s has p. The corresponding proposition in 1.211, when put into words, comes to the following: in *every* period, however short, which starts from t_1 there is *at least one* moment at which s has p.

It will be useful to compare with 1.111 and 1.211 the propositions which arise from contradicting both sides of the definitions 1.1 and 1.2. They are as follows:

$$\sim p(s, \to t_1) . \equiv :: (x) :. (\exists t) : t < t_1 . t \not< t_1 - x . \sim p(s, t) \tag{1.12}$$

$$\sim p(s, t_1 \to) . \equiv :: (x) :. (\exists t) : t > t_1 . t \not> t_1 + x . \sim p(s, t) \tag{1.22}$$

The expressions on the left-hand side of the equivalence sign here are negative in meaning as well as in form. For the proposition to the right of the equivalence sign in 1.12, when put into words, comes to the following: In every period, however short, which ends by t_1 there is at least one moment at which s lacks p. The interpretation of 1.22 is similar, *mutatis mutandis*.

We are now in a position to establish an important pair of correlated propositions, viz.,

$$p(s, \to t_1) \supset \sim \bar{p}(s, \to t_1) \tag{4.1}$$

$$p(s, t_1 \to) \supset \sim \bar{p}(s, t_1 \to) \tag{4.2}$$

The first of these becomes obvious if we compare 1.111 with 1.1. The argument runs as follows. If $p(s, \to t_1)$ is true, there is a period ending by t_1 such that s has p at every moment within this period. Now every period which ends by t_1 must be either contained in or coincident with or inclusive of this period. In either case, it will contain moments at which s has p. Therefore, if $p(s, \to t_1)$ is true, every period which ends by t_1 will contain at least one moment at which s has p. But the consequent of this hypothetical proposition is equivalent to $\sim \bar{p}(s, \to t_1)$ by 1.111. Therefore, $p(s, \to t_1) \supset \sim \bar{p}(s, \to t_1)$ This is 4.1. It is obvious that 4.2 can be proved by a precisely similar argument, *mutatis mutandis*. It should be noticed that the implications in these two

THE LOGICAL ANALYSIS OF CHANGE 299

propositions cannot be reversed. $\sim\bar{p}(s, \rightarrow t_1)$ is a weaker proposition than $p(s, \rightarrow t_1)$, and $\sim\bar{p}(s, t_1\rightarrow)$ is a weaker proposition than $p(s, t_1\rightarrow)$.

We can now define two other correlated propositions, viz., 's changes with respect to p at t_1' and 's is quiescent with respect to p at t_1'. I take the first to mean that s either gets or loses p at t_1. I take the second to mean that s has p at t_1, that it has had p continuously throughout a period which ends by t_1, and that it has p continuously throughout a period which starts from t_1. We will symbolise the two propositions respectively by $Ch(s, p, t_1)$ and $Q(s, p, t_1)$. Then we have

$$Ch(s, p, t_1) =_{df} G(s, p, t_1) . \vee . L(s, p, t_1) \tag{5.1}$$

$$Q(s, p, t_1) =_{df} p(s, t_1) . p(s, \rightarrow t_1) . p(s, t_1 \rightarrow) \tag{5.2}$$

If we apply 2.1 and 2.2 to 5.1, we get

$$Ch(s, p, t_1) . \equiv .. \ p(s, t_1) : \bar{p}(s, \rightarrow t_1) . \vee . \bar{p}(s, t_1 \rightarrow) \tag{5.11}$$

It is easy to see that $Ch(s, p, t_1)$ and $Q(s, p, t_1)$ are mutually exclusive. This follows at once from 4.1 and 4.2. But it is important to notice that they are not collectively exhaustive. We will now go into this matter which is of considerable interest.

Let us take the contradictory of 5.11 and combine each side with $p(s, t_1)$. The result is

$$p(s, t_1) . \sim Ch(s, p, t_1) \equiv: p(s, t_1) . \sim \bar{p}(s, \rightarrow t_1) . \sim \bar{p}(s, t_1 \rightarrow) \tag{6.1}$$

Next, take the contradictory of 5.2 and combine each side with $p(s,t_1)$. The result is

$$p(s, t_1) . \sim Q(s, p, t_1) \equiv .. \ p(s, t_1) :\sim p(s, \rightarrow t_1) . \vee . \sim p(s, t_1 \rightarrow) \tag{6.2}$$

We will now state these two propositions in words. In order to do this we have only to refer back to the definitions 1.1 and 1.2 and to propositions 1.111, 1.211, 1.12, and 1.22. The proposition on the right of the equivalence sign in 6.1 may be stated as follows: s has p at t_1; and in *every* period, however short, which either ends by or begins from t_1 there is *at least one* moment at which s has p. The proposition on the right-hand side of the equivalence sign in 6.2 may be stated as follows: s has p at t_1, but either in every period that ends by t_1 or in every period that starts from t_1 there is *at least one* moment at which s *lacks* p.

Now there is no logical inconsistency between these two propositions. But the conjunction of them would correspond to an extremely paradoxical state of affairs, as I will now show. Suppose that they are conjoined. Then it follows that either every period which ends by t_1 or every period which starts from t_1 contains at least one moment at which s has p and at least one moment at which s lacks p. Let us consider the first of these two alternatives. It follows, if that alternative is fulfilled, that in every period, however short, which ends by t_1 s alternates an infinite number of times between having p and lacking p. This is proved as follows. Take any moment t, before t_1, at which s *has* p. Then there must be a moment t′, *between* this and t_1, at which s *lacks* p. For, otherwise, there would be a period ending by t_1, in which there is a moment at which s has p but no moment at which s lacks p, and this is contrary to our hypothesis. But, for precisely similar reasons, there must also be a moment t″, between t′ and t_1, at which s has p. And so on, without end. If the second alternative be fulfilled, a precisely similar argument will lead, *mutatis mutandis*, to a similar conclusion.

Now, although this state of affairs is *logically* possible, we all assume, I think, that it is not *ontologically* possible. Let us consider a concrete example. Suppose that p were the property of being in the solid (as opposed to the liquid or the gaseous) state. Then, if the two propositions which we are considering were both true, we should have the following situation. On the first alternative, in every period, however short, which ends by t_1 the substance s would have alternated infinitely often between the solid and the non-solid (i.e., the liquid or the gaseous) states. On the second alternative, the same would be true of any period, however short, which starts from t_1. It is this kind of situation which, I think, we reject as ontologically impossible.

I am not concerned here to decide whether this rejection is a synthetic *a priori* principle or a generalisation from experience. In either case, we may put it on record here as a postulate, and call it the 'Postulate of Excluded Infinite Alternation'. It is easy to see that it is equivalent to asserting that $\sim p(s, \to t_1) \supset \overline{p}(s, \to t_1)$ and that $\sim p(s, t_1 \to) \supset \overline{p}(s, t_1 \to)$. The first of these asserts the following: If *every* period which ends by t_1 contains *at least one* moment at which s lacks p, then there is a period ending by t_1 at *every moment* of which s lacks p. The second of them makes the same assertion with 'starts from' substituted for 'ends by'. (See 1.12 and 1.11 for the first and 1.22 and 1.21 for the second.) We will denote these two propositions, which together make up the Postulate of Excluded Infinite Alternation, by Roman numerals, in order to distinguish them from those propositions which are logically dependent on our definitions. So we have

$$\left.\begin{array}{ll} \sim p(s, \to t_1) \supset \bar{p}(s, \to t_1) & \text{I, a} \\ \sim p(s, t_1 \to) \supset \bar{p}(s, t_1 \to) & \text{I, b} \end{array}\right\} \quad (I)$$

These should be compared with propositions 4.1 and 4.2 above, which are logical consequences of our definitions. If we combine I,a with 4.1, we get

$$(I, a) . \supset : p(s, \to t_1) . \equiv . \sim \bar{p}(s, \to t_1) \tag{4.11}$$

If we combine I,b with 4.2, we get

$$(I, b) . \supset : p(s, t_1 \to) . \equiv . \sim \bar{p}(s, t_1 \to) \tag{4.21}$$

If we combine I,a with 3.2, I,b with 3.3, and both of them with 3.41, we get the following three propositions about gaining or losing p at t_1.

$$(I, a) . \supset \therefore \overline{GL}(s, p, t_1) . \equiv p(s, t_1) . \bar{p}(s, \to t_1) . p(s, t_1 \to) \tag{3.21}$$

$$(I, b) . \supset \therefore \overline{GL}(s, p, t_1) . \equiv p(s, t_1) . p(s, \to t_1) . \bar{p}(s, t_1 \to) \tag{3.31}$$

$$(I) . \supset \therefore p(s, t_1) . \overline{GL}(s, p, t_1) := p(s, t_1) . p(s, \to t_1) . p(s, t_1 \to) \tag{3.411}$$

If we combine I,a and I,b with 6.1 and 6.2, we get the following propositions.

$$(I) . \supset \therefore p(s, t_1) . \sim Ch(s, p, t_1) := p(s, t_1) . p(s, \to t_1) . p(s, t_1 \to) \tag{6.11}$$

$$(I) . \supset :: p(s, t_1) . \sim Q(s, p, t_1) := . p(s, t_1) : \bar{p}(s, \to t_1) . \vee . \bar{p}(s, t_1 \to) \tag{6.21}$$

We saw that, without appeal to Postulate I, Q(s, p, t_1) and Ch(s, p, t_1) are mutually exclusive, but are not collectively exhaustive. We now see that, if Postulate I be granted, they are also collectively exhaustive.

EDITOR'S APPENDIX TO CHAPTER 3.4

Throughout this paper, Broad uses the notation of Whitehead and Russell's *Principia Mathematica*. Although Broad does use the *Principia*-style notation in several of his published papers (e.g., those collected in his 1968 book *Induction, Probability, and Causation*), the notation may nonetheless be somewhat alien to the contemporary reader. For that reason, in what follows, I provide a translation of Broad's formulae into a more modern – and therefore more generally familiar – formalism.

(1.1) $$p(s, \to t_1) =_{df} \exists x \forall t ((t < t_1 \land t \not< t_1 - x) \to p(s,t))$$

(1.2) $$p(s, t_1 \to) =_{df} \exists x \forall t ((t > t_1 \land t \not> t_1 + x) \to p(s,t))$$

(1.11) $$\overline{p}(s, \to t_1) =_{df} \exists x \forall t ((t < t_1 \land t \not< t_1 - x) \to \neg p(s,t))$$

(1.12) $$\overline{p}(s, t_1 \to) =_{df} \exists x \forall t ((t > t_1 \land t \not> t_1 + x) \to \neg p(s,t))$$

(2.1) $$G(s, p, t_1) =_{df} p(s, t_1) \land \overline{p}(s, \to t_1)$$

(2.2) $$L(s, p, t_1) =_{df} p(s, t_1) \land \overline{p}(s, t_1 \to)$$

(3.1) $$GL(s, p, t_1) =_{df} p(s, t_1) \land (\overline{p}(s, \to t_1) \land \overline{p}(s, t_1 \to))$$

(3.2) $$G\overline{L}(s, p, t_1) =_{df} p(s, t_1) \land (\overline{p}(s, \to t_1) \land \neg\overline{p}(s, t_1 \to))$$

(3.3) $$\overline{G}L(s, p, t_1) =_{df} p(s, t_1) \land (\neg\overline{p}(s, \to t_1) \land \overline{p}(s, t_1 \to))$$

(3.4) $$\overline{GL}(s, p, t_1) =_{df} p(s, t_1) \to (\neg\overline{p}(s, \to t_1) \land \neg\overline{p}(s, t_1 \to))$$

(3.41) $$(p(s,t_1) \land \overline{GL}(s,p,t_1)) \leftrightarrow p(s,t_1) \land (\neg\overline{p}(s, \to t_1) \land \neg\overline{p}(s, t_1 \to))$$

(1.111) $$\neg\overline{p}(s, \to t_1) \leftrightarrow \forall x \exists t ((t < t_1 \land t \not< t_1 - x) \land p(s,t))$$

(1.211) $$\neg\overline{p}(s, t_1 \to) \leftrightarrow \forall x \exists t ((t > t_1 \land t \not> t_1 + x) \land p(s,t))$$

(1.12) $\quad \neg p(s, \to t_1) \leftrightarrow \forall x \exists t\left(\left(t < t_1 \wedge t \not< t_1 - x\right) \wedge \neg p(s, t)\right)$

(1.22) $\quad \neg p(s, t_1 \to) \leftrightarrow \forall x \exists t\left(\left(t > t_1 \wedge t \not> t_1 + x\right) \wedge \neg p(s, t)\right)$

(4.1) $\quad p(s, \to t_1) \to \neg \overline{p}(s, \to t_1)$

(4.2) $\quad p(s, t_1 \to) \to \neg \overline{p}(s, t_1 \to)$

(5.1) $\quad Ch(s, p, t_1) =_{df} G(s, p, t_1) \vee L(s, p, t_1)$

(5.2) $\quad Q(s, p, t_1) =_{df} p(s, t_1) \wedge \left(p(s, \to t_1) \wedge p(s, t_1 \to)\right)$

(5.11) $\quad Ch(s, p, t_1) \leftrightarrow p(s, t_1) \wedge \left(\overline{p}(s, \to t_1) \vee \overline{p}(s, t_1 \to)\right)$

(6.1) $\quad \left(p(s, t_1) \wedge \neg Ch(s, p, t_1)\right) \leftrightarrow \left(p(s, t_1) \wedge \left(\neg \overline{p}(s, \to t_1) \wedge \neg \overline{p}(s, t \to)\right)\right)$

(6.2) $\quad \left(p(s, t_1) \wedge \neg Q(s, p, t_1)\right) \leftrightarrow \left(p(s, t_1) \wedge \left(\neg p(s, \to t_1) \vee \neg p(s, t_1 \to)\right)\right)$

(I) $\quad \begin{cases} (I, a) \\ (I, b) \end{cases} \quad \begin{array}{l} \neg p(s, \to t_1) \to \overline{p}(s, \to t_1) \\ \neg p(s, t_1 \to) \to \overline{p}(s, t_1 \to) \end{array}$

(4.11) $\quad (I, a) \to \left(p(s, \to t_1) \leftrightarrow \neg \overline{p}(s, \to t_1)\right)$

(4.21) $\quad (I, b) \to \left(p(s, t_1 \to) \leftrightarrow \neg \overline{p}(s, t_1 \to)\right)$

(3.21) $\quad (I, a) \to \left(\overline{GL}(s, p, t_1) \leftrightarrow \left(p(s, t_1) \wedge \left(\overline{p}(s, \to t_1) \wedge p(s, t_1 \to)\right)\right)\right)$

(3.31) $\quad (I, b) \to \left(\overline{GL}(s, p, t_1) \leftrightarrow \left(p(s, t_1) \wedge \left(p(s, \to t_1) \wedge \overline{p}(s, t_1 \to)\right)\right)\right)$

(3.411) $\quad (I) \to \left(\left(p(s, t_1) \wedge \overline{GL}(s, p, t_1)\right) \leftrightarrow \left(p(s, t_1) \wedge \left(p(s, \to t_1) \wedge p(s, t_1 \to)\right)\right)\right)$

(6.11) $(I) \rightarrow \left(\left(p(s,t_1) \wedge \neg Ch(s,p,t_1) \right) \leftrightarrow \left(p(s,t_1) \wedge \left(p(s, \rightarrow t_1) \wedge p(s, t_1 \rightarrow) \right) \right) \right)$

(6.21) $(I) \rightarrow \left(\left(p(s,t_1) \wedge \neg Q(s,p,t_1) \right) \leftrightarrow \left(p(s,t_1) \wedge \left(\overline{p}(s, \rightarrow t_1) \vee \overline{p}(s, t_1 \rightarrow) \right) \right) \right)$

NOTE

1   JW: Broad's own illustration: scanned from p. 3 of manuscript catalogue number BROD/C/2/39 in the Wren Library at Trinity College, Cambridge.

Part 4

PSYCHICAL RESEARCH

INTRODUCTION TO PART 4
Joel Walmsley

Broad is well known – indeed *infamous* – for his serious interest in that diverse subject matter that falls under the heading of 'psychical research'. This concern appears to have been life-long: in the first instalment of his 'Autobiography' Broad mentions that he 'can hardly remember a time when it did not exist' (Schilpp, 1959, p. 55). Then, in the 'Autobiographical Notes' of this volume (see Part 1, p. 66), he reports that over the course of his life, this interest had not diminished; in fact, says Broad,

> as my interest in and attention to contemporary philosophy have declined, my interest in psychical research has increased, and such philosophical abilities as I still have have been more and more directed to theoretical problems arising out of its ostensible findings.

Broad's *professional* interest in psychical research seems to have begun to find its way into print in the late 1910s. A 1917 paper on Hume's discussion of miracles ends with a comment, ostensibly on that particular subject, that would nonetheless be a fair characterisation of Broad's view of psychic research in general. There (p. 93), Broad says that we ought not to have

> such a strong belief in any of the alleged laws of nature as to make us at once reject an alleged exception, no matter how good the testimony for it may be. We ought to be very slow indeed in admitting an alleged exception to a well-established law; and it may well be that there never has been good

DOI: 10.4324/9781003081135-22

enough evidence for a reasonable man to accept any alleged miracle. But we have no right to say off-hand with Hume that no possible evidence could make it reasonable to suppose that a miraculous exception to some law of nature had taken place.

This was followed in 1918 and 1919 by a pair of papers in *The Hibbert Journal* concerning the desirability and the probability of the survival of bodily death, respectively, before Broad's joined the Society for Psychical Research in 1920, made his first of many contributions to its *Journal* in 1922, and eventually became President of the Society for two separate periods between 1935–1936 and 1958–1960.

Broad is often quite defensive about his interest in the paranormal, clearly recognising that many of his colleagues would have regarded such research as at best, marginal, and at worst, disreputable. In the preface to his (1925) *The Mind and Its Place in Nature*, he memorably writes (p. viii):

> I shall no doubt be blamed by certain scientists, and, I am afraid, by some philosophers, for having taken serious account of the alleged facts which are investigated by Psychical Researchers. I am wholly impenitent about this. The scientists in question seem to me to confuse the Author of Nature with the Editor of *Nature*; or at any rate to suppose that there can be no productions of the former which would not be accepted for publication by the latter. And I see no reason to believe this.

And yet Broad's main explicit defence of research into the paranormal – a 1949 essay entitled *The Relevance of Psychical Research for Philosophy* – is not really *per se* argument that we should *accept* ostensibly paranormal phenomena as veridical, or reports of them as true. Rather, his main aim seems to be to establish that psychical *research* is at least pursuitworthy, either because if such phenomena *were* veridical, they would dramatically conflict with what he calls 'basic limiting principles' about time, causation, and the relation between mind and matter (which are 'commonly accepted as constituting the framework of all possible natural phenomena'), or else because even if they are *not* veridical, they may still be of great psychological or sociological interest when we consider why such reports are widespread and often believed.

The two previously unpublished essays here exemplify this stance. At the beginning of 'Ostensibly Paranormal Physical Phenomena' (Chapter 4.1) Broad describes his position as one of *scepticism*, but goes on to explain:

> I use the word 'scepticism' here in its proper sense. I mean that I am uncertain *whether there are or are not* genuinely supernormal physical phenomena: I do *not* mean that I am practically certain that there are *not*.

This seems to be Broad's consistently held view; it is telling that the published version of his (1962) *Lectures on Psychical Research* begins with a dedication to Sidgwick, Myers, and Gurney (founders of the Society for Psychical Research, and by then deceased) and an epigraph from Hebrews 11:39: 'And these all, having obtained a good report through faith, received not the promise'. Both essays included here go on to assemble and catalogue the evidence in such a way as to conclude that – even though much of the evidence is unsatisfactory – there remains a '*residuum*' of positive results which cannot be simply denied or explained away. And Broad's definitive statement of his own views, which appears in the 'Autobiographical Notes' above (pp. 73–74) reiterates such a sentiment.

The two essays here are also unusual, for Broad, in another respect: they concern paranormal *physical* phenomena. In the 'Autobiographical Notes' above (p. 70), Broad says of his published work on psychical research – especially the *Lectures on Psychical Research* – with an air of regret: 'It does not deal with anything like the whole area of ostensibly paranormal phenomena. Nothing is said in detail about alleged *physical* phenomena'. Whereas Broad's published work on psychical research concerned paranormal mental phenomena (such as clairvoyance, telepathy, precognition, and mediumistic communication), the two essays in this section now also reveal his views on further topics such as poltergeists and telekinesis.

The essay 'Ostensibly Paranormal Physical Phenomena' is taken from a handwritten manuscript, dated 12 September 1955 with a note indicating that it was written – or at least, completed – in Stockholm. It may have been given (or intended) as a lecture during Broad's travels in Sweden because it includes some 'footnotes to self' with occasional items of Swedish vocabulary (e.g., for 'gamekeeper' and 'thimbles'). There is also a note in Broad's handwriting, indicating that it was expanded on 27 January 1965; the later additions were written in a different colour ink on separate pieces of paper

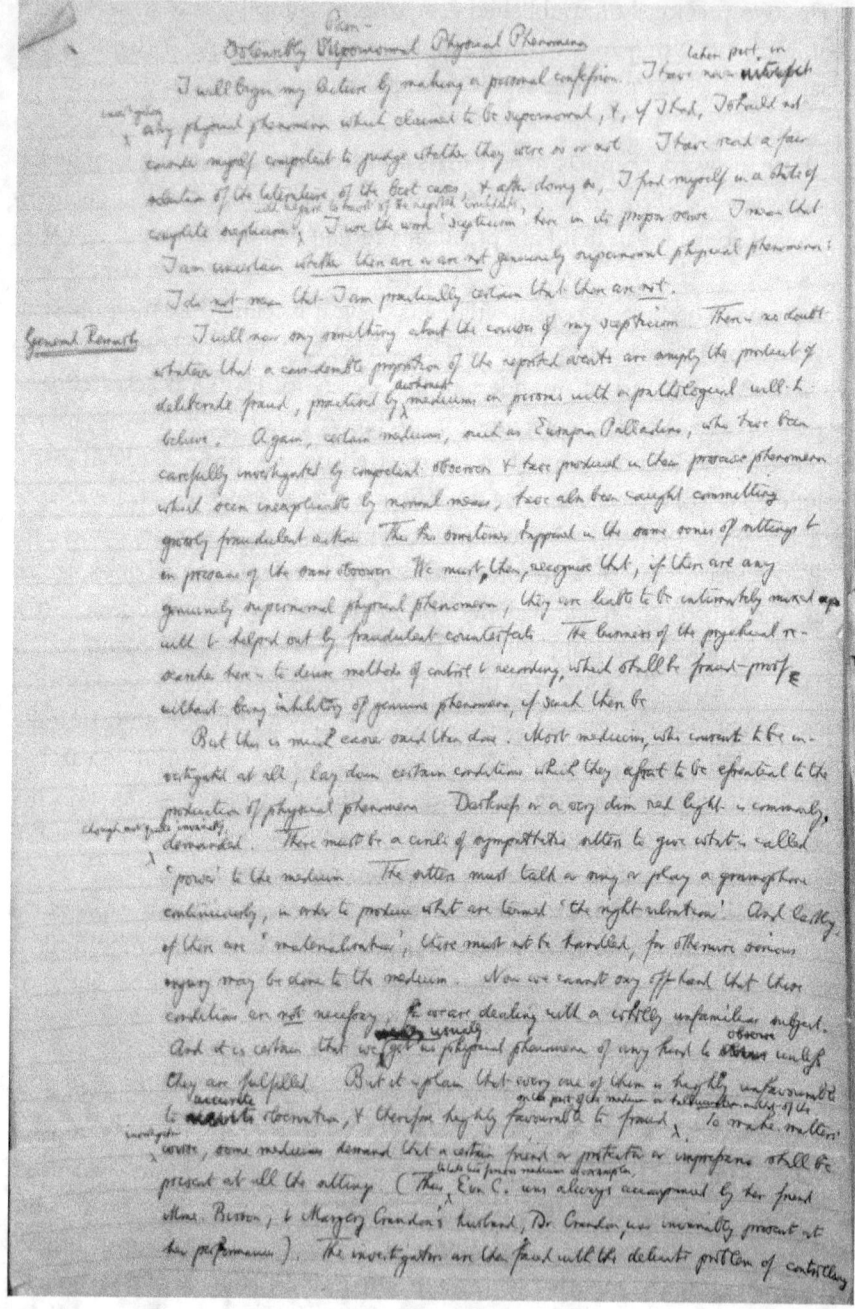

Figure 4.1 Original handwritten manuscript for Chapter 4.1

(literally copied and pasted in) and appear, almost *verbatim*, in the paper 'Poltergeists' (also included in this section) as an account of the 'Sauchie' case. To avoid repetition, I have therefore omitted those additions from the version here; it is thus, effectively, the 1955 instance of the manuscript.

The essay 'Poltergeists' is taken from a type-written manuscript, dated 29 January 1969. It was bundled with several items of correspondence indicating that it had been submitted to the Swedish magazine *Sökaren* ('The Seeker'), but returned because it was too long and too difficult from which to make an extraction. The correspondence also shows that copies had been sent to several of Broad's friends and colleagues in early 1969, and includes a return letter with comments from one Simon Blackburn (!) (then of Pembroke College, Oxford), who sums up nicely what is so alarming about poltergeists in particular, and paranormal *physical* phenomena in general. He writes:

> Psychologically I must say I find poltergeists more disturbing than other psychic phenomena. They seem to create a breach in expectations which are not just scientifically fundamental—telepathy may do that—but also so fundamental to the conduct of life, and therefore common, namely the expectations that objects will on the whole stay put.

Broad would surely agree; such cases seem to contradict a general point that he mentioned in 'Notes on Causation' in the previous section (p. 264): 'We think of things as tending to persist in certain quiescent states unless interfered with by some external agent' … what such 'external agents' may amount to is the subject-matter of this section.

4.1

OSTENSIBLY PARANORMAL PHYSICAL PHENOMENA

I will begin my lecture by making a personal confession. I have never taken part in investigating any physical phenomena which claimed to be supernormal, and, if I had, I should not consider myself competent to judge whether they were so or not. I have read a fair selection of the literature of the best cases, and after doing so, I find myself in a state of complete scepticism with regard to most of the reported incidents. I use the word 'scepticism' here in its proper sense. I mean that I am uncertain *whether there are or are not* genuinely supernormal physical phenomena: I do *not* mean that I am practically certain that there are *not*.

GENERAL REMARKS

I will now say something about the causes of my scepticism. There is no doubt whatsoever that a considerable proportion of the reported events are simply the product of deliberate fraud, practised by dishonest mediums on persons with a pathological will to believe. Again, certain mediums, such as Eusapia Palladino, who have been carefully investigated by competent observers and have produced in their presence phenomena which seem inexplicable by normal means, have also been caught committing grossly fraudulent actions. This has sometimes happened in the same series of sittings and in presence of the same observers. We must, then, recognise that, if there are any genuinely supernormal physical phenomena, they are liable to be intimately mixed with and helped out by fraudulent counterfeits. The business of the psychical researcher here is to devise methods of control and recording, which shall be fraud-proof without being inhibitory of genuine phenomena, if such there be.

But this is much easier said than done. Most mediums, who consent to be investigated at all, lay down certain conditions which they assert to be essential to the production of physical phenomena. Darkness or a very dim red light is commonly, though not quite invariably, demanded. There must be a circle of sympathetic sitters to give what is called 'power' to the medium. The sitters must talk or sing or play a gramophone continuously, in order to produce what are termed 'the right vibrations'. And lastly, if there are 'materialisations', these must not be handled, for otherwise serious injury may be done to the medium. Now we cannot say off-hand that these conditions are *not* necessary, for we are dealing with a wholly unfamiliar subject. And it is certain that we usually get no physical phenomena of any kind to observe unless they are fulfilled. But it is plain that every one of them is highly unfavourable to accurate observation and therefore highly favourable to fraud on the part of the medium or hallucination on that of the investigator. To make matters worse, some mediums demand that a certain friend or protector or impresario shall be present at all the sittings. (Thus, to take two famous mediums as examples, Eva C. was always accompanied by her friend Mme. Bisson and Margery Crandon's husband, Dr Crandon, was invariably present at her performances.) The investigators are then faced with the delicate problem of controlling this person in addition to the medium.

Now a very early result of the S.P.R's researches on physical mediumship was to show that human testimony about ostensibly perceived events is unreliable to a degree which we would hardly have thought possible. We are very apt to overlook details of events which are happening under our noses and to think that we have *perceived* events which we have in fact only inferred or unintentionally taken for granted. The experimental work undertaken by Mr S.J. Davey in connexion with the medium Eglinton, who claimed to produce messages in writing on the inner faces of a pair of superposed and interlocked slates, is one of the most important contributions which have ever been made to the psychology of malobservation. It is described in Vol. IV of the S.P.R.'s *Proceedings* under the title 'The Possibilites of Malobservation and Lapse of Memory from a Practical Point of View'. It was shown that intelligent persons, who knew that they were watching a trick and were trying to find out how it was done, would nevertheless misreport (both by omission and by supplementation), to an almost incredible extent what had actually happened in their presence. Any lapse of time between the events reported and the making of the report introduces further possibilities of mistakes, due to lapse of memory and unwitting elaboration, smoothing, and interpolation to fill the gaps. An account of another important series of experiments on the same subject, carried out by Mr Besterman of the S.P.R at a much later date, will be found in Vol. XL of the *Proceedings* under the title 'The Psychology of Testimony in Relation to Paraphysical Phenomena'.

A valuable result, which has emerged from carefully controlled sittings which were in other respects fruitless, is that we now know a great deal about the standard tricks of fraudulent mediums, about the extreme difficulty of keeping continuous control of their hands and feet, and so on. It has become clear that investigations of the physical phenomena of mediumship by unpractised amateurs, no matter what their scientific eminence may be, are worthless. Even with experienced investigators, it is most desirable that all alleged phenomena should be recorded automatically and permanently, by some photographic or electric or mechanical device, at the time when they happen. In any comparison that is made between the phenomena of physical mediumship and the performance of conjurors on the stage, it is necessary to draw the following distinction. At an ordinary spiritualistic seance, a fraudulent medium has far easier conditions than a stage-conjurer, but at a properly controlled sitting, conducted by experts, the exact opposite is the case.

Now the causes of my scepticism are as follows. On the one hand, it may fairly be said that the phenomena tend on the whole to become less and less impressive as the conditions are tightened up, and to fade out altogether just as the conditions become fraud-proof. On the other hand, there is a residuum of cases in which the experiments have been conducted under extremely rigid conditions by persons who were well acquainted with the methods used by fraudulent mediums, and positive results have been recorded. But even here there is a most unsatisfactory feature to be noted. One set of investigators working with a medium, and apparently using all needful precautions, will get interesting positive results. Then similar experiments will be done by other investigators with the same medium and the results will be purely negative.

Undoubtedly the psychological effect of all this on most students of the subject, who have not a strong will to believe, is to make them stress the negative results, and either ignore the positive ones or assume that these must have been due to fraud which happened to remain undetected. I am very conscious of this in myself. But I doubt whether this attitude is *logically* justifiable, and I propose to make some remarks on this point before passing from the general to the particular part of my lecture.

(1) Suppose that medium A produces certain physical phenomena, which he claims to be supernormal; and suppose that conjurer B produces precisely similar phenomena by normal means which he is prepared to reveal. Then it is very common to conclude that medium A *must* have produced the phenomena by the same means as conjuror B. This is quite illogical. Even if A was in a position to do the actions which B did, it does not follow that A in fact did them and that the phenomena were in fact produced in that way. For precisely similar observable effects can, and often do, come from different causes. And the reasoning is still more faulty if, as is often the case, there is no reason to believe, and strong reason to doubt that medium A was in a position to do what conjurer B did.

(2) No amount of subsequent negative results can logically wash out a previous positive result, if that was properly recorded at the time and the records remain for inspection. If the result of one experiment is positive, and that of others, performed under conditions which seem precisely alike, is negative, it is legitimate to conclude that there was *some* difference in the conditions. But, unless there is positive evidence pointing in that direction, it is not legitimate to infer that the difference *must* have been that the precautions against fraud broke down on the first occasion and did not do so on the other occasions. Obviously, the relevant differences *may* have been in the internal mental or bodily state of the medium. There is at least some reason to think that, if there are genuine powers of physical mediumship, they tend first to manifest themselves at the onset of puberty, then reach a maximum, and then often decline and fade out altogether in a few years. Now, if this were so, it would be likely that the time when such mediums were at their best

would be the time when they were still giving performances to uncritical audiences in their immediate circle of relatives and friends. There they would be under a strong temptation to practice tricks in order to increase their exploits and to eke out their genuine powers when they were not in good form. By the time they came to the notice of critical and experienced investigators, they would be likely to be well past their prime, though they might still have occasional bursts of genuinely supernormal achievement.

(3) It is a very common fallacy to put forward a normal explanation which covers nine-tenths of the reported phenomena of a certain kind, but fails to cover the remaining one-tenth, which are equally well-attested, and then either to ignore the recalcitrant residue, or to reject the reports of it, and claim that one's normal explanation covers *all* the alleged facts. As Professor Sidgwick said in his Presidential Address to the S.P.R. in its earliest days in 1883: 'It is not a scientific way of dealing with testimony to explain what you can and then say that the rest is untrue. It may be common sense, but it is not science.' I may add, on my own account, that, although it is not science, it has been a very common practice of scientists when dealing with such matters.

SUBDIVISION OF THE SUBJECT

I think that this should suffice by way of a general introduction. I will now come down to detail. Ostensibly paranormal physical phenomena may be divided into two classes, which invariably melt into each other. These are (1) *sporadic* cases, which have to be investigated where and when they happen and (2) those which can be studied at leisure in the laboratory or the seance-room in a series of experiments under the control of one or more skilled investigators. The latter can be subdivided into (2.1) those which require the presence of a medium and (2.2) those which can be carried out without a medium. The rest of the lecture will be occupied in describing some examples of each in turn.

(1) Sporadic Cases.

The commonest of these are the so-called 'Poltergeist' cases. In a house in which such phenomena take place bells will start ringing, crockery and fire-irons or lumps of coal and cinders will jump about or shoot through the air, stones or dirt will fall in closed rooms, windows will break without apparent cause, and there may be outbreaks of fire. It seems fair to say that the stories of Poltergeist phenomena have been relatively frequent and singularly constant in type for a very long period and over most of the Earth's surface.[1] So they do not seem to be dying out.

There have been several famous Poltergeist cases in England and the United States. An early one is the story of the disturbances at the house of Mr Mompesson at Tedworth in Wiltshire in 1661. The trouble began when Mompesson, in his capacity of Justice of the Peace, deprived a vagabond and rascally discharged soldier, called Digby,[2] of a drum, with which he had been making a nuisance of himself in the adjacent village of Ludgershall. Digby went his way and Mompesson took the drum with him back to his own house. Almost immediately Poltergeist disturbances started in Mompesson's house. A prominent feature in them was the loud sound of the beating of a drum. This continued after Digby's drum had been burned, and while Digby was lying in prison at Gloucester, many miles away. Mompesson's two small daughters were specially liable to be attacked and thrown out of bed; the floors and windows shook and heaved violently day after day, and these phenomena went on for about two years. The case was reported by Glanvill, one of the first members of the Royal Society, who had visited the town and witnessed the phenomena. The report may be read in his book *Saducismus Triumphatus* and there is other contemporary evidence still surviving. The case is generally known in literature as the *Drummer of Tedworth Case*.

The homes of clergymen and nonconformist ministers seem to have been peculiarly liable to the visitation of Poltergeist disturbances. One of the most famous English cases is that of Epworth Rectory, the home of the parents, brothers, and sisters of John Wesley, the founder of the sect of Wesleyan Methodists. It happened in the years 1716–1717. It is recorded in a contemporary diary by old Mr Wesley, father of John, who was himself a victim. There exists also an account written by him at the time for his son Samuel, who was then at school at Westminster. There are further accounts, written later for John, who was at school at Charterhouse when the phenomena were in progress, by his mother and several of his sisters. One of the most spectacular of the American cases happened in 1850–1851 in the house of an elderly Presbyterian minister, Dr Phelps, in the village of Stratford, Connecticut. This included such incidents as a brass candlestick falling from the mantelpiece and continuing to dash itself against the floor until broken, a shovel and tongs moving out from the fireplace, and proceeding to dance about in the middle of the floor, and a heavy dining-table rising in the air. A full account will be found in Carrington's *Historic Poltergeists*.

I will now describe in rather more detail a case, which happened in the village of Durweston in Wiltshire in 1894–1895 and was reported to the S.P.R. I choose it because it is typical, in being neither very strong nor very weak from the point of view of the evidence supplied.

It happened in the house of Mrs Best, an illiterate country-woman of about 60. In spite of her being a nonconformist, she was described by the Rector of the parish as 'an earnest Christian woman, who bears perhaps the highest character in the village'. She lived in a small semi-detached cottage, and her neighbour in the other cottage was Mr Newman, a gamekeeper.[3] He also receives high marks from the Rector for his honesty and truthfulness. Mrs Best had living with her as boarders two young sisters, named *Cleave*. The elder, Annie, was 13, and could write; the younger, Gertrude, was 4. Some months after the disturbances had begun a Miss Mason, Local Government Inspector for Boarded-out Children, took Annie to stay with her for a week in her flat in London and had her medically examined. She was pronounced to be of a markedly tuberculous tendency and apparently hysterical. Our information about the phenomena is derived from two sources. (1) From the notes taken by Mr Westlake, of the S.P.R., in an interview which he had on 23 January 1895, with Mr Newman, the Gamekeeper, who then described the experiences which he had had on 18 December 1894. (2) From an account written on 25 January 1895, by Mr Anderson, the Rector of the parish, of the experience had by himself and the village schoolmaster, Mr Sheppard, a fortnight earlier.

Mr Newman's story is as follows. He was sent for by Mrs Best between 10 and 11 in the morning of 15th December, and he alleged that he had then witnessed the following events, among others. (1) He was in the room on the ground floor with the two children, looking through the doorway into the garden. The door was open to its fullest extent. From behind the door there emerged at a height of about 5 feet

(1.5 metres) a succession of small shells and two thimbles.[4] Each travelled very slowly through the air, without apparent support, towards him. The two thimbles hit his hat. The impact was very gentle, so as to be scarcely perceptible, and immediately after hitting him, the objects fell to the ground. Some of the shells passed by him and descended slowly to the ground in a slanting direction. (2) A boot, which had been lying in front of the door, floated in, moving at a height of about 1 foot (30 cm) above the ground, and then fell at his side. It fell softly, as all the other objects had done. (3) Mrs Best threw this boot out into the garden, and Newman went out and put his foot on it. As he withdrew his foot, saying: 'I defy anything to move that boot', the boot rose up behind him and knocked off his hat. The boot and the hat fell to the ground together. There was no human being behind Mr Newman at the time.

So much for the gamekeeper; now for the Rector's and the schoolmaster's experiences. Mrs Best and the children had gone to stay in Mr Newman's cottages, and Messrs. Anderson and Sheppard visited them there on 10 January 1895. Mrs Best took the two children to an upper room and put them to bed, lying down herself on the same bed but in the opposite direction to the children. The room was adequately lighted by a hand lamp on the washstand.

Loud rappings were heard at once. At first, they tended to cease when Mr Anderson, the Rector, was in the room; but they soon became loud and continuous, whether he was there or not. He searched the room, the rest of the house, and Mrs Best's cottage next door. Then the Rector remained in the house with Mrs Best and the children, while Mr Sheppard, the schoolmaster, went outside to make sure that no one was playing tricks there. The noises continued throughout this period. Mr Anderson said that he could not detect any vibration in the wall, when he put his hand or his ear against it. But, when he put his hand on the rail at the end of the children's bed, he could feel a vibration there, varying in strength with the loudness of the knockings. He could see the hands of Mrs Best and of the children, and he kept a close watch on them, and he was convinced that the noises were not produced by them. There were also occasional scratching noises in the wall, and sometimes, as it seemed, in the mattress of the bed. No mysterious movements of objects were observed by these two watchers. When and only when the room was dark and the investigators were out of it and at the foot of the stairs, writing was produced on a slate placed about 4 feet (120 cm) from the bed. The Rector was convinced that no one could have left the bed, under the circumstances, without his hearing it: and Mrs Best said that she was willing to take an oath that none of them had done so. It will be remembered that the only one of the three who could write was the elder girl, Annie. I express no opinion on the likelihood of fraud at this point.

Later on in 1895, the children were removed to another house in the village. Similar disturbances took place there. Afterwards, the sisters were separated. It is said that the disturbances followed the elder and that they took the form of noises on the outside walls of the house in which she was then living.

This case is typical of the milder kind of Poltergeist cases. In the first place, it is certain that, in a significantly large proportion (though by no means all) of them, the phenomena start with and centre around a child or young servant-maid, often deformed or neurotic or unhappy. Again, they often, but not always, follow this person from one house to another. The occurrence of the phenomena tends to make such a person, who may hitherto have been neglected and despised, an object of wondering attention. Secondly, in a number of cases which have been carefully investigated, the child or young person concerned has been actually detected in fraud. Lastly, Newman's statement that the moving objects moved slowly through the air, that they fell gently, and that they did not hurt him when they hit him is characteristic of a number of such stories, whatever its significance may be.

In Vol. XVII of the S.P.R. Proceedings there is a valuable discussion on Poltergeist phenomena between Podmore and the Scottish ethnologist and historian Andrew Lang. I find myself sympathising with Lang's concluding remark:

> What we really desire is an answer to the question: 'How do these stories come to be told?' I am not too contented with the answer: 'Because young people play a few foolish tricks; the rest is all exaggeration and hallucination'. It is the extraordinary uniformity in the reports, from every age, country and class of society—the uniformity in hallucination—which makes the mystery.

I would add the following remark on my own account. In some cases, which are as well attested as the rest, there was *no* young person present. And in many of the cases, where such a person was present, some of the reported phenomena were of *extreme violence*. If they really happened, they were quite beyond the normal bodily powers of an adolescent child.

(2) Experimental cases.

Plainly, the case for there being something genuinely supernormal in sporadic physical phenomena, such as Poltergeist disturbances, would be greatly strengthened, if it were certain that somewhat similar events have repeatedly been observed by competent investigators in the laboratory or the seance-room under experimental conditions of control and record. So I will now pass to my second class, viz., Experimental Cases. We will begin with the first subdivision of it, viz., those in which a medium is involved.

(2.1) With Mediums

Among the phenomena, genuine or fraudulent, which have been observed, the most important are *Materialisation* and *Telekinesis* (i.e., the movement of objects without apparent contact).

I shall dismiss Materialisation in a few words because here I think that something more definitely negative than scepticism is justified. There has been in fact an immense amount of proven fraud, and, so far as I know, no completely satisfactory evidence for genuinely supernormal phenomena. The two most celebrated instances of materialising mediums investigated under fairly satisfactory conditions of control are Eva C. and Mrs Marjory Crandon.

I find it very difficult to doubt that both were fraudulent. The case of Mrs Crandon raises extremely interesting psychological and moral problems. If she was fraudulent, as I cannot doubt that she was, her husband must, I think, have been deeply involved in the fraud. Now he was a well-known and fairly successful medical practitioner in Boston. There was, so far as I can see, no possible *financial* motive here for fraud, and the notoriety of the case and the controversies to which it gave rise can scarcely have been helpful to his practice. I met him once in Cambridge, and heard him talk and lecture on his wife's performance, and he produced a not unfavourable impression. It would be most interesting to know something more of the background of this couple, and of their conscious and unconscious motives in a long and elaborate career of gratuitous fraudulent mediumship.

All that I will add on the general topic of materialisation is this. If a medium, who claims to produce materialisations, is to be investigated, the following conditions are essential. He or she must consent to a thorough bodily examination by a competent medical practitioner before and after each sitting. When I say 'thorough' I mean it; I will not labour the point in speaking to a mixed and non-medical audience. During the sitting, the medium should be dressed in a costume provided by the investigators. It is desirable that he or she should be enclosed in a bag of gauze[5] sewn up on each occasion by the investigators. Lastly, attention must be paid to the possibility of what is known as 'regurgitation'. Some persons have the capacity of swallowing quite large objects, keeping them at leisure in what is known as an *oesophageal diverticulum* or secondary stomach, bringing them up at will for the purpose of producing apparent materialisations, and then drawing them back into the mouth and swallowing them again. So the investigating medical man should be on the lookout for the possibility that the medium has this anatomical peculiarity and is utilising it for the purposes of fraud. Anyone who wishes to study this aspect of physical mediumship will find an interesting account of it in *Bulletin I* of the *National Laboratory for Psychical Research*. The article is entitled 'Regurgitation and the Duncan Mediumship' and it is by the late Mr Harry Price.

I pass now to alleged cases of Telekinesis. Here the evidence is considerably better. I will take as examples, the Italian medium, Eusapia Palladino, and the Austrian mediums, Willi and Rudi Schneider.

Eusapia Palladino was an ignorant, but extremely shrewd and cunning, Italian peasant woman. She was repeatedly investigated, with increasingly rigid control and increasingly careful recording, in Italy, France, and England. It is admitted that she cheated whenever she was given the least opportunity to do so. Mrs Salter, a distinguished member of the S.P.R., who as a child saw much of

Eusapia when the latter was being investigated in Cambridge, has told me that Eusapia cheated in every game that the two played together.

Much the best investigation of Eusapia's powers was that conducted for the S.P.R. during November and December 1908 in a room at the Hotel Victoria, Naples, by three of its members. The investigators were Hereward Carrington, W.W. Baggally, and Everard Feilding. The first two of these were skilled amateur conjurors, and all three of them had had a long experience in the investigation of physical mediumship and had detected many mediums in fraud. They were therefore well aware of the kind of tricks against which they had to be on guard. They held eleven sittings. The nature of the control, the arrangements of the room, and the state of the illumination are minutely described. The phenomena were reported verbally as soon as they were observed and the report (with a note of the time) was taken down at once by a stenographer. The account of these sittings will be found in Vol. XXIII of the S.P.R. *Proceedings*, where it occupies 260 pages. It is worth reading as a model of the best that could be done without the electrical methods of control and observations and record which are now available.

In all the experiments, a corner of the room was screened off with curtains by the experimenters before the sitting began, to form what is called a 'cabinet'. The medium and her two controllers sat outside the cabinet, in front of these curtains, her chair being between 1 ft and 1 ft 6 inches (30–45 cm) from the curtains. A total of 470 phenomena were observed and recorded. Of these, 350 took place when the medium was being controlled by two of the three S.P.R. investigators in conjunction, whilst the third was watching. We will confine ourselves to this selection, since they are the incidents that took place under the most rigid and expert conditions of control. They include 34 complete levitations of the table and 41 movements of other objects in the room *outside* the cabinet. On a further 28 occasions, there were movements of objects *within* the cabinet. Lastly, on three occasions *hands*, and on five occasions objects resembling *heads*, issued from and returned into the cabinet. All three investigators came to the conclusion that a large proportion of the phenomena witnessed and simultaneously reported and recorded could not have been produced by normal means. Anyone who reads their paper is provided with such complete details that he can judge for himself. So much for Eusapia.

Willi and Rudi Schneider were sons of a compositor in Braunau. Their mediumship started in their taking part in experiments with a planchette in their home. Willi began his career as a medium in 1918 at the age of 15. He was taken to Munich by Baron von Schrenck-Notzing in 1921, and elaborately investigated in his laboratory there. The control and recording seem to have been careful, but Schrenck-Notzing was an unreliable and uncritical investigator, and it would be unwise to attach much weight to his sole testimony. The findings were published in 1924 in a book entitled *Experimente de Fernbewegung*. In Vol. XXXIV of the S.P.R. *Proceedings*, there is a review by Dr Dingwall of this book and of certain criticisms which it had called forth in Germany.

In 1924, when Willi was 21, he came to England and was elaborately investigated in the S.P.R.'s seance-room by a committee of the Society. This included Dr Dingwall, who is a highly competent amateur conjurer with an immense experience of mediumship. An account of these sittings will be found in Vol. XXXVI of the S.P.R. *Proceedings*. The phenomena were far less numerous and far less spectacular than those reported by Schrenck-Notzing. But there is no doubt that levitation of small objects did from time to time happen, under conditions which seem to rule out any normal explanation. If Willi had genuine mediumistic powers, as I am rather inclined to believe, they were evidently on the wane at this time. In 1926, when he was 23, his powers vanished completely, and, as far as I know, never revived. He became a dental mechanic, a profession for which he was being trained during the course of his mediumship.

Willi's younger brother, Rudi, started his mediumistic career in the home circle at the age of 11 in March 1919. He also was in course of time taken to Munich by Schrenck-Notzing for training and experiment. After Schrenck-Notzing's death, Rudi came to London and had a number of sittings with Mr Harry Price during the latter part of 1929 and again in 1930. In these sittings, the sitters themselves were controlled electronically, and the phenomena were recorded photographically. In Harry Price's book, *Rudi Schneider* are to be seen photographs of waste-paper baskets apparently unsupported in the air, whilst Rudi's hands and feet are visibly being controlled.

From 1930 to 1931, Rudi took part in a very interesting series of experiments conducted by Dr Osty in Paris. They are described in Osty's book *Les Pouvoirs inconnus de l'Espirit sur la Matière*. An account of these experiments was subsequently given to the S.P.R. in a lecture by the English physicist Lord Rayleigh, son of a still more eminent mathematical physicist. The essential point of these experiments was the following. Osty arranged for a beam of infrared rays to be reflected to-and-fro across the surface of a table and then to be focussed on a photo-electric cell in a circuit connected with a bell. The effect of this device was that, if anything capable of absorbing or deflecting infrared rays should enter the region immediately above the table, the bell would thereupon ring. (In other experiments the bell was replaced by a recording device which would leave a permanent mark on a moving band of paper.) Cameras with flash-light were directed on the space above the table, so that an instantaneous photograph would automatically be taken if and when the infrared beam should be intercepted. The results were as follows. On a great many occasions, when Rudi claimed to be influencing the region above the table, the bell rang or the recording apparatus showed a mark on the moving band of paper. This showed that *something*, which interfered with the infrared beam, was present in that region at those times. On the other hand, the photographs automatically taken at the same time, when developed, depicted this region as *empty*. This showed that whatever was causing the interference was *not ordinary visible matter*.

This seemed very promising, but then came the usual disappointing sequel. In the latter part of 1932, Rudi came to London and gave a series of sittings to Lord Charles Hope, a member of the S.P.R. These were designed to repeat Osty's experiments, and also, if possible, to take infrared silhouette photographs of the intervening substance by a method devised by Lord Rayleigh. The phenomena were now very feeble. Osty's results were indeed confirmed by the occurrence of interferences with the infrared beam, but it was found impossible to get silhouette photographs. These experiments are described in Vol. XLI of the S.P.R. *Proceedings*.

Finally, between October 1933 and March 1934, Rudi gave another series of sittings for the S.P.R. in their seance room in London. These experiments were conducted with extreme care by Mr Besterman and the late Mr Oliver Gatty, who was an expert in electrical technique. The report is in Vol. XLII of the *Proceedings*. The results were completely negative. If Rudi ever had supernormal powers – and it is very difficult to believe that he had not – they had completely faded away. He married soon afterwards and became a motor mechanic in Germany or Austria. I do not know whether he survived the Second World War. If he did, I am afraid that telekinesis is for him now only 'eine schöne Erinnerung'.

I think that the Schneider boys provide the best evidence available up to date for the occurrence of super-normal physical phenomena under controlled conditions and automatically recorded. It must be said for them that they both submitted themselves most readily to every test and precaution which the investigators demanded. Moreover, it is much easier and pleasanter to work with tough young men, mainly interested in football, than with neurotic females, ever ready to fly into hysterical tantrums and apt on occasion to accuse their investigators of sexual impropriety.

I may sum up this part of my lecture as follows. Though there are unsatisfactory features even in the best cases, there is plainly good enough prima facie evidence to make it highly desirable to investigate further those few mediums who will consent to submit themselves to proper conditions. It is a waste of time to investigate those who will not. We have now a good method of research in the beam of infrared rays, as used by Osty. For mediums have committed themselves to the position that dim red light is not hurtful to the delicate psycho-physical structures with which they claim to produce the phenomena. Moreover, we may hope in the near future to be able to take continuous cinematic photographs by infrared light of the whole course of a sitting. I do not think that the question can be settled until these methods are applied to investigate physical mediums who are held to be still at the height of their powers. I venture to predict that very few such persons will consent to be investigated in this way, and that a large proportion of those who do will either accomplish nothing or be promptly detected in fraud. But I shall be somewhat surprised, if there is not a residuum of genuinely supernormal physical phenomena concealed in the mass of dross.

(2.2) Without Mediums

I will end my lecture with a very brief account of experimental work on telekinesis with ordinary persons, as distinct from mediums. Until 1943, there would have been nothing to describe under the heading. In March of that year, there appeared an important article in the *Journal of Parapsychology* by Professor Rhine of Duke University, North Carolina, in what he called *Psycho-Kinesis*. Since that date, the *Journal of Parapsychology* has contained a number of papers on 'PK' as it is called for short. In Vol. XLVIII of the S.P.R. *Proceedings*, there is a valuable review by Dr D.J. West of the American work up to the date of writing, and there are also reports of two independent attempts by English experimenters to obtain similar results.

The procedure in the American experiments was as follows. In all of them, the agent threw one or more dice. In some of them, he willed that the dice should fall with a certain face, e.g., the 6, upwards. In others he threw two dice and willed either that the total score should be *high*, i.e., 8 or more, or that it should be *low*, i.e., 6 or less, in each throw. In either kind of experiment, the question is this: Does the desired type of result happen with significantly greater frequency in a long run of throws than might have been expected if the wishes of the agent were causally irrelevant to the way in which the dice come to rest? If the answer is in the affirmative, the next question is whether any normal explanation can be found. For example, the dice might be slightly biased in favour of certain faces and these might by chance or by design be those which the agent willed to fall uppermost. Or, again, the agent in throwing might be able consciously or unconsciously to modify his way of throwing so as to favour any face that he wished to turn up. If neither these nor any other normal explanations can be admitted, we shall have tentatively to accept some kind of super-normal influences of a person's desires over physical events outside his body.

The following methods were used for casting the dice. Usually they were shaken by hand in a cup, and then either thrown down a sloping board with a corrugated surface or else bounced against a vertical partition. In some of the experiments, the dice were, instead, cast mechanically in an automatically revolving wire-cage. In one of the experiments, some trials were made with manual throws and other with mechanical throws, and the results were compared. There was no significant difference in the proportion of successes scored in the two cases. In two of the experiments, another method of casting was used in some of the trials. The dice rested on a ruler and were released by sliding the ruler away and letting them fall by their own weight. Significant positive results were scored in both experiments with this method. Dr West points out that mechanical devices can never be trusted to give random sequences, and that it is never safe to assume that a die is absolutely devoid of bias.

The results of the American experiments may be summarised as follows. Up to the date of Dr West's article, 13 experiments had been reported. Of these four were aimed at high or at low total scores, and the remaining nine at assigned faces. The aggregate number of throws in the four experiments of the first kind was 38,488. The aggregate excess of high scores, when these were aimed at, and of low scores, when these were aimed at, over the most probable number on the hypothesis of chance coincidence, was 1184. This is 12.25 times the standard deviation. In the nine experiments of the second kind, the aggregate number of throws was 382,596. The aggregate excess of occurrences of the face aimed at over the most probably number on the hypothesis of chance coincidence was 3121. This is 15 times the standard deviation. It should further be noted that in all 13 experiments the deviation was *positive*, whereas in the hypothesis of chance coincidence it would be equally likely to be positive or negative in each experiment. The odds against the deviation being all positive, on the hypothesis of chance coincidence, are about 8,300 to 1.

It seems plain that *some* factor other than chance coincidence was involved in these American experiments and it is very difficult to suggest any plausible normal explanation for the results. But I must end by recording the usual disappointment, which seems to cloud all attempts to establish super-normal physical phenomena in England. In the same number of *Proceedings* which contain Dr West's review of the American work, there are papers describing the careful attempts to repeat similar experiments by members of the S.P.R. One consisted of 6,480 trials of which $^1/_6$ were aimed at each of the six faces. There was no significant departure from what might have been expected on the hypothesis of chance coincidence. These experiments were done by Mr Dennis Hyde. Another set of trials were conducted, with the same completely insignificant results, by Mr Denys Parsons using several different agents to throw the dice. 4,608 trials were made with manual throwing, and a further 5,660 with a rotating cage. In neither was there any significant departure from what might have been expected on the hypothesis of chance coincidence. I believe I am correct in saying that, up to the present date, no one in England has had any appreciable success in PK experiments.

As I said at the beginning of the lecture, negative results do not logically wash out previous positive results or prove that there must have been some deficit in the precautions taken by the first set of investigators. But it obviously contributes to the difficulty of the subject, and to one's feeling of intellectual dissatisfaction, when results obtained under apparently rigid conditions in one place and by one set of investigators cannot be reproduced under apparently similar conditions in another place and by another set of investigators.

4.2

POLTERGEISTS

The word 'poltergeist' is of German origin, and *poltern* in German means to make a rumpus by knocking or throwing things about. The word seems to have been introduced into English by Mrs Catherine Crowe (née Stevens), who was born about 1,800 and died in 1876. Her book *The Night Side of Nature*, published in 1848–1849, contains a chapter entitled *The Poltergeist of the Germans*.... Here she gives examples of cases (to use her own words) of '... what the Germans call the Poltergeist or racketing spirit'. The name is highly appropriate. For, as we shall see, the alleged phenomena are such as to suggest that, if they be produced by non-human agents, these may fairly be described as the 'oiks' of the Astral Plane.

The kinds of phenomena alleged to happen in a typical Poltergeist case may be roughly enumerated as follows. Inexplicable rappings, cracklings, sounds as of sawing or threshing, and other noises, sometimes quite loud, may be reported as being heard. Lighter bits of furniture, such as crockery, fire-irons, etc., may be alleged to have danced about or to have shot through the air without visible human agency. Heavy objects, such as chests-of-drawers, dining-tables, etc., may be asserted to have been shifted, overturned, or even raised into the air, without human contact. Individuals may claim to have had stones, dirt, etc., come towards them, and in some cases to have been hit by these, without those missiles having been thrown by any human hand. It may be alleged that certain persons in a house are repeatedly victims of inexplicable minor assaults, such as having their bed-clothes pulled off, their beds overturned, themselves raised involuntarily above their beds, their hair pulled, and so on. The list is not exhaustive. Nor do many cases, if any, combine all the features just enumerated. But the typical Poltergeist case is characterised by several of them being alleged to have happened, simultaneously or in close succession, on fairly frequent occasions over a certain not very long period in a certain house or room, in presence of members of the family. And in many cases, it is claimed that these incidents have been repeatedly witnessed by visitors.

In many, but by no means in an overwhelming majority, of such cases, the phenomena seem to centre about a certain one or two individuals living in the house at the time. In a few, they seem to be associated rather with a certain person who has lived and has lately died there. And in a certain number, there is a still living person, not a member of the afflicted household, who has been offended by one of the latter, and who claims to be producing the phenomena in revenge by some kind of 'magical' practice.

I shall in due course give an example of each of these three kinds of cases. But, before doing so, I wish to give some idea of the very wide diffusion of accounts of Poltergeist cases, of one kind or another, both in time and in space. In order to do this, I would refer first to a list, entitled *Historic Poltergeists*, published by the late Mr Hereward Carrington, an experienced and careful psychical researcher, in 1936. In this list are 318 reported cases, with references given in each instance. They range in date from 530 A.D. to 1935 A.D. Before 1600, there are nine reported cases; in the XVIIth century are 16; in the XVIIIth 17; in the XIXth 134; and in the first 55 years of the XXth 141. Of these 318 reported cases, 74% came from Europe, 20% from America, and the remaining 6% from Africa and Asia. Of the 235 European cases, 25% were from France, 43% from Great Britain and Ireland, 11% from Germany, 6% from Italy, and the remaining 15% from other European countries, including 12 cases from the old Austro-Hungarian Empire and four from Iceland. Of the 63 American cases, 16% come from Canada and Nova Scotia, 66% from the United States, and the remaining 18% from S. America and the West Indies.

I think we may fairly assume that the increase in the number of recorded stories in successive centuries merely reflects the increasing facilities for putting them on record provided by the printing-press and the daily newspapers.

Again, the preponderance of France, Great Britain, and the United States as the sources of such stories is, no doubt, explicable partly by their larger population, partly by the fact that psychical research has been pursued more actively and longer in those countries than in others of comparable size, and perhaps partly by the fact that Hereward Carrington was an Englishman who had for long been settled in the United States. It seems reasonable to conclude that stories of Poltergeist phenomena have been fairly frequent, and singularly constant in type, for a very long period and over most of the inhabited world.

Carrington's list of cases can now be supplemented from the following two sources. (1) In 1953, Father Crehan, S.J., published, under the title *Ghosts and Poltergeists*, a collection of all the main writings on those subjects of Father Herbert Thurston, S.J. Thurston was a most acute and learned man, who was an active member of the S.P.R. from 1918 to his death in 1939. His book contains in all 54 cases, the latest of which is dated 1934–1935. Of these 33 are also to be found in Carrington's list, but the remaining 21 can be added to Carrington's 318 cases, giving 339 in all. Thurston had, naturally, special opportunities of receiving accounts of cases from Roman Catholic priests in various parts of the world. (2) The second supplementary source which I would mention is the following. Shortly before 1959 W.E. Cox, in the United States, compiled a list of cases, dating from 1850 to 1958. He included only those which he considered to have good *prima facie* claims to contain features not readily explicable by normal causes. His purpose was to make a statistical analysis of their main features. This he published in a valuable article in the *Journal* of the American S.P.R., under the title 'Introductory Comparative Analysis of Some Poltergeist Cases'. I shall mention some of the results of this analysis later, but for the present, I am concerned only with numbers of cases. There were 46 in all. Any of these which are dated after 1935 can occur neither in Carrington's nor in Thurston's lists. There are ten of these. So we may add at least 10 to the total of 339 cases reached above, reaching the grand total of 349.

I have now, I hope, said enough to show that the aggregate number of stories of Poltergeist cases on record at the present day is pretty considerable. It is reasonable to suppose that it is only a small fraction of the total number of actual cases, especially of those in the remoter past and in the less literate parts of the world. I shall now proceed to give, in some detail, accounts of three cases, each of a typically different kind.

My first case is taken from Dr A.R.G. Owen's admirable book *Can we Explain the Poltergeist?* (1964). It is quite recent, and it was investigated by Owen personally. It may be called 'The Sauchie Case', from the place in Scotland where it was located. The essential facts are as follows.

The events happened, mostly in November 1961, in one or another of a few houses in or near Sauchie, near Alloa, in Clackmannanshire, Scotland. Owen's attention was called to it in mid-December 1961. He visited the place from 13th to 16th January 1962, and interviewed the main witnesses. These were Mr Lund, the parish minister of Sauchie; Dr W.H. Nisbet, the medical attendant of the family concerned; his partner Dr Logan, and the latter's wife, also a qualified medical practitioner; Miss Margaret Stewart, a teacher at the school attended by the little girl, Virginia Campbell, who was the centre of the phenomena, and Virginia's much older married brother Mr Thomas Campbell and the latter's wife Isabella, at whose house Virginia was living. All these witnesses collaborated in a very helpful and friendly way with Owen.

The background of the case is as follows. Virginia Campbell, at that time aged 11, was the youngest child of James Campbell and his wife Annie. James was a small-holder in the depths of the country in Co. Donegal, Ireland. His older children had all grown up and left home, and in particular, his son Thomas had moved to Scotland, and had married and settled down in Sauchie, where he was employed in a neighbouring coal mine. In the autumn of 1960 Virginia and her mother, Mrs Annie Campbell, came to live with the Thomas Campbells in their house at Sauchie, leaving Virginia's father, James Campbell, for the time in Ireland arranging for the disposal of his small-holding. Virginia went to school at Sauchie elementary school, and her mother got a daily job in the neighbourhood.

Up to that time, Virginia had lived an extremely lonely life in Ireland. Her only companions had been a beloved dog, Toby, and another little girl Anna, both of whom she had to leave behind her on moving to Scotland. In her new home, there were two young children, viz., Thomas Campbell's daughter Margaret, aged nine, and his son Derek, aged six. Virginia slept in a double bed with Margaret, who was of course her niece. Owen visited the house and interviewed the Thomas Campbells, and while he was there it happened that Virginia and the two other children returned from Sunday school. He says that the house was exceptionally well kept and well furnished, that the Thomas Campbells seemed pleasant and friendly people, and that the family relationships appeared to be easy and harmonious.

Miss Stewart, Virginia's teacher at school, states that Virginia was at first extremely shy, and that this was accentuated by the fact that her northern Irish mode of speech differed very much from that of the other children. In other respects, Miss Stewart found her completely normal. She made friends easily, was somewhat above normal in intelligence, and was obedient, responsible, and well liked.

Dr Nisbet, the family doctor, who witnessed some of the phenomena, reported that Virginia's bodily health had been good, and that he had noted no sign of any fundamental psychological abnormality. But she was large in stature for her age, and was passing through a phase of very rapid pubescence.

So much for the background; now for the phenomena. These happened in three places, viz., (i) at home, (ii) at another house a few miles away, while Virginia was there on a short visit; and (iii) at school. The main events reported are the following:

(1) On Tuesday, 22 November 1961, after Virginia and Margaret had gone to bed, the Thomas Campbells heard a noise, like that of a bouncing ball, going on in the bedroom above. The children came downstairs to the living-room, and the noise followed them. It ceased (as all other phenomena were found to do) when Virginia was asleep.

(2) On the next day (23rd November) Virginia, was kept at home from school, and the following events are reported. (i) At teatime Mr and Mrs Thomas Campbell were in the living-room with Virginia, who was sitting in an armchair next to the sideboard. Both saw the sideboard move out some 5" from the wall and then return to its original position. Virginia was not touching it. Owen, who examined it for himself, reports that it would have been quite impossible for her to have moved it by normal means even if she had tried. (ii) That night, after Virginia had gone to bed, but before she had gone to sleep, loud knocks were heard all over the house, not only by the Campbells but also by several of their neighbours. At about midnight the Campbells called in the parish minister, Mr Lund. He found that the noises came from the head of the double-bed in which Virginia was lying, and he satisfied himself that this was not being struck or shaken by Virginia or by anyone else. He grasped the bed-head, while the knocks were going on, and felt it vibrating. (iii) While in the bedroom Mr Lund observed a linen chest, which was standing between the side of the bed and the wall, first rock,

then rise slightly, then travel some 18" over the linoleum towards the bed, and finally move back to its original position. The dimensions of the chest were 27" × 14" × 17"; it was full of linen, and the total weight would have been about 50 lbs. During these phenomena, Margaret, who usually slept in the double bed with Virginia, had been transferred to a single bed in the same room.

(3) On the following day (24th November) Virginia was at home from school all day. Mr Lund came in to watch after she had gone to bed, and Dr Nisbet came in later and watched. Mr Lund made the following observations. (i) He saw Virginia's pillow, on which her head was resting, rotate horizontally through about 60 degrees toward the length of the bed. (ii) He saw rockings of the linen chest, and he heard knockings. Dr Nisbet's observations were as follows. (i) He heard knockings and a noise as of sawing. (ii) He saw a rippling or puckering motion pass over the surface of the pillow on which Virginia's head was resting.

(4) On 25th November, Virginia went to school in the afternoon. The witness to the events which took place there is Miss Stewart, her class teacher. The children were seated at their desks for a period of silent reading. Miss Stewart had not previously heard of the alleged occurrence of Poltergeist phenomena in general and had no reason to expect anything odd in connexion with Virginia. Nevertheless, she observed the following events. (i) She was astonished to see Virginia trying to hold down the lid of her desk, which had apparently raised itself steeply two or three times. She noted that Virginia had her two hands palm downwards on the lid, and had both feet squarely on the floor in normal sitting position. (ii) About a quarter of an hour later a child, seated at the desk immediately behind Virginia's, left it in order to get a book. While that desk was thus vacant Miss Stewart saw it rise slowly to about 1" above the floor. It then settled down again, slightly to the right of its original position. Miss Stewart informed the headmaster of these two incidents on the same day, as soon as conveniently possible.

(5) On the evening of the same day, Dr Logan (Dr Nisbet's partner) kept watch in Virginia's bedroom while she went to sleep. (i) He heard spells of knocking. These continued when he removed the upper bedclothes and could see Virginia lying motionless on the mattress. (ii) From time to time he saw the linen chest move on the floor by amounts up to 1 foot. Once he saw the lid open and shut several times in succession.

(iii) He saw a horizontal rotation of Virginia's pillow through about 90 degrees, and he noted a curious puckering pass from time to time over the bedclothes in a kind of ripple. Dr Logan observed these phenomena again on the following night.

(6) On 28th November, Virginia was at school in the morning. Miss Stewart observed the following incident. Virginia left her seat end came to Miss Stewart's table in order to ask for some help in solving the problem on which the children were then engaged. While doing this Virginia stood to the left of the chair on which Miss Stewart was sitting. She was facing Miss Stewart's table, which was between the latter's chair and the class. Virginia had her hands clasped behind her back. On the table was lying a blackboard pointer. While Miss Stewart was sketching out the solution of the problem for Virginia this pointer began to vibrate, moved to the edge of the table, and then fell to the floor. Meanwhile, Miss Stewart could feel the desk vibrating. It began to rotate counter-clockwise about its left-hand corner, ending up in a slightly skewed position relative to Miss Stewart's chair. After these incidents, Virginia began to cry, and said: 'Please, Miss, I'm not trying it'.

(7) That night Virginia was taken to the neighbouring village of Dollar to stay the night with a relative. Dr Nisbet visited her there, and loud knocks were heard all over the house by him and by the others.

(8) On the next evening (29th November), while Virginia was still at Dollar, Dr Logan, accompanied by his wife, paid a visit. Both of them heard several outbreaks of knocking. These varied from gentle taps to a series of violent agitated raps when the Logans were about to leave. Mrs Logan, who had previously taken a sceptical attitude towards the accounts which she had heard from her husband and others, now satisfied herself that the sounds came from *within* the room, and that they could not have been made *normally* either by Virginia herself or by anyone else there.

(9) Later on the same night, Dr Logan was summoned by telephone to the house because Virginia was in a kind of hysterical fit. He found her talking in a loud, unnatural voice, calling for her dog Toby and her friend Anne, and throwing herself about on the bed. Her eyes were closed, but she heard and answered questions. After about 10 minutes, she awoke in a normal state, requested and was given a cup of tea, and soon fell into an ordinary sleep. A similar phase of hysterical trance had already

been noted by Mr Lund on the night of 27th November, and it was to recur in the presence of him and the two doctors on the night of 1st December.

(10) Virginia returned to her home at Sauchie on 1st December. That evening was a fairly lively one for her. Before she went up to bed the two doctors set up a movie camera in her bedroom, and also arranged for sound recording. (Owing to technical difficulties no satisfactory photographs were made by the camera. But the tape-recorder worked well, and the record was played to Owen when he visited Sauchie.) Virginia went up to her bedroom at about 9 p.m., and thereafter the following events happened. (i) From 9 to 10.30, there were continual noises, ranging from barely perceptible taps to loud agitated knocks. There was also occasional rippling of the bedclothes. (ii) At 11 p.m. Mr Lund arrived with three other ministers. They held a service of intercession from 11.15 to 11.30. During this, there was some more knocking. (iii) Between 11.30 and 12.15, a variety of sounds were heard and recorded. They included a series of loud peremptory knocks, and a harsh rasping sound, as of sawing. After 1 December 1962, the phenomena became less and less pronounced, and, so far as I am aware, they soon ceased altogether.

I will make some brief comments on this case before I pass to my next example. (1) It is typical of a substantial number of cases, having the following features, positive and negative. (i) The phenomena centre about a certain member of the household, generally a child, and often one who shows occasional hysterical symptoms. (ii) There is nothing to suggest that any 'spirit', whether non-human or the ghost of some deceased human being, is in any way responsible for the phenomena. (2) It seems certain that in this case, we can exclude *hallucination* on the part of the witnesses as a complete explanation. It is most unlikely that each of the witnesses would be hallucinated, on several occasions and in different surroundings, independently of each other. And it is impossible that the tape-recorder should have been hallucinated in respect of the sounds recorded by it. (3) It seems to me also quite incredible that such witnesses as we have in this case should have deliberately constructed a cock-and-bull story. (4) The sounds and the movements in this case are not, as they are in some alleged instances of 'haunted houses', such as might well be due to underground water, rats, or other unsuspected normal causes. The only possible normal explanation is repeated undetected trickery by Virginia herself. The witnesses were on the lookout for this, and they were not ignorant or credulous persons. Three of them, viz., Dr Nisbet, Dr Logan, and Mrs Logan, had had the kind and amount of scientific and practical training which a person has to undergo before qualifying as a medical practitioner. And some of the movements of heavy objects witnessed seem to have been quite beyond the power of a girl of 11, lying in bed, to produce normally, even if she had been unwatched and had been deliberately trying. (5) I am, therefore, obliged to hold that it is considerably more likely than not that in this case the central figure effected, by means not at present recognised by orthodox science, the motions of the air, resulting in sounds of various kinds, and that she produced or contributed to produce the movement of solid objects not in physical contact with her body. And, if one is forced to this conclusion in this case, where the available evidence is particularly cogent, it seems not unreasonable to think that similar action may have been present in other cases where the phenomena and the conditions alleged are very much the same but the evidence available is less overwhelming.

My second example is taken from Vol. XIII of the S.P.R. *Journal*, March 1908, It may be prefaced by the following introductory remarks.

The narrative is dated 24 February 1908. It was written by the head of the household concerned, who will be referred to as Mr 'R.D.' It is signed by him; by his wife Mrs C.M.D.; by the two of his sons, J.D. and F.D. (both over 20) then living at home; and by a daughter-in-law, Mrs M.R.D., who was living in the house, and had been doing so for some time, during the absence in Africa of her husband, Mr R.D.'s second son. Mr R.D. was a professional man, and asked that the names of himself and the others concerned should not be published. He was induced to write his report, to append the signature of himself and the other members of his family concerned, and to submit it together with several relevant photographs to the Editor of the *Journal*, by a member of the S.P.R. in the locality who knew the D.'s and had himself made contemporary notes of the case. The actual names end the address are all in possession of the S.P.R., and the Editor at the time saw all the original correspondence and the allegedly corroborative photographs. Finally, it should be remarked that the document is attested by a Glasgow lawyer in an accompanying letter dated 26 February 1908. This states that the writer has acted for about 20 years as solicitor to Mr R.D., and that he is quite certain that the latter, his wife, and the other members of the family concerned would not have signed such a document unless they had believed every word of it.

So much for the document; I pass now, to the scene of the incidents detailed in it. The house was a completely detached cottage on two floors. Mr and Mrs R.D. slept on the ground floor, and the living-rooms were there too. The first floor consisted of two bedrooms, each on the opposite side of a landing. These will be called 'Room 1' and 'Room 2'. Room 1 was to the right, and Room 2 to the left, of the landing. At the time when the incidents began Room 1 was the bedroom of the two grown-up sons, J.D. and F.D. Room 2 was the bedroom of the daughter-in-law Mrs M.R.D. At the beginning, there was sleeping with her, in Room 2, a married daughter of the D's, named 'H', who was on a temporary visit while her husband was in France.

It remains to mention what appears to be a highly relevant part of the previous history of the house. Ever since the death of Mr R.D.'s mother in 1875 his widowed father had lived with the M.D.'s. He had died there, in Room 1, at the age of 90, in March 1907 after a long illness. The daughter-in-law, Mrs M.R.D., had been a nurse before her marriage, and had nursed the old father during his last illness. From the nature of that illness, there had been, throughout it, a very strong and characteristic smell in the room. After the death, and before it began to be occupied as a bedroom by the two sons, the room had been thoroughly cleaned, the walls washed with carbolic and then re-papered, some of the old floor taken up and replaced with new boards, and the woodwork repainted.

We are now in a position to consider the events reported, which began on 13 August 1907 and would seem to have ceased after 23 January 1908. They were as follows:

(1) From 13 August 1907, i.e., some five months after the old gentleman's death, knockings began to be heard night after night in Room 2 around about 12 pm. After some days they ceased in Room 2 and started in Room 1.

(2) On the night of 30–31 August, Mr and Mrs R.D., sleeping in their room on the ground floor, were awakened by a crash in Room 1 above them. They immediately went upstairs, hearing knockings as they did so. In Room 1, they found that a small wooden press, which normally stood against one of the walls, had been moved out by some 9". In the course

of this a mahogany box, which normally stood on top of the press, had fallen to the ground, causing the crash. (It is not stated whether either or both of the sons J.D. and F.D. were sleeping in Room 1 at the time, but it is to be presumed that they were. If so, it seems possible that one or other of them had been sleep-walking, and had moved the press normally while doing so).

(3) Up to 3rd September, Mr R.D.'s married daughter H., who was on a temporary visit, had been sleeping along with his daughter-in-law Mrs M.R.D. in Room 2. On that date, H. left and thereafter M.R.D, slept alone in Room 2. After this, M.R.D. occasionally felt her bed in Room 2 shaken, whilst the son J.D. in Room 1 sometimes felt as if a hand were trying to draw away his pillow from under his head. In the meanwhile, the knockings continued. The sons also heard sounds as of someone coming upstairs, turning the handle of the door of their bedroom (No. 1), and walking about the room.

(4) On 8th December, at about 2.20 am, Mrs M.R.D., sleeping in Room 2, seemed to see on her pillow a long hand with knotty joints. She mentioned this later to the sons, and J.D. thereupon stated that he in Room 1 had seemed to see some nights earlier a hand come out of the wall. But, thinking that this might have been an illusion, he had refrained from mentioning it.

(5) On 16th December, rappings were heard, as usual, round about midnight. On this occasion, J.D. happened to be lying awake at the time in Room 1. He stated that he saw a small washstand, with a folding writing desk on top of it, move out some 6"–8" from the wall. He at once called to his parents, who came upstairs and found the articles shifted as stated.

(6) On 27th December, at about 10.15 am when no one was in the house except Mrs D. and her daughter-in-law Mrs M.R.D., the latter had been cleaning out Room 1. She went downstairs to fetch a scuttle of coal. On her return with it, she found Room 1 in extreme disorder. Two basket chairs were overturned; the ash pan and the front of the grate had been removed and laid on the carpet; clothing from pegs, a towel from the washstand, and a box from the top of the chest of drawers were all on the floor; and four pictures and been taken from the wall and laid face-downward on the bed. There had been no noise, and nothing was damaged. The two women were so frightened that they rushed into the garden, where they stayed in the rain until it happened that a girl came

on an errand to the door. Through her, they sent a telegram to Mr R.D. to get him to come home. He arrived at about 1 pm. Thereafter, the family vacated Rooms 1 and 2 altogether, and all slept downstairs.

(7) On the next day, 18th December, at about 10.15 am, the contents of Room 1 were again found overturned. That evening, at about 11 pm, J.D. took a photograph of the room and its contents as it then appeared. This was submitted to the Editor of the S.P.R. *Journal* as 'Photograph A'.

(8) On 21st December, in the evening, Mr and Mrs R.D. were in town. In the house were J.D., Mrs M.R.D., and a visitor. All of them heard three loud blows on the wall of the lobby, accompanied by knockings.

(9) On 24th December, Mr R.D. and his wife were at a Christmas Eve service at church. The two sons and the daughter-in-law were at home. All three of them heard at about 12.30, the same kind of noises as had been heard on the evening of 21st December.

(10) On 1 January 1908, at 5.40 pm, three loud blows were heard on the lobby wall by all those in the house, including some visitors. On the next day, a similar three blows were heard by F.D., Mrs M.R.D., and a visitor.

(11) On 13th January, between 10 and 11 am, when only the two women were in the house, they found the chest of drawers in Room 1 to be shifted some 18″ from the wall, and a number of objects to be on the floor. This time they were so frightened that they shut up the house and went into town. On their return at 4.30 pm, they found that an armchair in the kitchen, which had been standing in a corner when they left, had been moved and was now placed close to the fire. It was in a position in which the old man was wont to sit when he came in from the garden on a cold day.

(12) On 15th January, before noon, the chest of drawers in Room 1 was again found to be shifted. This time the bed was also out of place, and an armchair had been moved about four yards from the fireside corner to a place near the window. This was a position in which the old man used often to sit and watch the return of the family in the evening from work. This armchair was again shifted in a similar way on 18th January.

(13) On 20th January, the bed in Room 1 was found to have been moved during the day from its normal position with its head against the wall. Mrs C.M.D. replaced it in its usual position, but it was found to have been again moved in the course of the day.

(14) 21st January was a lively day in the house. (i) At about 10 am, the mattress of the bed in Room 1 was found tilted up against the rail at the foot of the bed. (ii) At about 11 am, the daughter-in-law, Mrs M.R.D., was in the downstairs room and had occasion to stoop down and get a box from under one of the beds there. As she did so, the mattress and the bedding appeared to be pulled over her, and she felt herself held down on the floor. She cried out and was released in a fainting condition by her mother-in-law, Mrs C.M.D. (iii) At about noon, the bedclothes of the bed in Room 1 were found to have been dragged off the bed and laid on the floor. A large chest in the room, containing bedding, etc., was found open and some of the contents emptied. The armchair had again been moved. By this time, Mrs C.M.D. and Mrs M.R.D. had had enough. They were thoroughly frightened, and again shut up the house end went out. In the evening, two photographs of Room 1, as it then appeared from two different positions in it, were taken. These were submitted to the S.P.R. along with the report as 'Photographs B1 and B2'.

(15) On 22nd January, the chest of drawers was again found moved from the wall, and chairs displaced. Mrs C.M.D. rearranged the latter, but within three minutes they were found displaced again.

The cessation of these domestic disturbances was, however, at hand. On 23rd January, knockings were heard downstairs. But these were not very loud; and from that date, all had been peaceful up to 24th February, the date of the report. It remains, however, to mention one rather gruesome circumstance. It is alleged in the report that, whenever any of these disturbances of the furniture in Room 1 took place, the smell, which had been characteristic of the sick-room, returned there as strong as ever.

I will now make some comments on this case, before passing to my next example:

(1) The evidence here is, of course, much less cogent than in the Sauchie Case. There are no independent witnesses, such as Drs Nesbit and Logan, Miss Stewart, etc., and there is no interviewing of witnesses, comparing of testimony, doing experiments on the spot, and so on. In considering a set of statements such as we now have before us, we should distinguish and consider the following questions. (i) Did those who reported themselves as having had such and such experiences in fact have

experiences of at least approximately the kinds which they reported? (ii) If so, how shall we classify those experiences? What proportion, if any, of them were *veridical sense perceptions*, such as any normal person in a normal condition would have had if he had been in the place where the experiment was at the time when the latter had his experience? What proportion, if any, of them were *hallucinatory quasi-perceptions, as* of seeing, hearing, etc., such and such physical events and/or situations, though in fact, none such were then and there present to the experient's sense organs? (iii) Supposing that there were hallucinatory *quasi*-perceptions, were any of them *repetitive*, i.e., recurring in the same individual on a number of successive occasions when placed in a certain situation? And were any of them collective, i.e., occurring simultaneously in several individuals who were together at the time, and correlated with each other more or less as the normal sense-perceptions of such persons would have been? (iv) If some of the experiences were ordinary veridical sense-perceptions, is there a plausible normal explanation of the particular physical events and/or situations which then existed and were perceived? If some of the experiences were hallucinatory *quasi*-perceptions, is there a plausible normal explanation for the occurrence of just such experiences in the individuals concerned, at the times and places when they did happen, and under the circumstances then prevailing? In particular, if some of these hallucinatory *quasi*-perceptions were either repetitive or collective or both, is there a plausible normal explanation of these special features in them?

(2) Subject to the fact that such investigations as would be needed in order to try to answer these questions cannot now be made, and were not made at the time, I must content myself with expressing the following tentative personal opinions. (i) I feel pretty sure that the report was not just a hoax. (ii) I think it considerably more likely than not that the persons concerned in fact had experiences substantially like most of those which they are reported as having. (iii) Supposing that to be so, then quite a considerable number of those experiences were normal veridical sense-perceptions of noises of various kinds, such as are described, of articles of furniture, clothing, etc., being in certain places other than those which they normally and recently occupied, and so on. (iv) Some of the experiences, however, were most likely hallucinatory *quasi*-perceptions. I should think that Mrs M.R.D.'s experience in the

early morning of 18th December as of seeing a knotty jointed hand was of this nature. And I should think that J.D.'s experience, a few nights earlier, as of seeing a hand emerging from the wall of his bedroom, was pretty certainly of that kind. I should be very much inclined to think that the experiences as of smelling the odour which had been characteristic of the sick-room were hallucinatory. If so, they were certainly instances of *repetitive* hallucinations, and it is possible (though it is not clear from the report) that some of them were also collective ones.

(3) Supposing that the above tentative opinions of mine are correct, as to the different natures of certain of the experiences reported, several questions as to causation remain. We can formulate these, and we can suggest certain conjectures about them, but we are in no position to go further. As regards those odd physical events and circumstances which actually existed and were perceived normally by the experients, is there any plausible normal explanation some or of all of these? As to *noises*, it is always wise to bear in mind that there are often normal but unsuspected causes of odd noises, for example, rats in old drains, water in pipes, underground streams swollen by heavy rains or by high tides, and so on. Such normally caused noises may be misinterpreted, for example, as the sounds of footsteps. And it is certainly conceivable that actual sense-perceptions misinterpreted may, under suitable psychological conditions, e.g., a state of fearful expectation, give rise to hallucinatory *quasi*-perceptions of one kind or another. But I can make no plausible conjecture as to normal causes for such knockings, etc., as began to be heard on 13 August 1907, continued to be heard pretty regularly for the next five months, and ceased to be heard after 23 January 1908. (ii) As to the repeatedly perceived alterations in the positions of various articles of furniture, the following observations seem to be worth making. Most of the reports are of *finding an object shifted*, not of seeing or feeling one *shifting*. Unless I am mistaken, the only report of an experience of the latter kind is that of J.D., lying awake in Room 1 on the night of 16th December, seeing a small wash-stand moving out from the wall, and calling his parents who then found it shifted. It is plainly impossible to feel sure that J.D. may not have moved the article himself, by normal means, possibly in a kind of half-dream. We are, then, left with the very numerous reports of finding this or that object shifted on repeated occasions. The only possible normal explanation of

this is to suppose that one or more persons in the house again and again moved the articles by ordinary physical means and that the others later saw the results without witnessing the actions.

(4) If we are to contemplate the above hypothesis, I think we should concentrate our attention on the daughter-in-law, Mrs M.R.D. It seems to me that, if anyone repeatedly shifted articles of furniture by normal means, the culprit was almost certainly neither Mr R.D. nor either of his sons, J.D. and F.D. This leaves the two women, the mother Mrs C.M.D, and her daughter-in-law, Mrs M.R.D. I do not think that there is the least reason to regard the former as either main agent or accomplice. So we are left with Mrs M.R.D. If she shifted the furniture by normal means and then showed the results to the other members of the household as something paranormal, she may have done this quite wittingly and deliberately. But I should think it much more likely that, if she did it at all, she acted half-unwittingly in some kind of dissociated state. However that may be, we should need to know (what we no longer can, if anyone ever could) whether on every relevant occasion she had time and opportunity to perform the actions needed without betraying the fact that she was doing so. A few of the incidents, if correctly reported in detail, seem hard to reconcile with that supposition. Others do not.

(5) Whatever view we may take of the above hypothesis, I think there is no doubt that Mrs M.R.D. was in some sense the central figure in the drama. She appears as such from the beginning and up to the spectacular events of 21st January, when she was allegedly attacked by the bedclothes in the ground-floor room, pinned to the floor, and finally rescued in a fainting condition by her mother-in-law. It is true that the central character was, in a sense, the deceased grandfather, since many of the events seemed to suggest his persistent, if barely deliberate or intelligent, influence. But, whether the phenomena were completely explicable by normal actions on M.R.D.'s part, or whether paranormal causation has to be invoked to account for at least some of them, M.R.D. appears to be the living human being at the centre.

One would like to know a great deal more than one does about her. She had evidently been for some considerable time member of the household, though her husband was alive and was apparently settled in Africa. She must have gone through a gruelling experience as nurse to the grandfather in his long and distressing last illness. It would certainly not be surprising if she were in a disturbed emotional state, and if that were closely bound up with her memories of the old gentleman and of the circumstances of his last days. This may well have been an essential precondition of her agency in connexion with the phenomena, whatever form that may have taken. It might have been so, whether that agency was purely normal, viz., nothing but well-concealed physical shifting of bits of furniture, or whether it was wholly or partly paranormal. And, on the latter alternative, she might have been the central agent, whether the paranormal activities proceeded entirely from herself, or whether they were in part determined by some element or aspect of the deceased persisting in some way independently of her and her memories of him.

My third and last example is of the following rather bizarre kind. Here a certain person, living in the neighbourhood at the time, claims, and is believed by the sufferers, to have caused, by some kind of magic and in revenge for an alleged injury, the poltergeist disturbances. Such cases were by no means uncommon, especially when and where belief in witches or warlocks was prevalent. Our picture would be seriously incomplete without at least one instance. A classical English case is that of 'The Drummer of Tedworth', which happened in and around Ludgershall in Berkshire from 1661 to 1663, and which was investigated personally by Glanvill, one of the earliest Fellows of the Royal Society. It is described by him in his posthumously published book *Saducismus Triumphatus*. (1682) Since this case has been discussed *ad nauseam*,[6] I prefer to take as my example the Cideville Case, which happened in France so late as 1850–1851, and became the subject of legal action, the records of which still exist.

A pretty full account of the case will be found in a paper by Andrew Lang, entitled 'The Poltergeist at Cideville', in S.P.R. *Proceedings* Vol. XVIII (1903–1942), pp. 454–463. He had already described it at some length in the chapter entitled *A Modern Trial for Witchcraft* in his book *Cock Lane and Commonsense* (Longmans: 1896). Through the good offices of the Marquis d'Éguilles, Lang eventually obtained an attested copy of the original documents of the trial before the local *juge de paix*. These he handed over to the S.P.R., and they are presumably still in the latter's possession.

The background of the case is as follows. Cideville is in Seine Inférieure, in the depths of the country, lying N.N.W. of Rouen, which is the nearest city. The principal characters concerned are, on the one hand, M. Tinel, the curé of the place, and his two resident pupils, Masters Lemonnier (aged 12) and Bunel (aged 14).[7] On the other side, the main personage is a local shepherd, named Thorel, about 40 years of age, who is described as dull, illiterate, but given to boasting about his alleged magical powers. He was believed by his neighbours, perhaps correctly, to be a pupil of a certain old shepherd living nearby who was regarded as a 'wise man' and had considerable practice as such. According to local gossip, the curé had visited in March 1849 a sick parishioner, then under treatment by the 'wise man', and had advised the patient to entrust himself to a more orthodox medical practitioner. The wise man had heard of this, had been angry at it, and had uttered threats of what he would do to the curé and his pupils. Not long afterwards the 'wise man' had been prosecuted for illegally practising medicine without a license, and he had believed, rightly or wrongly, that the curé was largely responsible for this. It was popularly thought that, in revenge, the 'wise man', through his pupil Thorel, induced a series of poltergeist phenomena in the curé's house, centring on the latter's two resident pupils.

However that may be, it is certain that such phenomena had been happening in the presbytery. As described by the curé in an official document, they included such incidents as the following. Raps would be heard behind the wainscot. A voice, responding to the summons of the boys, would be heard, and it would answer questions, make promises or threats, sing certain popular airs, and so on. There would be vigorous movements of shovels and tongs, tables and chairs, etc. Knives, inkstands, and similar articles would suddenly leave the table on which they were lying, fly off and break a window, end then return quietly to their places. Lastly, as a *pièce de resistance*, a visible hand without visible body would occasionally be seen, and would inflict heavy blows on the cheeks of the boys.

The legal case arose as follows. The curé had accused Thorel of being the agent responsible for the phenomena centring on the boys; once, when Thorel was calling at the presbytery the curé had made him go on his knees to the younger of the two boys and beg the latter's pardon; and the curé had on one occasion struck Thorel with his cane when the latter was at the presbytery. In respect of all this Thorel brought an action for defamation of character against the curé. Preliminary judicial proceedings took place on 7 January 1851, before the *juge de paix* at the adjacent town of Yerville. He adjourned the case till 3rd February, and on that day and the next, it was fully argued in court. Many witnesses, on either side were heard and questioned.

The judge gave his verdict on 15 February 1651, The essential points in it are the following:

(1) The result of all the evidence is that the cause of the events at the Presbytery at Cideville remains unknown. (2) The plaintiff Thorel had certainly himself spread a report that he was the cause of the disturbances; he had on two occasions expressed contrition; and the curé had struck Thorel with his cane only in self-defence when the latter had tried deliberately to handle him. So, Thorel lost his case and had to pay the equivalent of some £6 in costs.

Witnesses of various classes of society and various degrees of education, ranging from labourers, shopkeepers, and farmers to a neighbouring curé and members of the local squirearchy and aristocracy, testified to what they believed themselves to have experienced and to the conditions under which they believed themselves to have observed phenomena. There is a little testimony to cheating on the part of the boys, and a good deal more to the occurrence of phenomena under conditions where the witness believed that the possibility of cheating had been completely excluded. It is not worthwhile to go into detail about this, but it is of interest to consider the testimony given by the boys themselves.

Lemonnier, the younger pupil, stated that he had begun to hear raps on 26th November, when he was alone, and that they had continued since. All kinds of objects had flown about, and he had been struck by a black hand. He had been haunted by a spectre of an unknown man in a blouse. He first met Thorel when the latter was paying a call at the Presbytery and he then recognised him as the spectre in the blouse. The elder pupil, Bunel, stated that Lemonnier had lost consciousness and had had a nervous attack after meeting Thorel. Bunel alleged many odd movements of objects, and exhibited a black eye, which he stated to have been caused by a stamping-iron which had flown at his face.

The boys were eventually removed from M. Tinel's care, and became residents at another presbytery, where, it is stated (on what authority, I do not know) that they had no further trouble with poltergeists. The elderly 'wise man', as director-of-studies to Thorel, should on the whole have been satisfied with the way in which his pupil carried out his set exercise in black, or at any rate, grey magic; for the offending curé lost his two pupils after a fairly upsetting series of incidents in his presbytery.

As to the case as a whole, I will make only the following comments. (1) It certainly looks as if the younger boy, Lemonnier, at any rate, displayed at the time hysterical or perhaps epileptic symptoms. Whether these were contributory causes, collateral effects, or both together, of the poltergeist phenomena, I would not venture to guess. (2) Even if some of the phenomena should have been genuinely paranormal, I would certainly not put it past two boys in such circumstances to have eked them out by occasional larks to mystify their elders and enhance their own importance. Which of us would not have done so, at that age and under those conditions? (3) The one outstanding fact, from an evidential point of view, is that the *juge de paix*, after having heard all the available testimony and having examined the witnesses, decided that there was something in the phenomena which remained inexplicable by any normal cause that would suggest itself as probable. (4) As to whether Thorel played any essential part in initiating and sustaining the phenomena, and, if so, whether any other influence on his part than normal suggestion was involved, I can express no opinion. It is certain that he *claimed* to have been an essential agent, and to have wrought his effects by some kind of magic. It seems quite likely that he may have believed this. Beyond this, I cannot with any confidence venture.

(5) Finally, the case throws a most illuminating light backward on the allegations made in trials for witchcraft. Not so many years earlier Thorel would pretty certainly have been burned as a warlock instead of merely having to pay the equivalent of some £6 in costs. And it shows us that as late as the 1850s, in remote country districts in one of the world's most highly civilised nations, Daphnis was liable to employ his leisure in much less innocent activities than in piping to Chloe.

I have now given examples of three different kinds of Poltergeist cases, and have made some detailed comments on each. I will conclude with some observations on Poltergeist cases as a whole.

(I) From Cox's analysis of his 46 cases, *prima facie* involving a paranormal element, dating from 1850 to 1958, the following statistical facts emerge:

(A) *Presence or Absence of a Central Figure.* (1) A central figure was certainly present in 61% of the cases, and apparently absent in 22%. Information is lacking in the remaining 17%. (ii) Of the 28 cases in which there clearly was a central figure, the latter was a *child or adolescent* in 82% and an *adult* in the remaining 18%. (iii) Of the 23 cases in which the central figure was a child or an adolescent, the latter was *male* in 43% and *female* in the remaining 57%. Of the five cases in which the central figure was adult, the latter was *male* in 40% and *female* in the remaining 60%. (iv) In the 28 cases in which there clearly was a central figure, the latter was stated or implied to be *seriously maladjusted* in 11%, and *mildly so* in 16%. In the remaining 71% no maladjustment, serious or mild, is stated or implied to have been present. (v) In 32% of the same 28 cases, the phenomena are said to have *followed the central figure from one place to another*.

The upshot of the above is this. There seems to be a significantly, but not overwhelmingly, large proportion of cases in which there is a central figure. Where that is so, the central figure is, in a highly significant proportion of cases, a child or adolescent. Beyond that it would not, I think, be safe to draw any conclusions from the data. For example, the mere fact that in 32% of the central-figure cases, the phenomena followed the central figure when the latter was transferred from one place to another, tells us nothing of interest. For we do not know in what proportion of the remaining 68% the central figure *was* transferred *without* the phenomena following it, and in what proportion the central figure simply remained throughout in the same place. Obviously, nothing of interest could be inferred unless we knew the former of these two proportions.

(B) *Various Kinds of Noises*. In 24 of the 46 cases, i.e., about 52%, noises of one or more kinds were reported. Cox arranges the various kinds of noise under five heads, and the percentage of these 24 cases are as follows: 'Heavy blows' 17%; 'Raps and/or Knocks' 41.5%; 'Bell-ringing' 21%; 'Scratchings, Footsteps, and/or Cries' 29.5%; 'Other Kinds of Noise 41.5%. It will be seen that, of the specific kinds of noise, much the commonest is *Raps and/or Knocks*, which are reported in rather more than 40% of the cases in which noises were observed, Next to them come *Scratchings, Footsteps, and/or Cries*, which are reported in nearly 30% of such cases. 'Heavy Blows' are perhaps the most difficult to account for by normal causes.

(C) *Certain Kinds of Flights*. It happens that flights of objects, of one kind or another, are reported in the same number of cases as are sounds, viz., 24 of the 46 cases. Cox arranges the main kinds of flight reported under heads, end the percentages are as follows: 'Deliberate

Aim' 21%; 'Deliberate Timing' 25%; 'Arbitrary Erratic Routes' 21%; 'Evading Efforts to Catch Object' 6.5%; 'Swerving around Obstacles' 6.5%; 'Hovering' 25%; 'Landing Lightly or Noiselessly' 21%; 'Slow Throughout' 37.5%; 'Slow at first, then suddenly becoming Fast' 13%.

As to these, I would draw particular attention to the heading 'Erratic Routes', 'Swerving around Obstacles', 'Hovering', and 'Landing Lightly or Noiselessly'. The occurrence of one or other or several of these features is reported in regard to so many poltergeist cases that they must be regarded as fairly characteristic of those in which flights of objects are noted. Either the experiences reported were normal veridical sense-perceptions, or they were hallucinatory *quasi*-perceptions as of movements which did not in fact happen at all, or, if they did, did not really have the peculiar features which they appeared at the time to have. On the former alternative, the movements seem not to be wholly explicable in terms of normal physical causation. On the latter, we have to account for the frequent occurrence of certain very specific kinds of hallucinatory *quasi*-perceptions. On either alternative, we are in presence of a pretty puzzling mystery.

(D) *Certain other Features of Cases.* Cox tabulates a number of other features which occur among his 46 cases. Of these, I will mention only the following. (1) *Damage or Destruction* in 39% of the cases, and *Injuries to Persons* in 13%. Yet it is to be noted that there are a few cases (6.5%) in which it is particularly remarked that, although witnesses were struck by flying objects, yet, to their surprise, they were *not* hurt. (2) In 22% of the cases *particularly heavy* objects were shifted.

As regards these features, I would make the following remarks. (1) The not being hurt, as one might have expected to be, by a flying object which hits one, suggests one or other of two alternatives. One is that the experience as of seeing an object flying at one, and as of feeling it strike one, was wholly or partly *hallucinatory*. The other is that the movement *really did happen*, and really did have those peculiar features which it was perceived as having. On the former alternative, we have the problem of accounting for the occurrence of this very odd kind of hallucinatory *quasi*-perception in quite a respectable proportion of Poltergeist ceases. On the latter, it is difficult to suggest any causal explanation for such movements compatible with the accepted laws of macroscopic physics. (2) Among his 46 cases, Cox mentions a small proportion (6.5%) in which the stones or other small objects flying around were observed to be *notably warm*. He does not, however, explicitly mention a feature which is characteristic of a number of cases on record, viz., what I will call 'fire-raising'. By this I mean the repeated setting on fire of objects in various parts of the house concerned. It may be that Cox includes these under his 39% of cases involving 'damage or destruction'. However that may be, I think it desirable to mention them explicitly. They look very much like the tricks of mischievous or hysterical inhabitants of the house. Perhaps many of them can be plausibly explained in that way. But we must remember that *all* Poltergeist phenomena are very suggestive of the work of mischievous children. And we must ask ourselves whether the conditions under which fire-raising is reported to have happened were not in *some* cases incompatible with any such explanation. (3) Movements of particularly heavy objects cannot be due to tricks by young children.

(II) Leaving the statistical details which emerge from Cox's valuable paper, and the probable inferences which seem to be justified by them, I would conclude by mentioning certain writings in the early S.P.R. *Proceedings*, by Frank Podmore and by Andrew Lang, which should be carefully studied by anyone who wishes to form a reasonable opinion on the subject of Poltergeists. Podmore and Lang were both highly intelligent men, of deep and wide culture, who had studied carefully the reports then available of all cases which seemed worth serious attention. There can be few, if any, now living in England with so wide as background of accurate relevant knowledge as was possessed by both of them.

The series begins in Vol. XII of the S.P.R. *Proceedings* (1896–1897) with a long paper by Podmore, entitled 'Poltergeists' (pp. 45–115). In it he discusses in detail eleven then recent cases, all investigated by members of the S.P.R., and some by himself. There was thereafter a pause until 1903. In the February of that year, there appeared in Vol. XVII of *Proceedings* a paper by Lang entitled 'The Poltergeist Historically Considered'. This deals *inter alia* with such famous cases as that of 'The Drummer of Tedworth' and that of the phenomena reported at Epworth Rectory, the home at the time of the parents and sisters of John end Charles Wesley. It refers critically to the arguments and the conclusions of Podmore's paper. It occupies pp. 305–326 of Proceedings. It is followed immediately by a reply by Podmore (pp. 327–332) entitled 'Remarks on Mr. Lang's Paper', in which Podmore reiterates and defends his views. This is immediately followed by Lang's 'Further Remarks' (pp. 333–336).

Essentially Podmore's contention is this. When one has eliminated exaggeration and distortion in the stories, due to misperception, false memory, and dramatisation, the residue is completely explicable by a mixture of conscious or unconscious trickery on the part of a mentally unstable individual, generally a child, and of illusion and hallucination on the part of credulous and suggestible spectators.

Podmore's views are always worth serious consideration. Nevertheless, the final impression left on me by his discussion of this and similar matters is unsatisfactory. Often, it seems to me, his criticisms are so finical that hardly any report of an ordinary historical event, of the evidence on which cases are decided in the law-courts, or even the report of scientific experiment, would survive such treatment. Again, the suggestions which he puts forward conjecturally to account normally for ostensibly para-normal phenomena seem to me to be often so far-fetched and so devoid of all independent evidence as to be almost as incredible as the reported phenomena themselves.

I felt such objections before I was aware of such cases as that at Sauchie, and of a recent case in the United States investigated by persons as expert as Podmore himself and at least as well aware as he of trickery to be expected and of the means of detecting it and of making it ineffective. In these cases, Podmore's explanation pretty certainly does not cover the whole of the facts.

I feel a good deal of sympathy with the following sentence (p. 323) in Lang's paper:

What we really desire is an answer to the question: How do these stories come to be told? I am not too contented with the answer: Because young people play a few foolish tricks; the rest is all exaggeration and hallucination. It is the extraordinary uniformity in the reports, from every age, country, and class of society... that makes the mystery.

I would end with the following remark of Henry Sidgwick's made to the S.P.R. in an address in 1883. It was about normal explanations of alleged para-normal phenomena in general, but it is perhaps particularly relevant to those of alleged Poltergeist phenomena. 'It is not a scientific way of dealing with testimony to explain what you can and say that the rest is untrue'. To this, I will only add that, though not 'scientific,' it is only too common with persons pontificating in the name of 'science' about matters which they have never troubled to study accurately and in detail.

NOTES

1. CDB: A book, published in 1955, entitled *Exploring the Supernatural* by R.S. Lambert contains a chapter describing a sequence of ten typical Poltergeist cases, reported from various parts of Canada from 1877 to 1951. The latest, and one of the best, books, *Can We Explain the Poltergeist*, by Dr A.R.G. Owen of this College, published in 1964, contains a full account of a case in Scotland in 1960–1961, which Owen himself investigated carefully.
2. JW: Actually, one William Drury according to more recent accounts, e.g., Hunter, Michael (2005) 'New light on the 'Drummer of Tedworth': Conflicting Narratives of Witchcraft in Restoration England' *Historical Research* 78(201): 311–353.
3. CDB: Skogvaktare. [JW: Swedish for 'Gamekeeper'.]
4. CDB: Fingerborgar. [JW: Swedish for 'Thimbles'.]
5. CDB: (*gas*).
6. JW: for example, in 'Ostensibly Paranormal Physical Phenomena', Chapter 4.1 of this volume.
7. CDB: In the earlier account by Lang in his 'Cock Lane and Commonsense' (1896) Lemonnier's name is spelled with one 'n', and it is stated that the ages of him and of Bunel were respectively 15 and 12. I follow Lang's account in S.P.R. *Proceedings*, Vol. XVIII (1903–1904), which is based on the copy of the legal proceedings, which he had then obtained.

Part 5

MISCELLANY

INTRODUCTION TO PART 5
Joel Walmsley

To conclude the volume on a somewhat light-hearted note, I have included two short pieces that illustrate the kind of intellectual playfulness that is often found in fragments elsewhere in Broad's published work. Although both are amusing in their own right, it would also be reasonable to detect (or infer) an oblique pedagogical goal in both of them.

The first piece, entitled 'The Necromantic Tripos', is a parody announcing the establishment of a new Cambridge degree in Necromancy, together with the syllabus, course requirements, and regulations covering all the elements of witchcraft, magic, and the occult that one would expect of an accredited programme. This piece has *technically* already seen the light of day in two places. According to the bibliography in Schilpp (1959), it was originally published in the *Trinity Magazine* (a now-defunct Cambridge undergraduate publication) in 1926. More recently Emily Thomas (2020) published an essay on, and an abridged version of, the piece, in which she points out that this was probably Broad's attempt to amuse his students. Indeed, since it was written early in Broad's career – over 30 years before he was able to deliver the officially sanctioned *Lectures on Psychical Research* (see p. 70 of the 'Autobiographical Notes' above) – it may represent one of Broad's first attempts to nudge students in the direction of his own interest in psychical research.

The paper reproduced here is transcribed from a handwritten version found amongst the papers of Montague Summers in the archives of Georgetown University. Summers was the first to translate the *Malleus Maleficarum* into English, so perhaps he would have understood all of the references and inside-jokes, which are intended both for philosophers, and for those with some familiarity with writings on the occult. Final-year students are required to obtain a 'certificate of immoral character' from their tutor, and are strongly encouraged to attend 'Dr Tennant's lectures on Sin' as a pre-requisite (F.R. Tennant was then lecturer in Theology and Fellow of Trinity College, Cambridge, and did indeed give the Hulsean lectures, in 1901–1902, on *The Origin and Propagation of Sin*). One of the required readings is entitled *Über die Stellung der Höhren Zauberei im System der Exacten Wissenschaften* ('On the position of high sorcery in the system of exact sciences'), presumably a play on *Ueber Die Stellung Der Philosophie Zu Den Exacten Wissenschaften*, an 1861 work from Lotze, on whom Broad had written a Burney Prize-winning essay in 1910. This kind of humour is, of course, not to everyone's taste, but even the uninitiated will perhaps appreciate proposed regulations such as that 'The manure-heap in the Fellows' Garden may not be used for the incubation of Homunculi without special permission of the Garden Committee' or the important health and safety reminder that 'Hands of Glory count as oil lamps, not as candles; and their use as illuminants in college rooms is absolutely forbidden'.

The second piece in this section is slightly more serious – with a more obvious pedagogical intent – but nonetheless diverting. It is taken from a bundle of handwritten lecture notes, entitled 'Logic for R.A.F. Cadets', that were likely given during the time in which Broad was a lecturer at the University College of Dundee (then a part of St. Andrews) during the First World War; judging from the notes, it seems that Broad either assigned, or intended to assign, this puzzle as an examination question.

A version of the puzzle had originally appeared as 'Knot II: Eligible Apartments' in Lewis Carroll's (1885) *A Tangled Tale* (p. 84) as follows:

> *Problem.*—"The Governor of Kgovjni wants to give a very small dinner party, and invites his father's brother-in-law, his brother's father-in-law, his father-in-law's brother, and his brother-in-law's father. Find the number of guests."
> *Answer.*—"One."

There, Carroll *states* one solution. Broad, however, gives not only two non-equivalent solutions, but also goes through a step-by-step proof for each of them, with detailed family tree diagrams to illustrate (which I have recreated). Although the *problem* is therefore not one of Broad's own devising, his *solutions* are novel enough to be worthy of inclusion here.

In Lewis Carroll's fanciful tale where the puzzle first appears, two pupils say, of both the stories in their Latin textbook *and* their tutor's anecdotes, that 'vagueness in detail was more than compensated by their sensational brilliance'. It perhaps wouldn't be too much of a stretch (and I think Broad would agree) to say that the inverse applies not only to Broad's solution to the problem of family relationships but also to much of his other writing: what he lacks in sensational brilliance, he more than compensates for with painstaking *attention* to detail.

5.1

THE NECROMANTIC TRIPOS

(It is generally known that, in consequence of the munificent gift of a benefactor who prefers to remain anonymous, the University is proposing to establish a Tripos in the subject of Necromancy. We have much pleasure in giving an abstract of the syllabus which the recently established Board of the Faculty of Necromancy intends to issue in the next edition of the *Student's Handbook*. The College Council proposes to issue a set of regulations which will apply particularly to members of the college studying for the Necromantic Tripos, and we are privileged to print a synopsis of these regulations below.)

Part I of the Necromantic Tripos will consist of two papers on Astrology, two on Alchemy, two on the Elements of Magic, and a paper of essays. There will also be practical examinations in each of the three subjects.

Part II will consist of the following sections (A) the theory and practice of Divination, (B) Advanced Alchemy (C) Witchcraft and Black Magic. In each section, four papers will be set, and there will be a practical examination.

The schedule and set books for Part II are as follows.

Section A

(1) Astrology; genethliac, horary and judicial. The Radical and the Progressed Horoscope. Theory of Directions. The *Pars Fortunae*, the *Hyleg* and the *Anareta*. Influence of Comets. Planetary and Olympic Planetary Spirits.

(2) Geomancy and the Theory and Construction of Geomantic Talismans.
(3) Cartomancy. The Esoteric Meaning and the Practical uses of the Tarot of the Bohemians.
(4) Scrying. The Crystal & the Ink-Pool. Second Sight.
(5) Rhabdomancy. The Divining-Rod. Theory and Practice of Dowsing for Water, Oil, and Minerals.
(6) Miscellaneous Methods. The Teraphim. Urim and Thummim. Inspection of Entrails. Flight of Birds.

Section B

(1) Evocation of Elementals. Physiology and Psychology of Sylphs, Gnomes, Salamanders and Undines.
(2) Inorganic Alchemy. The Alkahest or Universal solvent. Potable Gold. Preparation and Properties of the Philosopher's Stone. Projection and Transmutation.
(3) Organic Alchemy. Preparation of Unguents, (a) for locomotion (b) for Bodily Transformations. Hands of Glory, their preparation and uses.
(4) Love Philtres. The three varieties of Hippomanes. Preparation and specific properties of each.
(5) Bio-alchemy. Methods of Rejuvenation. The Elixir of Life. Generation, nurture and uses of Homunculi.

Section C

[N.B. Candidates for this section must obtain a certificate of immoral character from their Tutor, and are strongly advised to attend Dr Tennant's lectures on Sin]
(1) Familiars. Their Evocation, Nutriment and Treatment in Health and Disease. Incubi and Succubi.
(2) Supernatural Locomotion. Aerodynamics of the Broomstick. Use of the Egg-shell for Transport and Locomotion. Levitation and Bilocation.
(3) The Law of Contract as applied to compacts with the Devil. Discussion of selected cases. Use of the Long Spoon.
(4) Organisation and Ritual of Sabbats. Ceremonial of Walpurgis Night. Theory and Practice of the Black Mass. Interpretation and Uses of Grimoires.
(5) General Theory of Putting and Lifting Curses. Storm-raising, crop-blasting and the Use of the Evil Eye. Construction, Liquefaction and Transfixion of Mommets.

(6) Theory and Practice of Vampirism and Lycanthropy. Properties of Ointments, Wafers and Garlic.

The following works are recommended by the faculty Board:

- Éliphas Lévi: *Dogme et Rituel de la Haute Magic*
- Alexius Skolechobrotos: *De Masticatione Mortuorum in Tumulis*
- Collin de Plancy: *Dictionnaire Infernal*
- Aphrodisius Pornographus: *De Incubis et Succubis*
- Caspar Peucer: *De Praecipius Generibus Divinationum*
- H. Baumberger: *Über die Stellung der Höhren Zauberei im System der Exacten Wissenschaften*
- B. Basin: *De Artibus Magicis*

SPECIAL COLLEGE RULES

The attention of members of the College in *statu pupillari* is called to the following regulations applying specially to candidates for the Necromantic Tripos.

Incantations

Incantations may be performed in College only on condition that they are inaudible outside the operator's room. This is possible if he moves widdershins round a suitably drawn pentagram, and the window be kept shut.

Evocation of Elementals

Owing to the terms of the fire insurance on the College Buildings, it is necessary to prohibit absolutely the evocation of Salamanders in rooms in College. It is an immemorial rule of the College that the baths are places for ablution and not for the evocation of Undines.

Infernal Compacts

No member of the college may contract himself either temporarily or eternally to the Devil without first satisfying his Tutor that he has obtained permission in writing from his parents or guardian. Members of the college who propose to enter into such contracts are advised to consult Mr Hollond before affixing their signatures to the document. Grave inconvenience in this world and the next may often be avoided by this simple precaution.

Familiar Spirits

A member of the college may not, without permission of his Tutor, keep a familiar in his rooms in college. Should the familiar take the form of a cat or (in the case of undergraduates living in New Court) a tortoise, permission will be generally granted. Spectral Hounds come under the general rule against keeping dogs. No member of the college may suckle a familiar in public, nor may he introduce his familiar into the Hall, Library, or Chapel.

Evocation of Planetary Spirits

No undergraduate may evoke a planetary spirit. B.A.s may invoke Planetary Spirits, but the privilege of invoking Olympic Planetary Spirits is strictly confined to Heads of Houses.

Homunculi

Homunculi may be kept in rooms in college during term, provided they be enclosed in stout and properly-stoppered bottles. Bottles suitable for this purpose may be obtained from the college Kitchen Office. The owner of a Homunculus is expected to take it away with him during vacation, or to make adequate provision for its maintenance during his absence. The manure-heap in the Fellows' Garden may not be used for the incubation of Homunculi without special permission of the Garden Committee, which will be granted only in very exceptional circumstances.

Mommets

No member of the college may make, have in his possession, melt, or transfix a mommet of the Master or any of the Fellows, Chaplains, Librarian, or Organist. Bedmakers have instructions to report immediately to the Dean of College the presents of any Mommets they may find.

Broomsticks

No undergraduate in his first year may keep a broomstick for purposes of equitation, or borrow a broomstick for such purposes. Undergraduates of higher years may keep broomsticks for this purpose provided that they obtain a licence from the Motor Proctor. The use of college roofs for starting or landing-places is forbidden. Three exeats in the year may be granted as a rule to bona fide candidates in Part II Section C of the Necromantic Tripos for the purpose of attending Sabbats. In addition, an exeat will always be granted to such candidates on Walpurgis Night.

Levitation and Bilocation

Levitation is strictly forbidden in Hall, Chapel, the Library, and during lectures. Any member of the college who has passed the qualifying exam in practical bilocation is expected, when he requires an exeat, to obtain two, one for himself & another for his wraith. Neglect of this rule is liable to lead to grave misunderstandings.

Black Masses

The Ante-Chapel is available from time to time for the celebration of Black Masses. All arrangements for such celebrations must be submitted to the Dean of Chapel and approved by him. Triangular wafers (black, red, or assorted), and sulphur candles, may be obtained from the Kitchen Office, but celebrants are expected to provide for themselves any other necessary materials. It must be clearly understood that the use of the Ante-Chapel is a privilege and not a right, and it is expected that celebrants will show their appreciation of this concession by leaving the building in a clean and tidy state. The small Writing-room next to the Senior Combination Room will be available at nearly all times for the private devotions of Fellows of the college who are Satanists.

Vampyrism and Lycanthropy

The number of bloodstains and human bones to be seen in the Courts of late shows that breaches of the rules against Vampyrism and Lycanthropy in college have become more numerous than they used to be, and that it is only by the maintenance of these rules that tidiness can be ensured.

Hands of Glory

Hands of Glory count as oil lamps, not as candles, and their use as illuminants in college rooms is absolutely forbidden.

5.2

PROBLEM IN FAMILY RELATIONSHIPS

Is it possible that a man's Father-in-law's brother, Brother's father-in-law, Father's brother-in-law & Brother-in-law's father should all be the same person?

DEFINITIONS

X's father-in-law	=	X's wife's father
∴ X's father-in-law's brother	=	X's wife's father's brother (1)
& X's brother's father-in-law	=	X's brother's wife's father (2)
X's brother-in-law	=	(a) X's wife's brother
	or	(b) X's sister's husband
∴ X's father's brother-in-law	=	(a) X's father's wife's brother
	=	X's mother's brother (3a)
	or	(b) X's father's sister's husband (3b)

DOI: 10.4324/9781003081135-28

366 MISCELLANY

& X's brother-in-law's father	=	(a) X's wife's brother's father
	=	X's wife's father
	=	X's father-in-law
	or	(b) X's sister's husband's father

(4a)

(4b)

We can reject (4a). For with this interpretation it would be impossible that X's brother-in-law's father should be identical with X's father-in-law's brother. For this would entail that one and the same person was X's father-in-law and X's father-in-law's brother, which is impossible.

Notation

The problem has two possible solutions which can be exhibited in two genealogical trees. I will denote males by capital letters and females of the same name by the corresponding small letters. I will denote those of the youngest generation considered by letters without suffixes, then of each generation above by letters with the suffix (1), e.g., X_1, and so on.

First Case

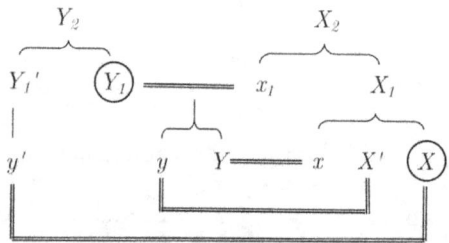

Figure 5.2.1 First case

Here Y_1 is X's wife's father's brother (1)
  X's brother's wife's father (2)
  X's father's sister's husband (3b)
  X's sister's husband's father (4b)

Second Case

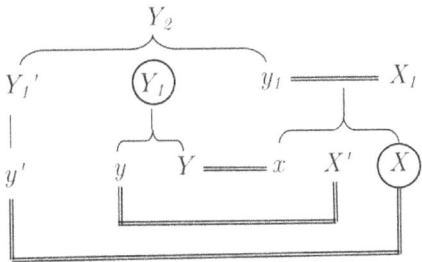

Figure 5.2.2 Second case

Here Y₁ is X's wife's father's brother (1)
        X's brother's wife's father (2)
        X's father's wife's brother (3a)
        X's sister's husband's father (4b)

The Argument

Case I

If conditions (2) and (4b) can be fulfilled by the same person then X's brother's wife and X's sister's husband must have the same father, or, X's brother and sister must have married two people who are themselves sister and brother. Thus, we have:

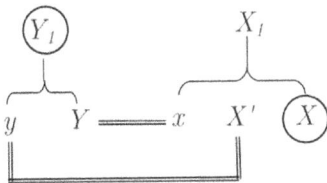

Figure 5.2.3

... where Y1 fulfils these two conditions. If further condition (1) is to be fulfilled by Y₁, Y₁ must be X's wife's father's brother. This is fulfilled if we have:

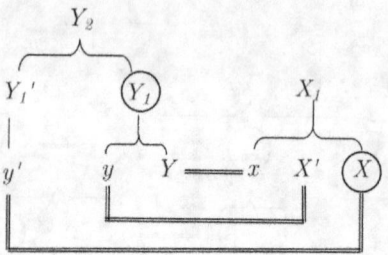

Figure 5.2.4

If further condition (3b) is fulfilled by Y_1, Y_1 must be X's father's sister's husband, i.e., must have married X_1's sister. Thus, we have:

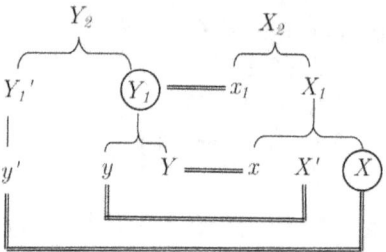

Figure 5.2.5

Case II

The argument proceeds as before till Figure 5.2.4 has been obtained. But now, if condition (3a) is to be fulfilled by Y_1, Y_1 must be X's father's wife's brother. So Y_1 must have a sister y_1 who is married to X_1. Thus, the third figure now becomes

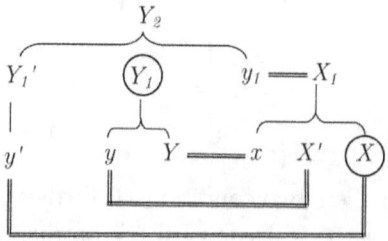

Figure 5.2.6

REFERENCES

Ayer, A.J. (1977) *Part of My Life* (London: William Collins Sons & Co).
Britton, K. (1978) "Charlie Dunbar Broad, 1887–1971" *Proceedings of the British Academy* 64: 289–310.
Broad, C.D. (1917) "Hume's Theory of the Credibility of Miracles" *Proceedings of the Aristotelian Society* 17(1): 77–94.
Broad, C.D. (1918) "In What Sense Is Survival Desirable?" *The Hibbert Journal* 17(1): 7–20.
Broad, C.D. (1919) "The Antecedent Probability of Survival" *The Hibbert Journal* 17(4): 561–578.
Broad, C.D. (1922) "A Neglected Method of Psychical Research" (Letter to the Editor) *Journal of the Society for Psychical Research* 20(283): 251–252.
Broad, C.D. (1925) *The Mind and Its Place in Nature* (London: Routledge and Kegan Paul).
Broad, C.D. (1926) *The Philosophy of Francis Bacon* (Cambridge: Cambridge University Press).
Broad, C.D. (1930) *Five Types of Ethical Theory* (London: Kegan Paul).
Broad, C.D. (1934) *Determinism, Indeterminism, and Libertarianism: An Inaugural Lecture* (Cambridge: Cambridge University Press).
Broad, C.D. (1935) "Mechanical and Teleological Causation" *Proceedings of the Aristotelian Society, Supplementary Volume* 14: 83–112.
Broad, C.D. (1949) "The Relevance of Psychical Research to Philosophy" *Philosophy* 23(91): 291–309.
Broad, C.D. (1952a) "Some Elementary Reflexions on Sense-Perception" *Philosophy* 27 (January): 3–17.
Broad, C.D. (1952b) "John McTaggart Ellis McTaggart" in His *Ethics and The History of Philosophy* (London: Routledge and Kegan Paul).
Broad, C.D. (1959a) "Autobiography" in Schilpp, P.A. (ed). *The Philosophy of C.D. Broad* (New York: Tudor), pp. 3–68.

Broad, C.D. (1959b) "A Reply to My Critics" in Schilpp, P.A. (ed). *The Philosophy of C.D. Broad* (New York: Tudor).

Broad, C.D. (1961) "Hume's Doctrine of Space" *Proceedings of the British Academy* 47: 161–176.

Broad, C.D. (1962a) "Wittgenstein and the Vienna Circle" *Mind* 71(282): 251.

Broad, C.D. (1962b) *Lectures on Psychical Research* (New York: Humanities Press).

Broad, C.D. (1967) "Some Personal Impressions of Russell as a Philosopher" in Schoenman, R. (ed). *Bertrand Russell: Philosopher of the Century* (London: George Allen and Unwin), pp. 100–108.

Carroll, L. (1885) *A Tangled Tale* (New York: Dover).

Earman, J. (2008) "Reassessing the Prospects for a Growing Block Model of the Universe" *International Studies in the Philosophy of Science* 22(2): 135–164.

Edmonds, D., and J. Eidinow (2001) *Wittgenstein's Poker: The Story of a Ten-Minute Argument Between Two Great Philosophers* (Faber and Faber).

Ewing, A.C. (1963) "The Philosophy of C. D. Broad [Review of The Philosophy of C. D. Broad, by P. A. Schilpp]" *Philosophy* 38(143): 78–82.

Farmelo, G. (2009) *The Strangest Man: The Hidden Life of Paul Dirac, Mystic of the Atom* (New York: Basic Books).

Jackson, F (1982) "Epiphenomenal Qualia" *Philosophical Quarterly* 32(April): 127–136.

McLaughlin, B.P. (1992). "The Rise and Fall of British Emergentism" in Beckermann, A., Flohr, H. & Kim, J. (eds). *Emergence or Reduction?: Prospects for Nonreductive Physicalism* (Berlin: De Gruyter), pp. 49–93.

Misak, C. (2020). *Frank Ramsey: A Sheer Excess of Powers*. (Oxford: Oxford University Press).

Moore, G.E. (1942) "An Autobiography" in Schilpp, P.A. (ed). *The Philosophy of G.E. Moore* (New York: Tudor), pp. 3–39.

Oaklander, L.N. (2020) *C.D. Broad's Philosophy of Time* (New York and London: Routledge).

Schilpp, P.A. (ed.) (1959) *The Philosophy of C.D. Broad* (New York: Tudor).

Thomas, E. (2019) "The Roots of C. D. Broad's Growing Block Theory of Time" *Mind* 128(510): 527–549.

Thomas, E. (2020) "A Magical Syllabus" *The Philosophers' Magazine* 91: 60–64.

Van Inwagen, P. (2008) "How to Think About the Problem of Free Will" *The Journal of Ethics* 12(3–4): 327–341.

White, A.R. (1960), "The Philosophy of C.D. Broad" *Philosophical Books* 1: 11–13.

INDEX

Absolute 107, 166–168; Bradley's positive account of 177–181; *ipso facto* contents of 181
Absolute Idealism 163–164, 186, 187
Absolute Idealists 164, 171
Absolute Space and Time 241, 247
Acting Stewardship 74–82
Adrian, B. D. 36–37
Adrian, Hester 25–26, 36–38, 83–86, 191–192
Advances in Applied Probability (Littlewood) 21
Alexander, Samuel 108; *Space, Time, and Deity* 186
Al Khwarizmi (Arabian mathematician) 224
Analysis of Matter (Russell) 184
Analysis of Mind (Russell) 184
Analyst (Berkeley) 254
Appearance and Reality (Bradley) 107, 120, 164, 183
Aquinas, St. Thomas 228
Aristarchus of Samos 229
Ayer, A.J. 2, 108; *Foundations of Empirical Knowledge* 186; *Language, Truth, and Logic* 186

Bacon, Francis 196–217; on academic philosophy 215–216; birth of 196; buried in 214; fourth centenary of the birth of 42; *Philosophy* 42, 106; as Solicitor-General 206; Viscount St. Albans 211
Bacon, Robert 196
Bacon, Sir Nicholas 196–197
Baggally, W.W. 323
Barham, Richard Harris: The 'Monstre' Balloon in the *Ingoldsby Legends* 19
Barrow, Isaac: *Geometrical Lectures* 254
Berkeley, George 105, 176; *Analyst* 254; *Defence of Free Thinking in Mathematics* 254
Bertrand Russell, Philosopher of the Century (Russell) 16
Bertrand Russell and Trinity (Hardy) 15, 190
Black, Max 4
Bosanquet, Bernard 3, 108, 129; *Philosophical Theory of the State* 183; *The Principle of Individuality and Value* 184; *The Value and Destiny of the Individual* 184

Bradley, F.H. 107–108; *Appearance and Reality* 107, 120, 164, 183; *Degrees of Truth and Reality* 164–168; *Essays on Truth and Reality* 107, 164; *Ethical Studies* 163, 183; philosophy of 163–181; *Principles of Logic* 163; positive account of the Absolute 177–181; Self 172–177; theory of judgment 168–172
Brahe, Tycho 229–230
Briggs, Henry 225
'British emergentists' 2
Britton, Karl 4, 10
Broad, C.D. 1; aphorisms 3; *Determinism, Indeterminism, and Libertarianism* 2; *Essays on Truth and Reality* 107, 164; *Ethics and the History of Philosophy* 42; *Five Types of Ethical Theory* 2, 106–107; 'growing block' theory of time 2; *The Mind and Its Place in Nature* 2; *Lectures on Psychical Research* 70, 309, 357; philosophical style 2–3; *The Philosophy of Francis Bacon* 2–3, 108; psychical research 307–308; Society for Psychical Research 308; and storytelling 106
Butler, Sir James 76

Caird, Edward 183
Cambridge xi, xii, 107, 111, 187, 197, 199; changes affecting 95–101; increase in number of visitors 97–99; increase in the number of fellows 99–101; increase of motor traffic in the streets 95–97; spread of bi-sexuality 101
Campbell, Virginia 333–338
Campbells, Thomas 333–334
Can we Explain the Poltergeist? (Owen) 333
The Cardinal of Lorraine and the Council of Trent (Evennett) 34
Carrington, Hereward 323, 331; *Historic Poltergeists* 318, 331
Carroll, Lewis 358–359; *A Tangled Tale* 358
causal laws 155, 260–261, 269–273, 295
causation 260–274
Cecil, Robert 204–207
changes: affecting Cambridge 95–101; affecting Trinity College 95–101; and continuity 275–294; and discontinuity 275–294; logical analysis of 295–304
Clark, Kitson 15
Cock Lane and Commonsense (Lang) 346
The Concept of Nature (Whitehead) 185
continuity: and change 275–294; and discontinuity 275–294
Copernicus 229–230; *De Revolutionibus Orbium Coelestium* 229
Cox, W.E. 332, 349–352
Crowe, Catherine: *The Night Side of Nature* 330

Dante, Alighieri: *Divine Comedy* 229
Darwin, C.G. 25
Davey, S.J. 313
death 88–89
Decline and Fall of the Roman Empire (Gibbon) 34
A Defence of Common Sense (Moore) 184
Defence of Free Thinking in Mathematics (Berkeley) 254
Degrees of Truth and Reality 164–168
De Revolutionibus Orbium Coelestium (Copernicus) 229
Descartes 105, 128, 222–225, 232, 237, 240–241, 245, 254–257
Determinism, Indeterminism, and Libertarianism (Broad) 2
Dingwall, E.J. 72, 324; *The Girdle of Chastity* 69; *Some Human Oddities* 69; *Studies in the Sexual Life of Ancient and Mediaeval Peoples* 69; *Very Peculiar People* 69
Dirac, Paul 3
discontinuity: and change 275–294; and continuity 275–294
Divine Comedy (Dante) 229
doctrine of the Self 145–162
Donaldson, J.G.S. 31
Drummer of Tedworth Case 317
Duff, Patrick 15, 86

Edmonds, D.: *Wittgenstein's Poker* 3
Eisenow, J.: *Wittgenstein's Poker* 3

emergence xi, 2, 187
Encyclopedia of the Philosophical Sciences (Hegel) 106
English absolute idealism 184
English travel 39–44
equality 89–91
Essays on Truth and Reality (Bradley) 107, 164
Ethical Studies (Bradley) 163, 183
Ethics and Language (Stevenson) 186
Ethics and the History of Philosophy (Broad) 42
Euclid 125, 221–223
Evennett, H.O. 25, 33–35; *The Cardinal of Lorraine and the Council of Trent* 34
evocation: of elementals 362; of planetary spirits 363
Évolution Créatrice (Bergson) 186
experimental cases 321–329; with mediums 321–327; without mediums 327–329
Experimente de Fernbewegung 324

familiar spirits 363
Farmelo, Graham 3
Feilding, Everard 323
Fellow or Felon (Pym) 32
Fellows of Trinity College 10, 15, 99, 193
Five Types of Ethical Theory (Broad) 2, 106–107
Foundations of Empirical Knowledge (Ayer) 186
Four Elements and the Quintessence theory 227
fraternity 89–91

Galileo 222, 231–233, 237–238, 240–249, 253, 272
Gardiner, S.R. 211
Gatty, Oliver 326
Gedanken von der wahren Schätzung der lebendigen Kräfte (Kant) 259
Geometrical Lectures (Barrow) 254
Ghosts and Poltergeists (Crehan) 332
Gibbon, Edward: *Decline and Fall of the Roman Empire* 34

The Girdle of Chastity (Dingwall) 69
Gomme, A.W. 28
Gow, A.S.F. 16, 22, 35, 191–192
Green, T.H. 183
Grimstone, Sir Harbottle 214–215
Gurney, Edmund 27, 309; *Phantasms of the Living* 73

hallucination 73, 122, 143–144, 313, 320, 337, 343–344, 351, 353
Hardy, G.H. 15, 20
Hazelius, Artur 50
Hegel, G.W.F.: 'after-thought' 113; certain or probable knowledge 127; *Encyclopedia of the Philosophical Sciences* 106; general images 112, 119; human emotions 116; Negative Reason 128; *Philosophy of Law* 121; Positive Reason 128; proper sense of 'idea' 119; reflexions 113, 115; on religion 116; Understanding 127–128; views on the nature of philosophy 111–129
Hegelianism 111, 129
Hellsten, Ulf 49, 53–54, 82
The Hibbert Journal 308
Hinks, David 26
Hipparchus (systematic astronomer) 226
historical development of scientific thought 218–234
Historic Poltergeists (Carrington) 318, 331
A History of Western Philosophy (Russell) 108, 194
Hollond, H.A. 16, 18–20
Homunculi 358, 361, 363
Hope, Lord Charles 325
Hume, David: Doctrine of the Self 145–162; *Enquiry* 273; 'Hume's Theory of Space' 63; memory-experience 154–155; Theory of Belief 130–144; *Treatise* 273
Hyde, Dennis 329

illnesses 59–66
induction 106, 112, 185, 216, 262
Introductory Comparative Analysis of Some Poltergeist Cases 332

Jones, Gareth 74–77, 79, 150, 158, 160
Jörpes, Pelle 51
Journal of Parapsychology 327
Joy, Sir George 68

Kallner, Sixten 51, 60–61
Kant, Immanuel 105, 121, 126–127, 142, 164, 187, 194, 259, 284; *Gedanken von der wahren Schätzung der lebendigen Kräfte* 259
Kantian ethics 163
Kepler, Johannes 222, 232, 245–246; birth of 230; First Law of Planetary Motion 249; *Laws of Planetary Motion* 230; Second Law 249–250; Third Law 249, 250–252
Ker, Alan 25
Keynes, Maynard 24, 189; *Treatise on Probability* 185

Lambert, G.W. 68
Lang, Andrew 320; *Cock Lane and Commonsense* 346; *The Poltergeist Historically Considered* 352
Language, Truth, and Logic (Ayer) 186
Law of Inertia 232
Laws of Planetary Motion (Kepler) 230
Lectures on Psychical Research (Broad) 70, 309, 357
Lectures on the Ethics of Green, Spencer, and Martineau (Sidgwick) 183
Leibniz, Gottfried Wilhelm 105, 176, 186, 222, 234, 237, 240–241, 247, 254–258, 284
Les Pouvoirs inconnus de l'Espirit sur la Matière (Osty) 325
liberty 89–91
The Library of Living Philosophers series 1, 9, 13
The Life of Louis Napoleon (Simpson) 16
Life and Reign of King James I (Wilson) 206
Littlewood, J.E. 16, 20; *On the Probability in the Tail of a Binomial Distribution* 21
Locke, John 105, 126–127, 169
Lord Adrian 15, 36
Lord MacDermott of Belmont, Lord Chief Justice of Northern Ireland 86
Lord Tedder 84

Malleus Maleficarum 357
The Master of King's Hall 32
Max Beerbohm on Lytton Strachey (Simpson) 16
McTaggart, J.M.E. 18, 36, 106–108, 186–187, 238
Meautys, Thomas 214
Methods of History (Simpson) 16
Milton, John: *Paradise Lost* 229
The Mind and Its Place in Nature (Broad) 2
Mommets 30–31, 363
The 'Monstre' Balloon in the *Ingoldsby Legends* (Barham) 19
Moore, G.E. 1–2, 52, 107–108, 111, 164, 187; *A Defence of Common Sense* 184; *Philosophical Essays* 184; *Refutation of Idealism* 184

Napier (Scottish mathematician) 224–225
Naturalism and Agnosticism (Ward) 183
nature of philosophy: Hegel's views on 111–129
Newton, Sir Isaac 36, 42, 84, 105, 108, 193, 199, 240–241, 246, 251–254, 257; law of universal gravitation 248–249; scientific thought 218–234; Third Law of Motion 232, 248
Nicholas, T.C. 16, 22–25
The Night Side of Nature (Crowe) 330
Nisbet, W.H. 333–336
Normal Cognition, Clairvoyance, and Telepathy 66
Nylander, Karl-Gustav 55

Olsson, Karl-Erik 55–56
Omar Khayyam 105
On the Probability in the Tail of a Binomial Distribution (Littlewood) 21
'organic sensation' 266

Original Sin 87–88
Osty 325–326; *Les Pouvoirs inconnus de l'Espirit sur la Matière* 325
Overbury, Sir Thomas 207
Owen, A.R.G. 333

Pantin, Karl 25
Paradise Lost (Milton) 229
Parsons, Denys 329
Perception (Price) 184
perceptions: hallucinatory quasi-perceptions 343; veridical sense 343
Phantasms of the Living (Gurney) 73
Philosophical Essays (Moore) 184
Philosophical Review 16
Philosophical Theory of the State (Bosanquet) 183
philosophy: of F.H. Bradley 163–181; Hegel's views on the nature of 111–129; 1900–1950 182–187
The Philosophy of C.D. Broad (Schilpp volume) 9, 13
The Philosophy of Francis Bacon (Broad) 2–3, 108
Pinsent, Dame Ellen 37
Plato 220–221, 225–226, 228
Polkinghorne, John 42
The Poltergeist Historically Considered (Lang) 352
poltergeists 330–354
population: increase in 91–95
Price, Harry 13; *Perception* 184; *Regurgitation and the Duncan Mediumship* 322; *Rudi Schneider* 325
The Principle of Individuality and Value (Bosanquet) 184
The Principle of Relativity (Whitehead) 185
Principles about Causation 260–261
Principles of Logic (Bradley) 163
The Principles of Natural Knowledge (Whitehead) 185
Probability and Induction (Kneale) 185
Process and Reality (Whitehead) 187
Propositions of Causal Connexion 260–261, 268–270, 273–274

psychical research xii, 19, 21, 27, 66–74, 307–311
Psycho-Kinesis 327
Ptolemy Soter, the first Greek king of Egypt 221
Pythagoras: *Pythagorean* Theorem 219; scientific thought 218–234
Pythagorean Theorem 219

quantitative methods 240–259
Qvarnström, Björn 52

rational beliefs 261
Refutation of Idealism (Moore) 184
Regurgitation and the Duncan Mediumship (Price) 322
Religion, Philosophy, and Psychical Research (Broad) 66
research, psychical 66–74
Robert Devereux, second Earl of Essex 200
Robertson, Dennis 25
Robertson, Donald 25
Ross, Sir David 187
Rudi Schneider (Price) 325
Russell, Bertrand 1–2, 8, 15–16, 106–108; *Analysis of Matter* 184; *Analysis of Mind* 184; *A History of Western Philosophy* 194; *Human Knowledge, its Scope and Limits* 184; *Marriage and Morals* 195; 90th birthday 188–195; *The Philosophy of Leibniz* 194; *Principia Mathematica* 239; *The Principles of Mathematics, Vol. I* 188; *Some Personal Impressions of Russell as a Philosopher* 16
Russell, F.W. 188
Ryle, Gilbert 9

Saducismus Triumphatus (Glanvill) 317, 346
Sällskapet för Parapsykologisk Forskning (Society for Research in Parapsychology) 53–54
Salter, W.H. 68

Scandinavia: countries other than Sweden 44–48; travels in Sweden 48–59
Schilpp, P.A. 357
Schopenhauer, Arthur 105, 176–177
Science and E.S.P. 70
Secret of Hegel (Stirling) 183
self 172–177
The Shame of the Shelfords (Winstanley) 32
Sidgwick, Henry 27, 108, 309, 316, 353; *Lectures on the Ethics of Green, Spencer, and Martineau* 183
Simpson, F.A. 16–18, 191–192; *The Life of Louis Napoleon* 16; *Max Beerbohm on Lytton Strachey* 16; *Methods of History* 16
Society for Psychical Research 308
Sökaren 311
Some elementary reflections on sense-perception (Broad) 2
Some Human Oddities (Dingwall) 69
Some Personal Impressions of Russell as a Philosopher (Russell) 16
Space, Time, and Deity (Alexander) 186
Spencer, Herbert 108, 163, 182–183, 186
Stewart, Margaret 333–334
Stirling, Hutchison: *Secret of Hegel* 183
Stratton of Caius 71
Studies in the Sexual Life of Ancient and Mediaeval Peoples (Dingwall) 69
Sweden: countries other than 44–48; travels in 48–59
'Synthetic Philosophy' 182

A Tangled Tale (Carroll) 358
Taylor, Sir G.I. 16, 21–22
theory of belief 130–144
theory of judgment 168–172
Thomas, Emily 357
Thurston, Herbert 332
Thurston, S.J. 332
Tractatus Logico-Philosophicus (Wittgenstein) 185
Tranøy, Karl-Erik 44, 46
travel 38–59; English travel 39–44; Scandinavian travel 44–59; in Sweden 48–59

Treatise on Probability (Keynes) 185
Trevelyan, G.M. 25
Trinity College: changes affecting 95–101; increase in number of visitors 97–99; increase in the number of fellows 99–101; increase of motor traffic in the streets 95–97; octogenarians still living 15–25; spread of bi-sexuality 101
Trinity Magazine 357

Underhill, Sir Thomas 206

The Value and Destiny of the Individual (Bosanquet) 184
Van Inwagen, P. 2
velocity 231–232, 241–259, 272, 275, 282, 285–287, 293–294
veridical sense perceptions 343
Very Peculiar People (Dingwall) 69

Wallace, Wm. 183
Ward, James 107–108, 190; *Naturalism and Agnosticism* 183
West, D.J. 327–329
White, A.R. 10
Whitehead, A.N. 108, 184, 186–187, 239, 302; *The Concept of Nature* 185; *The Principle of Relativity* 185; *The Principles of Natural Knowledge* 185; *Process and Reality* 187
Wiles, Maurice 4
Wilson, Arthur 198; *Life and Reign of King James I* 206
Winstanley, D.A. 17; *The Shame of the Shelfords* 32
Wittgenstein, Ludwig 1, 3, 108, 185–186; *Tractatus Logico-Philosophicus* 185
Wittgenstein's Poker (Edmonds and Eisenow) 3

Zotterman, Yngve 85